DESIGNING WOMEN

The Bucknell Studies in Eighteenth-Century Literature and Culture

The Bucknell Studies in Eighteenth-Century Literature and Culture aims to publish challenging, new eighteenth-century scholarship. Of particular interest is critical, historical, and interdisciplinary work that is interestingly and intelligently theorized, and that broadens and refines the conception of the field. At the same time, the series remains open to all theoretical perspectives and different kinds of scholarship. While the focus of the series is the literature, history, arts, and culture (including art, architecture, music, travel, and history of science, medicine, and law) of the long eighteenth century in Britain and Europe, the series is also interested in scholarship that establishes relationships with other geographies, literature, and cultures for the period 1660–1830.

Titles in This Series

www.bucknell.edu/universitypress

DESIGNING WOMEN

The Dressing Room
in Eighteenth-Century
English Literature and Culture

Tita Chico

BUCKNELL
UNIVERSITY PRESS
Lewisburg, Pennsylvania

First paperback edition 2023
ISBN: 978-1-68448-479-9

Library of Congress Cataloging-in-Publication Data

Chico, Tita, 1970–
Designing women : the dressing room in eighteenth-century English literature and culture
/ Tita Chico.
    p. cm. — (The Bucknell studies in eighteenth-century literature and culture)
    Includes bibliographical references and index.
    ISBN 0-8387-5605-0 (alk. paper)
    1. English literature—18th century—History and criticism. 2. Women and
literature—England—History—18th century. 3. Architecture, Domestic, in literature.
    4. Personal space in literature. 5. Clothes closets—England. 6. Dwellings in literature.
    7. Women in literature. I. Title. II. Series.
R448.W65C48 2005
820.9'3559—dc22   2004017669

A British Cataloging-in-Publication record for this book is available from the British
Library.

References to internet websites (URLs) were accurate at the time of writing.
Neither the author nor Bucknell University Press is responsible for URLs that may
have expired or changed since the manuscript was prepared.

∞ The paper used in this publication meets the requirements of the American National
Standard for Information Sciences—Permanence of Paper for Printed Library Materials,
ANSI Z39.48-1992.

bucknelluniversitypress.org

Distributed worldwide by Rutgers University Press

In Memoriam
Dorothy T. Fitzgerald
(1899–1999)

Contents

Preface: The Dressing Room Unlock'd

FROM THE LATE SEVENTEENTH CENTURY TO THE LATE EIGHTEENTH, the lady's dressing room changed from being a site of lasciviousness and secrecy for aristocratic women to an emblem for good and virtuous mothers. This transformation reflects the changing roles available to women over this time, from the sense that women improperly used eroticism to claim independence and autonomy to the model of ideal maternity that was impressed upon them. The dressing room captured the collective imagination of eighteenth-century England because it represented the possibility that women could act independently and selfishly, a fear that was ultimately reshaped into a celebration of the belief that women would not act independently or selfishly if they were good mothers. As a central feature of the eighteenth-century literary landscape, the dressing room was found with much greater frequency in poems and novels than it ever was in actual homes. The disparity between the imagined prevalence of the dressing room and its limited availability to upper-class women indicates the magnitude of this concern about the privileges and independence that women could assert in their dressing rooms, suggesting a widespread cultural preoccupation with the possibility that women would challenge patriarchal prerogative.

The dressing room encapsulates the history of gender roles in the eighteenth century, moving from women of a certain class having the ability to claim greater privilege to the widespread development of a submissive, maternal ideal. Throughout this book, I use the dressing room to think about gender. But gender also functions as a vehicle for writers to express *other* ideas as well; in this sense, I assume that gender always has a context—gendered subjects *do* things—and that this approach to gender offers a diachronic slice of eighteenth-century literary culture. The dressing room allows us to understand debates about privacy, theatricality, aesthetics, epistemology, education, and literature. When writers use the dressing room to voice a particular view, it may end up seeming normal or even natural. But it is not necessarily so. When Swift writes his dressing room poems, they are "about" women, beauty, and the body, but they are also "about" empiricism, experimen-

9

tation, and epistemology. Understanding literature in this expansive way will unearth the deep resonance of the question of women to seemingly unrelated questions about social order, aesthetics, philosophy, and literary authority.

For a book all about dressing rooms, the reader will find very little sex. With the dressing room so often a figure for the female body and sexuality, one would think that dressing room scenes regularly imagine women engaged in sex. I open chapter 1 with a reading of *A Court Lady's Curiosity*, which features a woman masturbating in her dressing room, though this example is rather unusual. Eighteenth-century pornography would certainly offer us a chance to see such scenes, but pornographic texts would ultimately be sensational and misleading about the dressing room's role in "mainstream" literary culture. Additionally, though seventeenth-century satires populate dressing rooms with erotica, such as lapdogs and dildoes, sex is not explicit in the self-consciously literary works that I consider. Looking instead at satire and the novel reveals that the dressing room trope and its associations with women's independence and objectification are woven into the fabric of eighteenth-century daily life, woven so tightly, in fact, that we may not even see them. The dressing room stands as a commonplace in eighteenth-century literary culture that has been treated as obvious, and has therefore suffered from an oversimplified view of its effects, connotations, and significance.

In this book, I aim first to recreate the historical setting of the dressing room and, at greater length, to illustrate its representational prevalence in eighteenth-century satire and domestic novels. We will see that the dressing room is a provocative space, one that produces narrative questioning and serves as an enabling fiction for writers throughout the long eighteenth century. In the early part of the century, satiric dressing room scenes design the female subject as an overwhelming figure of sexual excess, theatrical dissembling, and feminine agency, posited in tandem with (or as a provocation for) a text's mode of containment or censure. Later, writers, mostly domestic novelists, envisage the dressing room as both a narrative obstacle and goal, with the successful heroine in her dressing room a model of virtue and intellectual maturity. The dressing room trope in eighteenth-century literature contains simultaneously progressive and retrograde versions of femininity and reflects a problematic that is deeply generative of satiric and narrative production. The dressing room trope also redefines the gendered constitution of private spaces and exposes the shifting functions and protocols of literary forms in the eighteenth-century climate of generic experimentation.

I have divided *Designing Women* into three parts: chapters 1 and 2 constitute "Metaphor, Theory, and History," chapters 3, 4, and 5, "Satire, Art, and Epistemology," and chapters 6 and 7, "Domestic Novels, Education, and Motherhood." Within this three-part structure, there are two narratives—and two ways of reading the book. The first is chronological: from the late seventeenth to the late eighteenth century, the dressing room transformed from a measure of women's illicit sexuality and theatrical behavior to a site that confirmed a woman's virtue and her status as a good wife and mother. The dressing room likewise moved from a nearly exclusive association with satire to its programmatic inclusion, beginning with Richardson, in the domestic novel. This chronological and generic narrative illuminates changes in the period's gender codes, as women are first imagined as predominantly dangerous and subversive by satirists to having the potential for reform in domestic novels, particularly as young women negotiate the marriage market and assume the role of a good mother. The base narrative of the book also foregrounds the disparity between context and text—as literary works regularly reimagine the dressing room into a space open to nearly all women—and underscores the close connections between the development of eighteenth-century satire and the domestic novel, with their shared dependence on contradictory representations of women in private.

The second narrative structure of *Designing Women* is thematic, highlighting a cluster of associations that the dressing room evokes throughout the eighteenth century—art, epistemology, education, and maternity. In part II, I identify two significant preoccupations that are regularly associated with the dressing room. As chapter 3 demonstrates, satirists frequently pinpoint the dressing room as a site for rival artistry, as well as a space that both thwarts and invites classification. In chapters 4 and 5, I therefore draw out these associations in case studies of Pope and Swift, perhaps two of the most famous writers to use the dressing room metaphor in the eighteenth century. My readings of Pope and Swift elaborate the issues that preoccupy many of their predecessors and contemporaries, and point to the range of debates in which the dressing room figures. For Pope, the question of women's cosmetics—at the heart of the dressing room's primary function— segues easily into the question of what kind of art matters. And for Swift, the question of the dressing room's closed door—at the heart of the dressing room's architectural design—spills over into questions of how we come to learn things that are hidden from view.

Part III is dedicated to the mid- and late-eighteenth-century domestic novel. In chapters 6 and 7, I identify two additional aspects of the dressing room that come to the fore under the hands of domestic novelists. The issue of pedagogy was associated with the dressing room from the time of its inception in the seventeenth century, but regularly sidelined by satirists. Richardson, educational theorists, and other domestic novelists revive the legitimacy of the dressing room as a pedagogical space and use the trope to endorse women's education. In domestic novels, the dressing room becomes a transitional space through which heroines must pass in order to reach the conclusion of the female bildungsroman, finding a proper husband. And once they do pass, the problem of the dressing room returns, for it then becomes a litmus test for proper motherhood. The themes of a heroine's development and a mother's reformation form the endpoint of the book's chronological narrative, but I hope that they also foreground the fundamental plasticity of the dressing room as a metaphor and the variety of concerns that get voiced through its representation in literature.

I should say a few words about my title. *Designing Women* clearly plays with the title of the 1980s sitcom created by Linda Bloodworth-Thomason, a show that stars four interior decorators who play a delicate balance between self-fashioned, witty female entrepreneurs and demure Southern ladies. But my primary allusion is to the eighteenth century: Richardson's *Pamela*. This is a novel in which Mr. B regularly has "designs" on Pamela, designs that she spends her time resisting. When Pamela's father expresses his hope that "the good 'Squire has no Design" on her, Pamela naively responds, "My Master continues to be very affable to me. As yet I see no Cause to fear any thing. Mrs. *Jervis* the House-keeper too is very civil to me, and I have the Love of every body. Sure they can't *all* have Designs against me because they are civil."[1] The word "design" occupies a central position in Pamela's fight against Mr. B; it carries with it a pernicious tone and the suggestion of entrapment. Indeed, shortly before Mr. B abducts Pamela, he blames her beauty for evoking his desire to control her sexually: "you are so pretty, that go where you will, you can never be free from the Designs of some or other of our Sex" (85). During this interlude, the editor intervenes and inserts a copy of Mr. B's misleading letter to Pamela's father, which "will shew the base Arts of designing Men to gain their wicked Ends" (90). But the rhetoric of Mr. B's "designs" on Pamela is weighed against the suggestion that Pamela herself schemes. Mr. B writes, "I had vow'd Honour and Love to your Unworthiness, believing you a Mirror of bashful Modesty, and unspotted Innocence; and that no perfidious Designs lurked in so fair a Bosom. But now I have found you out, you specious Hypocrite!" (145–46). And readers from the beginning have seconded Mr. B's point of view by suggesting that Pamela herself is "designing" because she uses the guise of virtue to hide her vice.

If, in Mr. B, we have an example of "designing men," then in Pamela we have one of "designing women." I have chosen to adopt the phrase "designing women" as a title because it registers the tensions in the eighteenth-century dressing room that I foreground throughout this book. The dressing room promises women the potential to design themselves: literally, with clothes and makeup, or figuratively, through private reflection and education. It suggests that women make designs on the world and that they scheme to outwit and to ensnare men. But the dressing room also introduces the possibility that women are circumscribed, or designed, by others, drawn into roles that are not necessarily of their own choosing. *Designing Women* underscores all of the possibilities written into the century's gender codes, showing the potentially liberatory and constrictive nature of the eighteenth-century lady's dressing room. Finally, I hope that *Designing Women* opens our eyes to the organizational and conceptual centrality of the dressing room trope to eighteenth-century literary culture.

CHAPTER SUMMARIES

In part I, "Metaphor, Theory, and History," I position the dressing room trope within historical and theoretical debates about private life and consumerism and then propose a materialist account of the meanings of the dressing room, particularly as it developed spatially in seventeenth- and eighteenth-century English playhouses and homes. Chapter 1, "Women's Private Parts: The Politics and Aesthetics of the Dressing Room," argues that the dressing room trope is a particularity of eighteenth-century literary culture and offers a chronology of the metaphor and its specific associations with satire and the domestic novel. The study of architecture and literature raises the question of literature and context; I argue that the case of the dressing room highlights the problematics of contextualizing literary texts. The material record of the dressing room (presented in chapter 2) indicates that such a space of privilege was available to but a few wealthy women. This project is necessary because of several critical blind spots, including earlier feminist accounts of satires about women that regularly assume an unproblematic relationship between culture and literature, as well as a narratives of progress common to literary histories. Moreover, accounts of the domestic novel likewise neglect to acknowledge the figural influence of satiric dressing rooms on the spaces of novelistic domesticity, just as studies of satire and the novel fail to question the relationship between representations of women in satire and the domestic (rather than "comic") novel. Chapter 1 also illuminates the several conceptual and theoretical duties that the dressing room served in the late seventeenth and eighteenth centuries. I argue that the dressing room occupies a central (if neglected) place in the history of private life, which additionally calls into question the "separate spheres" thesis that has been defended and attacked by historians and critics. The dressing room allows us to understand the means by which certain women were able to negotiate the differences between public and private life through consumerism. I also investigate the theoretical nature of the dressing room, particularly its instability as an enclosed space and its very illusory promise of full disclosure, thereby pointing to the category of femininity that is erased from the postmodern theoretical closet and from studies of the historical closet. The theoretical implications of the dressing room extend to its materialization of the two-sex model of gender difference that emerged in the eighteenth century. The dressing room offers writers and commentators an imaginary solution to the problem of seeing beyond a closed door, and stands not only as an originary site for women's theatricality and false claims to beauty, but also as a surrogate for women themselves.

Chapter 2, "'The Art of Knowing Women': A History of the Dressing Room," draws on extensive archival research to argue that the cultural context of the dressing room trope includes the design and use of both domestic architecture and the playhouse tiring-room. The Restoration tiring-room—a space newly inflected following the introduction of female players to the stage in 1662—emerged as a venue for erotic objectification and exchange between the actresses and their male admirers at the same time that the domestic dressing room itself came to be incorporated with regularity in grand English homes. The tiring-room, drawn most vividly in the diary of Samuel Pepys, facilitates the production of voyeurism and *vanitas*, particularly insofar as the actress in the tiring-room was construed as sexually available. I turn to domestic spaces to argue that the ritual of the levee, the social structure in which wealthy women took visitors into their dressing rooms, explicitly domesticated the erotic politics of the tiring-room. Female objectification in the dressing room is all too smooth, as dressing rooms not only ready a lady for public display, but also serve as sites of display in their own right. The emphasis on the decorative, while always at the forefront of the dressing room trope, only tells part of the story. Architectural designs and domestic inventories (from diaries, auction lists, wills, credit reports, parliamentary foreclosures, and court cases) indicate that the emergence of the lady's dressing room in seventeenth-century English architecture signals the advent of female privacy. Against the backdrop of the early modern notion of privacy as a masculine prerogative, the lady's dressing room introduced a challenge to the traditional domestic hierarchy. Archival domestic records indicate that wealthy women used their dressing rooms to retire in private for a variety of activities, ranging from socializing with intimates to reading and writing. While many of the grand homes during this period continued to spatialize a gendered hierarchy, most frequently by isolating the female quarters from a house's conceptual center, these same designs introduced the potential for women from this elite class to claim a room of their own.

The chapters of part II, "Satire, Art, and Epistemology," give us our first turn to the dressing room as a literary trope. The dressing room became a stock-in-trade for satirists almost immediately following its development as an architectural space in seventeenth-century English architecture. Chapter 3, "'A painted woman is a dang'rous thing': Dressing Rooms and the Satiric Mode," refashions the current debate about satiric theory to argue that satiric dressing room scenes point to satire's uneasy reliance on context that is, in fact, a mask for its self-referentiality. Through readings of translations of Juvenal's *Satire Six* and texts inspired by and modeled after this *locus classicus*, I argue that the trope of the dressing room allows for the projection of duplicity, whether by a woman in her dressing room or by a satirist peering into it. The dramatic narrowing of historical context results in a notion of the dressing room as a space of unlicensed and rampant female sexuality or as a site for the production of female vanity. Borrowing from the Juvenalian model, satirists such as François Bruys, John Gay and Lady Mary Wortley Montagu, Andrew Marvell, John Breval, Elizabeth Thomas, and others use the trope of the dressing room to raise questions about the powers of art and artifice and the dressing room's resistance to epistemologies of order.

The following two chapters of part II elaborate the aesthetic and epistemological implications of satiric dressing rooms. Chapter 4, "The Arts of Beauty: Women's Cosmetics and Pope's Ekphrasis," takes as its subject debates about cosmetics, the material object most readily associated with the dressing room, and their perceived relation to women's sexual, aesthetic, and intellectual independence. Critics of cosmetics frequently contend that women can use the subterfuge of artifice to fool spectators by appearing more beautiful or virtuous than they are, while advocates imagine that cosmetics educate women to become well-regulated, pious individuals, with enhanced powers for critical thinking. Within the context of this debate about face painting, the objectification of women through cosmetics takes on a new meaning in Alexander Pope's poems *The Rape of the Lock* and *To a Lady. On the Characters of Women*. When Pope opens *The Rape of the Lock* with a toilet scene, he not only invokes debates about the efficacy and legitimacy of cosmetics, but also contrasts the aesthetics of face painting with the timelessness of poetic painting, or ekphrasis. Pope appropriates the dressing room trope as a means of setting up an aesthetic hierarchy between the cosmetic and poetic arts. The dressing room stages a battle of aesthetic proportions. Ultimately, Pope's use of ekphrasis in these poems not only functions as an aesthetic strategy to represent women, but also as an ideological means of displacing their art and its privileges with his own. This rivalry for aesthetic superiority is played out through the theme of painting, as Pope competes with the image of beautiful, if cosmetically constructed, women for readers' attention.

In Chapter 5, "The Epistemology of the Dressing Room: Experimentation and Swift," I argue for an explicitly epistemological reading of Swift's dressing room satires to understand the connection between fingering through a woman's belongings and coming to "know" a woman. Swift's dressing room poems explicitly critique women's potential for privacy, while also appropriating the model of experimentation associated with the rise of the New Science. Thomas Sprat's *The History of the Royal Society* calls for the "Arts of Mens Hands" to produce not only scientific conclusions, but also literary wit, a position that Swift implicitly adopts in the satiric survey of Celia's dressing room. However, as much as Swift satirizes Strephon and his method, the poem itself depends—albeit uneasily—upon the logic of observation and speculation to produce its own satiric truth, namely that the body of Celia is, indeed, disgusting, though it is the projection of a goddess that ought to be admired. Regardless of this difference (Strephon is naively horrified, the satirist wisely and knowingly entranced), Swift's adoption of the dressing room trope introduces a methodology for the production of general knowledge that itself depends upon the denigration of the female body.

In part III, "Domestic Novels, Education, and Motherhood," I posit that mid- and late-eighteenth-century domestic novelists refashion the trope of the dressing room to develop connotations that the satirists of the earlier generations had suppressed. Chapter 6, "Richardson's Closet Novels: Virtue, Education, and the Genres of Privacy," argues that *Pamela* and *Clarissa* use the dressing room to signal the dangers of female sexuality and transgression and the indecency of satire, as well as the exemplary nature of Richardson's virtuous heroines and the inherent superiority of his narrative form. I draw on texts defending and attacking women's education to argue that Richardson participates in a pedagogical debate that sees learning in the dressing room as a combination of the imperatives for female beauty with the rhetoric of religiosity and intellectual development. Faced with a literary culture that almost inevitably conjoined the dressing room trope with the satiric mode, Richardson foregrounds the educational potential of the dressing room while suppressing its association with dissembling and, in so doing, draws a generic distinction between the raillery and wit of satirists such as Pope and Swift and the narratives of virtue and subjectivity that Richardson himself produces. The novelist disentangles the trope from the satiric mode, and uses female privacy to enable his heroines to write out their virtue, but the dressing room throughout *Pamela* and *Clarissa* continues to introduce the possibility of dissembling and unlicensed sexuality. I conclude by arguing that Richardson's use of the dressing room trope achieves a key generic distinction—as an architectural analogue for the epistolary representation of a woman's mind and the occasion for his novelistic and epistolary innovations.

Following Richardson's innovations, the legacy of the dressing room shapes the plots of the domestic novel's female bildungsroman. Chapter 7, "From Maiden to Mother: Dressing Rooms and the Domestic Novel," argues that domestic novelists use the trope of the dressing room to represent women both before and after marriage. Through readings of novels by Oliver Goldsmith, Frances Burney, and Charlotte Lennox, I argue that the dressing room functions as a developmental stage from which heroines must graduate to progress along the lines of the bildungsroman, requiring them at once to embrace and resist the aesthetics and values of the dressing room. These novels likewise revert to the dressing room trope's satiric heritage by schooling young heroines through the threat of ridicule and mortification to thwart the allure of the dressing room and an excessive attraction to consumerism, clothing, makeup, and appearance. Remarkably, many domestic novelists revisit the married woman's dressing room, using the trope as a metaphor for a woman's success as a mother while still introducing the threat of satiric censure if a woman does not measure up. Johann Zoffany's portrait of Queen Charlotte (ca. 1765–66) and Lady Morgan's *The Book of the Boudoir*, in particular, point to the ideals of maternal virtue as producing a transparent privacy. The chapter concludes with a detailed reading of Maria Edgeworth's *Belinda*, a novel that plots the exposure of Lady Delacour's boudoir and her secret life enclosed therein as the paradigmatic occasion through which the idealized maternal role may be instituted. Within the terms of the novel, this revelation simultaneously facilitates the proper education of the young Belinda and justifies Edgeworth's narrative form, with its transformation of the "romance called the Mysterious Boudoir" into the "Moral Tale" called *Belinda*. In this final chapter, the trope of the dressing room shapes the developmental narratives available to women at the end of the century, often positing idealizations of female maturation through the same space that had been considered illicit and transgressive only one hundred years earlier.

Acknowledgments

I BENEFITED FROM THE GENEROUS FINANCIAL SUPPORT OF SEVERAL foundations and institutions while writing and researching this book, including the Mellon Postdoctoral Fellowship at the Newberry Library, the Research Enhancement Fund at Texas Tech University, and the MacCracken Fellowship, the Halsband Fellowship, and a grant from the Center for Medieval and Renaissance Studies at New York University.

My deepest gratitude goes to Carolyn Dever, Dustin Griffin, and Mary Poovey for their advice, encouragement, and mentorship. Their support has been unfailing, their standards high, and I cherish all that they continue to teach me. I also want to thank Donna Heiland, who first taught me about the eighteenth century and from whom I have benefited from years of conversation and friendship.

I am grateful to Greg Clingham at Bucknell University Press for bringing this project into print and to the two anonymous readers who helped me to see the project in a new light and to improve it in ways I could not have imagined. My many thanks, too, go to Christine A. Retz and Cathy Slovensky for their help with the production and copyediting of the book.

There are also several other individuals whose comments, conversations, and friendships have enhanced my thinking. A number of my colleagues at Texas Tech University have supported the work, including Sherry Ceniza, Bryce Conrad, Doug Crowell, Sam Dragga, Jenni Frangos, Sharon Diane Nell, and John Samson; Bruno Clarke, Madonne Miner, Marjean Purinton, and Jen Shelton deserve special thanks for their generosity as colleagues and readers. My colleagues at Vassar College, particularly Mark Amodio, Mita Choudhury, Bob De-Maria, and Susan Zlotnick, gave me early support and encouragement. At NYU, Margaret Cohen, Laurence Lockridge, Perry Meisel, and Marvin J. Taylor provided timely and generous assistance. I am also indebted to a number of extraordinary colleagues across the country, including Lisa Freeman, Bob Markley, Phyllis Rackin, Laura J. Rosenthal, Helen Thompson, Randy Trumbach, and Hans Turley. During my year at the Newberry, I greatly profited from conversations with Cathleen Cahill, Loretta Fowler, Jim Grossman, Hjordis Halvorson, Dale Van Kley, Sumathi Ramaswamy, David Spadafora, and Carla Zecher, and I am especially grateful to Sara Austin and George Hoffman for their intellectual comradery. My thanks to Morgan Britton Everett for her invaluable research assistance, and to all of my students for their lively engagement with the eighteenth century.

Researching this project has taken me to a number of collections and my thanks to the librarians at the British Library, the Newberry Library, the Folger Shakepeare Library, the New York Public Library, NYU's Fales Library, and Yale's Beineicke Library. I also want to thank the staff at Ham House, Marble Hill, Blenheim Palace, Attingham, and Windsor. Finally, the TTU Interlibrary Loan staff has been heroic in their efforts to locate texts for me.

I have been lucky in friendship and am happy to acknowledge my closest friends here — Mary D. Lewis, Gita Panjabi Trelease, Filiz Turhan, and Allison Pease. Aliza Wong and Stefano D'Amico helped to make moving to Texas from New York City a pleasurable change. Many thanks, too, to my family — Beverly Chico, Raymundo Chico, Gregory Chico, Matthew Chico, and Laura Shipler Chico — for their love, support, and laughter over the years. I am only sorry that my great aunt and godmother, Dorothy T. Fitzgerald, is no longer here, though her love remains.

Early portions of chapters 2 and 5 appeared, respectively, as "The Dressing-Room Unlock'd: Eroticism, Performance, and Privacy from Pepys to the *Spectator*," in *Monstrous Dreams of Reason: Cultural Politics, Enlightenment Ideologies*, ed. Laura J. Rosenthal and Mita Choudhury (Lewisburg, Pa.: Bucknell University Press, 2002) and as "Privacy and Speculation in Early-Eighteenth-Century Britain," *Cultural Critique* 52 (Fall 2002): 40–60. An early version of chapter 4 appeared as "The Arts of Beauty: Women's Cosmetics and Pope's Ekphrasis," *Eighteenth-Century Life* 26, 1 (Winter 2002): 1–23. I am grateful to the editors for their permission to include this material here.

My thanks to the Office of the Provost at TTU for subvention support.

DESIGNING WOMEN

I
Metaphor, Theory, and History

1

Women's Private Parts:
The Politics and Aesthetics
of the Dressing Room

In 1741, JOSEPH PEARCE PRINTED THE NOVELLA *A COURT LADY'S Curiosity; or, the Virgin Undress'd. Curiously surveying herself in her Glass, with one Leg upon her Toilet* and included this additional, suggestive description on the title page: "With a Curious Frontispiece, representing the Posture this Beautiful Chinese Lady was surprized in by Her Lover; and the Artifice he made Use of to accomplish his Design upon her."[1] The novel records the sexual exploits of a young Italian man named Davila visiting China, who becomes infatuated with the daughter of a "Mandarine, or Lord of the Country" (16). For this, his last adventure before returning home, Davila contrives to sneak into the daughter's dressing room and to remain hidden in a "large China Jar," from which he "took the Lady indulging her Fancy in the Glass" (17). The novel suspends the prose narrative to include a verse account by Davila himself. The poem opens with a description of the library in her dressing room (which includes romances, novels, plays, love poetry, and billet-doux) and produces a characteristic dressing table scene: "Behold the Goddess rise to view! / Her Helmet-cap with Jewels spangling" and "Her radiant Eyes — Her sable Curls — / Surpass the Brilliants and the Pearls" (22–23). But the poem deviates from the typical scenario to imagine this woman masturbating with the use of her dressing mirror, surreptitiously observed by the hidden Davila. In what I consider a metaphor for this project, the single extant copy I have discovered (at the British Library) does not have a frontispiece. Whether it was torn away for framing, for obscenity, or whether it never existed, I cannot know. I am left with only a hint of what might have been represented — a site of masturbation, unusual in dressing room scenes, and a structure of doubled voyeurism, as both the reader and the character Davila peep into this woman's private dressing room and, by synecdochic connection, her sexuality. *A Court Lady's Curiosity*'s incomplete status points to the difficulty of a project that is concerned with the emergence of a metaphor in eighteenth-century culture.

The tropes, conventions, and fascination with the lady's dressing room that *A Court Lady's Curiosity* capitalizes upon are typical for the eighteenth century. A lady's private dressing room houses the materials for self-construction, sex, and contemplation, a triumvirate of connotations potentially at odds with one another and richly suggestive for a variety of writers. Throughout the late seventeenth and eighteenth centuries, the lady's dressing room was a stock-in-trade for literary representations that celebrated female autonomy and for those that critiqued it. The dressing room was also evocative of a web of associations related to concerns about genre, gender, language, representation, and authority.

Designing Women considers how the space of the dressing room came to gain figural prominence in the literary culture of the eighteenth century. The dominant chronological narrative of this book details the dressing room's association in the early part of the century with the dangers of women's sexuality and independence, predominantly in satires, to its later incarnation as an image for women's education and maternity in domestic novels. But the thematic narrative of this book demonstrates that the dressing room also appears throughout the century as a figure for aesthetics, epistemology, education, and virtue in both satiric and novelistic texts. The dressing room heralds a legacy of doubled, even contradictory signification. If women's private parts — their rooms, their belongings, their behaviors are all seen as *metonymies* for their bodies — are indicative of a transgressive license, then these same private parts, particularly later in the century, might foreground the liberatory potential of the lady's dressing room as a site for knowledge production and domestic authority, much like the gentleman's closet. In our corpus of late-seventeenth- and eighteenth-century satires about women, the lady's dressing room is attacked as a realm of individual and social degradation. But in domestic novels from the second half of the century, this same space is celebrated as a site of moral, social, and personal amelioration.

The complicated nature of the dressing room's associations renders it a recurring scene in eighteenth-century literary texts, as well as a measure of cultural transformations in gender coding. As a literary setting, the dressing room offers a stage of representation that marks a boundary that is forever susceptible to violation. That boundary, the line of the dressing room door, is, in fact, defined through violation; if it were not, then the dressing room would remain a secret place, open only to speculation. Instead, eighteenth-century writers enthusiastically embrace the imaginative possibilities of the dressing room by rendering it,

over and over, in their texts. As we shall see, the act of closing the dressing room door and marking its perimeter only serves to heighten a literary and cultural investment in determining—or surmising—what,
indeed, the dressing room houses. For this reason, the dressing room in
eighteenth-century texts is immensely productive; it is a space of questioning and problems, for those inside and outside of its walls. Peering
into the dressing room generates narrative; it generates text. Just as the
existence of the dressing room provokes concern about what privileges
it might extend to women, the possibility of these privileges being secretly codified fuels much debate about the appropriateness of women's
privacy and the ability of literary texts to structure—through their representational strategies—appropriate responses and alternatives.

REPRESENTING THE DRESSING ROOM: METAPHOR AND GENRE

The eighteenth-century dressing room offered some women a room
of their own. By midcentury, the terms "dressing room" and "closet"
were interchangeable;[2] the term "lady's cabinet" could refer to this
space and "boudoir" entered the lexicon in the later decades of the century.[3] However, the emergence of the lady's dressing room—as distinguished from the closet or cabinet—in mid-seventeenth-century
English architecture registers only a passing reference in histories of
domestic building and interiors, such as those by Mark Girouard and
by John Fowler and John Cornforth, or it is omitted altogether.[4] Philippe Ariès and George Duby's *A History of Private Life*, which has an
admittedly Continental slant, fails to acknowledge the important symbolic presence of the dressing room, much less its status as a mechanism
for women's privacy. When Orest Ranum turns to consider "The Refuges of Intimacy," those particular spaces that were considered private
in the early modern period, his "scenes of intimacy" include the walled
garden, the chamber, the *ruelle* and the alcove, the study, and the cabinet—but not the lady's dressing room.[5]

If the dressing room has received scant attention from architectural
and domestic histories, then it has been neglected whole-scale by literary studies at the expense of the closet, that site of male prerogative.
The scenes of dressing rooms can trip off a reader's tongue—Pope's *The
Rape of the Lock*, Richardson's *Pamela* and *Clarissa*, Swift's scatological
poetry and *Gulliver's Travels*, and Edgeworth's *Belinda*, to name a few—
but literary critics have yet to acknowledge the dressing room's powerful entrance into the figurative landscape of late-seventeenth- and
eighteenth-century literature. Some critics have considered the topic of
literature and architecture in recent years. For Simon Varey, the eigh-

teenth century witnessed the "parallel development" of space and nov-els.[6] Varey reads architectural theory in conjunction with thematic manifestations of space (both public and private) in novels by Defoe, Fielding, and Richardson and concludes, in essence, that the space in architecture and city planning is, like the space in novels, political, al-though he admits that "an architect's spaces and a novelist's are rarely identical."[7] Philippa Tristram likewise sees space and literature in an associative relation, arguing that houses themselves are fictional just as novels are domestic (and therefore like houses): "Because the novel is invincibly domestic, it can tell us much about the space we live in; equally, designs for houses and their furnishing can reveal hidden as-pects of the novelist's art."[8] Tristram's analysis focuses on the sense of space one has in a novel (rather than the details of furnishings), sug-gesting that this reflects domestic organization as well as social status.[9] While both Varey and Tristram offer perceptive insights into the func-tioning of space—defined variously as the boundaries of architecture as well as the areas in between—their readings assume a mimetic relation-ship between architectural context and novelistic rendering. The dress-ing room, and its widespread adaptation in literary texts (making it more common figuratively than literally), demands that we investigate the particular protocols of each mode of representation and the extent to which they not only corroborate but also diverge from one another.

A more productive approach to literature and architecture finds a voice in Lee Morrissey's *From the Temple to the Castle: An Architectural History of British Literature, 1660–1760.* Morrissey does not merely collate architectural references in familiar literary texts, but also charts a unique intellectual history to expose a preoccupation with structure, whether in architecture or in literature, that ultimately contributes to the period's redefinition of nature: "Literature and architecture are here both understood as types of purposeful metaphor, a larger rendering of the process of positing connections between unlike things, or perhaps a type of purposeful metonymy, a larger rendering of the process of as-cribing a variety of different names to things (or, conversely, the same names to different things)."[10] Morrissey introduces unique and valuable cultural contexts for understanding now familiar literary works by studying writers who were also concerned with architecture.[11] These definitions of form determine one's sense of constructed space and also constitute the formal foundations of each writer's text. Morrissey pro-ductively points to the variety of relations that structure and text may have, and reminds contemporary readers that the disciplines of archi-tecture and literature were not so distant as they are now.

The necessary interrelationship of a figure of space with a literary text's form resonates with the dressing room. A point of convergence in the representation of privacy with its presence in literary texts can be found in the practice of reading; as William B. Warner reminds us, "the relative cheapness of small formats opened books to broader reader-ship, while their small size made them easy to carry in one's pocket into private-reading spaces, such as the bed, the garden, or on a journey."[12] Silent reading came out of the "closet culture" that J. Paul Hunter associates with Protestantism, which "involved habits of privacy and solitude."[13] Frequently a silent affair, reading established a zone of privacy for the reader that replicated the zone of intimacy that satiric and novelistic texts imagine when they peer into the dressing room; moreover, this exemplifies a central problematic of the dressing room trope: the representation of private life for the public's pleasure.[14]

However, the case of the dressing room raises a particular set of issues that highlight the limitations of contextualizing literary texts. History tells us that only wealthy women had dressing rooms, but literature extends this privilege to women of nearly all classes. This disjunction between context and text has implications for literary study more broadly: how do we understand a literary history that rewrites its material context? In other words, how can we make room for the history of a *metaphor*? Moreover, in what ways is the dressing room a particular feature of the eighteenth-century literary landscape? What is its relation to the development of genres during the century and to the range of concerns voiced by writers through the figure of the dressing room?

The chronological boundaries of the dressing room are quite specific: it is an eighteenth-century metaphor. While one might consider other feminine spaces of privacy—Gertrude's closet in *Hamlet*, for example, which is more famous than it is representative, and precedes the historical incorporation of the dressing room into English domestic architecture—the fact that architectural change gives us a point at which to note the appearance of "dressing room" as a figure of speech. When William Wycherley's Horner boasts in *The Country Wife* (1675) that he has unfettered access to women's dressing rooms, he uses the dressing room as a sign of female sexuality.[15] On the other end of the century, the dressing room as a representative of femininity becomes diffused into the feminization of domestic space more generally, as evidenced in Maria Edgeworth's *Belinda* (1801) and Jane Austen's *Pride and Prejudice* (1813) (discussed at length in chapter 7). Well into the nineteenth century, English novels may include a dressing room, but they are most commonly associated with the rise of suspense and mystery in the nineteenth-century sensation novel. In Mary Elizabeth Braddon's *Lady Audley's Secret* (1862), for example, Lady Audley's boudoir and her dressing room are featured prominently in this story of a bigamous heroine who has deserted her child, murders her first husband, and contemplates poisoning her second. Lady Audley's dressing room cloaks the mystery of her identity, a half-finished portrait and the secret of her criminality. Adding to this connotation are the circumstances of a notorious scandal novelist's death; Caroline Archer Clive (1801–73) was sensationally burned to death while writing in her boudoir.

The metaphor is also an especially English one, at least until several decades into the eighteenth century. Studies of the boudoir in French literature, such as Peter Cryle's *Geometry in the Boudoir* and, more recently, Michel Delon's *L'Invention du boudoir*, demonstrate that the predominant connotation of the French boudoir is sexual. Cryle uses the boudoir motif to address the structures of eighteenth-century erotic and pornographic French literature, while Delon analyzes the emergence of the boudoir as a literary scene in the eighteenth-century and its later manifestations in the nineteenth century.[16] However, the timing of this metaphoric emergence is later in the French manifestation: I argue that the English dressing room gained figural status in the late seventeenth century, while Delon dates the boudoir's appearance as a variant of the cabinet in French literature to 1735.

The generic implications of this metaphor are likewise significant: the dressing room trope is a figure associated with the genres of satire and, later in the century, domestic narrative. Apart from lyric and epic, in which dressing rooms often foreground the subjection of a lover to his beloved's beauty or stage the effeminizing seduction of epic heroes, many dressing room scenes seem inevitably to revert to a satiric mode.[17] Even an encomium such as Mary Molesworth Monck's "On *Marinda's* Toilette" (1716) includes satiric censure of a dressing room. Monck's poem is a tribute to the *naturally* beautiful Marinda and therefore begins by satirizing women who use dressing room cosmetics to make themselves beautiful: "hence vulgar Beauties take their pow'rful Arms, / And from their Toilette borrow all their Charms."[18] By midcentury, the Richardsonian domestic novel in effect disengages the dressing room trope from the satiric mode and aligns it with his narrative form in a battle for aesthetic superiority, consolidating the domestic narrative as a vehicle for virtue and education.

As I conceptualize it here, the trope of the dressing room does *not* figure as a dominant metaphor in the dramatic literature of the late seventeenth and eighteenth centuries. While there are famous dressing room scenes from several plays in this period—including Lady Wishfort's anxious efforts at her toilet to make herself look young again and Lord Foppling's foppish pretensions and machinations in his dressing room—the drama at this time did not suppose a "fourth wall." In other words, the space of the Restoration and eighteenth-century stage did not institute a boundary between the players and the spectators to per-

petuate the illusion that these scenes took place in private. The antithe-
atricalist Jeremy Collier, writing in 1698, warned that the theater was
dangerous *because* there was no "fourth wall": the actors played on stage
and in the audience, ready to "remove from Fiction into Life."[19] It is
only later in the eighteenth century that the playhouse itself changed its
scopic regime such that audience members assumed a more voyeuristic
role as they watched the players act on stage.[20] Catherine B. Burroughs
provocatively argues that female Romantic dramatists—most prominently Joanna Baillie—used the trope of the closet drama as a means
of revealing that the "private sphere is inherently theatrical" and that
the closet itself provided "a smaller stage that permit[ted] the more subtle dramatization of public and private realms, a more naturalistic acting
style, a lighting design that would allow audiences to read psychological
shifts."[21] Burroughs contends that even the phrase "closet drama"
"serve[d] as a metaphor for privacy and intense intellectual engagement, but it also identified a literal space in which a variety of theatrical
activities—many particular to women—took place."[22] But this is a phenomena of the late eighteenth century, and is clearly available to these
dramatists as a result of the widespread cultural play of the dressing
room in the literary culture of the late seventeenth and eighteenth centuries.

Designing Women argues that over the course of the eighteenth century
the dressing room's connotations and relations to genre changed from
accusatory to celebratory, but this is not necessarily a story of improvement or advancement. In contrast, most critics who consider the representation of women in satiric texts implicitly read the century as one of
"progress." Felicity Nussbaum's *The Brink of All We Hate* and Ellen Pollak's *The Poetics of Sexual Myth*, both pioneering works of feminist literary history, provide metanarratives of sympathy in their readings that
privilege one kind of satirist over another. For example, Nussbaum associates the comparative decline of satire's prominence in the later eighteenth century with an increase in concern for women's "plight."[23] Read
this way, the corrective element in satires about women—the latent desire to improve the readers of a particular satiric text—confirms for
Nussbaum a larger cultural concern with the labors of femininity, and
this awareness, in turn, precipitates the demise of satire; she adds, "as
the blame shifts from woman's inherent sexual characteristics to her social plight, the path from the whore to the fallen woman is a path
toward greater understanding and greater sympathy for the sex."[24] The
demarcation that Nussbaum foregrounds sets up satirists such as Pope
as voices of sympathy for women, just the sort of argument that has
subsequently permeated studies of satire. Pollak replicates Nussbaum's
focus on the sympathetic poet but argues, in contrast, that Swift is

"kinder to women" than Pope is, positioning her interpretation in contrast to New Critical readings of Pope that recuperated his reputation
and made space for the admiring view (corroborated by the formally
beautiful poetry that Pope produces).[25] Swift, Pollak argues, has received primarily biographical attention, as critics speak to his personality and pathologies in any reference to his attitudes toward women
without addressing the texts as texts.[26] *The Poetics of Sexual Myth* proceeds to do just that to prove that it is Swift—not Pope—who is ultimately more sympathetic to women and that the "graciousness" of
Pope's poetry "belies contempt."[27] For Pollak, the century is one of
progress, too, through the development of a genre arguably more incipi-
ently "feminist" than satire—the novel.[28]

As important as these studies have been to the field, both sides of this
argument are limited. The "either/or" model of interpretation narrows
our appreciation for and understanding of satiric texts to those that
seem to be more genial. It also eradicates the spectrum of satiric models
operative during this period.[29] The dressing room trope offers a powerful alternative through its conflicting imperatives—which range from
containment to liberation and from censure to celebration—that themselves illustrate the unstable nature of satiric rhetoric. Moreover, this
focus on the trope of the dressing room allows us to consider the shift
from satire to the domestic novel while resisting the same narratives of
progress that have been associated with this transformation. Margaret
Ezell offers a powerful historical model that questions the development
thesis, noting in particular that it assumes a conclusion or ripening in
the nineteenth-century domestic novel: "What we do need is an arche-
ology of an early body of writings which strips away layers of assumptions between us and these past texts without seeking to impose
immediately a preconceived hierarchy of literary values and the progress of feminist thought on what we find."[30] In this spirit, I offer a generic understanding of this kind of representation through the lens of
the dressing room trope. If, following the Richardsonian novel's labored
separation of the satiric mode from the dressing room, the domestic
novel comes to be the locale for the imaginary presence of the dressing
room, then this transformation does not necessarily reflect a larger concern for the sufferings of women. Instead, this indicates a shift in representational strategies that envisages women as potentially—but not
fully—intelligent agents, even though this potential is ultimately subsumed under the rubric of wifely and maternal selflessness.

Rather than read in an approving or disapproving manner, as the satires themselves ask us to do, it is much more productive to interpret
these satiric texts in their fullest tensions and to capitalize on the unease
that Patricia Meyer Spacks associates with satire more generally.[31] The

satirists' views may be indefensible or admirable, but this is not the point of analyzing their texts. Pope himself anticipates this kind of reaction when he confesses that *The Rape of the Lock* is at once inoffensive and satiric.[32] We must reframe the questions that earlier critics implicitly pose: assuming that Swift and Pope represent (and in so doing, *de*-limit) women as objects, how does this strategy of representation corroborate or reveal the interconnections of the dressing room as a figure for gender difference to art, knowledge, morality, education, and motherhood? Required is a rereading of the meanings of these texts that undeniably satirize women. Laura Brown and Laura Mandell point us to the ways in which representations of women are culturally ramified. According to Brown, the female figure is linked with both commodification and trade as well as with violence and difference, associations that "play a central role in the constitution of [a] mercantilist capitalist ideology" that shapes eighteenth-century cultural productions.[33] Following Brown, Mandell extends the category of "misogyny" to consider its cultural ramifications, arguing that misogyny "is not about women but rather about society: representations that inspire passionate hatred of women and disgust with the female body provide a place for people to work out passionate feelings about changes in economic and social structure."[34] While both Brown and Mandell offer compelling readings of eighteenth-century texts that disparage women, I argue that we must calibrate the extent to which truisms of gender difference—played out dramatically through the trope of the dressing room—resonate in and give form to other realms of conflict, which is why I offer double narrative that describes a chronological and generic change, as well as a cluster of themes that regularly find a voice in the dressing room.

On the other side of the critical divide in eighteenth-century studies, *Designing Women* offers a corrective to debates about the domestic novel that fail to acknowledge the influence of the satiric tradition on the novel's development. Typical accounts of the novel's "rise" in the eighteenth century generally assume a fundamental disjunction between the aesthetics and protocols of satire and those of novelistic discourse. The trope of the dressing room offers a persuasive means of revising this debate. Nancy Armstrong sees in the novel's origins an anxiety about what women were, as eighteenth-century domestic novels subordinate "all social differences to those based on gender . . . [to] bring order to social relationships."[35] For Armstrong, the question of delimiting women—refashioning them as proper, middle-class subjects—was at the heart of novelistic discourse, and ultimately in line with the poetic tradition that looked to women as muses. Women for novelists, therefore, "became instead a function of imagination that provided figurative language with a psychological source of meaning."[36] But while Armstrong looks to the conduct book tradition (which she argues predates the existence of the class identity that it projects) to find an analogy for novelistic representations of women, particularly those following the Richardsonian model in *Pamela*, this approach neglects the generic — and therefore ideological — antecedents that Richardson himself appropriates.[37]

If we use the dressing room trope to think about the relationship between satire and the domestic novel, then we likewise see that their connection is equally unacknowledged by critics whose focus is satire and fiction, generally because the reading of satire is itself narrow. Michael McKeon, for example, conceives of satire itself as a corrective mode of representation — a limited definition in itself — and only in relation to a reading of Swift's *Gulliver's Travels*.[38] A more expansive reading is available in Mikhail Bakhtin's *Problems of Dostoevsky's Poetics*, which vigorously contends that Menippean satire — particularly with its focus on the carnivalesque — gave birth to the novel, but this argument, too, confines our understanding of the novel to the specifically comic novel of writers such as Fielding and Sterne.[39]

Not since Ronald Paulson's 1967 *Satire and the Novel in Eighteenth-Century England* have we benefited from a sustained analysis of novelistic and satiric forms. Paulson predominantly focuses on self-identified satirists such as Fielding, Smollett, and Sterne, but simultaneously opens a space for the consideration of narrative and satiric forms more broadly because both, he argues, are invested in "realistic" accounts of the world.[40] Like G. S. Rousseau, who argues that satire and the novel "did not get along,"[41] Paulson cautiously limits the relationship: "The English novel did not, of course, grow out of satire; they are two discontinuous forms."[42] Even so, Paulson argues that satire in the Richardsonian novel (an author whom he calls a "satiro-novelist") functions as a vehicle for the heroine to defend herself from the encroachment of others.[43] Satire in these novels ultimately shows "how a realistic work could be moralistic and still realistic."[44] If both forms are mimetic, however, then Paulson's argument seems to be more suitable to the self-consciously domestic novels of Richardson and others, rather than to the comic novels of Fielding and Smollett.

The focus of critics considering the relationship between satire and the domestic novel has preempted a thoughtful consideration of the extent to which the tradition of satirizing women contributed to the development of narratives about female subjects, even though the novelists themselves were acutely aware of the precedent. Eighteenth-century satiric and novelistic discourses share an investment in the representation of femininity, but the question of this relation to a cultural context (the question of whether this is, indeed, a *reflection* of the eighteenth-century world) is a vexed one. By examining the trope of the dressing room, I offer a means to correct this literary history of generic influence and development between satire and the domestic novel: once the satirist showed the way into the lady's dressing room, the eighteenth-century novelist never stopped looking.

THE DRESSING ROOM'S OTHER CONTEXTS: PRIVACY, CONSUMERISM, AND THEORY

If the trope of the dressing room is a powerfully *literary* phenomenon, then it likewise resonates with debates about the history of private life and consumerism that are central to the study of early modern culture and with debates about theories of privacy that explore our postmodern preoccupation with the "closet."

The history of the dressing room is inextricably tied to the history of private life. In England, the country that Philippe Ariès calls the "birthplace of privacy," domestic architecture and design instituted spaces that were differentiated and demarcated, including the dressing room.[45] For Lawrence Stone, the spatialization of privacy contributed to the eventual rise of affective individualism. Stone contends in *The Family, Sex, and Marriage In England, 1500–1800* that architectural innovations in domestic structures were designed not only to give individual family members increased privacy (in smaller and more diversified rooms), but also to allow the family as a unit to "escape from the prying eyes and ears of the ubiquitous domestic servants, who were a necessary evil in every middle- and upper-class household."[46] Stone also attributes a "refinements of manners"—reflected in increased hygiene and increasingly elaborate dress—to a "desire to separate one's body and its juices and odours from contact with other people, to achieve privacy in many aspects of one's personal activities, and generally to avoid giving offence to the 'delicacy' of others."[47] Stone's analysis illuminates the implications of having access to privacy: even if individuals could not be physically isolated, then their behaviors and manners were designed to keep certain things private. In this climate, individuals from wealthier classes developed a kind of shield that, in Stone's historiography, allowed them to keep themselves conceptually separate from one other; moreover, we must remember that "privacy" during this period could very well not indicate solitude but familial society.[48]

Pace Stone, how that privacy manifested itself in the English context is an object of debate among historians. Lena Cowen Orlin, for example, links the early modern history of property rights to the cultural construction of privacy in sixteenth- and seventeenth-century English

culture. The state both depended upon private households as genera-
tors of national income, and remained wary of households' "internal activities," insofar as they might be sites for government resistance.[49] The
household facilitated the consolidation of a patriarchal form of privacy,
Orlin argues, through its "reinvention as a unit of social control, the
empowerment of the householder as defender of political order, and,
finally, the promulgation of an enabling ideology of domestic patriar-
chalism."[50] Through Orlin's work, we can measure an antecedent to the
eighteenth-century household, in which the Habermasian public sphere
finds not only its capital resources, but also—as Addison and Steele's
Mr. Spectator imagines it—a pool of women to be educated (and to buy
the paper).

Consider a famous appropriation of the dressing room, when Mr.
Spectator strategically adopts the dressing room in his announcement
that the periodical will be especially valuable for women:

> there are none to whom this Paper will be more useful than to the female
> World. I have often thought there has not been sufficient Pains taken in
> finding out proper Employments and Diversions for the Fair ones. Their
> Amusements seem contrived for them rather as they are Women, than as
> they are reasonable Creatures; and are more adapted to the Sex, than to the
> Species. The Toilet is their great Scene of Business, and the right adjusting
> of their Hair the principal Employment of their Lives.[51]

The domestic sphere becomes a matter for public debate and intervention; thus, Mr. Spectator hopes that his periodical, designed (in the
words of Terry Eagleton) for the exchange of free rational discourse,
finds its way to the tea tables of every reputable English family and
produces civil conversation on manners and morals.[52]

But the "separate spheres" thesis—the idea that women were confined to this domestic sphere—has come under recent criticism. Armstrong's *Desire and Domestic Fiction* locates the rise of the middle-class
subject in the figure of the domestic woman.[53] To Armstrong, this female figure is the model political citizen; she represents the paradox of
modernity, forever embodying the apparently apolitical (the family, the
home) even though these same categories are inevitably politicized.[54]
Lawrence E. Klein takes issue with Armstrong's readings and argues
that while the theory of social organization conceptualized women as
"private" subjects, eighteenth-century women actually led public lives
and had public experiences (and were not just the private figures that
Armstrong imagines), thereby undermining the strict division envisaged by our anachronistic "public/private distinction."[55] Amanda Vickery approaches this question differently by looking directly at women's

domestic experiences: if it is incontrovertible that women "were primarily associated with home and children," then it is likewise notable that
conduct literature instructed women of the genteel class to exercise
power and authority within the household.[56] Vickery contends that domesticity was engaged with the outside world in practical terms (unlike
Armstrong's symbolic relation), whether through social interactions or
by means of reading and other forms of cultural consumption.[57] To confine our understanding of privileged women's lives in the eighteenth
century to the paradigm of separation is to accentuate "distinctions of
limited significance" and to miss "central preoccupations."[58]

The *Spectator* paper cited above imagines one form of cultural consumption that bridged private and public spheres: shopping. If Mr.
Spectator laments that "the Toilet is [women's] great Scene of Business,
and the right adjusting of their Hair their principal Employment of their
Lives," then his frustration is redoubled by women expending energy
dressing to shop and, if they are particularly industrious, *actually* shopping: "The sorting of a Suit of Ribbons is reckoned a very good Morning's Work; and if they make an Excursion to a Mercer's or a Toy-shop,
so great a Fatigue makes them unfit for any thing else all the Day after.
. . . This, I say, is the State of ordinary Women."[59] Mr. Spectator's concerns that women "shop 'til they drop" find an economic explanation in
Neil McKendrick's famous proclamation that "there was a consumer
revolution in eighteenth-century England"; others date the phenomenon more precisely to the 1720s.[60] McKendrick suggests that the implications of consumerism in the eighteenth century were far-reaching, as
shops sprang up where eighteenth-century consumers could purchase,
rather than inherit, luxury items and, indeed, would imagine these luxury items as necessary to leading one's life.[61] "Shopping" for fashionable clothing enabled women to self-fashion themselves,[62] but also made
consumers out of people across classes. Servants, as McKendrick notes,
were a "vital chain" in the promulgation and consumption of fashion, a
model of emulation that satirists and domestic novelists frequently ridiculed.[63] The eighteenth-century shop produced a "world which blurred
rather than reinforced class divisions and allowed the conspicuous lead
of the fashion leaders to be quickly copied by the rest of society."[64]

While economic historians debate the specificities of McKendrick's
claims, the value of foregrounding consumption in our discussion of the
dressing room is clear.[65] As we shall see in chapter 2, the dressing room
was a perfect repository for women's material consumption, whether in
the form of furniture, china, lacquer, books, paintings, clocks, or, of
course, clothing. Dressing rooms in all sorts of houses had versions of
the same things, frequently differing only in quality or price. There are
two points to be made about consumerism and the dressing room. First,

following the explosion of shopping venues throughout England in the early decades of the eighteenth century, even a woman of a certain means in a country farmhouse could have her toilet.[66] Second, as Harriet Guest notes, there was a pervading belief that fashionable activity was "a synecdochic representation of commercial culture."[67] Thus, Mr. Spectator's complaint that women's attention is captured by their dressing rooms and shopping, to the exclusion of any productive behavior, astutely conjoins a feminized materialism of the domestic sphere with a feminized commerce available in the public.

Consumerism made the concept of fashion available to a greater range of people, and this availability had a particular parallel to eighteenth-century notions of femininity. "Consumption" alludes both to material acquisition and to the physical disease; as John Brewer and Roy Porter note, "consuming is thus both enrichment and impoverishment."[68] Addison and Steele's *Spectator* picks up on this contradictory meaning, but only to suppress its potential benefits. Mr. Spectator condemns women for exhausting themselves shopping (or the paler version, just *thinking* about it), all the while supporting the notion that the accumulation of material goods at a mercer's or a toy shop is entirely frivolous. Addison and Steele's paper likewise points to shopping as a form of behavior regularly and insistently associated with women, reflecting what Elizabeth Kowaleski-Wallace argues is an "ongoing process of constructing female subjectivity" through consumerism.[69] Even though the shopkeeper was figured as masculine and the shopper, feminine, female consumption in the eighteenth century was paradoxical; writers imagined that women were either "supremely disciplined" and submissive to the (male) shopkeeper or "disruptive and disorderly" and threatening to patriarchal order.[70] The satiric associations between luxury goods and prostitution fed on this model of female consumption.[71] The dressing room, both as an architectural space and as a metaphor, predates the widespread consumption of luxury goods and the role of consumerism in eighteenth-century definitions of femininity by a generation or so, but the parallels are instructive. If, as Kowaleski-Wallace's analysis suggests, the gendering of consumerism in the eighteenth century constructed a double bind for women, then we are well served by seeing this conflict replicated in the feminized materialism associated with dressing rooms that writers across the century could claim either enhanced a woman's moral exemplarity or confirmed her lack of it.

The various correctives offered by recent historical scholarship on private life and on consumerism collectively ask us to reconstruct the possibilities available to eighteenth-century women. In spite of these contributions, however, a critical question lingers: such historical debates do not always illuminate the vexed *theoretical* connotations of privacy and its relation to subjectivity, issues also at the heart of the dressing room. Historian Yves Castan provocatively argues that "there was no mystery about privacy," but mystery—or at least, secrecy—was written into the possibility of claiming privacy from the start.[72] If, as Peter Brooks argues, the Enlightenment witnessed a "new and intense concern for privacy," then it also saw the advent of the *violation* of such private domains or the construction of "an inviolable space opened only by an invasion of privacy."[73] The dressing room itself is a case in point. A dressing room might have easily functioned as a threshold to the public; its primary function was to house a woman as she prepared for the day and disrobed at the end of it (although Samuel Johnson defines the term more narrowly as the "room in which clothes are put on").[74] But the dressing room also had four walls and a door (or two or more), boundaries to partition a woman from many aspects of and people in her household. Individuated physical spaces and locked objects were indelibly associated with the potential for individualism.

These material facts of life also gave rise to the domestication of secrecy. In an admittedly different context, seventeenth-century French court culture, Norbert Elias studies the implications of this new kind of privacy to argue that a self-detached subjectivity results; there is a foundational association between "alienation and the increase in consciousness, the ascent to a new level on the spiral staircase of consciousness."[75] For Elias, this is all an effect of "distancing"—distancing oneself from nature and from others.[76] "Reality" itself becomes a series of layers, with each individual assuming an external mask for public consumption and self-consciously inserting a gap between "the affective, spontaneous impulse to act and the actual performance of the action in word or deed."[77] Elias focuses on a specifically French context (leaning here on a reading of Honoré d'Urfé's novel *L'Astrée*) and implicitly conceives of this "ascension" as psychological development, but his arguments have profoundly influenced subsequent studies of "private life," particularly in the monumental series of that same name.[78] The essence of Elias's argument allows us to conclude that privacy allows for a separate domain, first of body (at least to some extent) and then of mind. The alienation of which Elias speaks is not the postmodern self-alienation of, say, psychoanalysis, but of the separation between what a person thinks she or he is in private and how that person knows she or he is understood in public.

While Elias's topic is exclusively Continental, his work is not too far afield from readings of privacy in seventeenth- and eighteenth-century England. Patricia Meyer Spacks's recent *Privacy: Concealing the Eighteenth-Century Self* contends that "psychological privacy" garnered the most attention and debate, for "it appeared to encourage hypocrisy, a major focus of anxiety in the period: people might employ masks of various kinds in order to retain control of secret thoughts, feelings, and imaginings."[79] Spacks's use of the mask image suggestively alludes to Elias's spiral staircase, but Francis Barker's earlier *The Tremulous Private Body* allows us to reconsider the layers of disguise that Elias's model presupposes and to differentiate between the French court culture that Elias studies and the history of English domesticity relevant to the dressing room. Barker contends that this period witnessed a radical privatization of the self and locates the scene of this transformation in English writing. The language and subject matter of the seventeenth-century diarist Samuel Pepys lead Barker to conclude that private, domestic spaces are scenes of reading, writing, and sexuality. Opening with Pepys's ambivalent evocation and denial of his penchant for buying, reading, and burning French pornography in the privacy of his own home, Barker demonstrates that even the realm of the private does not always deliver full disclosure. Pepys uses a "plainness" of speech to keep still other things private. The diary "employs massive means — not of repression, for everything is said, eventually, even if it is not acknowledged as having been said — but of diversion: we are asked to look 'by the way' at 'other things.' "[80] For Pepys, it is the fact of pornography that must remain diverted from the reader's eye, even though that reader is always himself and even though the text is produced and stored in his closet and written in code.

The idea that there is an original lurks behind theories of privacy as a mask or as the distanced self-spectatorship of a spiral staircase, but Barker's reading of Pepys's diary challenges this assumption of authenticity. Instead, the process of hiding may implicate even the most intimate moments of truth-telling, calling into question the very project of exposing a private space to public scrutiny.[81] In other words, things may still be hidden, a dressing room — even a dressing room with its doors thrown wide open — may still contained its own purloined letters, evidence of the unseen, sitting in plain view. Barker's private tremulous body indicates that the suggestion that privacy is in some way authentic is itself illusory, with every exposure precipitating yet another obfuscation. The promise of disclosure — indeed, even the *fact* of disclosure — only introduces yet another opportunity for enclosure. Even Pepys, writing to himself in a made-up language and in private, cannot submit to openness with himself.

The uneasiness that the dressing room produces for satirists and domestic novelists originates in this contradiction. Just as Pepys's desires for illicit texts (pornography) produces an opacity that refuses to clear, all the while pretending to transparency, the dressing room's association with female sexuality and desire both engenders narrative and thwarts resolution. To understand the vexed theoretical nature of privacy in this way draws on contemporary theories of the closet, particularly from Eve Kosofsky Sedgwick's *Epistemology of the Closet*. For Sedgwick, the queer closet is an open secret that functions as a narrative structure and as an ideological form. It is the "telling secret" that simultaneously—and contradictorily—promises to expose things to view while also keeping them hidden away.[82] Building on D. A. Miller's insights from *The Novel and the Police*, Sedgwick contends that open secrets such as the closet seem to conflate categories—mixing the private and the public, for example—but that they actually reinforce those very binaries. The closet, a resilient metaphor for homosexuality, embodies the theoretical incoherence that has ensured the existence of an excruciating system of double binds for gays and lesbians. Commenting on the legal decisions in cases of gay discrimination (such as Bowers v. Hardwick and the suit brought by Acanfora), Sedgwick writes that "the space for simply existing as a gay person . . . is in fact bayonetted through and through, from both sides, by the vectors of a disclosure at once compulsory and forbidden."[83] Gayness is neither private nor public, and the symbol of the closet aptly and profoundly reflects this conundrum. Coming out of the closet does not—and cannot—offer epistemological or even ideological certainty; nor does staying inside.

In all of these instances—Pepys's pornography, the lady's dressing room, the queer closet—secrecy is subsumed by the secrecy of sexuality. The figure of the closet opens up the question of knowledge. To open the closet or to go inside is to acquire sexual knowledge, but the violation of this conceptual (if not experiential) boundary signals the acquisition of knowledge more generally. An epistemology of the closet is the modern-day tree of knowledge, the fruit of knowing that is inextricably linked to sex. Sedgwick explains that "knowledge meant sexual knowledge, and secrets sexual secrets, there had in fact developed one particular sexuality that was distinctively constituted *as* secrecy"—namely, homosexuality as it emerged (conceptually) in the nineteenth century and gained currency in the twentieth.[84]

The applicability of Sedgwick's closet to other periods and sexualities is promised through her claim that this epistemology of the closet does not solely implicate lesbians and gays. The closet figures centrally in the construction of all kinds of cultural categories and divisions that have given rise to or defended the hierarchies of the status quo:

> The epistemology of the closet has also been . . . inexhaustibly productive of modern Western culture and history at large. While that may be reason enough for taking it as a subject of interrogation, it should not be reason enough for focusing scrutiny on those who inhabit the closet (however

equivocally) to the exclusion of those in the ambient heterosexist culture who enjoin it and whose representational needs it serves in a way less extortionate to themselves.[85]

The closet functions to compel gays and lesbians both to come out and to stay hidden, and it likewise contributes to and supports the heteronormative social structure located outside of its walls. The closet embodies the apparent but illusory binary between the categories of heterosexuality and homosexuality. In more general terms, the reliance of cultural hegemonies on the categories that they attempt to exclude becomes extraordinarily clear. The epistemology of the closet throws light on the relation of "homosexuality to wider mappings of secrecy and disclosure, and of the private and the public, that were and are critically problematical for the gender, sexual, and economic structures of the heterosexist culture at large."[86] The fundamental instability of the closet—it is neither wholly private nor wholly public—exposes the idea that self-consciously public discourses depend upon the closet's existence and its apparently problematic status, banking on the assumption that everything outside of an epistemologically fraught closet would be stable, clear, and impervious to interrogation. What we learn from Sedgwick's analysis is that the instability and incoherence of the closet is shared equally by the normative structures that depend upon its marginalization, resulting in a "crisis of definition."[87] Such categorical crisis relates specifically to the interdependence of the two terms that are conceptualized as inherently distinct, even though their differences are theoretically and practically blurred.

Sedgwick's groundbreaking work productively exposes the theoretical instability of the interconnections among secrecy, sexuality, and knowledge, as well as the means by which hierarchical binaries seem to perpetuate confusion on the one hand and order on the other. The closet as such seems to be made-to-order for studies of the early modern masculine closet because, while feminist in methodology, Sedgwick's focus is unwaveringly on masculine homosexuality.[88] For Sedgwick, the risk of ignoring women pays off: "a great deal depends . . . on the fostering of our ability to arrive at understandings of sexuality that will respect a certain irreducibility in it to the terms and relations of gender," even though those understandings of sexuality will be of masculine sexuality.[89] This turn from feminism to queer theory depends upon the refiguration of patriarchy into heterosexism, accompanied by the redefinition of misogyny as homophobia.

While Sedgwick's contributions to the development of queer theory are significant, critics have noted this glaring absence of women, specifically lesbians, from her work. As Carolyn Dever explains, Sedgwick "inaugurates an era in which feminist practitioners fixate on male homoeroticism as an interesting problematic while dismissively relegating the 'dyke' to the outer reaches of feminist discourse."[90] In the introduction to her earlier *Between Men: English Literature and Male Homosocial Desire*, Sedgwick acknowledges that "the isolation, not to mention the absolute subordination, of women, in the structural paradigm on which this study is based . . . is a distortion that necessarily fails to do justice to women's own powers, bonds, and struggles."[91] In effect, Sedgwick's method—privileging men over women—replicates her thesis about the conceptual erasure of women in a homosocial economy. The queer theory in Sedgwick's work therefore institutes a simultaneously structural and theoretical elimination of women, whether gay or straight.

Sedgwick's model of the closet also allows us to apprehend the dressing room's centrality in the cultural imagination of the eighteenth century as a repository for a range of debates about femininity, the arts, epistemology, education, and motherhood. Adapting Sedgwick's reading of the queer closet, with its contested status and its relation to the maintenance of cultural categories more generally, to the eighteenth-century lady's dressing room does not suggest a symmetry between the experiences of gays and lesbians, on the one hand, and those of a group of women with the privileges of the dressing room, on the other. While the occasional text pursues the homoerotic or autoerotic potentialities of women's sexuality in the dressing room, as we shall see in the reading of Maria Edgeworth's *Belinda*, the majority of texts that represent women in their dressing rooms imagine women as heterosexist—that is, women sexually active only with men or with phallic substitutes such as lapdogs or dildoes.[92] My work instead offers a beginning corrective for the erasure of women in general from theories of the closet.

There certainly were dressing rooms for men—Lord Chesterfield conducted (in)famous business in his—but they were provinces for male prerogative (linked in type to the gentleman's closet) rather than sites of anxiety. When men's private parts came under scrutiny, the effect was much more likely to suggest that the particular man was a deviant, rather than that an entire gender was. Examples such as the Baron's altar in *The Rape of the Lock*, Colley Cibber's account of Pope's impotence with a prostitute in his *"Tom-Tit"* story, and Lady Mary Wortley Montagu's satire of Swift's impotence with another prostitute all suggest that these men fail individually, rather than collectively. In contrast, responses to the lady's dressing room registered a desire to produce the heterosexist gender difference that Randolph Trumbach argues emerged in the eighteenth century.[93] During a time when women were increasingly acquiring material and legal privileges, the trope of the dressing room gave writers a vehicle to express concerns about the roles of women by arguing for the differences not only between men and women, but also between good and degenerate women.[94] In this way we can see that, while conceptually analogous in terms of privacy, the dressing room differs from the closet in another especially important way: to many writers throughout the period, the materialism of the dressing room itself stood as a direct metonymy not only for female sexuality, but also—in very precise terms—for the female body. When Swift's Strephon tiptoes into Celia's dressing room, he imagines that he sees her body everywhere, even though she has left for the day. The objects decorating the dressing room are regularly imagined as surrogates for the female body, and this characteristic "embodiment" of the dressing room assumes physical differences between men and women that constituted this gender difference. Or, in the terms Thomas Laqueur presents, the dressing room makes evident the eighteenth-century "invention" of sex as grounded in the body.[95] This two-sex system rendered the female body the site of "incommensurable difference," and if the dressing room was so often read as a figure for women's bodies and their sexuality, then we can understand that its representation staged a "battleground for redefining the ancient, intimate, fundamental social relation: that of woman to man."[96] This "fundamental social relation" underscores the stakes of representing the dressing room in the eighteenth century. That the dressing room was first primarily associated with women's *illicit* sexuality (and theatricality) and later with its legitimate forms (through the marriage market and motherhood) indicates the century's shifting codes of gender, as well as the dressing room's persistence in and adaptability to a variety of contexts and genres.

To get inside the dressing room was not only to see metonymies for women's bodies and their sexuality, but it also allowed one to emphasize the metonymic relationship between space and body that the sexualization of the dressing room presupposed and, in so doing, derive the authority of stripping away the surface of femininity to expose its dirty little secrets—to *name* that incommensurable difference. This strategy is most predominantly associated with satirists from the late seventeenth and early eighteenth centuries, but even domestic novelists in the later part of the century, a time when the dressing room contributed to the idealization of female virtue and maternity, would evoke its tawdry associations with difference in order to critique characters or signal danger. The dressing room was, for many, an overdetermined place of mystery—the texts analyzed throughout this book work on a set of common expectations—and this was a situation that invited speculation and censure, rewarding those who circulated these images with the authority of "discovery" and truth-telling, but always leaving open the possibility that not everything was found. The dressing room came under the pressure of investigation regularly and thoroughly by a vast number of writers, commentators, and critics.

2

"The Art of Knowing Women": A History of the Dressing Room

Should any daring Pen attempt to show
What sorts of Dress our Modern Females know,
What antick habits their own *Mothers* wore,
And what was us'd an hundred years before,
Their *Fardingales*, *Stiff-Ruffs*, and all the train
Of Fashions us'd in old *Queen Bess*'s Reign;
Could he describe the Rise and Pedigree
Of Monumental *Top-Knot* Gallantry,
Expose their arts (which they esteem no sin)
To mend the Face, and Meliorate the Skin,
Of *Washes, Paints, Perfumes*, display their skill,
The bare relation would more Volumes fill,
Than are in *Oxford* or the *Vatican*,
And reach from thence to *China* or *Japan*.
   —Richard Ames, *The Folly of Love* (1691)

DRESSING ROOMS FOR WOMEN BEGAN TO APPEAR IN ENGLISH HOMES in the mid-seventeenth century, and increased in number and frequency with the return of Charles II and his courtiers, whose restoration sparked a rise in the number of country houses designed and built.[1] In this chapter, I chart an archaeology of the dressing room that foregrounds both its placement in the domestic hierarchy, as well as its relation to the kinds of roles available to women. Keeping in mind Lorna Weatherhill's methodological caution that inventories and official statistics might be misleading, I rely on a variety of sources, including inventories taken at death and those associated with property seizures (following the South Sea Bubble), diaries and letters, furniture designs, architectural plans and theories, court cases, and popular literary texts.[2] The picture that results is one of sexuality and artifice, on the one hand, and education and autonomy, on the other.

The dressing room produced an architectural innovation for some of the wealthiest women in England that brought the theatricality and eroticism associated with the newly reconfigured Restoration tiring-room into newly reconfigured homes. The ritual of the levee, and its popularization in the cultural imaginary, corroborated the increasingly close connection between the sexualized female body and a model of female consumerism desirous of luxury goods. The objects most readily associated with the dressing room, including the dressing table, were often beautifully designed and expensive, thereby conceptualizing the lady's dressing room as a space for display and as a space of treasure. The dressing room's material history indicates, however, that it was also a space of privacy that could stage any number of activities, ranging from tea parties and card games to reading and writing in solitude. These uses of the dressing room indicate its status as a descendent of the early modern closet, that site of patriarchal privilege; women's dressing rooms thus challenged the spatial hierarchy of the early modern home. The lady's dressing room might be designed as an inferior counterpart to the gentleman's closet, isolated by architectural marginalization. This form of spatial privacy, however, could just as likely allow some women the autonomy and independence to behave as they wished in their own rooms.

The purpose of this chapter is to bring the dressing room's history to light and, in so doing, illuminate its varied connotations. The dressing room was always associated with the female body, sexuality, and artifice, an association that came to implicate the precious items housed there. In this way, we can identify the means by which consumerism and global commercialism, which spiked in the eighteenth century, contributed to the objectification of women, who in turn came to be represented through the objects they collected in their dressing rooms. These are the very connotations that satires about women throughout the late seventeenth and early eighteenth centuries exploit, and which have come to shape our commonsensical understanding of the dressing room's role. But the documents I examine in this chapter foreground another connotation of the dressing room that is suppressed by the satirists: the lady's dressing room as a pedagogical space. If privacy had been exclusively extended to male heads of households, then the emergence of the lady's dressing room not only rivaled that exclusivity, but also introduced the possibility that women could educate themselves by retiring to their dressing rooms to read or write. This connotation, which points to the increasing sense that women have a claim to intellectual independence, within certain parameters, of course, is the potential of the dressing room that domestic novelists entertain in the later half of the eighteenth century.

Perhaps most remarkably, the lady's dressing room throughout the eighteenth century remained a privilege available to only the wealthiest of women, though its prevalence in the literary culture of the time suggests otherwise. While there are records of dressing tables in bedchambers of more modest homes during the eighteenth century, the image of a woman at her dressing table, engaging in all the possible modes of behavior suggested by just such a space, disproportionately haunts our corpus of eighteenth-century literature.

THE TIRING-ROOM: VOYEURISM AND VANITY

The primary purpose of the earliest tiring-rooms in English Renaissance playhouses was to house actors as they prepared for stage. The Theatre, the first permanent playhouse built in London, had three galleries, a yard, and an "Attyring housse or place where the players make them ready."[3] An early usage of "tiring-room" in James Mabbe's prefatory verse to *Shakespeare's Works* associates the space with withdrawal: "we wondered, Shakespeare, that thou went'st so soon / From the world's stage to the grave's tiring room."[4] Perhaps the most familiar reference to the "tiring-house" is in the theater that Peter Quince imagines for his midsummer night's production of "Pyramus and Thisby": "This green plot shall be our stage, this hawthorn brake our tiring-house, and we will do it in action as we will do it before the Duke."[5] But the tiring-room also instituted a place where select audience members could gather to see the actors up close. According to theater historian Andrew Gurr, the tiring-rooms of the playhouses built from 1600 to the closing of the theaters in 1642 actually had a double function: housing actors offstage and serving as a separate theater entrance for wealthy patrons.[6] Gurr speculates that the sixpence admission to the "lords' rooms" on the balcony would have been collected at the tiring-room door, and that these wealthy audience members must have gone through the tiring-room on the way to their seats.[7] The Rose even included a separate room for "visitors of position" above the tiring-room.[8] These privileged audience members were entitled to peer into the tiring-room. Going backstage was a part of the price of their expensive tickets.

The Restoration tiring-room inherited the double function of the Renaissance tiring-room when the playhouses were reopened by Charles II. Actors and actresses used the tiring-room to prepare for the stage and it was typically open to certain privileged members of the public. Descriptions of Restoration tiring-rooms are rare, but one measure of the audience's presence backstage can be found in the various attempts to regulate their access to and behavior in the tiring-room. The Lord Chamberlain issued public protests and royal warrants to seal off the tiring-rooms from the audience on 25 February 1663/64 and again on

16 May 1668.[9] A similar pronouncement was made under Anne on 17 January 1704 "for the better regulation of the Theatres."[10] A 1675 agreement between the players and managers of the Theatre Royal stipulated that the door to the tiring-room be guarded, "To avoyd the future inconveniency of strangers frequent Egresse and regresse when a play is done in ye House."[11] These edicts reflect an effort to construct the tiring-room as a space marked off from the public stage, but likewise highlight the fact that the Restoration tiring-room, just like its Renaissance predecessor, instituted a theater within the playhouse.

The presence of women players in the Restoration theater changed the implications of going backstage. Indeed, two generations later, Colley Cibber's *Apology* (1740) attributes the expansion of the theatergoing audience during the Restoration to the sexual appeal of actresses: "The additional objects then of real, beautiful women, could not but draw a proportion of new admirers to the theatre."[12] One of these new admirers was Samuel Pepys; he hated a production of *A Midsummer Night's Dream*, but the sight of pretty actresses rescued the evening for him ("[he saw] some handsome women, which was all [his] pleasure").[13] These "handsome" and "real, beautiful women" were not the boy actors of the Renaissance playhouses, and Restoration productions turned the female body into a public spectacle, often in a controversial way.[14] Nearly one-fourth of all women's roles from 1660–1700 involved crossdressing, a fact that underscores the extent to which the female body was a spectacle on the Restoration stage.[15] In 1663, Pepys enjoyed a performance of John Dryden's *The Slighted Maid* primarily because of the cross-dressed actresses, "being most pleased to see the little girl dance in boy's apparel, she having very fine legs" (23 February 1663). Not only did these actresses wear breeches and show off their legs, but these roles also frequently required them to expose their other body parts as well. The cross-dressed Fidelia confesses her gender in William Wycherley's *The Plain Dealer* (1676), only to have her hair taken down and breasts groped.[16] The sexual desirability and presumed sexual availability of the female players prompted the diarist John Evelyn to condemn them for threatening the young noblemen of London: "Women now (& never 'til now) permitted to appear & act, which inflaming severall young noble-men & gallants, became their whores, & to some their Wives, . . . any of these, who fell into their snares, to the reproch of their noble families, & ruine both of body & Soule."[17]

Given the design and function of the playhouse tiring-room from its beginnings, these "real, beautiful women," who inflamed their audiences, presumably drew new admirers backstage as well. This observation has become a commonplace in histories of the stage, and critics regularly imply that these visits were part of a well-established sexual ritual in which "the wits and beaux came flocking backstage as never before" to flirt with the actresses.[18] Elizabeth Howe productively outlines the climate of accessibility that characterized the tiring-room — "Men were free to go behind the scenes and watch the actresses dressing"—but her analysis assumes that getting backstage was a universal possibility for all theatergoers, male or female.[19] Howe uses this assumption to emphasize the dangers actresses could face as a result of this practice: a woman "would have found it impossible to avoid sexual advances if she worked in the theatre," nor could she depend on protection from the playhouse managers or even from the law.[20] While the point of view of an actress productively underscores her legal and practical vulnerability, an important question remains: how was the potential for access to the tiring-room construed by contemporaries?

There has been much disagreement about whether or not these actresses were also prostitutes, and what that might have meant to their audiences, but it is clear that the private, even sexual, lives of actresses captivated the theatergoing audience.[21] If Restoration actresses were some of the earliest "stars," in the contemporary sense of fame, then the tiring-room stood as a figurative doorway into the actresses' "private" lives that so fascinated their public, as Pepys's unique and extensive accounts of the Restoration playhouse culture document. Pepys recollected in his diary numerous visits to the theater, including the two previously mentioned, balanced by just as many vows to stay away from it. For six months in 1662, he avoided the playhouses and their associated pleasures before falling into the Restoration version of wine, women, and song—what he called the "practice of loving plays and wine" (30 September 1662) and going backstage to visit the actresses. If the playhouses were like "a House of Scandal" to contemporary critics, then the tiring-room was at the center of this dubious, erotic locale.[22] Pepys's diary marks an intense ambivalence regarding this access and the actresses' presumed sexual availability. While the tiring-room offered Pepys sexual access to one of those "real, beautiful women" described by Cibber, getting backstage did not always give Pepys an entirely pleasurable experience. These visits more frequently forced him into unsettling reflections on theatrical performance and female sexuality.

Pepys's entries confirm that the imitative nature of theatrical performance simultaneously intrigued, pleased, and troubled the spectator. Going backstage gave Pepys the opportunity to reflect upon the difference between the effects of performance and the materials that produced those effects. In a visit behind the scenes that featured just this discordance, Pepys arrives at the disconcerting conclusion that theatrical performance parodied the real world:

my business here was to see the inside of the Stage and all the Tiring-roomes and Machines; and endeed it was a sight worthy seeing. But to see their clothes and the various sorts, and what a mixture of things there was, here a wooden leg, there a ruff, here a hobby-horse, there a Crowne, would make a man split himself to see with laughing—and perticularly Lacys wardrobe, and Shotrell's. But then again, to think how fine they show on the stage by candlelight, and how poor things they are to look at too near-hand, is not pleasant at all. (19 March 1666)

Pepys notes that the sight of props and costumes is simultaneously comedic and disturbing. The markers of status are bathetically reduced to their representative function, jumbled together with all categories of objects; even symbols of authority are not convincing when seen up close. Pepys's visit backstage punctures the allure of a playhouse performance, yet this realization does not keep him from returning, nor does it fundamentally diminish his efforts to satiate his sexual desire there.

Two visits to the actress Elizabeth Knepp, with whom Pepys was first acquainted in December 1665, exemplify the particular pleasures that Pepys derived from interacting with actresses in the tiring-room, as well as the concomitant anxieties about legitimacy that the tiring-room provoked. As a threshold to the stage, the tiring-room was potentially a site of authenticity, the place where props should be put aside and the performances should be dropped, even if these props and performances were themselves ultimately ridiculous. Standing in a tiring-room filled with players and activity, Pepys focused his attention on the materials that made up the actresses' onstage performances, costumes and cosmetics, reasoning that the actresses' appearance was unnatural and—significant to Pepys's nearly insatiable concupiscence—repulsive:

> To the King's house; and there going in, met with Knipp [sic] and she took us up into the Tireing-rooms and to the women's Shift, where Nell was dressing herself, and was all unready; and is very pretty, prettier then I thought; . . . and then below into the Scene-room, and there sat down and she gave us fruit; and here I read the Qu's to Knepp while she answered me, through all her part of *Flora's Figarys*, which was acted today. But Lord, to see how they were both painted would make a man mad—and did make me loath them. (5 October 1667)

Although seventeenth-century spectators mostly considered a female player's behavior offstage "an extension of her histrionic function," offstage behavior is the very thing that concerns Pepys here.[23] Pepys sets the scene with his enchantment by the beautiful Nell Gwyn and his participation in the profession of acting (helping Knepp to remember her

lines). In spite of his complicity in the work of the stage, Pepys abruptly
distances himself rhetorically from the "painted" actresses, using his
characteristic expression of reversal, "But Lord," to do so. While the
Restoration tiring-room allowed this spectator the chance to enjoy the
pretty actresses, it also forced him to see them as cosmetically constructed performers, who "would make a man mad—and did make me
loath them." But, as we shall see, Pepys's loathing never lasted for long
and never obscured his chances to exploit the tiring-room as a sexual
marketplace.

If shabby props call the pleasures of stage performances into question, then so, too, does the actresses' use of cosmetics call their desirability as sexual partners offstage into question. Amid all the props and
costumes visible backstage, Pepys reserved special criticism for the actresses because they used cosmetics. Face painting is not just unsettling,
as the use of props is, nor is it comedic. Cosmetics infuriate him. Face
painting exposes the inherent tension between Pepys's notion of an authentic femininity (particularly as a by-product of feminine decorum)
and its imitation. Elsewhere in his diary, Pepys sharply rebukes Elizabeth Pearse, the wife of James Pearse, surgeon to the Duke of York,
for using paint; she is "still very pretty but paints red on her face, which
makes me hate her" (26 October 1667) and when "I find her painted
([it] makes me loathe her)" (16 September 1667). Pepys's tiring-room
argument that the actresses' makeup "would make a man mad—and did
make me loath them" underscores the limits of perception: cosmetics
thwart a spectator's power of interpretation. How can a woman's face
be legible if it is obscured by paint? How can a spectator know if an
actress really is beautiful, as she seems to be onstage? These concerns
point to the voyeuristic pleasure Pepys derives from the picture of Nell
Gwyn without theatrical makeup and costume, who is "prettier then I
thought."

Pepys's attitude toward cosmetics implicitly links sexual desire to
epistemological certainty, but whether he confines himself to this position is another issue entirely. Pepys's visits to meet with Elizabeth
Knepp backstage at the King's Playhouse foreground the sexual promiscuity that was also associated with the playhouse tiring-room (just
the possibility that Evelyn feared would "ensnare" all the young noble-
men of England, to the ruin of their families). Pepys's relationship with
Knepp was clearly sexual and Elizabeth Pepys, his wife, was clearly
jealous; he records his wife's anger about the actress in eleven entries
throughout the *Diary*.[24] Beginning in January 1666, Pepys documents
the erotic nature of his encounters with Knepp, ranging from his "play
[ing] with her breasts and [singing]" (2 January 1666) to "putting my
hand abaxo de her coats and tocar su thighs and venter—and a little of

the other thing, ella but a little opposing me; sus skin very douce and I mightily pleased with this" (21 April 1668). When he visits the King's Playhouse in May of 1668, Pepys knows that the tiring-room was the threshold to a sexual liaison with Knepp. Following their meeting, they take a coach ride, during which "I all the way having mi mano abox la jupe de Knepp con much placer and freedom" (7 May 1668).

But if we consider Pepys's account of this rendezvous more closely, it is apparent that while Pepys benefits from the commodification of Knepp's sexuality, he is also oddly critical of it:

> Thence called Knepp from the King's house; where going in for her, the play being done, I did see Becke Marshall come dressed off of the stage, and looks mighty fine and pretty, and noble—and also Nell in her boy's clothes, mighty pretty; but Lord, their confidence, and how many men do hover about them as soon as they come off the stage, and how confident they [are] in their talk. (7 May 1668)

As in the earlier description, Pepys's fascination is initially with the beautiful women, but his entry swiftly turns to their behavior, or at least to his perception of their behavior. He registers surprise when these women seem to express themselves, associating this confidence with the way they talk and the men who admire them. His reaction to their behavior not only suggests a general concern about how women ought to behave, but it also reflects a specific ambivalence about actresses' availability to men backstage.

In spite of this ambivalence, Pepys himself then plays the lover with an actress: "Here I did kiss the pretty woman newly come, called Pegg, that was Sir Ch. Sidley's mistress—a mighty pretty woman, and seems, but is not, modest" (ibid.).[25] Pegg is both actress and mistress, two roles inextricably linked. The disjunction between an actress's performances onstage and her life off it was, by this time, a familiar convention. Dryden famously foregrounded this contradiction in the epilogue to *Tyrannick Love; or, The Royal Martyr* (1669) in which Nell Gwyn announces, "Here *Nelly* lies, who, tho' she liv'd a Slater'n, / Yet dy'd a Princess, acting in S. Cathar'n."[26] Gwyn, like Pegg, seems modest, but is not. She may play the role of the virtuous Valeria in *Tyrannick Love*, but she is also the soon-to-be "Protestant Whore" of Charles II.[27] What concerns Pepys is Pegg's, and presumably the other actresses's, performance of modesty, what Wycherley will later call a "mask of modesty."[28] Pepys's commentary introduces the possibility that feminine decorum may be parodied. It also attempts to contain femininity and masculinity within an emergent heterosexual ideal, where women were actually modest and men desired them that way.

The frequency of Pepys's censure of the female players does not merely respond to an anxiety about gender roles; it also reflects his own sense of dislocation as a spectator in the tiring-room. He is critical of the other men backstage there, sensitive to the differences in class and status among them: "what base company of men comes among them, and how lewdly they talk — and how poor the men are in clothes, and yet what a show they make on the stage by candle-light, is very observable" (5 October 1667). Pepys was a gentlemen, the players professionals. Pepys recorded these experiences in his private diary, itself written in code and hidden, but he experienced the playhouse tiring-room among competing spectators. He was never alone with the actresses backstage, so he labored to distinguish himself from the actors by emphasizing their professional status as performers. But Pepys's disdain inadvertently reiterated the possibility that not only is gender performed, but class as well, whether in a theater or on the street: every time he critiqued the players' performances in the tiring-room, he was simultaneously self-conscious about playing the proper role himself.

Access backstage was never uniform, but the trope of peering into the tiring-room and participating in its implied erotic economy nevertheless characterized the role of the theatrical spectator. In some instances, these activities were merely imagined. The reputations of actresses were inevitably tied to the erotic politics of the tiring-room, even if they were defined in opposition to them. At the turn of the century, Anne Bracegirdle (?1663–1748), one of the most accomplished actresses of her time, maintained a reputation for chastity. Bracegirdle cultivated this persona in large part because she reputedly did not participate in the sexual opportunism of the tiring-room and also because the roles she played onstage were consistently of chaste women.[29] *A Comparison Between Two Stages* (1702), attributed to Charles Gildon, claims that Bracegirdle maintained the appearance of modesty by appearing *not* to act when playing virtuous roles. Known as the "Romantick Virgin," hers was a "Reputation for not acting."[30] Cibber's *Apology* argues that Bracegirdle was popular because her private life was just that, a circumstance that corroborated her reputation for chastity. He explains, "Never any woman was in such general favour of her spectators, which, to the last scene of her dramatick life, she maintain'd, by not being unguarded in her private character. This discretion contributed, not a little, to make her the Cara, the darling of the theatre."[31] Cibber's litotes "not being unguarded" and "not a little" stress that Bracegirdle successfully managed the conventions of the playhouse culture to her own benefit. Bracegirdle's status as an object of desire, "the Cara, the darling of the theatre," was a function of the fact that direct access to her was pure fantasy for everyone — a prototype of our modern-day star system. Cibber's characterization of the audience's response shows not only that the sight of femininity on display prompted desire, but also that this response itself became a sort of cultural practice: "few spectators that were not past it, could behold her without desire. It was even a fashion among the gay, and young, to have a taste or *tendre* for Mrs. Bracegirdle."[32] Bracegirdle's admirers converted the male competition that concerned Pepys in the tiring-room into a pleasurable fraternity of looking and collective desire. From this point of view, Bracegirdle projected an idealized model of femininity onstage that could never be contradicted by spectators' reports of an erotic performer backstage.

If getting backstage and into the tiring-room were perceived as the first step in getting access to the actresses' bodies, an association that eroticized the very act of looking behind the scenes, then this connotation survived well into the eighteenth century. Boswell relates that Samuel Johnson frequented the green room as his tragedy *Irene* was in production, but finally told Garrick, "I'll come no more behind your scenes, David; for the silk stockings and white bosoms of your actresses excite my amorous propensities."[33] The tiring-room itself fueled the "amorous propensities" of many a visitor, even if this same space might fundamentally call into question the authenticity of a player's beauty.

A "GREAT SCENE OF BUSINESS": THE LEVEE AND EROTIC OBJECTIFICATION

Moving from the tiring-room of the Restoration playhouse to the dressing room of domestic architecture, the ritual life of the levee, popular in seventeenth- and eighteenth-century grand households, introduced means by which the category of femininity was constructed as a process of erotic objectification. The levee featured women of high social standing, in contrast to the professionalized actresses, but instituted a process that implicitly drew the sexual marketplace of the Restoration tiring-room in a domestic context. The levee was popularized during Charles II's reign and practiced by both men and women up through the eighteenth century. As Simon Thurley and Anna Keay have recently argued, Charles II appropriated the French custom of the levee and the couché by adapting it to the English royal tradition of the private bedchamber.[34] The form of the ceremony was imported from the French tradition, but the exclusivity, intimacy, and even privacy of its use was particularly English. In general, only men attended other men's levees, while both men and women attended women's.[35] The design of Marble Hill House demonstrates that a dressing room's primary function could have been to hold levees.[36] This Palladian villa was built in 1724–29 for Henrietta Howard, the mistress of the Prince of Wales and later King George II.[37] Howard was a close friend of Pope, Swift, and Gay, and served as an important intermediary for Swift with the court when he visited England in 1726 and 1727. Swift, in turn, memorialized her home with the poem, "A Pastoral Dialogue between Richmond Lodge and Marble Hill" in 1727, when George II ascended the throne. In Marble Hill, Howard's dressing room did not sit next to her chamber. Instead, her bedchamber was on the west side of the central Great Room and her dressing room on the east of it, with all three rooms opening to a view of the Thames.[38] Although the house had this separate dressing room, Howard's bedchamber actually doubled as her dressing room, insofar as the bedchamber housed all of her furniture and accessories for dressing, including "Two looking Glasses," "A Dressing Table," "Two large looking Glasses and one Dressing Ditto."[39] Howard's dressing room proper, on the other side of the Great Room, was filled almost exclusively with tables and chairs, suggesting that a small party might convene there.[40] Given its size and that the dressing table was in her bedchamber, Howard's dressing room was probably used more to receive informal company in the morning than for dressing.

By 1711, the levee was familiar enough for Addison and Steele's Mr. Spectator to pronounce that "the Toilet is [women's] great Scene of Business"[41] and to satirize one Sempronia for holding a levee, while only upholding the *appearance* of discretion: "[she] is so modest as to admit her Visitants no further than her Toilet. It is a very odd Sight that beautiful Creature makes, when she is talking Politicks with her Tresses flowing about her Shoulders, and examining that Face in the Glass, which does such execution upon all the Male Standers-by."[42] Sempronia, like the actresses, seems modest, but is not. The fourth plate of William Hogarth's *Marriage à la Mode* likewise portrays a fashionable levee, with the countess at her dressing table enraptured by the addresses of one "Silvertongue," who instructs her as to his plan for their rendezvous at a masquerade that evening.[43] The furnishings of the countess's dressing room confirm the sexual license that this encounter suggests, as they include an erotic novel by Crébillon and paintings of seduction and rape. If the toilet is women's great scene of business, then this business seems to be self-indulgence, performance, delusion, and unlicensed sexuality. These examples of early-eighteenth-century popular representational culture also point to the meaning that access to a lady's dressing room held: a woman's toilet suggested not only that she dressed for a performance in public and that she was already engaged in such a performance in the dressing room, but also that the dressing room gave admirers access to a woman's sexuality.

The seventeenth-century diarist John Evelyn responded to just such a scene of performance, sexuality, and desire when he was brought to the levee of Louise Renée de Kérualle, Duchess of Portsmouth, an influential mistress of Charles. By 1672, she had borne the king a son (later Duke of Richmond) and, in 1673, was created the Duchess of Portsmouth and, by Louis XIV, Duchesse d'Aubigny. In 1675, Evelyn noted the magnificence of the duchess's "splendid Appartment at Whitehall, luxuriously furnished, and with ten times the richenesse and glory beyond the Queenes, such massy pieces of Plate, whole Tables, Stands etc: of incredible value."[44] Several years later, in October of 1683, Evelyn had the occasion to accompany Charles to the duchess's dressing room. I quote from his remarkable diary entry at length:

> Following his Majestie this morning through the Gallerie [at Whitehall], [I] went (with the few who attended him) into the Dutchesse of Portsmouths dressing roome, within her bed-chamber, where she was in her morning loose garment, her maides Combing her, newly out of her bed: his Majestie & the Gallants standing about her; but that which ingag'd my curiositie, was the rich and splendid furniture of this woman's Appartment, now twice or thrice, puld downe, and rebuilt, to satisfie her prodigal and expensive pleasures, whilst her Majestie dos not exceede, some gentlemens Ladies furniture and accommodation: here I saw the new fabrique of French Tapissry, for designe, tendernesse of worke, and incomparable imitation of the best paintings; beyond any thing, I had ever beheld: some pieces had Versailles, St. Germans and other Palaces of the French King with Huntings, figures, and Landscips, Exotique fowle and all to the life rarely don: Then for Japon Cabinets, Skreenes, Pendule Clocks, huge Vasas of wrought plate, Tables, Stands, Chimny furniture, Sconces, branches, Braseras etc they were all of massive silver, and without number, besides of his Majesties best paintings: Surfeiting of this, I din'd yet at Sir Steph: Foxes, and 5 went contentedly home to my poore, but quiet Villa. Lord what contentment can there be in the riches & splendor of this world, purchas'd with vice & dishonor.[45]

In the beginning of this entry, Evelyn could be replaying a scene from the playhouse tiring-room, with a beautiful actress surrounded by a bevy of admirers while she dressed. Notably, royal scopic pleasure seems to take the same form as that of a theatrical spectator (Charles took the actress Nell Gwyn as a mistress, too), even though this event occurs within the confines of a luxurious apartment in Whitehall, rather than just off a stage of make-believe. More than a characteristic scene of a woman at her dressing table holding court, however, Evelyn's entry reflects a displacement of the duchess's body on display with her beautiful room. His writerly eye is quickly drawn to the luxury of the duchess's dressing room, and the bulk of the passage is dedicated to inventorying its adornments; this is the thing, after all, "which ingag'd my curiositie." Again, we are reminded that the duchess's furnishings outshine those of the queen, a rivalry of interior decoration that mimics the rivalry for the king's affection and attention. The duchess's dressing room showcases the newest and the best, and Evelyn notes that it has been made over several times to please her. Evelyn's attention to the material objects of the dressing room results in a methodical survey of the contents. In addition to the French tapestry, which was "beyond any thing, I had ever beheld," the room is adorned with a multitude of cabinets, screens, vases, tables, silver sconces, and some of the finest paintings from the king's art collection. Evelyn's account emphasizes the excess of the place, even though, as we shall see in the following section, the items (if not their quality) adorning the duchess's dressing room were common enough decorations on their own.

Evelyn's diary not only provides a rare glimpse into the world of the dressing room, but it also demonstrates the powerful ways in which such a room produced meaning for viewers. Wedged into a single sentence following this survey, Evelyn concludes that the material riches of the duchess's dressing room were procured as a result of her being sexually available to the king. Once at home in his (comparatively) "poore, but quiet Villa," Evelyn has the space of mind to critique the scene: "Lord what contentment can there be in the riches & splendor of this world, purchas'd with vice & dishonor." Notably, Evelyn does not censure the king or the duchess directly, but implies—without great subtlety—that the dressing room was decorated in return for sex. Within this sexual economy, the dressing room is a marker of a woman's (sexual) commodification. The more beautifully and luxuriously decorated the dressing room, the greater the market value a woman's sexuality commands. The duchess's dressing room is also a sign of her power as a mistress of the king, who can claim valuable treasures as her own. But the focus on these objects in Evelyn's diary entry confirms that he sees them as representative of her; one wonders if he may gawk at the furnishings as surrogates for the desirable duchess precisely because she is off-limits to him. Evelyn's account productively exposes the fluidity of association between a sexualized female body and the room that not only encases it and, in some senses, produces it (putting her in beautiful clothes and so forth), but the room that also comes to stand *for* the female body. For Evelyn, the duchess's dressing room represents her sexually promiscuous behavior, as well as her sexualized female body, and the desiring male spectator who will barter for it. No wonder, then, that in 1675 William Wycherley's Horner describes his sexual success through the figure of the dressing room. Playing a eunuch, Horner boasts that he "was made free of [women's] Society and dressing-rooms for ever hereafter," without being detected by "the grave Matrons, and old rigid Husbands [who] think me as unfit for love, as they are."[46]

The Objects of the Dressing Room:
Form, Function, and Display

Evelyn's collusion between a desirable female body and beautiful furnishings is played out again and again in dressing rooms throughout this period, and is especially evident in the kinds of items that were commonly found in and associated with the lady's dressing room. Most remarkable for readers of eighteenth-century literature, the materials of the dressing room were not merely the tawdry tools of beauty that a satirist like Swift envisages, such as dandruff-filled combs, grime-covered basins, filthy clothes, and noxious chamber pots. Instead, the historical record I have unearthed shows that dressing rooms were furnished with items for display in their own right—a fact that underscores the function of display inherent to the dressing room. Just as the emergence of the dressing room developed alongside an increase in the individuation of interior spaces, it likewise coincided with a shift in English domestic interior decoration. Before the return of Charles II, grand houses contained comparatively little luxurious furniture; by the mid-eighteenth century, furniture designers and makers were busy generating enough items to fill all sorts of lesser domestic spaces, responding to the fashion of interior decoration.[47] This shift is attributable both to the importation of the French trend to "invest private space with public meaning" as well as Britain's increased commercial wealth, especially overseas trade.[48] As Lorna Weatherhill explains, the image "of a society falling over itself to consume clothes, furniture, houses, possessions and leisure" was fostered, an image that was regularly emblematized by the luxury housed in the dressing room.[49]

Of course, the dressing room's central (and defining) piece was the dressing table. Descriptions from auction lists, estate sales, credit reports, and furniture designers tell us that the dressing table was both beautiful *and* functional. It might be inlaid.[50] Other times it was made from deal or mahogany or walnut (one such table sold for £1.10.0 in 1740).[51] Dressing tables were topped by mirrors, perhaps gilt, framed with mahogany, or a "swing glass."[52] In the late eighteenth century, Thomas Sheraton introduced "side-glasses" that folded up to make a U-shaped mirror.[53] The tops of wooden dressing tables consisted of two panels that opened to expose several compartments for cosmetics below, and a mirror that might be tilted up for viewing.[54] These dressing tables also had several compartments, drawers, and small cupboards.[55] A bureau dressing table or a commode dressing table had a similar design, but included drawers for clothing.[56] One such cabinet dressing table had drawers "intended to hold all the ornaments of dress, as rings, drops, &c."[57] The dressing chairs in William Ince and John Mayhew's *The Universal System of Household Furniture* (1762) are all one-armed, and the dressing stools especially ornate.[58] The difference between dressing tables and toilets centered on the degree of decoration. Dressing tables had a more simple design than toilets, and toilets were draped with luxurious fabric that skirted the bottom and framed the mirror.[59] The cost of the toilet generally exceeded that of the dressing table; "a fine green velvet toylet, on a walnut tree frame, with a dressing glass, boxes &c. compleat" sold in 1729 for £5.5.0.[60] While most of the compartments were designed to hold cosmetics, accessories, and clothing, Sheraton's cabinet dressing table featured a "washing-drawer," fit with drainage.[61] The tops of these pieces of furniture may have also been covered with scented powder, if the room did not have an incense burner.[62]

The design and decoration of dressing rooms throughout the period suggest that they were spaces not only for the assemblage of a woman's dress, but were also places where women could show off their belongings. Black-lacquered furniture was particularly popular throughout the eighteenth century, having been first introduced by Queen Catherine in 1662 (she brought from Portugal "such Indian Cabinets and large trunks of Laccar, as haad never before ben seene" in England).[63] Such furniture was described as "japanned"; a "Japan dressing table and two scones" sold in 1729 for £0.6.00.[64] Occasionally the furniture was from Japan, but more frequently, these items were produced in Europe and designed to look as if they were imported from Asia. A dressing room in Ham House was decorated in this fashion (it was called the Green Drawing Room or Queen's Antechamber even though it was actually a dressing room). The room was refurbished when the entire house was remodeled extensively in 1672, following the marriage of Lady Dysart and John Maitland, the 1st Duke of Lauderdale and secretary of state for Scotland.[65] This room was furnished with lacquered furniture of European origin, including a cabinet and stand, lacquer chairs (which had cushions matching the wall hangings), a lacquer side table (which was probably Dutch), and a lacquer close-stool.[66] It also had lacquer screens and porcelain.[67] All sorts of lacquered items could be procured during this period and many were adapted to the functions of the dressing room. A dressing-box sold in 1739, categorized under the heading "curiosities of various sorts," was described as "A fine japan dressing box"; a "japan corner cupboard" from a dressing room was auctioned by Thomas Fitzgerald in 1740 (a japan corner cupboard owned by Lady

Betty Master had glass doors); and a "small japan desk and bookcase, with dressing boxes & a glass door" along with "a japan dressing table and two sconces" were sold in 1729.[68] One Col. John Mercer had a "japan Bed Chamber" in his house on Denmark Street in Soho, which featured an "8 day clock in a japan case."[69] Dressing rooms also featured other forms of orientalized decoration, such as the "*India* Cabinet" and "Blue *China* Hangings" owned by Lady Lambert.[70] China became an increasingly popular commodity in the eighteenth century and "drew the female consumer into a national debate about the debilitating effects of a home economy indebted to foreign trade."[71] The orientalized appearance of this furniture rendered the dressing room a site for the display of global loot, even if the items were actually made in England. Mr. Spectator reflects, when celebrating the internationalization of the Royal Exchange, that "Our Rooms are filled with Pyramids of *China*, and adorned with the Workmanship of *Japan*."[72] The female body and the room that made up that female body were regularly imagined as being adorned with the fruits of England's international trade.[73]

The imperative to display the female body and a woman's beautiful possessions in the dressing room extended to curiosities and wall hangings, as well as to the overall design of the room. Celia Fiennes, the daughter of a parliamentarian officer, traveled throughout the kingdom in the late seventeenth century and kept an extensive diary, in which she recorded seeing a curiosity cabinet in Lady Exeter's dressing room, among the room's many luxurious furnishings: "the wanscoate of the best Jappan, the Cushons very Rich Work: there is a great deale of fine worke under Glasses and a Glass case full of all Sorts of Curiosityes of Amber stone Currall and a world of fine things."[74] A dressing room might also feature "Family Pictures" (Lady Betty Master's dressing room had fourteen), black-and-white prints (the dressing room in one Richard Wooley's Highgate house had thirty-eight), or engraved reproductions of the Old Masters.[75] Women regularly pasted engravings they had purchased in Europe on the walls of their dressing rooms. The walls in the Print Room in the Vyne in Hampshire (remodeled in 1754) are pasted up in this style.[76] Dorothy Noel, Countess of Gainsborough, displayed several pictures and other works of art in her dressing room, including a "pheasant and other Birds, by Bogdani," "A triumph, a bass-relievo in wax, from the antique, by Mr. Gosset," "His Royal Highness, the beauties at Hampton-Court, and 6 others," "Five oval bass-relievo's, and a drawing after Rubens" among others.[77] More luxurious dressing rooms featured elaborate tapestries. The Gold-Tapestry Dressing Room in Houghton Hall (Norfolk), built for Sir Robert Walpole beginning in 1722, was lined with five Mortlake tapestries of Stuart monarchs: James I, Anne of Denmark, Charles I, Henrietta Maria, and Christian IV of Denmark.[78] The North Sitting Room at Holkham Hall (1734–64) in Norfolk, which originally served as a dressing room, was decorated in Brussels tapestry of the seasons by Peemans.[79] The East Dressing Room in Mereworth Castle, Kent, built from 1720 to 1723 by Colin Campbell, was also lined with a Brussels tapestry, along with a highly ornamented fireplace, dark and light wood parquetry floors, and a ceiling painted by Sleter.[80]

Later in the eighteenth century, dressing room decoration increasingly reflected French influence, as the term "boudoir" became fashionable.[81] The circular boudoir at Attingham Park was probably decorated by the French émigré painter Louise André Delabrière in the 1780s. Its color scheme of naturalistic greens, reds, and pinks, framed with gold leaf, explicitly adopted French fashion.[82] The circular boudoir in Syon (Middlesex), designed in 1770 by Robert Adam (who had remodeled all of Syon in 1762), featured a color scheme of pale pinks, grays, and blues, and was also considered to be French.[83] Hanging in the center of this circular boudoir was an ornate birdcage, on the bottom of which was a large clock.

These examples demonstrate that the domestic dressing room allowed women a space both to prepare their bodies to be seen in public and to display their decorative taste and style for the consumption of an intimate circle. This continuum of display is at the heart of William Congreve's satire of Lady Wishfort at her toilet in *The Way of the World*. When this mature woman complains that her makeup needs improvement, else she will never "keep up to my picture," her maid Foible points to the fact that Lady Wishfort's portrait in the dressing room now stands as the model, rather than the other way around.[84] Once a beauty ages, ever the threat facing such women, she must labor to be as beautiful as her dressing room—and as beautiful as her dressing room makes her seem.

CLOSET PRIVILEGES: AN IDEOLOGY OF PRIVACY

If the eighteenth-century dressing room could be seen as a domestic version of the tiring-room, particularly as a signifier of female sexuality and as a space to display the female body and its surrogates (beautiful objects), then it was also conceived of as a potentially *private* space for some of England's wealthiest women, a prototype of a room of one's own. The violation of a woman's private space (and her husband's presumed privileges there) is at the heart of a late-eighteenth-century adultery case. One Sir Richard Worsley sued one George Maurice Bissett for criminal conversation with his wife, Lady Worsley. The defendant's lawyer makes much of the plaintiff's reaction to the presence of *other* men in Lady Worsley's dressing room, as part of his case that Lord Worsley regularly prostituted his wife. A witness for the defense, one Lord Deerhurst, was called to testify to his affair with Lady Worsley in 1779, a relation that they claim was condoned by Lord Worsley. Given this past disregard for his wife's faithfulness, the defense argued that Lord Worsley did not deserve damages from Bissett. The central fact in this affair from 1779 is the husband's discovery of Lord Deerhurst in Lady Worsley's dressing room, a room adjacent to her bedchamber—at four o'clock in the morning. Although in his testimony Lord Deerhurst does not recall how Lady Worsley was "dressed at that time," whether "in a dress, or undress," he does relate that Lord Worsley discovered them.[85] Bisset's lawyer, Lord Mansfield, summarizes this episode in his concluding comments to the jury, focusing on the explicitly sexual connotations of a man being discovered in a married woman's dressing room:

> once the Plaintiff found him in Lady Worsley's dressing-room at four o'clock in the morning; and he only says to him, 'Deerhurst, how came you there?' And there is no further explanation or examination between them. Is it not *extraordinary* to find a Gentleman in his Lady's dressing-room at four o'clock in the morning, *and nothing further said*? All is well; they are all good company the next morning; and some few days afterwards Lady Worsley is going to Southampton. At the same time Sir Richard goes eight miles with her, and leaves Lord Deerhurst to go on with her to Southampton: he goes on with her to Southampton; he stays there twenty-four hours, and she stays three or four days:—*yet there is no appearance of Jealousy in the Husband!!*[86]

From the perspective of the witness, Lord Deerhurst, his presence in Lady Worsley's dressing room (particularly at four o'clock in the morning) is evidence of his "intimacy" with Lady Worsley.[87] Although Lord Deerhurst ultimately declines to say whether he had "any particular intimacy" with Lady Worsley on that or any other night, his trespass into Lady Worsley's dressing room would have clearly been understood as having a sexual meaning.[88] In character with the language of Criminal Conversation cases, rhetorical discretion marked accusations of sexual infidelity just as domestic spaces or pieces of furniture, particularly the state of a bed in the morning, came to stand for the act of adultery.[89] (But even the most explicit accounts follow a decidedly reserved and descriptive vein, such as the following report from a servant, one Mary Palmer: "Mrs. *Conner*, was sitting on the chair, and Mr. *Atkinson* a-cross her, with his *breeches down.* —Seeing this, she [Mary Palmer] thought proper to go away."[90])

At issue in the Criminal Conversation case between Worsley and Bis-

sett is a sexual transgression that is most visible through a spatial violation. While the tradition of the levee legitimized visitors to a lady's
dressing room, the presence of another man in a woman's dressing
room at an inappropriate hour had decidedly erotic and illegitimate
connotations. Thus the defense lawyer questions: "Is it not *extraordinary*
to find a gentleman in his lady's dressing-room at four o'clock in the
morning, *and nothing further said?*" The feature of eighteenth-century domestic life that the reported liaison between Lord Deerhurst and Lady
Worsley reflects is the increasing sense that women had privacy as well,
even if it were deeply implicated in the ideology of female sexuality and
its commensurate threat of betrayal.

As Lena Cowen Orlin reminds us, the sixteenth- and seventeenth-
century English household promoted a specifically patriarchal understanding of privacy.[91] Therefore, the possibility for some women to
claim privacy was a revolutionary concept, particularly insofar as the
notion of privacy was first thought to be a masculine prerogative and
associated with the privilege of the closet. While the potential for privacy within the home was a result of the larger architectural development of different kinds of domestic spaces in England and Europe, the
first exclusively private place within these interiors was the man's
study, or *studiolo*, which probably began as a locked writing desk in the
husband's bedroom and later turned into a room that housed the family
papers and library.[92] In 1672, Charles Hoole described the study as a
"place where a Student, a part from men, sitteth alone."[93] The emergence of the gentleman's closet and the possibility of privacy that it offered started with the fifteenth-century architectural innovations of the
wealthy Florentine merchant Leon Battista Alberti. The type of privacy
that Alberti created in the closet was linked to "thinking, writing, and
masculinity," a condition that simultaneously figured the female body as
one of the family's prized possessions that needed to be secreted away.[94]
Alberti's *On the Art of Building in Ten Books* stipulated that each house
ought to be divided into public, semiprivate, and private zones, but embedded in these designs was an effort to perpetuate gender and class
hierarchies. This system of differentiation operated on the principle that
access to these different types of spaces was a function of a person's
status within the household. The closet, marked as the most private of
zones, would have been available only to the man of the house and to
his secretary. Mark Wigley argues that the sanctum of the man's closet
became "the true center of the house" and the center of patriarchal control for two reasons: it spatialized the power hierarchy of gender difference in the Renaissance household and created "an intellectual space
beyond that of sexuality."[95] The fact that the family's papers were held
in the husband's closet leads Stephanie H. Jed to argue that these pri-

vate papers came to be equated with patriarchal order and hierarchy.[96] Alberti's mandate in *The Book of the Family* that a wife be prohibited from seeing her husband's papers demonstrates that the closet became the intellectual and legal headquarters of the domestic sphere. Conversely, married women were allotted a semiprivate dressing room off the bedroom, but this was not an exclusive place. Instead, Alberti imagined that the young children, maidens, and the household's nurse would have slept there.[97]

Alberti's plan not only created a separate and privileged zone for the head of the household, but it also instituted regulatory mechanisms to ensure that this hierarchy remained stable. In fact, Alberti argued that a wife "could not read" or "lay hands on" her husband's papers or even enter his closet.[98] These rules installed a double prohibition for women and a double freedom for men. The design of the house was intended to regulate the behavior of women and their thinking. Women were not permitted access to learning either outside or inside the house. Men, however, were permitted to go beyond the limits of the home and to be utterly private within it. Claiming privacy in the closet paradoxically became a public and privileged act that created and confirmed a gentleman's authority.[99] The difference between a Renaissance husband's closet and his wife's dressing room reflected the different roles that married men and women were expected to play: the husband's private study housed documentation of the family's worth and status; the wife's more public dressing room housed clothing, cosmetics, children, and servants.

The second of Wigley's points—that the closet was an intellectual space beyond sexuality—has been revised by readings of the potential for homoerotic exchanges within the closet.[100] Plans for husbands and wives to have separate bedrooms created a physical separation between intellectual activity and conjugal sex. Mary Poovey argues that the mandate to divide the husband and wife's bedroom created two new kinds of privacy for the family's resources: the privacy of the man's closet and the privacy of the marriage bed.[101] The import of this pairing resides in the equation between the two. The privacy of the closet was extended to female chastity and reproduction.

An important effect of this system was to limit the potential for women's power, be it intellectual, sexual, or social. Alberti's anxiety about female embodiment and exposure motivated his theoretical attempt to contain women's independence. The potential for women to assume agency represented a threat to the patriarchal authority that Alberti carefully constructed. These great efforts to keep women away from the texts that represented a family's status—the books and records in the closet—indicate that a man's control of his family could be fundamentally, and even dangerously, provisional. A gentleman's status depended upon *exclusive* knowledge and control of the family's history. Such a model of masculine authority was necessarily contingent upon the strict exclusion of competitors, whether strangers or female family members or servants, from the material position of privilege.

SPACING OUT IN THE EIGHTEENTH CENTURY: GENDER AND EXCLUSION

The influence of Alberti's work on English architectural theory is evident beginning with Sir Henry Wotton's *The Elements of Architecture* (1624), which adopts Alberti's principle that domesticity itself necessitated additionally private spaces.[102] When we turn to late-seventeenth- and early-eighteenth-century domestic architecture, we can see that the placement of the English dressing room was regularly incorporated into a design that maintained the division envisaged in early modern notions of privacy, with one notable difference: the principle of exclusion was modified to one of separation. Writing in ca. 1695–96, Roger North explains that upper-class English husbands and wives needed dressing rooms because they shared a bedchamber. In more expensive houses, "one would add to [the bedchamber] a dressing room, nay more, one for a man, and another for a woman, with chambers for the servant of each to lodge to be within call; so that at rising each may retire apart, and have severall accomodations compleat."[103] After sleeping, men and women withdrew to separate, private places for different types of activity, activities that defined their roles and positions. In English domestic architecture, the lady's dressing room was most often conceptualized as a female counterpart to the masculine closet. This hint of equation, however, depended upon separation, suggesting the limits of the justification "separate but equal." Men's and women's private spaces were certainly distinct and, in many ways, certainly not equal. This spatialization of gender difference resonates with Sir Robert Filmer's idealization of the father in *Patriarcha; or, The Natural Power of Kings* (1680) as owner, with all other family members as subjects in this domestic kingdom. As Laura J. Rosenthal reminds us, Locke's attack on Filmer focuses on political power deriving from patriarchal authority, but does not challenge "fatherly authority as such"; moreover, "modern patriarchy subordinates women by representing masculine domination as nonpolitical."[104]

The layouts of period country houses, a genre of opulent building particular to the English, exemplify the ideological interconnection between a principle of separation and a spatialization of a domestic hierarchy that concretizes both Filmer's and Locke's brand of patriarchal order.[105] Sir John Vanbrugh was famous in the seventeenth century as a playwright and in the eighteenth as an architect of, among others, Castle Howard in Yorkshire and the Orangery at Kensington Palace. In the early eighteenth century, he drew up plans for Blenheim Palace in Oxfordshire (1705–20), and organized the palace's domestic space around two pairs of apartments. One pair was reserved for the duke and duchess and the other for state apartments along the south front of the palace.[106] As James Dallaway (who harbored an admitted prejudice for the neo-Greco designs of Robert and James Adams) observed in 1806, "By the sarcastick wit of Swift, the censure of Pope, and the elegant criticism of Walpole, Blenheim was long condemned to be spoken of, if without contempt, rather as a monument of gratitude than of the taste of the nation."[107] But the exemplarity of Blenheim is an important feature of its conception; after all, the palace was a gift from Queen Anne to the Duke of Marlborough to commemorate his military successes and contributions to the nation's well-being. In his correspondence, Vanbrugh suggested that Blenheim ought "to be consider'd as both a Royall and a National Monument," and that the "Qualitys proper to such a Monument" included "Beauty Magnificence, and Duration."[108] Through this viewpoint, Vanbrugh places himself in the tradition of Sir Christopher Wren, who advanced the political use of architecture by arguing that it "establishes a nation" and "makes the people love their native country, which passion is the original of all great actions in a commonwealth."[109] However, Blenheim was simultaneously conceived of as a private residence, and therefore required the application of additional architectural principles. Other grand houses, Vanbrugh observed, did not have the uniformity of design that Blenheim would: most large estates "are generally ill favour'd by Scrambling about, And look like a Ragged Village Wheras [Blenheim Palace] being all Compriz'd within One regular Handsome Wall, (And being likwise regularly dispos'd within) Form a Court, which by this means Adds to the Magnificence of the Dwelling, but not to the Quantity of it."[110] (Vanbrugh's pride of uniformity was to become to later viewers a tyranny of "sameness" evident in the "constant monotony of lengthened fronts.")[111]

But even behind this unified exterior wall, Vanbrugh's plan allowed for the spatialization of the domestic hierarchy, what the editor of Vanbrugh's letters calls "an arrangement suited to the ritual of their [the duke's and the duchess's] daily lives."[112] In other words, the domestic plan needed to facilitate the daily activities of both husband and wife. Vanbrugh's design conjoins "magnificence" with "intimacy," and this is particularly evident in the arrangement of the apartments.[113] Both pairs of apartments were divided by a vestibule, such that a large salon separated the state apartments and a dining room separated those of the duke and duchess. Conjoining both pairs was the Grand Cabinet. As historians have agreed, a "cabinet" in this context was a space associated with political power. This was the place where Charles II "discussed policy with his inner circle of advisers; the king's cabinet council was the ancestor of the prime minister's cabinet of today."[114] Well into the eighteenth century, the king's closet or cabinet stood as both a symbol and tool of royal power, even as the king's role in daily policy making shifted over time. George II, for example, was requested to give the "favour of your closet and the power of it" to various advisors.[115] As William Pitt's political status rose, so, too, did his desire to gain entry to the king's closet (as did the king's desire to exclude him); in 1756, as a condition of Pitt's ministry, he demanded unimpeded access to the king's cabinet.[116]

If one accepts that the placement of the Grand Cabinet in the design of Blenheim represented a lynchpin of power, then it is notable that this same Grand Cabinet was not only accessible from the duke's apartments and from the state apartments, but that it also linked them to each other conceptually. The proximity of the duke's bedchamber to the Grand Cabinet explicitly reflected — and facilitated — the duke's own relation to political power, even if this relationship proved to be tenuous in 1712, when the duke was dismissed from all his employments.

While the duke's rooms placed him in an analogous position with the state apartments (and with state power), the duchess's kept her away from both. Following the early modern model of exclusion, the duchess's access to the state apartments was mediated by the duke's insofar as her own apartment was at a remote end of the palace, away from the highly politicized space of the Grand Cabinet. Therefore, Vanbrugh's placement of the Duchess of Marlborough's dressing room, wardrobes, and closets marks a difference that is simultaneously political and gendered. The duchess was a powerful woman, who enjoyed a close relationship with Queen Anne before falling out of favor following Abigail Masham's ascendancy at court.[117] As powerful as the duchess was, even in her domestic affairs (she famously quarreled with Vanbrugh and temporarily halted the building of Blenheim in October 1710, accusing the architect and his contractors of inflating prices), she was, of course, no equal to her husband.[118]

Without overstating the exemplarity of Blenheim, it is important to remember that its underlying principle of divided and not-so-equal informed the design of houses throughout this period, with explicitly masculinized spaces systematically given access to and conceptual allegiance with the sites of knowledge and power. In the 1690s, Celia Fiennes described the private apartments of one Mr. Foley and his wife in Stoake; off their shared bedchamber was her dressing room and "a Large studdy for him."[119] The Scottish architect George Steuart's design of Attingham (1783), one of the grandest houses in the west Midlands, for the 1st Lord Berwick similarly brings the gender politics of domestic organization into focus.[120] Lady Berwick's circular boudoir counterbalanced Lord Berwick's study on the other side of the building, and was linked to an anteroom and to the "Sultana Room." Lord Berwick's octagon-shaped study adjoined its own anteroom and the Library.[121] These were separate and inherently different zones of the domestic plan and, in the words of Lord Berwick's biographer, the interior was designed "with wings leading from each side of the entrance hall, one 'masculine,' the other 'feminine.'"[122] The library's proximity to Lord Berwick's study reiterated the sense that learning is for men; Lady Berwick's apartment incorporated the exotic with her orientalized "Sultana Room." The household's collection of textual knowledge was rendered masculine, and stood in additional contrast to the foreignness of the east and a kind of orientalist fantasy of femininity.

A ROOM OF ONE'S OWN: WOMEN'S AUTONOMY IN THE DRESSING ROOM

Many accounts of the dressing room show that its design and decoration upheld the early modern notion of the sexualized female body. But an important part of my thesis is that the domestic dressing room was a flexible space. In other words, the dressing room might be marshaled to confine women to a particularly objectified status within a household. It just as easily could set the stage for female subversion and autonomy; several aspects of the dressing room support this latter view, particularly the fact that the dressing room was often also a female study. The spatialized hierarchy that shaped English domestic architecture was not as stable as the plans would seem to imply. Dressing rooms were frequently part of floor plans where rooms were separated only by connecting doors. Celia Fiennes describes moving within just such a house: "You go thence into parlours, dineing rooms, drawing roomes and bed Chambers one leading out of another."[123] Without the innovation of hallways, the boundaries between rooms were both necessary and immensely vulnerable; a closed door could block access both to a particular room as well as to a wing of apartments.[124] Moreover, each of these rooms would have a jamb-door to the house's interior servants' passage; Fiennes recounts the jamb-door in one lady's dressing room that led to the back stairs used by the servants.[125] These kinds of alternative entrances and exits suggest that as separated or isolated as the dressing room might be from the center of household power, the room's varied thresholds could well be put to uses not intended by architectural design. These were the passageways that could allow private, even unauthorized, visitors a secret entrance.

The tension between the concepts of exclusion and privacy, between a paternalistic control of a woman's space and her own prerogative, highlighted by these structural features of seventeenth- and eighteenth-century domestic architecture, shape the famous marriage negotiation that William Congreve stages between Millamant and Mirabell in *The Way of the World* (1700). Millamant demands, among many things, the right to "dine in my Dressing-room when I'm out of Humour, without giving a Reason. To have my Closet inviolate. . . . And lastly, whereever I am, you shall always knock at the Door before you come in."[126] If women's spaces were sometimes figured as inferior, then this same quality of exclusion could be converted into an advantage. As Millamant's demands imply, this woman wants a room of her own to control, arguing that she does not want to "dwindle into a Wife."[127] And it is this desire for autonomous control that most concerns Millamant's suitor Mirabell, who responds to her by declaring that he wants to be "enlarg'd into a Husband."[128] These competing spatial metaphors speak to the challenge women's privacy posed to the traditional structure of a paternalistic household. Millamant undermines Mirabell's claims to unconditional authority through the technology of privacy, arguing that even a husband must respect the boundary of a closed door. Mirabell subsequently counters her demands with his own, stipulating that Millamant "admit no sworn Confidant, or intimate of your own Sex," no "she Friend."[129] In the face of Millamant's privacy, Mirabell imagines ways of monitoring it, fearful that his future wife will internalize her physical privacy and keep secrets from him. Although Congreve stops short of representing Mirabell and Millamant's married life, and fails to resolve their marriage negotiation, *The Way of the World* reflects the tension that women's privacy produced in the late seventeenth and early eighteenth centuries—the conflict between autonomy and exclusion. If a woman shuts the door, then she claims autonomy; if that door is shut by someone else, then she is excluded.

Even the hierarchy of gentleman's closet and lady's dressing room, upon which so many plans depended, could be called into question. A letter from Queen Mary to King William reveals that the conceptual subordination of the lady's dressing room to the gentleman's closet was not necessarily fixed. Mary's letter describes the renovations that still needed to be completed at Kensington House (alterations that were designed by Sir Christopher Wren), and suggests to her husband that they temporarily share an apartment: "tho mine can not possible be ready yet awhile, I have found out a way if you please . . . we may ly in your chamber & I go throw [through] ye councel roome down or else dresse there."[130] This letter demonstrates that the rooms just beyond the bedchamber—the most intimate space of the apartments—housed the acts that defined each gender, just as Alberti would have liked it. Mary's suggestion that the king's "councel roome" may double as the queen's dressing room shows how the difference between masculinity and femininity could be represented spatially. One space produced the actions of a king, while the other produced the looks of a queen. This was (royal) gender difference.

Nearly one hundred years later, Frances Burney, who served as Second Keeper of the Robes to Queen Charlotte from 1786–91, richly describes this queen's daily dressing schedule, just the kind of ritualistic preparation that Mary implies in her letter. Upon the queen's rising, her hair was adorned and then she was dressed by Burney and Burney's immediate superior, the ill-tempered Mrs. Elizabeth Schwellenberg; notably, "no Maid ever enters the [dressing-]Room while the Queen is in it."[131] Around midday, the queen again retired to her dressing room "to begin Dressing for the Day," a process that took upward of two hours:

> These times mentioned call me to the irksome and quick returning labours of the Toilette. The Hour advanced on the Wednesdays and Saturdays is for curling and craping the Hair, which it now requires twice a Week.
>
> A quarter before one is the usual time for the Queen to begin Dressing for the Day. Mrs Schwellenberg then constantly attends; so do I. Mrs Thielky of course at all times. We help her off with her Gown, and on with her powdering of things, and then the Hair Dresser is admitted. She generally reads the news-papers during that operation.[132]

Following the preparation of her hair, Charlotte removes to her "state Dressing Room," where her dress is finished; the queen's decouché takes decidedly less time, only twenty to thirty minutes, sometime between eleven and twelve o'clock at night.[133]

The remarkable aspect of Queen Mary's letter the century before resides in the fact that gender difference was not absolute, but somewhat unstable. The simple fact of Kensington House's renovation required that the spatialization of gender difference be reconsidered. The possibility for redefining the spaces that represented masculinity and femininity indicates that the architectural regulation of gender difference was provisional and that this condition introduced the possibility that such a gender hierarchy could be interrogated or even parodied.

The separation of women's rooms from men's institutionalized additional circumstances through which the hierarchy between men and women could be challenged.[134] While a dressing room might be remote—and far away from the conceptual center of a household such as Blenheim—the privacy of the dressing room could just as well connote a sense of privilege, as Millamant's desire for control over her apartments suggests. Consider, for example, Wren's renovation of Cardinal Wolsey's old palace of Hampton Court for William and Mary. Engaged by the queen, Wren designed a pair of royal apartments and two suites of them were completed just before Mary's death in 1694; William reportedly praised Wren's design of the royal apartments as unparalleled by any palace in Europe for their "good Proportion, State, and Convenience."[135] (The alterations to Hampton Court were not finished by the time of William's death nor of Queen Anne's; George II employed Willaim Kent to finish the project.[136] The royal apartments were finally used beginning in 1716, when they were set up for the Prince and Princess of Wales, the future George II and Queen Caroline, but were left empty after their departure.)[137] As in other grand houses of the day, the queen's and king's apartments were separate, connected by a gallery decorated with Lely's portraits of Charles II's "Windsor Beauties" (and the apartments were 330 and 328 feet long, respectively).[138] The queen's dressing room was the final room in a series of interconnected rooms that made up the queen's apartment. Each room had a grand view of the Fountain Court, an arrangement that reflects what Mark Girouard calls an "axis of honour."[139] The interior spaces were figured as increasingly private, so entering rooms farther along this axis simultaneously conferred and denoted a higher status. The first room in the apartment was the queen's drawing room, followed by her private bedchamber, which was fitted with special hinges that enabled the king and queen to lock themselves in at night.[140] Only the dressing room was beyond this intimate bedchamber. Such a floor plan assigned the greatest status of all to the dressing room—and to those who could gain admittance to it. Later in the following century, John Soane's design for William Colhoun's home near Thetford in Norfolk likewise assigned a significant status to the lady's dressing room; it is the largest of all the rooms on the chamber floor, measuring 21.6 by 27 feet, centrally positioned, and immediately above the drawing room on the ground floor (see figure).[141]

The dressing room's potential for privacy likewise introduced the question of how women would spend their time. Inventories help us to determine that women used these spaces to engage in the same kinds of

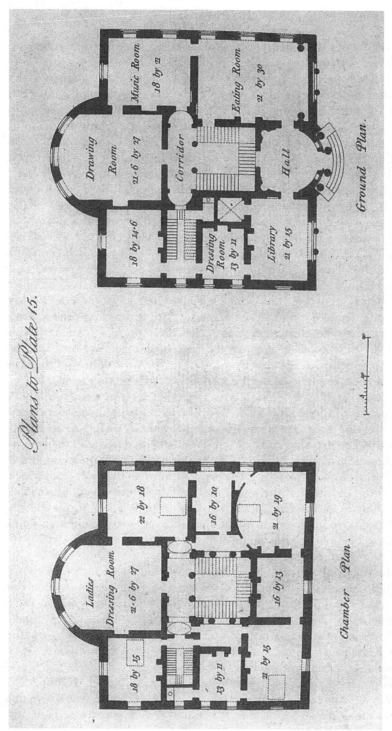

Plans to Plate 15.

Ground Plan.

Drawing Room
21-6 by 27

Music Room
18 by 21

18 by 14-6

Corridor

Dressing Room
13 by 21

Eating Room
21 by 30

Hall

Library
21 by 15

Chamber Plan.

Ladies Dressing Room
21-6 by 27

22 by 18

18 by 15

16 by 12

13 by 21

21 by 19

16 by 13

21 by 15

John Soane, *Sketches in Architecture. Containing Plans and Elevations of Cottages, Villages, and Other Useful Buildings* (London, 1793), plate 15. Courtesy The Newberry Library, Chicago private pursuits that men could. Remarkably, the dressing room was not merely a space for dressing and undressing; instead, a wide range of activities were possible within it, many of which were aligned with a sense of independence and autonomy. The dressing room of Lady Betty Master is one such example. A snapshot of her dressing room exists because her husband, Sir Harcourt Master, was a director of the South Sea Company and had all of his assets seized after the bubble burst, including their two residences. Confiscated from Lady Betty's dressing room in their Greenwich house were pieces such as a "Dressing-Glass," "a Toylet," and a "Dressing" chair, obvious enough furnishings for such a space.[142] But the inventory lists additional items that suggest Lady Betty spent time in her dressing room engaged in activities other than getting ready for the day or disrobing after it. These included "an Easy-Chair," "a parcel of China Cups and Saucers, Dishes and Basons," "a Card Table," and "a Tea-table and China."[143] The dressing room in her Tower-Hill townhouse also featured a service for tea ("parcel of China Plates, Cups, Sawcers, and som Delf[t] Plates").[144] One could relax, play cards, or take tea in either of Lady Betty's dressing rooms. Lady Lambert, the wife of another South Sea director, had a similarly furnished dressing room in her townhouse in the East End on Mincing-Lane.[145] And a 1762 design by Ince and Mayhew confirms that the dressing room facilitated social gatherings; a side section from *The Universal System of Household Furniture* shows that a large settee "compleat with cushions in form of a Turkish Soffa" is set back in the alcove of a lady's dressing room and flanked on either side by exaggerated rococo mirrors.[146] The dressing room of one Stephen Child's wife in their house in Richmond had such a "Satee."[147] As these objects suggest, the dressing room could well play host to social gatherings that were not necessarily in the tradition of the levee. Instead, these women could socialize with intimates in a secluded setting, free to take tea or to play cards. The dressing room was not just a space for potential male lovers like Horner to cuckold the husbands of London; it could also be a space for "she Friends" to congregate.

If the material history of the lady's dressing room indicates that it provided women with a space for informal social gatherings, then this same history points to the fact that the dressing room was also often used as a study. This was, perhaps, its most radical function, especially as the dressing-room-as-study conjoined a signifier for female sexuality with the material circumstances for female knowledge production. Various inventories bear out the fact that women regularly used their dressing rooms for solitary activities such as reading and writing. The Duchess of Lauderdale's "White Closet" in Ham House was a dressing room in the first two senses described above: here she dressed and undressed, and also played host to close friends, serving them tea as they relaxed in lacquered furniture.[148] But the White Closet was also a study where the duchess could read and write in private.[149] Her writing-cabinet, described in 1683, was "One Scriptore of Prince wood garnished with silver."[150] Dorothy Noel, Countess of Gainsborough, kept volumes of Donne's poetry in her dressing room.[151] In Monsieur Calonne's house, a mahogany dressing glass stood by a "ladies sheffinger, writing or work table, with a drawer, expensively furnished" and elsewhere a mahogany writing desk was paired with a mahogany dressing table.[152] Likewise, the property lists of one Edward Dennis indicate a similar domestic arrangement, with a "Dressing table and Cover" in company with a "walnut-tree Desk and Book-case."[153] Sir John Blunt, another director of the South Sea Company, shared a bedchamber with his wife in their Stratford home, off of which stood her dressing room, which was put to varied uses. This room featured not only a dressing table, three "Looking Glasses," an "Easy Chair, "66 Pieces of China," "32 Cups and Saucers," and several chairs of various designs, but also an "Escretore" [sic].[154] The dressing room was still a space for private contemplation early into the nineteenth century. When Maria Edgeworth stayed with the Strutts in 1813, she observed that "In each dressing room there was a writing desk and table with everything that could be wanted for writing."[155] The dressing room stood as a site for the production of women's knowledge.

The space of the dressing room remained, by and large, available only to wealthy women with rank in their households. Bedchambers in many houses did not always have adjoining dressing rooms. Eltham Lodge, a late-seventeenth-century prototype of the "middling" country house built in Greater London, contained three bedchambers, two of which had adjoining dressing rooms; the 1774 sale catalogue of Scotney Castle in Kent, which had existed since before the fourteenth century and had undergone several renovations by this time, listed five bedchambers and two dressing rooms.[156] But these same inventories and catalogues reveal that many of those bedchambers had dressing room furniture — and presumably served similar functions, allowing women to dress, socialize, and think with some amount of privacy. A 1721 inventory of Richard Houlditch's house at Casehorton, Surrey reveals that "Madam's Room" contained both a bed and the kind of furniture normally associated with the dressing room, including "six Dutch matted Chairs," "a walnut-tree Chest of Drawers," and "a Table and Looking-Glass."[157] In 1760, the house of a Mrs. Masters at Brook, near Wingham, had a single dressing room, but the several bedchambers contained items that facilitated the same function of the dressing room. There was a "dressing table and draw, lin'd with pink satten" and "dressing glass, two stands" in the Wrought Bed Chamber; there was a "dressing glass" as well as a "pier glass" in the Worsted Damask Chamber; the Blue Room and Closet held "a dressing table with a muslin twilight"; and the Crimson Silk Damask Room contained a "dressing glass in a swing frame and drawers," "one wallnut-tree desk, and dressing-table," and "two dressing boxes."[158] When a Miss Lampreys of Canterbury died in 1764, her house did not contain any dressing rooms, but there were dressing tables and dressing glasses in the two bedchambers.[159] The 1782 auction list for the farm of a Mr. Thomas Laugher in Worcester lists dressing tables in each of the two bedchambers, one made from walnut and the other featuring a glass.[160] These documents attest that even if there were not separate dressing rooms, many bedchambers in more modest dwellings would have contained the materials normally associated with the dressing room, suggesting that such a space could likely enable a similar range of intimate and potentially independent activities.

The seventeenth- and eighteenth-century domestic dressing room in England offered some women a room of their own, in the Woolfian sense of this phrase. Its primary association was with its primary function—the acts of dressing and undressing, the fashioning and dismantling of a woman's cosmetics and clothing. This association produced a nearly one-to-one correspondence between the dressing room and the female body and sexuality, a connotation that maintained the early modern notion that the female body was a prized possession. But this chapter's history of the lady's dressing room demonstrates that it was also a space over which women might have a certain amount of control and in which they could engage in various social and intellectual activities. The seventeenth- and eighteenth-century English dressing room allowed women to claim their own position of privilege, a situation that had the potential to rival the exclusive privacy generally reserved for men. By institutionalizing privacy for some women, allowing them a place to retire by themselves or with close associates, the lady's dressing room transformed the central paradigm of privacy developed in the early modern period and dismantled its system of surveillance. If the closet offered men an intellectual space beyond heterosexuality that publicly represented their authority, then the lady's dressing room potentially rivaled that claim of authority and staged a conflict between the imperatives of public decorum and the freedom available to some women in private. When one looks carefully at the historical record (a record that itself must be culled from a variety of sources), it becomes clear that a number of seventeenth- and eighteenth-century English women of privilege spent their time in spaces that provided the materials for independent thought and acts.

However, just as notable is this fact of association: the coexistence of the materials of beauty and sexuality with those of social intimacy and private reflection necessarily implicated one another. Therefore, if the opportunity or option for some women to retire in private translated into a wide-scale discursive preoccupation for eighteenth-century writers, then the interchangeability of these connotations—women's education is like cosmetics and vice versa, for example—likewise offered writers a rich and ambiguous metaphor for appropriation to a range of ends. On the level of figuration, the trope of the dressing room came to represent women's potential for independence in a variety of areas, whether it be through sexual license, social gatherings, or the production of knowledge. The question of representation—how this "actual" space came to be represented in literary texts—will be addressed in the following chapters.

II
Satire, Art, and Epistemology

3

"A painted woman is a dang'rous thing": Dressing Rooms and the Satiric Mode

This is the Fool, fair Ladyes, that does haunt yee,
That will from Dressing-Room to Play gallant yee.[1]

THE DRESSING ROOM METAPHOR IS SHAPED EARLY IN THE CENTURY by the supposition that women are theatrical and excessive, whereas by the late eighteenth century the dressing room becomes a place for heroines and mothers to consolidate and represent their virtue. The history of the dressing room metaphor is also shaped by its initial predominance in satires about women and later by its regular incorporation into the domestic novel. The dressing room trope reflects changes in genre and gender across the century, but it is also tied to a specific set of thematics in each case. In this chapter, we will take up the topic of the dressing room and satire not only to analyze the difficulty of reading satiric texts that presume and thwart referentiality, but also to suggest a mode of interpretation that takes satirists' stated and unstated strategies into account. Satires repeatedly imagine that women are "fallen" and are consumed by a vanity that itself presupposes the *absence* of beauty and authenticity. But, as we shall see, satires about women also use the dressing room to foreground the theme of artifice, all the while expressing their own preoccupation with which kind of artifice — women's or satirist's — is ultimately more persuasive. This aesthetic rivalry sets up two kinds of responses, one that produces a form of scopic apprehension unique to the satirist, what I shall call the "satiric double take," and the other that reverts to seemingly neutral epistemological orders to create the conceptual boundaries that women's dressing rooms seem endlessly to threaten, namely the satiric inventory. In all of these instances, we see that satires about women consistently attend to both the aesthetic and epistemological implications of the lady's dressing room, thematic implications that we will also explore in greater depth in chapters 4 and 5.

"SOME NEW MODE PRODUC'D A NEW LAMPOON":[2] DRESSING ROOMS AND SATIRIC THEORY

Nearly every satire about women reverts in one form or another to a dressing room scene. Regardless of their class, gender, religion, or politics, famous writers (Dryden, Pope, Swift, and Wortley Montagu) and infamous writers (Ned Ward, John Oldham, and Elizabeth Thomas) all use dressing rooms. The texts analyzed in this chapter—many of them forgotten satires by forgotten writers—use the dressing room and its associated activities to ridicule and censure women's assumed theatricality and narcissism. While the particularity of these examples might suggest that this is a minor literary tradition, collectively these texts illuminate the prevalence and significance of a representational strategy central to eighteenth-century literary production. The satiric dressing room was a commonplace in the period's literary culture.

Unlike any other mode or genre during this time, satire is inextricably linked to the dressing room; later in the century, domestic novels systematically incorporate the dressing room, but in the Restoration and early eighteenth century, the genre is satire. One might begin to explain this phenomenon by explaining that dress—and women's dress, in particular—holds a uniquely powerful status in the rhetoric of the fall, and that satirists were quick to draw upon this association between clothing and the story of Adam and Eve. From the reprimanding perspective of these satires, Eve's hubris ruined the innocence and purity associated with the naked body and introduced the necessity for concealment. As the speaker in *The Original of Apparel; Or, the Ornaments of Dress* (1732) laments, "Unhappy Cause! Thus from the Fall of Man / Garments invented were, and Dress began."[3] According to this satiric genealogy, dress is a *result* of deception.

But satirists also regularly characterize dress, again, specifically women's dress, as a *tool* of deception. Daniel Defoe attempts to preempt sartorial dissembling by instructing readers that determining the meaning of a woman's "Monstrous Dress" is notoriously difficult.[4] William Wycherley contends that dress no longer functions as an accurate indicator of a woman's status in the "Epistle Dedicatory" to *The Plain Dealer* (1676): "For by that mask of modesty which women wear promiscuously in public, they are all alike, and you can no more know a kept wench from a woman of honour by her looks than by her dress."[5] Consider, too, the warning that François Bruys issues in his lengthy prose satire *The Art of Knowing Women; Or, The Female Sex Dissected* (1730), a catalogue of female types: "Women, in order to inhance the Lustre of their *Beauty*, or to drown their Defects in that invaluable point, have recourse to *Dress*."[6] This "recourse to Dress" allows women to deceive people about their true physical appearance (they may appear even more beautiful or even not so ugly) and, implicitly, about their true moral quality. Women's "recourse to Dress" is both a means of deception and an effect of original sin, thus making every woman a descendant of Eve—at least to the satirists. Ironically, the naked body in the postlapsarian, dressing-room-filled world is just as likely to signify female debauchery as dress is.

If dress enables women to conceal themselves with a duplicitous surface, and if any kind of adornment by this definition is misleading, then dressing rooms enhance and institutionalize this project. But it is likewise remarkable how the ability of dressing rooms to hide things also opens the way for satire. John Breval—a career army man and diplomat, famous, too, as one of Pope's dunces—explicitly ties the "problem" of the lady's dressing room in seventeenth-century English court culture to the production of satire. In *The Art of Dress* (1717) Breval tells us that dressing-boxes, which are "fatal" and contain "more Ills" than Pandora's box, date from the Restoration of Charles II, a chronology concurrent with the architectural developments analyzed in the previous chapter.[7] Breval's focus is on the spectacle of female beauty that accompanied the king on his return to England: when "The Second Charles fills up th' *Usurper*'s Room, / Unnumber'd Beauties flock[ed] from ev'ry Part" and "*Mantuas, Pendants,* and *Commodes* appear'd."[8] The fashion show of Charles's court, with women's identities firmly supplanted by the clothes and adornments they wear, precipitates a satiric response. Women's style generates satire: "Sackville and Wilmot then sat Censors here, / Kind to the Sex, but to its Faults severe; / Such *Satire* flow'd from their abounding Store."[9] Within the context of dress as misleading, women's appearances are their "Faults" and figured as a *provocation* to satiric writers. In a phrase that jumbles monthly cycles, women's dress, and literary production, Breval's speaker argues that "ev'ry Moon / With some New Mode produc'd a new Lampoon."[10] The more women express themselves "With some New Mode," the more satire is produced as a corrective to women's excesses, a sequence of events that renders a causal relation between a particular social condition (women's inappropriate dress) and a literary response. *The Art of Dress* succinctly names women's reputed penchant for fashioning themselves in their dressing rooms as the catalyst of Restoration satire.

Breval's assessment is not too far off the mark, at least when we consider the body of satires circulated throughout the late seventeenth and

eighteenth centuries. This is not to say that the emergence of the dressing room "caused" this satiric tradition, but that their chronological
conjunction is true. Yet this literary phenomenon has received little critical attention. In spite of the fact that the dressing room pervades satires
about women, Felicity Nussbaum is one of the few critics to consider
the relationship between the dressing room and satire in the seventeenth and eighteenth centuries. Nussbaum's *The Brink of All We Hate*
astutely identifies satires about women as a literary tradition that had
not been considered previously and points to many of the suppositions
that make up satirists' use of dressing room scenes, including the claim
that women use the dressing room to plot machinations that endanger
men and that the satirist has the authority, indeed the mandate, to expose such a space to public view.[11]

In spite of these contributions, Nussbaum's account also raises several interpretive problems, primarily because her description of the satiric dressing room replicates satirists' self-justification. Elsewhere,
Nussbaum explains that her readings provide a catalogue of the conventions satirists used to indict women, though this inventory does not
call the satirist's presumptions or methods into question.[12] Indeed, when
satirists expose the dressing room to public view, they depend upon the
idea that this space *deserves* invasion. Such claims ought to be analyzed,
especially since self-justification is a satiric convention dating back to
Juvenal's argument that it is difficult not to write satire in such a debauched society. Rather than wholly subscribe to the satirist's point of
view, one needs to consider how these claims succeed and the extent
to which they attempt to render certain issues invisible to the reader.
Moreover, to describe the dressing room as "morbidly fascinating" and
as a "living metaphor for women's mystery" reiterates the stereotypes
upon which these satires depend, leaving the significance and function
of these assumptions as literary tropes unquestioned.[13]

Returning to Breval's satire can help us to unpack these stereotypes.
The Art of Dress's genealogy of the conjunction of the satiric mode and
the dressing room trope raises an issue central to the current critical
debate about satire. Breval is quick to defend Restoration satirists by
presenting attacks on women as a result of what women themselves did.
But one must also consider the extent to which the artifice of satire itself
is obscured by the satirists' overt preoccupation with the dissection of
feminine artistry. Reading *The Art of Dress* or any satiric dressing room
scene forces one to consider whether they are discursive responses to
particular material conditions or whether satires are formal experiments, divorced from any cultural context.[14] In the first model of satiric
theory, textual details are tied to historical particulars, as the critic provides a historical key that illuminates the allusive literary text. These

kinds of historicist interpretations see the factual in the satiric, linking the King of Lilliput to the King of England. In this vein, feminist critics regularly look to a satirist's cultural context to explain misogynistic representations. Ellen Pollak, for example, turns to the social and economic possibilities for women in the eighteenth century and to representations in domestic novels to sketch the context of "passive womanhood" that she argues pervades the satires of Pope and Swift.[15] Nussbaum argues that a tradition of satires about women resulted from the variety of threats that women posed to men in the post–interregnum era.[16] These comparisons between signifier and referent do not always hold and force critics to admit that the contextual parallel does not completely work; as Nussbaum admits, "we cannot know how accurately the satires reflect society."[17] Given this limitation, it is tempting to read satires as sealed off from their contexts. Rose Zimbardo argues that "there is no historical reality" that satire parodies; instead, satiric texts consist of "inauthentic constructs [that] erase each other in a continuous process that exists for the sole end of undoing itself."[18] An exclusively formal reading opens us to the discursive play of satiric texts, and to the performative strategies that frequently characterize this play, but it likewise blinds us to the material conditions of Restoration and eighteenth-century literary culture that these texts regularly ask us to examine. Reading satire requires consideration of the "outside" world, in some manner, in order to register the meanings that satires generate and exploit.

The satiric dressing room is an important case in point. Satirists seem to refer to the world outside of the text by evoking a space that had a newly defined, and potentially subversive, place in some English households. But satiric texts regularly *misrepresent* the material reality of this space, imagining women solely through the lens of illicit sexuality and artifice. For these reasons, dressing room scenes in Restoration and eighteenth-century satiric literature challenge us to think through the implications of satiric referentiality. If, as Fredric V. Bogel argues, "referentiality" and even "factuality are essential conventions, products of certain rhetorical strategies," then the problem of the satiric dressing room, as well as of satire more generally, comes down to that of context versus text.[19] How do we handle the contemporary analogues that these texts imply, while acknowledging their difference?

Dustin Griffin suggests that "the historical particulars in satire always have a curious in-between status, neither wholly fact nor wholly fiction"; it is this "curious in-between status" that most fully characterizes satirists' appropriation of the dressing room trope.[20] Satiric accounts of the dressing room are remarkable for both their frequency and their explicit misreading of historical context. Although the material conditions of the dressing room suggest that it facilitated women's private contemplation and writing, satiric texts throughout this period systematically suppress the intellectual connotations of the dressing room in favor of the stereotype of women's widespread sexual promiscuity and physical degeneracy. A space that historically represented a site of emancipation for the elite is transformed by satirists into a house of lewdness, often for women on the edge of social appropriateness, such as prostitutes. Such a disjunction and a radical misreading of cultural context require us to rethink not only the new historicist project, but also to develop strategies for reading satiric texts that themselves posit a superficial and distorted relationship to their cultural context. We need a method of reading the satiric mode that takes into account its fundamentally unstable nature as well as its productive, if vexed, relation to context.

A solution to the double bind inherent to reading satire —is it a purely formal activity or a historicist one —is to consider that satire simultaneously uses and distorts society. For satirists, the very existence of *some* dressing rooms implicates *all* women in an economy of duplicity. As readers, however, we can see that this projection is two-sided, and speaks to that "curious in-between" status of satiric rhetoric. The satiric projection of duplicity through the dressing room allows writers to claim that a social problem, namely that women are out of control, requires their redress; by locating the cause of satiric attacks outside of the text, the satirist then avoids the suggestion of impropriety or voyeurism. The claim that women are duplicitous can also be seen as a strategy to render satiric texts legitimate and even necessary; in other words, the projection of duplicity allows satirists to create problems that they can likewise resolve by peering into the dressing room and then writing about it. By foregrounding the "real" threat of the dressing room (and implicating readers in this concern), many satirists create foils for their own rhetorical leaps of logic. As we shall see, there are two primary concerns at the heart of satiric dressing rooms that relate to art and artifice and to theories of knowledge, concerns that I will discuss below as well as in the following two chapters.

Dangerous Pleasures: Artifice, the Toilet, and Satire

As a literary tradition, seventeenth- and eighteenth-century satiric dressing rooms draw heavily on the example of Juvenal's *Satire Six*. This satire, perhaps more than any other, shaped the form and content of satires about women throughout the seventeenth and eighteenth centuries.[21] Even a cursory view of satires from this period reveals the influence of the dressing room scene from *Satire Six*, be it in the form of an epigraph, an allusion, or a translation. Mary Evelyn, the daughter of the diarist John Evelyn, penned her satire *Mundus Muliebris; or, The Ladies Dressing-Room Unlock'd And her Toilette Spread* (1690) (which was published posthumously by her father) in the form of a guidebook for young men to seduce women with clothing and jewelry. In character with such satires, Evelyn's epigraph quotes *Satire Six*: "Such care for a becoming Dress they take, / As if their Life and Honour were at Stake."[22] The simile that Evelyn selects to open *Mundus Muliebris* foregrounds the misapprehension that such texts inevitably attack, namely a woman's belief that her appearance is ultimately a matter of essence. The couplet suggests that dress for women is tantamount to the armoring of a warrior (a strain that Pope adopts in *The Rape of the Lock*) and that traditional physiognomy, which equates one's appearance with one's moral value, is potentially at risk under the tyranny of "dress." These are words, of course, from ancient Rome, easily adopted by the young Evelyn for the England of 1690.

Evelyn's use of Juvenal underscores two related notions regarding women's dress that structure satiric dressing rooms throughout the period. The first supposition that satirists used was to contend that a woman has many sartorial options at her disposal to fool those who view her; the second was that women inappropriately value their physical appearance. Taken as commonplaces, this reading of female beauty simultaneously introduced the problems of deception and frivolity and then linked them. While there was debate about Juvenal's method and doubts about the efficacy of the satiric mode more generally, Juvenal's "insights" were the stock-in-trade of seventeenth- and eighteenth-century satirists, a perception facilitated by an increasing number of translations that made his work more widely available to English audiences. Sir Robert Stapylton—a Benedictine monk in his youth, before converting and securing a position in the privy chamber of the future Charles II—produced the first complete translation of the satires published in English. Although Stapylton's is regarded as a literal rendering with little poetic merit, his work and John Dryden's more well-known 1693 translation illustrate the satiric strategies that Juvenal's text promulgates.[23] The narrator of *Satire Six* explicitly warns one young "Posthumous" not to marry and voices a series of scenarios to dissuade the young man. The dressing room scene offers the satirist an opportunity to reveal what wives become, promising to show, in Stapylton's words, "How married women spend the day."[24]

As Evelyn's allusion indicates, Juvenal's satiric attack is two-pronged: the dressing room scene in *Satire Six* focuses on a woman's behavior in private and how this behavior is shaped by an obsession with her looks. The satirist also urges the reader and Posthumous to conclude that this is a representative account of married women, rather than an anomalous one. By the time we arrive on the scene, there are already several casualties suffering from this woman's domestic torture: "Her chief maid's dead, her dresser ready stript, / . . . [Her chair-bearer's] head / Breaks her tough cane."[25] "She rules and governs in no milder sort, / Then if her *house* were a *Sicilian Court*," according to Stapylton.[26] Dryden's translation paints her as crueler: "Compar'd with such a proud, insulting dame, / Sicilian tyrants may renounce their name."[27] Both versions elaborate the comparison between an implicitly contemporary urban (English) woman and ancient Sicilian rulers. In the editorial apparatus, Stapylton explains that "A *Sicilian Court*," particularly the "Reigns of *Sycily's* cruellest Tryants, *Phalaris* and the *Dionisii*," was an especially despotic government, just as Dryden wryly observes that "*Sicilian tyrants* are grown to a proverb, in Latin, for their cruelty."[28] The simile renders women and Sicilian despots degenerate and autocratic, acting out their undisputed rule, only women are worse. Stapylton sharpens the political aspect of Juvenal's satire by calling the assembly of her servants at the dressing table a "councel." While the term has obvious political connotations and extends the initial simile between a woman at home and rulers in a despotic government, this "councel" has a particularly ridiculous mandate—to confer about the trivial matter of "dressing my Lady."[29] Thus the language of *Satire Six* reconfirms the message of its content; a married woman at home is at once powerful and ridiculous. The allusion to a Sicilian tyrant moreover implies a homology between a tyrannical wife and an abusive government, drawing a connection between a disordered domestic structure and an authoritarian political system; the abusive, out-of-control wife is not as innocuous or as easily contained as might be imagined.

But then again, Juvenal's text makes the reader think that this woman is ultimately ridiculous by pairing its allusion to abusive rule with women's vanity. The satire moves seamlessly from domestic abuse to the dressing table in a narrative that links a woman's power and its commensurate waste of energy to her desire for a beauty that cannot be achieved; this transition works to contain the potential damage of a powerful wife, by reasoning that she will exert her energy for futile and inherently self-destructive ends. The woman treats her attendants poorly because she anxiously hopes to project an awesome image of feminine beauty; her ill-temper only increases as their efforts fail to produce results. Stapylton's narrator humorously reprimands her with questions, the end-rhymes of which intensify the satirist's mockery: "*What hath your woman done deserves these blows? / Is't her fault, Madam, you dislike your nose?*"[30] Eventually, the cause and effect structure of this woman's autocratic behavior and the inability of her body to be beautiful is blurred. One condition feeds the other so that her abhorrent character merely grows, as does her figure.

Late-seventeenth- and eighteenth-century English appropriations of Juvenal specifically focus on the satirist's exposure of female beauty as both a fraud and as ultimately trivial. Bruys's *The Art of Knowing Women* praises Juvenal's dressing room scene for the acumen of its satiric mode: "Nothing can be more judicious, than JUVENAL'S *Ideas*, when he introduces us to a *Lady* at her TOILET, attended by her Chamber-Maid, in the greatest Confusion for want of Time to dress her self."[31] Juvenal is "judicious" to represent the lady in her dressing room, and Bruys's selection of nouns is relevant. Departing from conventional readings of Juvenal's satiric mode as "declamatory," Bruys suggests that the Juvenalian dressing room scene is marked by wisdom and good sense.[32] Sound judgment, rather than vengeful ire, motivates Juvenal to satirize a woman in her dressing room. Bruys follows this satiric principle by including a Juvenalian-inspired portrait of one "Lucinda," who spends "three or four Hours together dressing or undressing her Head, till her Glass tells her, nothing can be nicer."[33] These three or four hours are wasted hours, spent on the trivial and repetitive task of arranging one's cosmetics, hair, and clothing (and satirists always suppose that it takes three or four hours). The author of another satire, *Female Taste* (1745), extends the ridicule of the importance women place on their appearance by drawing a portrait of a woman who arranges for a post-mortem toilet, determined that a maid will "spread, / A few soft teints of lively red" on her dead cheeks.[34] If one is appropriately made-up, the satirist ironically promises, "No saucy worm shall ever dare / To breakfast on a form so fair."[35]

Satirists in this period also develop the implications of Juvenal's message by turning the artifice of the dressing room back onto women: if women are deluded to think that cosmetics improve their looks, then they should know that they will become, in the words of Bruys, a "ghastly Sprite" whether they use cosmetics or not.[36] Just as Pope's Clarissa warns near the end of *The Rape of the Lock*, Bruys's satiric speaker admonishes that female beauty is destined to fade. The lecture encapsulates the conceptual double bind that ensnares women:

> Then, to be sure, wilt thou endeavour to conceal the Ravages of Age, and with all the deceitful Powers of Cosmeticks, smooth and plump up the Wrinkles of thy Brow. The natural *Lillies* and *Roses* of thy Bosom being withered, thou wilt be for laying on artificial Colours: But all to no Purpose; for maugre all the Art and Paint in the World, the Deformities of Old Age will show themselves.

> And whatever Secret the Tire-Woman may bragg of, all her Skill cannot recover fading *Beauty*; and she is so far from giving it *new Life*, that she only hastens its *Death*.[37]

In all of these satires, the artifice of the lady's dressing room ultimately confirms the absence of beauty and the presence of vanity, but it likewise foregrounds the artifice of satire. Keeping in mind Bogel's argument that referentiality is a convention of satiric rhetoric, consider the extent to which satirists implicitly draw a correlation to the world outside the text by suggesting that "women" in general threaten them. The oft-repeated threat to satire functions as yet another claim of causation that assumes the world beyond the text shapes a satirist's rhetorical possibilities. In the "Argument" to *Satire Six*, Dryden argues that Juvenal's "bid" that men "beware of [women's] Artifices is a kind of silent acknowledgment, that they have more wit than Men: which turns the Satyr upon us, and particularly upon the Poet; who thereby makes a Complement, where he meant a Libel."[38] Dryden's commentary highlights two concerns that resonate with the question of context versus text that I discussed in the previous section. First, the fact that women supposedly need to be satirized suggests that they are already out of (men's) control and subject men to their (sexual) power. Second, women's artifice (emblematized by the dressing room) already outwits men's satiric artifice. As spaces of female prerogative and (sexual) agency, the dressing room is figured as a site for the emasculation of *other* men. It is the place where weak men can lose their heads, as it were, seduced by the sight of a beautiful woman up close who is, potentially, sexually available; one is reminded of Michael Seidel's argument that the satirist "hopes, almost prays that whatever out there threatens him does not by a stretch of his own imagination absorb him" and emasculate "him."[39] Edmund Waller's "Of her Chamber" (1645) ridicules the shuffling and jockeying of men during a visit to a beautiful lady's dressing room.[40] This space is a "Paradise," even better than heaven because the woman's visitors are alive to enjoy it.[41] Waller's dupes forget who they are, and "stand amaz'd and gazing on the fair, / Loose thought of what themselves or others are."[42] These men are paradoxically united in their competition with one another, even though each and every one of them runs the risk of becoming emasculated by the sight of a beautiful woman in her dressing room.

Women are simultaneously objects and agents within the satiric economy: they provoke with their reputedly debauched behavior, but they also threaten to upstage the satirists with their skill for duplicity and artifice, and are therefore actually aesthetic *rivals*. We will discuss this aesthetic tension in great detail in the following chapter, particularly

Pope's appropriation of the dressing room as a vehicle for the articulation of a poetics that undercuts the value of spectacle. But whether in the poetry of Pope or others, the satiric tension foregrounded in the dressing room may very well come down to who can manufacture the more convincing spectacle, a woman or a satirist.

John Oldham—the poet mourned by the likes of Dryden at his early death—conceives of female beauty not only as artifice, but as *criminal* when he argues that a woman killed his friend with her "Falshood [*sic*] and Scorn."[43] The satirist sees this amorous betrayal embodied in her physical beauty and is appalled that she continues to be an object of desire for other men, that her "criminal Beauties . . . / in their old Lustre still prevail."[44] To counteract her hold over people, Oldham first uses a satiric dressing room scene to show that this woman's smiles "Are but an Ambush to hid Treachery" and her good looks "a gawdy Case" for a "nasty Soul."[45] Apprehended properly, she is a concoction of artifice. But in Oldham's text we also see what happens when a satirist acknowledges that peering into the dressing room does not exact a satisfactory revenge. As with the postmodern closet, opening up the dressing room to public view only invites additional anxieties and questions. Thus we can reclassify Oldham's dressing room scene as a failure that actually intensifies the satirist's ire, thereby introducing the tool of *satiric* artifice; this is, in effect, what Pope will do in *The Rape of the Lock*. "Arm'd with dire Satyr, and resentful Spite," the satirist promises to "haunt her with the Ghosts of Wit."[46] By evoking the power of satire, Oldham exposes the functioning of injurious speech; considered performatively, as Judith Butler notes, "hate speech is an act that recalls prior acts, requiring a future repetition to endure."[47] Oldham installs his text as a participant in the literary tradition of satires about women (its title uses the familiar and often recycled "A Satyr Upon A Woman") *and* as the words that will be forever identified with this particular woman. The satirist's dream is that his words—his satiric artifice—will come to define not only this woman's physical appearance, but also her social and moral standing:

> Grant I may fix such brands of Infamy,
> So plain, so deep grav'd on her, that she,
> Her skill, Patches, nor Paint all join'd can hid
> And which shall lasting as her soul abide.[48]

If, indeed, Oldham's fantasy of injurious speech were to pass, then these "brands of Infamy" would permanently displace her physical beauty. Oldham's desire undercuts this woman's self-presentation, threatening to represent her instead with a more powerful and damning form of artifice, satire. By criss-crossing the divide between the material world and the literary text, the satirist yearns to rewrite the female body by supplanting the transformative powers of the dressing room with that of a satiric text. In this formula, the agent of representation also changes, as the satirist appropriates a woman's ability to construct herself.

Oldham's dream confounds the opposition between the "real" world and the literary text, between a historicist mode of reading and a formalist, in part through its evocation of the law. To render this woman branded with infamy is not only to give her "evil fame or reputation," according to the *Oxford English Dictionary*, but also to challenge her civil rights. The term "infamy" carried legal ramifications in the seventeenth and eighteenth centuries; it was "the loss of all or certain of the rights of a citizen, consequent on conviction of certain crimes."[49] Historically, most defamation cases concerning women focused on their sexual behavior, but such accusations often masked the real object of dispute.[50] Attacking a woman's sexual reputation was merely a vehicle, and the charge of infamy in Oldham's satire clearly depends upon this slippage. By using the word "infamy" to question her sexual reputation, Oldham's satirist also questions her *legal* status. The satirist's (imagined) textual inscriptions on this woman's body mark her as criminal and constitute a single act of rhetoric that produces two effects, naming and punishment. This twofold desire is encapsulated in a single wish: "help me rhime her dead."[51] The satirist not only conflates the branches of the judicial system by claiming to be her "Witness, Judge, and Executioner," but also renders the power of these various offices into an effect of language.[52] As Ann Van Sant has recently argued, "satire and law aim at the absence of women."[53] Naming explicitly installs regulation and effectively takes the dressing room — and a woman's ability to name herself — out of the picture.

Thomas D'Urfey, famous as a lyricist and dramatic poet, emplots the "failure" of a dressing room scene, but in a different vein. The poem "Paid for Peeping" (1690) details what can go wrong when a man is overpowered by the sight of a woman in her dressing room, and explains this "defeat" specifically in terms of genre. D'Urfey's modern-day "Actæon" had "hop'd to see, / Something well worthy Raillery," but instead produces an encomium.[54] If we consider D'Urfey's text a failed satire, then we can see that the speaker does not maintain the critical distance necessary to produce satire and that he instead develops a sympathy of intimacy. By the end of the poem, the woman in question has discovered his scopophilia and blocked the peeping hole into her chamber; the speaker believes that his punishment is his unending desire to see her once again. In the context of a tradition of satires about women, we can also determine that the speaker is, in effect, paying for his transgression of falling for a woman who *should* have been satirized. Satire collapses into desire, rather than the other way around. Likewise, Joseph Thurston suggests in the three-part verse satire *The Toilette* (1730) that "When half reveal'd, your Charms invite to Love; / Our active Fancy will the rest improve."[55] The gentleness of Thurston's language portends the production of amatory and speculative verse, rather than a satiric exposé that the dressing room more often provokes.

Given that satires about women seem to hinge on the satirist's ability to remain critically distant, a satirist such as the Scottish poet, wigmaker, and bookseller Allan Ramsay imagines an alternative relation to a female beloved than complete supplication, even though this response still models itself in terms of artifice. Ramsay's "The Morning Interview" (1721) tells the story of one "Damon" who exacts revenge upon one "Celia" for resisting his sexual advances. In a scene reminiscent of Belinda's mock-epic dressing table, Celia's dressing room holds various "implements of death," including "lac'd shoes and her silk stockings," "garters," and a "petticoat."[56] Ramsay's Damon finds himself overwhelmed by the metonymic associations of these objects, for the beau believes that he is looking at the sartorial equivalent of Celia's naked body: "His dazzled eyes almost deserted light, / No man before had ever got the sight"—the sight of this lady's garters, that is.[57] Ramsay holds Damon in a familiar predicament. He is weakened by the very sight of a beautiful woman up close in her dressing room. But Ramsay converts this potential for paralysis into an occasion for action. When Cupid takes the form of Celia's lapdog Shock, Ramsay artfully reformulates the satiric anxiety about masculine sexual displacement that preoccupies satirists in earlier generations, for lapdogs and dildoes are explicitly identified with female masturbation. The dildo was a common object in Restoration satires about women, beginning most famously with "Signior Dildo" (1673–74), a satiric ballad attributed to Rochester in which the dildo functions as a secret substitute for the penis that is hidden easily under women's clothing or even in their bodies.[58] The lapdog was similarly figured as an erotic object and expressly associated with the dressing room, as Donald Posner has noted.[59] Thus Richard Ames writes in *The Folly of Love* (1691) that "Lap Dogs and D—s serve . . . to cure / [women's] am'rous customary Calenture."[60] In opposition to this satiric tradition, the lapdog in Ramsay's "The Morning Interview" is *not* a rival of Damon's, but his coconspirator. Cupid-cum-Shock shoots "two barbed darts" in Celia's eyes to blind her will to resist Damon.[61] Even though the narrator claims that "both were conquerors, and both did yield," the poem concludes with a satiric comeuppance for Celia: while Celia attempts to use her dressing room to overpower Damon, he secures the upper hand by usurping her tools of defiance, with a little help from divine intervention.[62] This contrast satirizes and belittles (literally) the power that women derive from their dressing rooms, while suggesting that women are ultimately ideal objects for men's sexual desire and mastery.

The speaker of the anonymous *Woman in Miniature* (1742) similarly identifies satire as a means of countering female artifice. The poem's "sportive rhimes" demonstrate that "Satire is but the shadow of a rod"; this satirist "hurts no patient, while he cures the wound."[63] The woman in question is, of course, located in a dressing room, which contains her "rubbish" "Plac'd in irregular oeconomy."[64] This "Cosmelia" is a "mistaken fair" and a "Fair sloven!" who threatens to "encroach on man."[65] While Ramsay's "The Morning Interview" reconfigures a battle of the sexes in the dressing room, *Woman in Miniature* argues that the excesses of Cosmelia shall be contained if "thy husband be a poet" like this satirist.[66] Satire takes care of women—it puts them in their presumed places and even marries them off to controlling, satiric husbands. Some texts even go so far as to envisage the erasure of women as a means of guaranteeing the genre's existence. Richard Ames and Andrew Marvell both conclude their satires with masculine utopias, specifically an Eden without Eve; "Such was that happy Garden-state, / While Man there walk'd without a Mate," Marvell observes in *The Garden* (?1652).[67] However, this masculinist desire runs its own generic risks: when Ames's *The Folly of Love* imagines that, in paradise, the poet would "*never, never* think on *Woman-kind*," this fantasy obscures satire's investment in designing women.[68]

To return to John Breval's *The Art of Dress*: this satirist acknowledges that artifice—whether a woman's or a satirist—is integral to the production of satiric literature. Perhaps all too knowingly, Breval's speaker argues that a female body in the sunshine, as it were, would render the deconstructive nature of satiric rhetoric unnecessary. Without a surface to contest, satirists are themselves impotent:

> White Breasts, and Shoulders bare, invade the Eye,
> And Legs no more conceal'd, our Jests defy,
> Those pretty Legs so Taper, and so Smart,
> By which Men guess at ev'ry other *Part*.[69]

If, indeed, legs are no longer concealed, warns Breval's satirist, satiric rhetoric has no place and no potency in the realm of cultural exchange. Instead, the exposed female body has the potential to overwhelm the viewer ("invade the Eye"). All is not lost, however, for the sight of women's legs propels observers to drop the mantle of satire in favor of speculation about female sexuality, or, in the language of Breval's verse, to "guess at ev'ry other *Part*." The scenario Breval envisages, therefore, conjoins a displacement of traditional satiric artifice with both an acknowledgment of the productivity of the surface and the continuum of association (legs with genitalia). Therefore, while the clothed and manufactured projection of femininity, by satiric definition, invites censure and ridicule, Breval contends that the most extreme of the dressing room aesthetic (featuring a naked female body) still produces sexual and even satiric meaning.

If Looks Could Kill: Satiric Double Takes

In the previous section, we considered the range of ways in which satires about women deploy the dressing room trope to accuse women of artifice, while explicitly using the artifice of satire themselves. These efforts attempt both to delimit the category of femininity to its superficial construction and to establish a hierarchical opposition between the artistry of women and that of satirists. In this section, we will take up the structural implications of the dressing room as satirists use its potential as a conceptual portal into women's secrets, a vision of apprehension designed to teach readers how to acquire legitimate knowledge about women. If only people see into the dressing room *properly*, reason satirists, they will themselves censure and ridicule women. But this issue of appropriate apprehension is a tricky one in satires about women. *Satire Six*, for example, does not rest at the level of imagery or even content. In case readers are not convinced by this exposure of the dressing room's cosmetic function and women's penchant for delving into domestic tyranny, *Satire Six* reverts to another mode of persuasion: the satiric "double take." With this phrase, I describe Juvenal's transformation of the *gaze* of desire into one of satire, a change that is accomplished by the emplotment of a double perspective as well as the jarring collision between them. The satiric double take is manifested in the form of a surreptitious glance, stolen without permission and upending the terms of apprehension that a woman in her dressing room establishes. Its necessarily clandestine character does not merely offer a second view of the satiric object, but implies that this alternate viewpoint contains the truth of a spectacle because it does not subscribe to a woman's self-presentation. This coinage "double take" is designed to describe the dynamic of scopic apprehension that allows satirists to negotiate the conceptual and epistemological slipperiness of women's cosmetic surfaces by introducing another viewpoint, and to explicate a model of satiric scopophilia that carries with it, in the words of feminist

film theorist E. Ann Kaplan, "the power of action and of possession."[70]
In the context of the aesthetic rivalry we described in the previous section, the satiric double take ensures that the satirist's view of things —
namely female artifice — is taken as *the* legitimate view.

The satiric double take is powerfully utilized in Juvenal's *Satire Six*.
At first glance, Juvenal's satirist tells the reader what the woman seems
to look like: from the front, "You see *Andromache*," which is desirable
enough.[71] But from behind, "She's less, you there *another woman* find."[72]
The image of beauty that the woman in question hopes to project is that
of Hector's wife, but apprehending the female body from behind exposes her subterfuge and the disparity between surface and essence that
the labors of the toilet cannot completely conceal. Dryden's translation
capitalizes on this disjunction:

> With curls on curls, they build her head before,
> And mount it with a formidable tow'r.
> A giantess she seems; *but, look behind*,
> And then she dwindles to the pigmy kind.
> Duck-legg'd, short-waisted, such a dwarf she is,
> That she must rise on tiptoes for a kiss. (emphasis added)[73]

Looking at a woman's backside magically offers a view of the "real"
thing. Rather than being subject to the projection of duplicity and artifice that this woman and her attendants manufacture, looking askance,
paradoxically, allows one to see clearly and truthfully. To emphasize
this unlikely insight, Dryden does not even let the line conclude, but
interrupts the frontal view to change the angle: "but, look behind," the
speaker urges after the line's third foot. Faced with a towering image,
the satirist's gaze shrinks the woman's projection, such that she who
pretended to be Andromache "dwindles" in front of our eyes. The word
"dwindle" aptly captures the deflating effect of the satiric mode since it
operates on physical and conceptual levels, for the term means both to
become gradually smaller and to lose importance. Dryden's redirected
gaze, his "double take," simultaneously diminishes this woman's stature
and her value. And the satire leaves her this way: *Satire Six* critiques
this woman's behavior in her dressing room by exposing her as ridiculous, deluded, and trivial. The racial implications of "pigmy" demonstrate that the rejection is not solely the discarding of something
ephemeral or inconsequential. Indeed, the satirist is anxious to inflect
an element of the grotesque in the portrait to ensure that this woman's
fixation on the trivial is appropriately abhorred. In this light, one understands retrospectively that the comparison to Sicilian tyrants functions
analogously.

In the face of an image that threatens to set the terms of view—from the front, she looks awesome—the satiric double take manufactures a gaze for the satirist (and, implicitly, for the reader/spectator) that appropriates the potential agency of this image. If a woman in her dressing room, surrounded by the materials of self-construction, threatens a satiric viewer, it is on the level of meaning making that this rivalry occurs. Ever dependent upon the metaphor of revelation, and its corollary, the interiorization of truth, the satiric perspective eradicates the legitimacy of the satiric object in the service of constructing its own.

Peering into the dressing room sets the parameters for this scopic apprehension, tied as it is to claims of superiority, and satirists throughout the late seventeenth and eighteenth centuries adopted the satiric double take to great effect. Andrew Marvell's "The last Instructions to a Painter" (1667) ridicules an older woman for her sexual promiscuity in one telling gesture. Once naked, this woman is a picture of incongruities that embody her transgressions. "Stript to her Skin, see how shee stooping stands," urges Marvell's satirist.[74] In the face of her attempts at discretion (she cleans herself "lest the Scent her Crime disclose"), the satirist looks beneath her layer of deception to discover the physical truth that resonates with her moral standing (or lack thereof).[75] Even Lady Mary Wortley Montagu and John Gay's satire "The Toilette. A Town Eclogue. Lydia" (1716/20) utilizes the double perspective. Lydia, the object of satire, too, is an older woman, and the text enjoins the reader to "see" her delusion up close, namely her fantasy of beauty and desirability that is facilitated by the material objects of the dressing room. Just as she continues the "dumb devotion of her glass," this Lydia believes that her youthful clothing allows her to pass off her age, and that the "Shocks, monkeys, and mockaws" peopling her room will make up for the absence of lovers "catch[ing] her at her Toilette half-undrest."[76] Throughout this portrait, the satirist pauses to emphasize how readers really ought to see the objects visible in Lydia's dressing room, including her clothing and her pets, and the extent to which these things function as merely faint imitations of her youthful past. In this way, the satirist offers the reader a double perspective—what a woman reveals and what the satirist claims *needs* to be revealed—to make a satiric meaning out of the dressing room.

But if we are going to resist capitulating entirely to the satiric position, then this satiric scopophilia needs to be open to view as well. The satiric perspective, which shifts the reader's gaze from a woman's self-projection to an often surreptitious glance at the satiric object, allows the text to develop alternate ways of beholding things. Following Michel Foucault's opposition between spectacle and surveillance in *Discipline and Punish*, Jonathan Crary reconsiders the question of vision and observation and identifies the camera obscura as the paradigmatic structure for scopic relations in this period. Crary argues that the camera obscura defines the observer as "isolated, enclosed, and autonomous within its dark confines" and neatly separates "the act of seeing from the physical body of the observer, to decorporealize vision."[77] The camera obscura "*a priori* prevents the observer from seeing his or her position as part of the representation."[78] The spectator Crary describes appears, too, to be manifest in the satiric double take. The satiric spectator in the dressing room scene from *Satire Six* is an implied position, subject only to the empirical report of the object in view, and apparently comfortable in its disembodied authority.

Juvenal's strategy of looking in a different way foregrounds the satiric object's reputed weakness or element of debauchery, and this model of apprehension succeeds to the extent that satiric texts presume that satiric objects *are* weak or debauched. These satires all *assume* that these objects are different and, therefore, deserve our censure and ridicule for being other than what they *should* be; they assume, too, that this ideal is supported by a consensus. The difference between a woman in her dressing room and the satirist implies preexisting deviance to which satirists merely respond, a supposition all the more alluring because of the material presence of dressing rooms in the outside world. This understanding of satiric structure informs much contemporary criticism of satire, and speaks to the problem of referentiality discussed earlier. But the ability of satire to convince readers of its conclusions about reality limits our understanding of satiric censure. Critics regularly engage in a conversation about whether the satirist's attack is *justified*, but this question obscures the way in which satires manufacture these responses. Ronald Paulson, for example, explains that "satire's purpose ordinarily is not to create something new but to expose the real evil in the existing."[79] Penelope Wilson takes this position to task by suggesting that the satiric perspective is, in fact, a coercive one because of its attempts to foreclose disagreement: "Augustan satire is perhaps uniquely adept at constructing the terms of its own criticism and at preemptive disablement of the opposition."[80] Even though Paulson and Wilson disagree about whether the satirist's response to the satiric object is appropriate, they both assume that satirists are responding to something that really exists. Critics disagree about whether a satirist should or should not attack, but rarely pause to consider that this question itself adopts the satirist's point of view.

These observations return us again to the pull in satiric theory between understanding satire as allusive or as solely self-referential. The tension may very well come out of satires themselves, if we consider that satirists often admit creating the oppositions that they claim to describe. Fredric V. Bogel's recent insights are particularly illuminating on this point: "acts of exclusion, efforts of boundary-policing, and introductions of difference and distinction . . . create—rather than grow out of—an opposition between the satirist and the satiric scene or world."[81] Bogel traces this effort to differentiate to various kinds of connections, whether as tenuous as shared language or as integrated as an "intimate knowledge" of the satiric object, and subsequently extrapolates this categorical confusion as applicable to the triangle of the satirist, satiric object, and reader.[82] But the case of the dressing room demonstrates how literary this knowledge is. The satiric appropriation of the dressing room trope actively divorces this space from its material reality; satires suggest that nearly every woman had a dressing room and that she inevitably used it to dubious ends, while the historical record analyzed in chapter 2 demonstrates that this was not necessarily the case. Thus, satirists are left representing the space in its literary configuration as a site for the production of sexual promiscuity and transgression. While Bogel rightly thinks about satire as rhetoric in a most complicated sense, his theory also runs the risk of lapsing into awkward stereotypes from the "real" world. The satirist's "intimate knowledge," therefore, may be as fictional as everything else. In other words, Bogel threatens to slip away from a rhetorical argument to something more experiential, even though the satiric texts do not bear this out. Satires about women posit either a fantasy or a horror story staged in the dressing room, and are endlessly shaped by their own literary conventions, including the satiric commonplaces that women are sexually insatiable, socially untrustworthy, and physically diseased.

Therefore, we must consider that if satires make the differences they report to describe, then they likewise reveal the constructed nature of the disembodied scopophilia they utilize or how their "satiric double takes" really work. Robert Gould's vitriolic attack on women in *Love given o're; or, a Satyr against the Pride, Lust, and Inconstancy, &c. of Woman* (1682) depends upon the persuasive power of Juvenal's double perspective and also embodies the contradictory nature of the satiric gaze. Gould, a predominantly self-educated writer of moderate success, presents a catalogue of lustful women from Messalina to Restoration actresses in a sequence that precedes the satire's most self-consciously revealing verse paragraph. This is the moment when the satirist takes stock of women's private spaces—in this case, he calls the space a closet, though the items are more regularly associated with dedicated dressing rooms—and what they conceal:

> And now, if so much to the World's reveal'd
> Reflect on the vast Stores that lie conceal'd:

How, when into their Closets they retire,
Where flaming Dil — —s does inflame desire,
And gentle Lap-d — —s feed the am'rous fire:
Lap-d—s! to whom they are more kind and free,
Than they themselves to their own Husbands be.[83]

One could contend that Gould ultimately "resorts to a conventional scene attacking women's artful attempts at the dressing table to delude themselves that they are avoiding their own mortality," but such a view fails to interrogate the means by which the satirist accomplishes the goal of ridiculing and censuring women.[84] First, Gould's satirist corroborates the imperative to expose the private by emphasizing that so much is already known to be dubious about women. The reader is expected to wonder, then, just what is not known. The word "reflect" deliberately sets up this shift from description to speculation, as the satirist instructs readers to think for themselves. But when Gould's satirist urges readers to imagine the objects that "lie conceal'd" in a woman's private space, he swiftly provides suggestions as to what those items might be, specifically indicating that the lady's dressing room must conceal dildoes and lapdogs. By means of a speculative imperative, a methodology that we will see again in Swift's dressing room poems, the text's satiric mode can pretend to offer an objective account, even though it explicitly induces readers to imagine the dressing room in very particular ways. Think about what is hidden, says the satirist, and you will see dildoes and lapdogs.

The success of Gould's satire resides in its subtle manipulation of a reader's imagination made possible through its exploitation of the satiric mode's ability to spread from one realm of discourse to another. To continue thinking about the term "reflect," the word indicates both a shift from description to speculation and from description to judgment: "to reflect" also means "to cast a slight or imputation, reproach or blame on or upon a person or thing; to pass a censure on."[85] The idea of reflection is not solely grounded in neutral meditation, but also in the idea of rebuke. Speculation leads to judgment. The satirist need only offer the barest of examples for the reader to censure women's private places. The dildoes and lapdogs thought to populate ladies' dressing rooms serve this secondary function of reflection perfectly. Gould's manipulation of the call to reflect demonstrates that the satiric convention of looking properly (and seeing what the satirist points out) is itself a constructed gaze that shapes what comes into view. Just as Juvenal's look from behind promises another, more truthful perspective, Gould's satiric mode urges readers to align themselves with the satiric point of view—literally and conceptually.

Satiric dressing rooms conjoin satiric exposure with speculation and this strategy rests on the premise that a lady's dressing room contains illicit secrets. Early in Gould's satire, we can identify the intricate tension between satiric exposure and satiric creation that renders these scenes simultaneously persuasive and problematic. In the opening lines of the poem, Gould's satirist insists:

> Unvail 'em quite to ev'ry vulgar Eye,
> And in that shameful posture let 'em lie,
> Till they (as they deserve) become to be
> Abhorr'd by all Mankind, as they're abhorr'd by me.[86]

One could argue that Gould's text does what it says it does, following Paulson's argument; this would assume that Gould's satirist appropriately exposes debauched women to public censure and ridicule. But the command to "Unvail 'em" instead calls into being that which the satirist claims to reveal. The lesson here is key: the *process* of satiric exposure promises to make the satiric object "shameful." It follows, then, that the satirist "unvails" women by arguing that they are shameful, and also by making them into shameful objects—this is no disembodied viewer, but a satirist manufacturing the view. The satire's projection is reflected in the claim that this exposure will make women "Abhorr'd by all Mankind," implying that satiric "unvailing" creates its objects of derision.

The doubled message of this method is that the satirist will use the means of representation available—in this case, unveiling—to describe *and* to prescribe the satiric object. If, as Kaplan argues, "the gaze is not necessarily male (literally), but to own and activate the gaze, given our language and the structure of the unconscious, is to be in the masculine position," then this satiric structure demonstrates that such a view is itself necessarily constructed.[87] The astute reader must note that there are *two* projections of duplicity or forms of artifice operating here—the woman's, which refers to the outside world, and the satirist's, as evident in the satire's language. Understanding satire's delicate negotiation between the realm of referentiality and producing the *effect* of referentiality again gives credence to a methodology that interrogates the tension between materialist and formalist interpretive strategies. A satirist such as Robert Gould ultimately depends upon the slippage between the satiric perspective and the mind's eye, as he enjoins readers to see—and therefore to think—as his satirist does. Considering satiric "double takes," the technique of presenting two perspectives, reveals strategies of exposure that satirists frequently use to counteract the powerful allure of a female spectacle. The thematics of the dressing room, a space for the production of artifice, combines with its structural potential as a window into women's secrets.

INVENTORIES AND CATALOGUES:
THE LIMITS OF SATIRIC EPISTEMOLOGY

Much of this chapter has been devoted to discussions concerning the
ways satires about women adopt both the thematics of the dressing
room (particularly the associations with theatricality and sexuality) and
the scopic assumptions written into each of these scenes, which allows
writers to claim that they describe a preexisting scene of deviance or
debauchery. In this concluding section, we will examine more fully the
epistemological implications of the dressing room for satirists. The coupling of satire with the dressing room embodies a strategy of representation that anxiously creates boundaries, only to expose in the process
that those very boundaries are under threat, evoking the epistemological problems that several theorists associate with the postmodern queer
closet. We considered at length the theoretical similarities between the
dressing room and the closet in chapter 1; both conceptual spaces are
neither wholly private nor openly public, but introduce repeatedly the
problem of pinning down the subjects within them to a specific kind of
identity. In light of the slipperiness of satiric rhetoric, the question of
the dressing room's epistemological status becomes additionally
pressing.

The structure of the dressing room embodies a simultaneous promise
of enclosure and disclosure that in effect brings what Rose Zimbardo
calls satire's "continuous process . . . of undoing itself" into sharp re-
lief.[88] If the desire to expose the dressing room in Restoration and eighteenth-century satire is so great because it promises clarity and a
resolution to the problem of women's potential autonomy and the threat
this poses to men's satiric productions, then we must also acknowledge
that these moments of exposure merely provide the illusion of clarity
and, implicitly, order, an illusion that masks a failure of the mechanism
of categorization.

The modern-day "closet" and "coming out" similarly promise redefinition and also manifest analogous structural and epistemological
problematics. The idea of "coming out of the closet" promises a certain
amount of clarity and definition. Yet, as Judith Butler notes, this coming out depends upon its corollary, being "in": "Hence, being 'out' must
produce the closet again and again in order to maintain itself as 'out.'
In this sense, *outness* can only produce a new opacity; and *the closet* produces the promise of a disclosure that can, by definition, never come."[89]
Enclosure is equated with opacity of meaning and evokes disclosure,
which is associated with transparency of meaning, and vice versa. Butler's point is that their interdependence signals each category's funda-

mental unviability, or, as Jean Marie Goulemot argues in the context of early modern genres, "the paradox is that the secrecy of private space produces its effect only by ceasing to be private."[90] Butler demonstrates that this instability is inherent not only to categories of exclusion, but also to the categories of normalcy as well, and applies her insight to the process of *naming*. Just as anything private is vulnerable to visibility by becoming public, language threatens to install private subjects into public roles solely by naming them. To this extent, Butler's analysis confirms our understanding of the vexed theoretical nature of the dressing room trope. Conceptually, privacy and language converge at the point of classification, though even that effort at order is inevitably compromised; in other words, if coming out of the closet promises a clarity that can never be achieved, so, too, does the process of naming. Naming reflects, in Butler's words, "regulatory regimes" that presuppose classificatory systems *and* that create those orders through the process of naming itself. The origins of naming and classification are intertwined and complicit in one another's effectiveness.[91]

Several hundred years before our postmodern preoccupations, satiric dressing rooms promised clarity of meaning—confirmation of a woman's duplicity and a satirist's abilities—that they could not deliver. In response to this built-in failure, many satirists created their own kind of order, an inventory. These catalogues of women's dressing rooms are presented as self-evident, transparent, and stable texts. Jonathan Swift's "The Lady's Dressing Room" is perhaps the most famous example of a dressing room inventory and, as we shall see in chapter 5, Swift's dressing room satires not only ridicule women, beauty, and the female body, but they likewise raise epistemological questions. Three less well-known satires—Mary Evelyn's *Mundus Muliebris; or, The Ladies Dressing-Room Unlock'd* (1690), Daniel Defoe's *The London Ladies Dressing-Room* (1705; Defoe borrows heavily from Evelyn's satire), and Elizabeth Thomas's "An Inventory of a Lady's Dressing-Room" (1738)—also adopt the structure of an inventory as a means of offering epistemological clarity in a space that seems to thwart it.

While it may be tempting to read these texts solely in the context of female consumerism in the eighteenth century, a context that is valuable to understanding the trope of the dressing room more generally, we also need to think about how these satires reflect the dressing room's and satire's shared resistance to order and classification. Notably, each of these poems uses the dressing room as evidence of a preexisting disorder and as a sign of women's excess. Each text also offers a rhetoric of naming in the form of a list to clean things up, as it were, and to subsume women to satiric control. Thomas—rendered infamous herself through her correspondence with Dryden, her successive bankruptcies, and Pope's spite in *The Dunciad*—opens her text with an invocation requesting that the muse "sing a *Catalogue* in *verse*."[92] This is a particularly rough challenge indeed because "No *formal order* here is found / But *gay confusion* strows the ground."[93] Defoe's satire also self-consciously announces its form: "And to make the short of this long Story, / I'll let you see the Inventory."[94] One can make sense of the dressing room, goes the logic, if one can scan through an inventory of it. In both cases, an inventory supplants story and functions as an ordering device; when narrative fails, a list takes over. Underlying this claim is the supposition that a list of items will render not only the objects within the dressing room transparent, but also the meaning of the dressing room itself clear, unequivocal, and stable.

Following the traditional satiric critique of female artifice and consumerism, satiric inventories represent the dressing room as a container for innumerable expensive and trivial objects. Dressing rooms are filled, in Evelyn's words, with "Implements, / Of Toilet Plate, Gilt, and Emboss'd, / And several other things of Cost."[95] There are "*Washes, Unguents*, and *Cosmeticks*"; "Snuffers, and Snuff-dish, Boxes more, / For Powders, Patches, Waters store"; "Hoods by whole dozens," a "store of Coiffs" and "Velvet Scarfs"; a "*Tea* and *Chocolate* Pot" with "*Porcelan* Saucers, Spoons of Gold."[96] The list goes on and on. For Thomas's satirist, the indictment against women is intensified by a focus on all the objects littering the dressing room that fail to perform their intended functions. This is a site where beauty refuses to "reign," leaving "All other *ornaments* . . . vain."[97] One might be tempted to argue that Thomas's inventory catalogues items just as an advertisement for an eighteenth-century auction or estate sale would. But Thomas's list focuses on items that no longer have any use, ranging from a "*watch* that never minds the hour" and a "*mantile*, that has lost a wing" to "*boxes* flying from their *hinges*" and "shatter'd *hoops* of plyant cane / Exil'd from their *Elysian* reign."[98] Everything in this inventory is broken, bears only the residue of its original appearance, and no longer functions as it should. Thomas's dressing room is a "*Magazine* of female airs"; it is both a stock of women's clothing and, figuratively, a store of women's pretensions, all of which fail to fool the satirist.[99] The text that begins as an encomium to beauty—"Inspir'd by *Beauty* I presume / To sing the *Lady's Dressing-Room*"—concludes with the dismissal of those who attempt to muster only superficial attraction.[100] These are "Vain arts!" that "Attempt to wound with borrow'd charms."[101] Thus, Evelyn and Thomas produce a body of evidence to suggest that the dressing room is a site of failure and delusion.

If naming itself is a failed effort to regulate and contain subjects, then it is a question as to whether these attempts at "order," albeit satiric, manage to contain their subjects within the lines of these inventories. Each of these lists is threatened by the chaos that apparently rules in the dressing room. This threat of epistemological, if not material, chaos is reflected in the privileging of excess that the satirists attribute to the women who hold sway over the dressing room. Evelyn's satirist succinctly reflects that "She's a poor Miss [who] can count her store," but even this observation projects the satirist's limitations onto the woman herself.[102] The satiric drive to itemize is developed—we are told—as a response to excess, but it also points to the limitations of the inventory. This kind of satiric naming jerks awkwardly toward a resolution, as Evelyn's abrupt ending indicates: "tir'd with numbers I give o're, / Arthimetick can add no more."[103] Defoe's satirist, too, is "Tir'd with Numbers," but admits that this inventory barely represents the entirety of the collection ("Tho' I could count up ten times more").[104] These conclusions imply that the dressing room needs to be regulated by more than the conceptual order of an inventory. Both texts strive to derive meaning from these lists, but the lists themselves come to constitute most of what these satires convey. There is no narrative in these poems or a change of topic. Instead, they labor to name item after item, such that each satire is made up almost exclusively of these descriptive lines, framed by the minimal statements of purpose. If the meaning of an inventory is, indeed, transparent, then these inventories suggest that the satirist's ability to utilize the inventory for mastery fails as these texts become studies in detail, limited to particularities and only as comprehensive as a list can be.

In this chapter I have argued that the *metaphor* of the dressing room gained a prevalence in seventeenth- and eighteenth-century satiric texts that is at odds with its material presence, and I have used this significant disjunction to analyze both the effects of this representational divergence as well as the metaphor's structural suitability to the satiric project more widely. If the trope of the dressing room offers satirists a *locus classicus* for the censure and ridicule of women's propensity to be, in the words of Mr. Spectator, "smitten with every thing that is showy and superficial" to the detriment of everyone else, then the dressing room allows for the creation of the satirist as a self-appointed social arbiter.[105] A satirist who peers into the dressing room does so, ostensibly, for the reformation of a female readership and for the education of a male readership. But this synopsis, as I have demonstrated, speaks only to the stated occasions for the production of satires about women and obscures—as does the satiric mode—the extent to which such texts are implicated in the artifice that they critique.

Whether a satirist implies that women threaten satire or that women's behavior generates satire, the effect is the same: while satiric dressing room scenes operate on a level of referentiality, pointing as they do to a feature of material culture unique to the late seventeenth and eighteenth centuries, they are simultaneously self-consciously rhetorical affairs. This hanging between referent and self-referential finds a correlative in the myths of generation that surround satiric dressing rooms; dressing rooms (and the women who occupy them) are simultaneously objects of satiric censure and subjects of satiric destruction. That telling projection of duplicity I analyze functions as both a satiric occasion and a satiric tool, exposing the contradictions that constitute the claims of objectivity and order that satiric dressing room scenes labor to make.

If satiric dressing rooms give us an occasion to evaluate satiric theory and satiric structures, then they also point to the vexed relationship between privacy, secrecy, language, and authority. For all of its promise of clarity and stability of meaning, the exposure of the dressing room, in effect, produces not a resolution, in many instances, but a provocation for additional questioning and the production of additional text. The lack of formal closure, endemic to the satiric mode, points both to an instability in the nature of language, particularly in its efforts to name, quantify, and thereby control the dressing room trope, and to the vulnerability of an authority structure that defines its legitimacy through this very project. To order—to organize and to command—functions as a likely resolution in many satires about women, but the likelihood of these orders remaining stable is limited. The dissembling woman, seated at her dressing table, thereby exists in the late seventeenth and early eighteenth centuries as a paradigmatic provocation—for satire, for observation, and for text.

4

The Arts of Beauty:
Women's Cosmetics and Pope's Ekphrasis

A Painted Skin stuff'd full of Guile and Lies[1]

Fraud and Deceit, are in her painted face[2]

Maybe she's born with it. Maybe it's Maybelline!

IN CHAPTER 3, WE SAW THAT THE SATIRIC DRESSING ROOMS OF THE
late seventeenth and early eighteenth centuries return time and again to
the question of women fashioning themselves with their cosmetics. The
labors of the dressing room produce a surface beauty that could be perceived as alluring but which, the satirist endeavors to show, is more
rightly conceptualized as illegitimate and dangerous. At the heart of
these representations is an implicit debate about the gender politics of
art and artifice, its manifestations in low and high culture, and the
power of a spectacle that is itself an embodiment of betrayal. These concerns are expressed powerfully through the figure of cosmetics and in
debates about face painting during the late seventeenth and early eighteenth centuries.

Makeup is the thing most likely to be identified with the dressing
room. After 1558 and then again after 1660, women's use of cosmetics
in England increased dramatically for a variety of reasons, including
increased wealth and consumerism, the weakened influence of the
Church, and Charles II's importation of French styles and modes into
the English court. For women of the privileged classes, a toilet set was
a requisite, often given to a bride by her new mother-in-law. Patching
was more common than face painting until about 1700, at which point
using red rouge on the cheeks rose in popularity. The cosmetics market
was centered in London, but the products were decidedly foreign and
came primarily from France, Italy, and Turkey. Toilet waters, oils, and
face creams were increasingly imported through the eighteenth century,
encompassing such a bustling trade that a tax was imposed in 1786 on
a range of toiletries. Tax was due on "every packet, box, bottle, phial or

other enclosure containing any powders, pastes, balls, balsams, ointments, oils, waters, washes, tinctures, essences, liquors or other preparations commonly called by the name of sweet scents, ordours or
perfumes; or by the name of cosmeticks."[3] Cosmetics were an international trade and, increasingly, considered a daily necessity for some English women. Thus, as critics have frequently noted, "an eighteenth-
century lady in all her perfume, powder, and paint was truly a symbol
of international trade."[4]

The dressing room scene in canto 1 of Alexander Pope's *The Rape of
the Lock* (1712/14) has long been considered an icon of female consumerism. Louis A. Landa famously argues that the image of Belinda at her
toilet "would generate in a contemporary reader responses appealing to
the geographical imagination and related to the romantic image of an
England made magnificent by maritime activity," specifically global
trade and the national debates about luxury.[5] As has become commonplace to note, the lady of fashion embodied both a threat to the national
economy and a justification for its expansion. Several kinds of luxury
items associated with the dressing room, as well as the tea table, were
symbols of this double bind. Elizabeth Kowaleski-Wallace draws our
attention to the representation of "china" in Pope's poem as representative of Belinda's "dual status" as a commodity and as a consumer of
luxury items.[6]

If the luxury-status of imported objects were one way that the dressing room codified eighteenth-century women as the consumers of a
global market, then cosmetics also raised aesthetic and ideological questions about the women who used them. Writers in the satiric tradition,
some of the most detailed observers of the cosmetics industry in the
eighteenth century (perhaps ironically, some of the richest sources for
information about seventeenth- and eighteenth-century cosmetics are
satiric texts), regularly conflated women's character with the artifice of
makeup, suggesting that women painted themselves with "criminal
Beauties," in the words of John Oldham.[7] Face painting all too easily
suggested to such satirists more widespread subterfuge, concern about
women's roles, social order, and the value and purpose of artifice.

Therefore the dressing room scene in canto 1 of *The Rape of the Lock*
is also an icon of face painting and the objectification of women through
cosmetics. Unlike Clarissa, whose lengthy moralistic speech in canto 5
is *"to open more clearly the MORAL of the Poem,"* Belinda functions less as
a speaking subject and more as an object for a gazer's eye, a position
with both ideological and aesthetic implications.[8] Felicity Nussbaum
reads Pope's objectification as ultimately sympathetic toward the heroine and critical of the social constraints that limit her, arguing that the
poem "teases Belinda [for her failings and pretensions] while it displays

her entrapment in the rigid rules of courtship."[9] Ellen Pollak's assessment sharply critiques the poem's ideology of "passive womanhood," and contends that this ideal evacuates women's agency in order to confirm that of men.[10] More recently, Christa Knellwolf has shown us that Pope's characterization of Belinda depends upon a literal understanding of objectification: "much of Pope's poetry is primarily a description of lifeless objects while human subjects are metonymically characterised by the countless objects which are described as background to their actions."[11] Knellwolf suggests additionally that this process of objectification is gendered and that, for Pope, "the subject of aesthetic merit is intrinsically connected to his views of femininity."[12] In spite of these insights about the aesthetic implications of this objectification, Knellwolf refrains from articulating Pope's particular aesthetic register, and goes on instead to confirm Nussbaum's and Pollak's view that the bulk of Pope's points about women are primarily social in nature.[13]

To apprehend the objectification of a female figure such as Belinda in both economic and feminist terms, Laura Brown uses the structure of commodification, which illustrates that "as exchange value comes to usurp use value, and relations between things replace relations between people, human beings themselves can come to be redefined as objects."[14] Brown's analysis productively exposes the ambiguous distinctions between art and nature upon which eighteenth-century aesthetics depend; however, the positioning of women's "dress" as the justification for and cause of mercantilist imperialism depends, in Brown's analysis, equally (albeit uneasily) on the notion of "undress."[15] Therefore, Brown's contribution helps us to see the complex interdependency of economics and a characteristic feature of eighteenth-century representation (the tension between the mutually constitutive categories of dress and undress), but leaves the question of ornament on its own unanswered.

This chapter is concerned with cosmetics. The term "beauty," as Robert W. Jones has recently noted, "was perhaps most strikingly deployed in relation to the role of women in cultural and social debate."[16] Nowhere was this relation more apparent than in discussions of cosmetics, although the issue has not gained much critical attention.[17] Johnson's *Dictionary* links the cosmetic with beauty, defining the term as "having the power of improving beauty; beautifying." The word is also linked etymologically to "cosmos," Greek for "order, ornament, world or universe," ideas embedded within the term "cosmetic." Paradoxically, however, cosmetic adornment in the seventeenth and eighteenth centuries was often perceived to threaten social order. Texts debating the values of cosmetics often figure face painting as degrading women, even though this position frequently obscures a more profound concern that such art actually empowers women. According to critics, cosmetics not only alter nature, but also offer women an opportunity to function as artists or, alternately, artificers and as potentially independent and subversive agents within the social sphere. Cosmetics subsequently provoke questions about verisimilitude and art, and about the kinds of benefits that women might properly or improperly derive from face painting.

If the object most closely associated with the dressing room is makeup, then satirists regularly exploit the rhetorical ambiguity of the term "painting" as it relates to women in order to heighten a critique of women's self-construction. Consider, for example, Andrew Marvell's imperative: "Paint *Castlemain* in Colours that will hold / (Her, not her Picture, for she now grows old)."[18] Or this exchange in Lady Wishfort's dressing room from William Congreve's *The Way of the World*:

> *Lady Wishfort*: Let me see the glass.—Cracks, say'st thou? Why I am arrantly flayed. I look like an old peeled wall. Thou must repair me, Foible, before Sir Rowland comes, or I shall never keep up to my picture.
>
> *Foible*: I warrant you, Madam; a little art once made your picture like you; and now a little of the same art must make you like your picture. Your picture must sit for you, Madam.[19]

The art necessary to produce the public face of beauty is presented as a subspecies—or, to some, a bastard child—of proper painting. These are not portraits of Dorian Gray, but images that give lie to the natural deterioration of the female body, an entity that itself mandates the application of "a little art" to make a woman look as she should.

Pope's poetry is preoccupied with cosmetics, both literal and poetic. Belinda's dressing room scene, perhaps the most famous in eighteenth-century literature, focuses explicitly on the cosmetic process. While Pope's social commentary forms an important aspect of his poetic corpus, many earlier readings run the risk of privileging the social message over the poetry's aesthetic goals, even when those aesthetic goals embody ideological concerns. They threaten to obscure the fact that Pope was invested in becoming a great poet and that the representation of women posed a specifically aesthetic challenge for him, one that he needed to meet in order to succeed artistically. Pope's ideology of management, which objectifies a figure such as Belinda, reflects a particular aesthetic concern: what is the best kind of art? Pope's claim to manage character and beauty, enacted most vividly in Belinda's dressing room scene, implicitly evokes the contemporary debate about face painting, long understood to be a woman's art. This chapter explores Pope's rivalry with the cosmetic through his use of ekphrasis, which I argue is both a form of poetic painting and an aesthetic manifestation of the dressing room trope. Understanding this context allows us to see that Pope promotes his poetry as superior to the arts of cosmetics, especially for representing and apprehending women. Pope's aesthetic hierarchy has commercial implications, for the success of *The Rape of the Lock* helped to consolidate his own honor, name, and praise in eighteenth-century London. Addison praised the 1712 two-canto version as evidence of a "rising genius among my countrymen"; the five-canto version sold 3,000 copies within four days of its publication in 1714; and as Maynard Mack notes, *The Rape of the Lock* was "the talk of the town" the summer it was published.[20] Within this commercial literary culture, Pope's poetry was nearly as much of a commodity as Belinda's beauty would ever be. By rendering—and ultimately managing—women's beauty through ekphrasis, in both *The Rape of the Lock* and the later satiric verse epistle *To a Lady* (1735), Pope represents the agency of the spectacle of a cosmetically constructed woman only to displace that power with his own commodity—the perfect poem.

"PICTS": THE AESTHETICS AND POLITICS OF FACE PAINTING

The Art of Beauty: A Poem (1719) adopts the character of Pope's Belinda to satirize the powerful effects of cosmetics on women and the men who desire them. The author ironically lauds the dedicatee Belinda for having distinguished herself "in so remarkable a Manner by [her] admirable Skill and Knowledge in Cosmeticks, that [she is] now become without any Assistance from Nature, one of the most celebrated *Oxford* Beauties."[21] *The Art of Beauty* is part of a satiric tradition—see, for instance, *The St. James's Beauties: or, the Real Toast* (1744)—that parodies encomiums celebrating the beautiful women of a particular locale. This Belinda wins praise "as the most profound Adept in the Mysteries of *Venus*, the greatest Mistress of the Toilet" (vi). Quickly, the text distinguishes between the natural and the artificial and, in so doing, satirically subordinates so-called real beauty to its cosmetic counterpart. The poet ironically suggests that the unadorned female body is only an object of curiosity, and that the cosmetically produced image of femininity produces awe and, significantly, desire in those who view it:

> Nature undress'd, and stripp'd of all Attire,
> May raise our Wonder, but we can't admire:
> But where she takes Advantage from Disguise,
> When golden Roofs, and Marble Pavements rise,
> The stately Structure's sure to please our Eyes.

> The Milk-white Fleece, in glowing Purple dy'd,
> Blushes in all the Pomp of *Tyrian* Pride.
> The polish'd Iv'ry shines serenely bright,
> To grace the Toilet with its Silver Light.
>
> (10)

"Disguise" offers women the "Advantage" of representing themselves with the shining and lustrous objects of the dressing room, which
transforms the normal course of the blazon. Just as Nancy J. Vickers
observes that Petrarch's Laura is a composite of her body parts, *The Art
of Beauty*'s portrait displays no part of the female body.[22] Instead, one
sees only the metonymic displacement imitative of *The Rape of the Lock* —
"you [Belinda] were form'd . . . / To glitter in Brocade, and flame in
Gold" (11). Belinda is beautiful because she assumes the properties of
the brocade and gold that adorn her. Like them, she glitters and flames.
The passage quoted above also uses analogy to link the cosmetic construct and a "stately Structure" with "golden Roofs, and Marble Pave-
ments"; but this clumsy comparison only heightens the satire,
ludicrously suggesting that buildings and beautiful women produce the
same kind of pleasure in "our Eyes."

The Art of Beauty contains another ironic lesson: not only do women's
admirers derive pleasure (albeit ridiculous) from cosmetic beauty, but
women do, too. In fact, at the dressing table they lust after themselves,
in an extrapolation of Juvenal's warning about female vanity in *Satire
Six*:

> Then to the floating Mirrour they retire,
> Act o'er the Lover, and themselves admire,
> Survey the purling Streams with secret Joy,
> And smile with Pleasure as they whisper by.
>
> (13)

The Art of Beauty again alludes to *The Rape of the Lock* when expostulating
on such "Rites of Pride." With much less subtlety than Pope, *The Art
of Beauty* makes clear how enjoyable her cosmetic transformation is to
Belinda:

> But see! the Nymph begins the Rites of Pride,
> And these Cosmeticks ev'ry Blemish hide,
> Pleas'd to see Nature to her Skill give way,
> And her Cheeks dawn with the Approach of Day:
> She calls for specious Art's intenser Light,
> And fancy'd Conquests swim before her Sight!
>
> (17)

Whereas the cosmetics used in *The Rape of the Lock* seem to call forth Belinda's beauties, this Belinda's paint compensates her for her lack of beauty; she needs "Skill" not only to transform and obscure the natural but even to imagine conquering men. But *The Art of Beauty* carefully limits this potential—those "Conquests," after all, are "fancy'd" and "swim" in Belinda's image of herself.

The Art of Beauty critiques the use of cosmetics as a "specious Art" that enables women to dissemble and exert power over "Conquests," whether imaginary or not. Joseph Addison and Richard Steele's *Spectator* 41 more explicitly reprimands women who paint, calling them "*Picts*," for just these reasons. A correspondent complains to Mr. Spectator that he has been tricked into marrying a woman whose beauty was "all the Effects of Art," alluding to the deception of Ben Jonson's Morose in *Epicoene* to amplify his point.[23] By their "own Industry," warns the dupe, women will "make Bosom, Lips, Cheeks, and Eyebrows." Even the less naive Will Honeycombe reports an adventure with "a *Pict* . . . whose beauteous Form . . . every Day increased upon him, and [who] had new attractions every time he saw her." Sneaking into her dressing room, by this point in time a traditional strategy of satiric discovery, Honeycomb learns her secret: "The *Pict* begins the Face she designed to wear that Day, and I have heard him protest she worked a full half Hour before he knew her to be the same Woman." Prompted by these anecdotes, Mr. Spectator draws a satiric anatomy of a painted woman: "A *Pict*, tho' she takes all that Pains to invite the Approach of Lovers, is obliged to keep them at a certain Distance; a Sigh in a Languishing Lover, if fetched too near her, would dissolve a Feature; and a Kiss snatched by a Forward one, might transfer the Complexion of the Mistress to the Admirer. . . . [she is the] worst Piece of Art extant, instead of the Masterpiece of Nature." A "*Pict*" is a body of parts, a construction ready to come apart at any moment. A "*Pict*" is also clearly a picture, an art object, though explicitly an inferior one. Mr. Spectator thus implores "Men always to Examine into what they Admire" because it can be so difficult for spectators to tell the difference between a "Piece of Art" and a "Masterpiece of Nature," as even the similarity of these two phrases suggests. *Spectator* 41, like other critiques of cosmetics, attacks women's self-fashioning by degrading their artistry as artifice and renders it additionally suspicious because it gives women illegitimate power over men.

Satiric as they are, *The Art of Beauty* and the *Spectator* adopt old truisms common to more serious critiques of face painting. For example, "Miso-Spilus," author of *A Wonder of Wonders; or, A Metamorphosis of Fair Faces voluntarily transformed into foul Visages* (1662), complains that the cosmetic disguising of plainness reflects women's "Pride, Lasciviousness, impudence, and other Vices."[24] *A Wonder of Wonders* more explicitly associates cosmetics with the degradation of social order and with moral dubiousness; cosmetics threaten the harmony of the "cosmos." Underlying this view is the belief that women are, by nature, simultaneously deceitful and alluring. Thus an artificially beautiful woman turns masculine desire into impotence when her disguise is revealed, and her enjoyment of the entire process confirms her narcissism and danger to male hegemony.

John Gauden, the bishop of Exeter and Worcester and later Charles II's chaplain, refuted similar attacks in 1656 in a treatise reprinted in 1662 and 1692, *A Discourse of Artificial Beauty, In Point of Conscience Between Two Ladies*—which Neville Williams judges a "milestone in the history of the Englishwoman's toilet."[25] Prefaces to how-to-do-it manuals throughout the seventeenth and eighteenth centuries regularly endorse the use of cosmetics, albeit briefly.[26] But Gauden's text dismantles the opposition's views in detail and at length in a dialogue "Between Two Ladies," throughout which the second advocates face painting by rebuking the objections of the first. Gauden's defense in his "Epistle Dedicatory" is patriarchal, arguing that "since Woman is made for the Pleasure of Man, and that Pleasure consists in her beauteous Form, 'tis her Duty to keep her self capable of answering that End, as long and as much as she is able, by the assistance of Art or Nature." His central thesis, however, is potentially at odds with this notion of women as solely objects of masculine desire: Gauden posits that cosmetics are not inherently evil and subsequently conceives of women as independent agents who should be admired for making themselves beautiful. Within this paradoxical view of femininity, face painting serves as an important method for women's self-improvement and self-expression.

For Gauden, the face is properly the focus of a woman's beauty, *pace* the satirists' claim that the dressing room is a stage for a woman's "Rites of Pride." Gauden's mouthpiece protagonist argues that a woman's face is the "Cathedral of *Beauty*" (74) and the "chief Theatre, Throne and Centre of *Beauty*, to which all outward Array is subservient" (28) and that cosmetics cannot threaten a user's body or soul, for "the Heart [cannot have] received sinful Infection by any *Colour* or *Tincture* put to the *Face*, more than it doth moral *Defilement* by any thing that *enters into the mouth*" (81). Cosmetics are not inherently evil; moreover, they do not refashion women into things that they are not: "This makes no more a new *face* or Person, (so as to run any hazard of confusion or mistake) than usually befalls Women in their Sicknesses and ordinary Distempers" (52). Rather than claim that women hide their perversions and flaws behind cosmetics to deceive and subjugate beholders, Gauden's speaker contends that cosmetics complement nature: "Nor doth all this so terrible a Change amount to more than a little quickness of *Colour* upon the Skin; it alters not the Substance, Fashion, Feature, Proportions, Temper or Constitutions of Nature" (52–53). Gauden argues that cosmetics do not transform nature but that they produce an effect: face painting allows women to seem beautiful, without running the risk of actually changing.

Furthermore, the defense of cosmetics as morally neutral allows Gauden to point out that detractors use imprecise logic to misrepresent the properties of cosmetics and the intentions of those who use them, as when they "slide from the *abuse* of things to decry the *use* of them" (114). Gauden's "Objection IX" cites the Puritan divine John Downame's argument from *The Christian Warfare* that face painting is "The Devil's Invention, absolutely a Sin, not only in the Abuse, but the very Use; in the nature of the thing, and not only in the Intention of the Doer" (127). *A Wonder of Wonders'* "Miso-Spilus" celebrates Downame's equation between use and abuse, calling face painting "the Devils counterfeiting and mocking of God, by seeking to mend his works, as if God needed his enemies help to compleat his creatures, &c."[27] Gauden's insistence that critics blur the difference between "use" and "abuse" is central to the *Discourse's* defense of "auxiliary beauty," and demonstrates Gauden's appropriation and redefinition of his opponents' terms.

The *Discourse* redefines the debate about cosmetics by arguing at length that the proper use of cosmetics is permissible and even has the potential to be virtuous and godly. In response to Objection V, "Painting the Face against the Seventh Commandment forbidding all Adultery," Gauden's advocate posits that "where the Heart is upright, without any sinful warpings as to Piety, Purity, and Charity, it must follow, That the use of any thing God hath made and given to mankind must needs be good and lawful, both in Nature and in Art" (45). Likewise, "True Piety permits us to pay an Honour, Love and Reverence to our selves, as well as to others; and to our Bodies, as well as to our Souls" (58). Women who use paint do not suffer from "Pride, Arrogancy and Hypocrisie" (115) because "the remedying of [physical defects] by artificial Applications can be no more temptation to Pride, than the use of Crutches or Spectacles to those that are lame and dimsighted, or the applications of other Delights and Ornaments to our outward man or senses" (118–19). The *Discourse* does not promote vanity, pride, wantonness, or "self-adulterating" (41) — as critics would suggest — but endorses women's "innocent use of *auxiliary Beauty*" (89) to better themselves and to reflect their piety. And the author of *A Wonder of Wonders* even concedes that Gauden has a point.[28]

By focusing the debate about cosmetics on the question of their proper use, and by challenging the assumption that use leads to abuse, the *Discourse* implicitly conceptualizes women as autonomous, free-thinking, and free-acting subjects. Put to its most noble service, face painting is a reflection of divine devotion. Using cosmetics is not a sign of displeasure with "God's Works and Disposings" (61), but an index of a woman's commitment to "Industry" (63). Whereas the husband in the *Spectator* laments women's industriousness in the dressing room, Gauden's speaker argues that women should "excite [their] inventions and industries" (70); just as people should "repair [their] decayed Houses [and] . . . mend [their] torn Garments" (67), they should also improve their looks. Failing to do this is a sign of laziness, the "supine and sottish despondencies of mind" (70). The idea that face painting may signify piety and diligence opens up the possibility that observers cannot judge a woman's character by her appearance. Instead, women must be evaluated in terms of their *intentions*. This claim challenges the traditional principles of physiognomy by acknowledging the complexity of motivation and by viewing women as varied and independent agents, not as a homogeneous group that can be "read" quickly and easily dismissed.

Commensurate with the notion that women are independent is Gauden's imploring of women to judge their critics, who have "every one of them [holy men] had their Errours, greater or lesser, even in Points of greater Concern than this of Ladies *Beauties*" (134): "It is time for us at length to get beyond that Servility and Sequaciousness of Conscience, which is but the Pupillage, Minority and Wardship of Religion, inquiring and heeding, not what saith the Lord, but what saith such a Father, such a godly Man, such a Preacher or Writer" (214–15). The introduction of possible error simultaneously introduces a critical model for women to adopt: since "Good and great Men are not set beyond mistakes" (135), women must think for themselves. Gauden's *Discourse* offers women a blueprint for disagreement and independent analysis. Throughout the dialogue, the second speaker enacts this principle of intellectual skepticism by analyzing critics' discursive strategies and by contending that their attacks are rhetorical or satirical rather than logical.[29]

While Gauden's *Discourse* overtly defends the use of cosmetics as virtuous, an important side effect of the defense is its inadvertent rendering of women as independent subjects, not cosmetic objects. Subsequently, face painting is figured as a legitimate art that empowers women, physically and spiritually. Moreover, defending its practice enables women to develop intellectually. While the emphasis on personal improvement is not an unusual stance for devotional writing, Gauden's position shows his departure from the conventional rhetoric about face painting and the women who use it. Thus, a text such as Gauden's begins its defense of women's cosmetics by appealing to men's desire for beautiful women, only to conclude with a protofeminist message about women's rights as thinking and acting beings. In this most pious context, face painting gives women a forum to improve themselves and to be better Christians. And in the context of Charles II's restored court, this valuation of physical beauty is even less surprising. But Gauden's *Discourse* and the texts that opposed his view highlight the issues at stake in the debate about women and face painting. The use of cosmetics could suggest that women dissemble in order to subject men to their influence, and that such women are, in turn, deluded themselves. Or it could encourage women to act and to think freely, subject only to their consciences and admired for their virtue and independence.

One final implication of Gauden's argument, and one more area of departure from his contemporaries, is that art functions as a vehicle for truthful representation. Although, as Will Pritchard notes, women's cosmetics were frequently read as a sign of forgery and blasphemy, Gauden's text opens up the possibility that this kind of art conveys truth.[30] *A Wonder of Wonders* threatens that God will renounce made-up women on Judgment Day and may not even recognize them, but Gauden assures these women that cosmetics allow them to be better Christians.[31] In this way, Gauden's treatise implies that face painting has the ability to reveal a woman's goodness and that this art speaks to the most sacred of things—in Gauden's words, "True Piety" (58). To see both value and veracity in artifice sets up an unlikely convergence between Gauden and Pope, as we shall now see.

PRETTY AS A PICTURE: EKPHRASIS IN *THE RAPE OF THE LOCK*

Pope's famous appropriation of the dressing room trope in *The Rape of the Lock* explores in depth the disjunction between face painting and poetry as tools for the representation of women. The question that Pope raises is this: how does the poetic rendering of a beautiful woman at her dressing table challenge or displace her ability to fashion herself through face painting? In the dedicatory epistle to *The Rape of the Lock*, Pope offers a telling answer. He assures Arabella Fermor, the professed inspiration for the poem, that all she shares with her fictional counterpart is beauty: "the Character of *Belinda*," Pope writes, "as it is now manag'd, resembles You in nothing but in Beauty" (37–38). Pope's promise to Fermor developed from her indignant response to his 1712 edition; as he admitted to John Caryll, "the celebrated lady herself is offended, and, which is stranger, not at herself, but at me."[32] Pope designed the 1714 dedication to distance Fermor publicly from the coquettish Belinda, and the resulting address evidently alleviated her concerns. As Pope later confessed to Caryll, "the young lady approves" of the added dedication, but it "can neither hurt the lady, nor the author."[33]

Pope's effort to placate Fermor demonstrates not only his ability to use heavy-handed (and double-edged) flattery to get his way, but that an objective of *The Rape of the Lock* is the management of a woman's character, which in Belinda's instance is primarily determined by her beauty; we shall see that Pope's management of her character and beauty is a simultaneously ideological and aesthetic goal. The feminized quality of "Beauty" implicitly prefigures Edmund Burke's midcentury notion of beautiful objects as those that "submit" to their beholders and inspire love, a response that explicitly establishes a power relation between the spectator and the spectacle.[34] "Manage" likewise connoted a sense of control in the eighteenth century, thereby implicating the agent of this transformation. A "manager" in Johnson's *Dictionary of the English Language* was "one who has the conduct or direction of any thing," and "to manage" for Johnson implied government. Several of the *Oxford English Dictionary* meanings current in the eighteenth century clarify the notion that to manage something is to manipulate it, in one instance by "artifice, flattery, or judicious suggestion of motives." Moreover, the *OED*'s second definition of "manage" ("to make [an object] serve one's purposes") indicates self-interest. Further expanding the meanings, the promise that Belinda "is . . . manag'd" refers specifically to "a working out" of a particular subject in a "literary treatment" (*OED*); Fermor's beauty, first reported to Pope by Caryll and thus already a representation of her, is transformed into the fiction of Belinda.[35] To reiterate, and with this complex of semantic meanings in mind, we shall see that the address to Fermor in the dedication reveals an ideology of management that functions both ideologically and aesthetically.

This powerful association between the construction of female beauty in the dressing room and Pope's poem has long informed images linked to the mock-epic, from its original publication to the mid-twentieth-century publication of Pope's works in the *Twickenham Edition*.[36] The five-canto 1714 edition of the poem featured engravings that picture Belinda at her dressing table and asleep in her chamber, with her dressing table nearby. That the poem was accompanied by engravings is itself remarkable, for only six out of eleven hundred separately printed poems were illustrated with plates in the 1710s.[37] Over sixty years later, a full edition of Pope's *Works* used the image of Belinda at her dressing table as its icon for his poetic corpus.[38] In our own century, the editors of the *Twickenham Edition* have historicized the notion that the poem represents female beauty by using a portrait of Arabella Fermor as that volume's frontispiece—many readers begin the poem having gazed at the beauty who seemed to have started it all.

Narrowly read, *The Rape of the Lock* offers familiar examples of why women's cosmetics are chided. The famous toilet scene displays Belinda's beauty under construction and reduces her luster to cosmetics. Her beauty is the result of labor and, as in contemporary critiques of face painting, not "natural." When Betty, and the airy sylphs who attend Belinda, "call forth all the Wonders of her face" (1.142), those wonders turn out to be cosmetic. Her cheeks are painted with a "purer Blush" (1.143) than her natural one and the "keener Lightnings," or eye drops, "quicken in her Eyes" (1.144) to make them look bigger. Before beginning her toilet, Belinda admires the amenities on her dressing table for their "Cosmetic Pow'rs" (1.124). The poem throughout makes reference to the work necessary to construct Belinda's awesome beauty, the feminine industry that Gauden admires and that Mr. Spectator's correspondent despises. As the sun sets in canto 3, so cease the "long labours of the Toilette" (3.24), and the speeches by Thalestris and Clarissa amplify the toil of adornment. After the rape, Thalestris questions whether all the work was worth it, while detailing the art of Belinda's beauty:

> Was it for this you took such constant Care
> The *Bodkin*, *Comb*, and *Essence* to prepare;
> For this your Locks in Paper-Durance bound,
> For this with tort'ring Irons wreath'd around?
> For this with Fillets strain'd your tender Head,
> And bravely bore the double Loads of Lead?
>
> (4.97–102)

Thalestris's language underscores the mock-heroic mode of the poem, as "tort'ring," "strain'd," and "bravely bore" imply that Belinda has withstood the pains of the dressing room with great courage. Clarissa's later reprimand of Belinda in canto 5 reminds readers that her beauty, even if it is artificially constructed, cannot withstand the decidedly natural passage of time. While "Beauties" (5.9) such as Belinda are "deck'd with all that Land and Sea afford" (5.11), these adornments have never "Charm'd the Small-pox, or chas'd old Age away" (5.20). The transformation accomplished by the toilet cannot last; Belinda's is a "frail Beauty [that] must decay" (5.25), "Since painted, or not painted, all shall fade" (5.27). As Mr. Spectator's "*Pict*" is vulnerable to decomposition, so, too, is Belinda, another example of a made-up woman who duplicitously attempts to increase her power but ends up suffering for it.

Laura Brown notes, however, that Belinda's beauty is ambiguously both a product of nature and of art.[39] *The Rape of the Lock* is not merely another moral tale against face painting, for it seems to celebrate (and luxuriate in) the cosmetic details of Belinda's beau monde. To understand Pope's contribution to the debate about cosmetics, we need to consider instead the extent to which the poem meditates upon the value of face painting *as an art form*. Specifically, Pope's rendering of face painting as an art evokes the traditional distinction between the arts of verbal and visual "painting," a connection exploited in *The Rape of the Lock* and later in *To a Lady*.[40] Pope is not unique in considering cosmetics a type of pictorial art: for example, the textbook *Polygraphice* includes a chapter on face painting as well as chapters on the fine arts of drawing, engraving, etching, and painting, and Mr. Spectator conceives of his "Picts" as works of art.[41] But Pope adopts the trope of cosmetics as an example of visual painting in order to pit the art of face painting against the art of poetic painting, or ekphrasis.[42] *The Rape of the Lock* emphasizes the constructed nature of Belinda's beauty not only to call it into question, but also to set up a hierarchy between makeup and poetry. William Christie rightly notes the parallels between Pope and Belinda, asking if Pope is "after all is said and done, any less obsessed with 'dress'—whether Belinda's or his own poetry's?"[43] Christie observes that both figures are concerned with a "theory of *making*," but their similarity is more particular.[44] Pope's poetry and Belinda's cosmetics are analogous because both kinds of art aspire to a kind of truth by applying paint to display women as aesthetic objects. To insist that poetry is a superior form of "painting," Pope enacts an aesthetic contest within *The Rape of the Lock* that positions ekphrasis as aesthetically superior to Belinda's cosmetics.

Definitions of ekphrasis have proliferated in recent years, ranging from Jean Hagstrum's particular "quality of giving voice and language to the otherwise mute art object" to Murray Krieger's "general principle of poetics" that distinguishes literary language from ordinary language.[45] Yet these definitions either personify or dilute the rhetoric and context of ekphrastic representation. In contrast, James A. W. Heffernan productively suggests this definition for ekphrasis: "verbal representation of visual representation"; ekphrasis aims to represent a "work of representational art," or something that is itself the result of artistic labor.[46]

Therefore, to argue that Belinda's beauty, as represented by the poem, is also ekphrastic implies that her beauty is actually a work of representational art—and it is. Since Belinda is an imaginary figure (apart from her complicated relation to Arabella Fermor), this particular kind of ekphrasis is, according to Heffernan, "notional ekphrasis."[47] Belinda's beauty unequivocally results from her attendants' cosmetic labors; and, as the debates about cosmetics indicate, face painting is an art. If we understand that Belinda's beauty is ekphrastic, then we can see that embedded in ekphrasis is a contest between the writer and the piece of art, one that is repeatedly gendered:

> Ekphrasis speaks not only *about* works of art but also *to* and *for* them. In so doing, it stages—within the theater of language itself—a revolution of the image against the word, and particularly the word of Lessing, who decreed that the duty of pictures was to be silent and beautiful (like a woman), leaving expression to poetry. In talking back to and looking back at the male viewer, the images envoiced by ekphrasis challenge at once the controlling authority of the male gaze and the power of the male word.[48]

Beyond the drawing room melee, the real battle of *The Rape of the Lock* is between cosmetics and ekphrasis, between a woman's art and a man's (or Pope's, at least) poetry.[49] As in texts debunking women's use of cosmetics, Belinda is pretty as a picture. In other words, Pope's heroine is not necessarily beautiful, though she certainly seems it: we cannot be sure. This is precisely the problem that requires Pope's aesthetic management: "To represent a painting or sculpted figure in words is to evoke its power—the power to fix, excite, amaze, entrance, disturb, or intimidate the viewer—even as language strives to keep that power under control."[50] Belinda's art of beauty threatens to emasculate the viewer and, therefore, must be contained by Pope's art. Since the poet is explicitly male this conflict undeniably evokes early-eighteenth-century gender politics. The question, "what is good art?" plagued Pope throughout his career (as he ferociously attacked "hacks" and those who did not admire his writings) and took on increasingly gendered terms. Writers who ridiculed Pope's writing often did so in terms of his masculinity, specifically his body—he suffered from tuberculosis of the bone, an ailment that left him physically deformed—and questioned his sexual virility.[51] In 1716, John Dennis described Pope as "A Lump Deform'd, / for Shapeless he was Born"; and in 1729, Ned Ward referred to him as "A frightful, indigested Lump, / With here a Hollow, there a Hump."[52] In his account of the "*Tom-Tit*" story, Colley Cibber claims that "the little-tiny Manhood of Mr. Pope" could not handle sex with a prostitute.[53] The anonymous *Sawney and Colley* (1742) relates these perceived sexual inadequacies to Pope's writing, claiming that the poet is "As impotent in *Spite* as *Love*."[54] Such attacks ultimately prompted Pope to vindicate himself in *An Epistle to Arbuthnot*, but it is clear that even early in his career, Pope's poetic reputation took on gendered connotations that were regularly figured through failure.

Not surprisingly, this concern fuels his aesthetic rivalry with Belinda,

as well; face painting becomes an issue not solely about women's independence and power over men, but also about artistic superiority and
market value. The contest between Pope and Belinda as artists is
shaped by the poem's status as a mock–epic, for the ekphrasis in *The
Rape of the Lock* clearly alludes to the trope's heritage in the epic. Traditionally, Homer's elaborate description of Achilles' shield has been considered the *locus classicus* of ekphrasis, and Pope's involvement with his
translation of Homer while completing and publishing *The Rape of the
Lock* is well documented. By translating Homer's epic, Pope emulated
his poetic heroes Milton and Dryden, whose portraits he kept "in my
chamber, round about me, that the constant remembrance of 'em may
keep me always humble."[55] A translation of Homer would have also
been designed to impress readers with Pope's aesthetic skill in successfully rendering the heroism and poetic authority associated with the
Homeric epic.[56] In his correspondence, Pope reflects upon an epic
model of masculinity and his own fear of lack: "'Tis certain the greatest
magnifying glasses in the world are a mans own eyes, when they look
upon his own person; yet even in those, I appear not the great Alexander Mr Caryll is so civil to, but that little Alexander the women laugh
at. But if I must be like Alexander, 'tis in being complimented into too
good opinion of my self: they made him think he was the son of Jupiter,
and you persuade me I am a man of parts."[57] Although Edward Young
would later lampoon Pope's translation, complaining that "it is less par-
donable, by that effeminate decoration, to put Achilles in petticoats a
second time," Pope would prove himself through the translation of epic
poetry, even if this "Alexander" were not a classical hero.[58] As Pope
writes in the preface to the *Iliad*, he "hope[s] to pass some of those
Years of Youth that are generally lost in a Circle of Follies, after a manner neither wholly unuseful to others, nor disagreeable to myself."[59] The
epic, for Pope, serviced the construction of a specifically masculine poetic persona, with all its attendant privileges and fame.

    Appended to his translation of book 18 of Homer's *Iliad* (published in
1720) with its description of Hephaestus's creation of the shield, Pope's
critical essay "Observations on the Shield of *Achilles*" directly addresses
the topic of ekphrasis in the epic.[60] As Heffernan notes, "Exactly what
Hephaestus wrought on the shield is ultimately impossible to
visualize. . . . All we can see—and all that really exists in this passage—is Homer's language, which not only rivals but actually displaces
the work of art it ostensibly describes and salutes."[61] But in the "Observations," Pope flies in the face of critical tradition to argue that Achilles'
shield was possible to visualize. Others contend that "the Shield is
crowded with such a Multiplicity of Figures, as could not possibly be
represented in the Compass of it," while Pope argues that the shield is

not "one vast unproportion'd Heap of Figures, but [is] divided into twelve regular Compartiments [*sic*]" and even draws a picture so that "the Reader will have the Pleasure to be convinced of it by ocular Demonstration."[62]

Reflecting upon Pope's contention that Achilles' shield is an object that could be visualized, one could expect a similar fate for ekphrasis in epic's progeny, the mock-epic. With all of its references to paint and the toilet and for all of the descriptions of Belinda's cherished and beautiful sable locks, *The Rape of the Lock* is oddly silent when it comes to detailing Belinda's appearance. The dressing table scene in canto 1 promises the most descriptive account of the young woman; however "unveil'd, the *Toilet* stands display'd" (1.121) instead of Belinda. The poem displays the cosmetics more vividly than its heroine, in spite of her preoccupation with self-display. As in *The Art of Beauty*, the items that litter Belinda's dressing table connote her beauty: "Each Silver Vase" (1.122), the "glitt'ring Spoil" (1.132) of "Unnumber'd Treasures" (1.129), "India's glowing Gems" (1.133), combs of tortoiseshell and ivory described as "the speckled and the white" (1.136), and "files of Pins" in "their shining Rows" (1.137). These beautiful, sparkling items simply stand in for Belinda and imply that she, too, is beautiful and sparkling. So do the magical, even airy sylphs who paint and protect her, and who used to be women themselves. Their "Transparent Forms" (2.61) keep them invisible to the human eye, but they are described as luminous: "Loose to the Wind their airy Garments flew, / Thin glitt'ring textures of the filmy Dew" (2.63–64). Their wings are insectlike, "silken" (2.130), and colored in the "richest Tincture of the Skies" (2.65) that change "whene'er they wave" (2.68). When the sylphs convene, Ariel rises to a "gilded Mast" (2.69), spreads his "Purple Pinions" (2.71), and raises an "Azure Wand" (2.72).

By ekphrasis, Belinda's beauty is rendered metonymically: as a product of the dressing table and the sylphs' labors, it is characterized by shining, glittering, and expressly visual description, even as that description precludes our viewing Belinda herself. Whereas Pope draws a picture of Achilles' shield to prove the ekphrastic image's visibility, the frontispiece to the 1714 edition places Belinda in profile, sitting in front of a mirror as she applies cosmetics. Since Pope was probably involved in the production of the plates accompanying the poem, one can conclude that the frontispiece to the mock-epic refrains from supplying an "ocular Demonstration" of Belinda's beauty.

In spite of these constraints in the mock-epic, the poem meditates upon the effect of an ekphrastic image. To recall Heffernan, the ekphrastic image implicitly challenges the "controlling authority of the male gaze and the power of the male word."[63] One needs only to picture

Robert Browning's "My Last Duchess" to envisage the Duke's increasingly defensive posture in the face of his dead wife's portrait, the meaning of which he tries, unsuccessfully, to control. Like "My Last Duchess," *The Rape of the Lock* plays out (and tries to control) the effect that Belinda's beautiful image has on those who view her. As an ekphrastic image, Belinda's beauty functions much like Achilles' shield: her "awful Beauty puts on all its Arms" (1.139), a description that explicitly evokes the poem's epic antecedent. Although some readers have considered Belinda's petticoat the mock equivalent of the shield because of its circumference, her beauty is the parallel that the poem draws thematically and figurally.[64]

Belinda's beauty is her shield: it is an object of awe and admiration, beginning with her own awe and admiration as she sits at the dressing table. When Belinda seems to see herself in the mirror, "A heav'nly Image in the Glass appears" (1.125). Instead of "seeing" that "heav'nly Image" themselves, readers are given only the effect the picture has on Belinda: "To that she bends, to that her Eyes she rears" (1.126). This "heav'nly Image" prompts Belinda's apparent narcissism, recasting Eve's fascination with her own image from book 4 of *Paradise Lost*. Yet the ambiguity of the twice-repeated "that" keeps this image from being clearly defined as Belinda's face, suggesting instead that Belinda sees and desires not her literal self, but an imaginary picture of herself. Knellwolf interprets this disjunction as evidence that women were self-alienated, but just as important is Belinda's fascination with the image.[65] The supplication to it continues when she enters the Thames at the beginning of canto 2, where "ev'ry Eye was fix'd on her alone" (2.6), even though "Fair Nymphs, and well-drest Youths around her shone" (2.5). Belinda's radiance even competes with the brilliance of the rising sun, as she is "the Rival of his Beams" (2.3). The most famous effect of Belinda's appearance centers upon the apparent willingness of her admirers to forsake their beliefs and to honor her instead; thus, "On her white Breast a sparkling *Cross* she wore, / Which *Jews* might kiss, and Infidels adore" (2.7–8). Belinda's breast clearly empties out any religious meaning normally associated with the cross and renders its function ornamental, but the couplet also revitalizes the traditional meaning of the cross to prove the poet's point: Belinda subdues those who gaze upon her, even provoking radical conversions.

Belinda's power over her admirers embodies the fears shared by opponents of cosmetics. Her allure even drives the Baron to fetishize her hair. But in poetic terms, her ability to control viewers develops as an effect of ekphrasis, and the model for this power can be traced back to the *Iliad* once again. Even though Achilles' shield ultimately suffers attacks from Aeneas and Hector in books 20 and 21, it initially functions as an extension of its user's heroism. In 19, after the ekphrastic description in 18, Achilles' magnificent shield is called a "radiant Gift."[66] This radiance is significant because the shield's brightness blinds—and thus overpowers—those around it. In explicitly scopic terms, the ekphrastic image threatens to weaken those who gaze upon it: thus "Back shrink the *Myrmidons* with dread Surprize, / And from the broad Effulgence turn their Eyes."[67] As an emblem of Achilles' strength, the ekphrastic shield awes its viewers, subjecting them to the warrior's heroic presence.

We can begin to understand beauty's potential for power, especially as an emblem of feminine art and as a tool for female agency. Belinda's beauty serves as the figurative armor with which she will presumably devastate men, and it thwarts admirers' empirical analysis of her, giving her the upper hand. Pope does not leave Belinda in control for long, but promptly intervenes to disabuse those who gaze upon her. In so doing, he reveals the means by which he "manages" her beauty. Ten lines before the Baron expresses his desire to possess the symbol of Belinda's powerful beauty, those "bright Locks" (2.29), the poet addresses the reader:

> Yet graceful Ease, and Sweetness void of Pride,
> Might hide her Faults, if *Belles* had Faults to hide:
> If to her share some Female Errors fall,
> Look on her Face, and you'll forget 'em all.
>
> (2.15–18)

Many readers regard this pair of hypothetical couplets as proof of either of two opposite attitudes toward Belinda, ranging from Cleanth Brooks's suggestion that these lines are "sincerely meant" as a compliment to Ellen Pollak's argument that the couplets explicitly disparage Belinda.[68] Such readings consider satire in terms of its epideictic heritage by assigning praise or blame to the satirists themselves, and this critical trend has helped to shape the field of satire and Pope studies (and, as we shall see, Swift studies).[69] But the difference between Pope's censure and his praise can be hard to pinpoint and, as Laura Mandell notes, the limiting effects of idealization and satire on the female subject are similar.[70] Pope's own interpretation of the poem insinuates that both readings have validity, especially since he simultaneously celebrates and disavows the satiric mode. As Pope famously explained in a 1714 letter, it is "at once the most a satire, and the most inoffensive, of anything of mine."[71]

These couplets from canto 2 more accurately embody the ambivalence Pope felt toward Belinda and the arts of cosmetics, a mixture of rivalry and veneration characteristic of ekphrastic representation. The poet's address to the reader deliberately explains what happens when one takes in Belinda's appearance. The spectacle of Belinda's beauty reportedly overwhelms the hypothetical spectator, much as Achilles' shield forces the Myrmidons to "shrink back." With the imperative that the hypothetical spectator "Look on her Face," a face we see only in fragments and only in terms of cosmetics, the poet attempts to take agency away from Belinda and to reassign it to those who look at her. By instructing this fictional spectator how to "read" Belinda, Pope attempts to distinguish gazers from readers and to advance a model of physiognomy that is dependent upon reading texts. In *The First Epistle of the Second Book of Horace, Imitated* (1737), Pope explains this difference when he defends writers and requests that George II "Think of those Authors, Sir, who would rely / More on a Reader's sense, than Gazer's eye."[72] A "Reader's sense" is more valuable to Pope than the "Gazer's eye" because this sense implies that one has insight. A "Reader's sense" allows one to observe a woman such as Belinda knowingly and to see that the agency her cosmetic beauty allows her to hold is ultimately illegitimate. In contrast, gazers will always be subject to the power of the spectacle.

The poet's aside to the reader in canto 2, therefore, does not discount the ekphrastic power of Belinda's beauty. Rather, the poet demystifies the process by which one kind of spectator may become emasculated by Belinda's beauty. Even though Belinda's beauty thwarts evaluation—if we look on her face, we'll forget her faults—Pope suggests that reading can appropriate and subordinate the influence of Belinda's beauty. With the focus momentarily not on Belinda but on an imagined spectator, Pope labors to contain the influence of the ekphrastic image by exposing appearances as untrustworthy and by urging people to read texts instead. Only writing is reliable, for a poet such as Pope will tell the truth, whereas an image can be misleading. Pope's double move—the simultaneous use and deconstruction of ekphrasis—allows *The Rape of the Lock* to exercise moral and aesthetic superiority over a beautiful object. The poem's concluding apotheosis of Belinda's lock signals the conclusion of the aesthetic contest between cosmetics and ekphrasis: no one save the poet, with his "quick Poetic Eyes" (5.124), can "see" well enough to witness the lock's apotheosis; everyone else must read the poem. Pope firmly displaces Belinda's art of beauty with his own, even as he cajoles her into accepting his poem as compensation for her lost lock by promising that *"This Lock"* (5.149) shall outlive her cosmetic one. At long last, Pope ensures that the art of poetry will loom over the fading art of face painting, as *his* readers will outlive *her* admirers.

PAINTING WOMEN: FROM OBJECTIFICATION
TO ABSTRACTION IN *TO A LADY*

Over twenty years later, Pope revives the ekphrastic representation
of femininity in the verse epistle, *To a Lady*, only to replay the gendered
contest between cosmetics and ekphrasis once again. There is no originary dressing room in *To a Lady*, save the reference to "Sappho," who is
satirized for her use of cosmetics, particularly because they do not
work; her toilet is a "greasy task" that cannot possibly render her beautiful.[73] While Pope sheds the architectural setting of the dressing room,
he explicitly refines the aesthetics of ekphrasis that he developed there.
The narrative of *To a Lady* is a tour of a portrait gallery featuring images
commissioned by women. Here the ekphrasis, while still "notional," is
more obvious and depends more heavily on the poet's interpretation of
each portrait, which he describes to his nearly silent female addressee;
Pope solidifies the gendered ideological and aesthetic contests inaugu-
rated in *The Rape of the Lock*. The portraits, which uncritically reproduce
a series of (in)famous women's self-conceptions—including "Arcadia's
Countess" (7), "Pastora by a fountain side" (8), "Fannia" (9), "a naked
Leda with a Swan" (10), "Magdalen" (12), and "Cecilia" (13)—are at
odds with the poet's interpretation of them; this contradiction produces
satire. As Alison Conway notes, Pope uses the multiplicity of poses assumed by women to confirm the "profound instability and vacuity at
the heart of female identity" and to suggest that such women are narcissistic.[74] These portraits also suggest another venue for female consumerism—the commissioning of one's portrait—as well as the period's
association between the pictorial representation of femininity and female sexuality. Ranging from Aphra Behn's "sign of Angellica" in *The
Rover* (1667) to Arbuthnot and Pope's account of the portrait of the
"Double Mistress" in Martinus Scriblerus's *Memoirs* (published 1741)
that inaugurates Scriblerus's erotic journey, a number of writers figured
the public display of femininity—even in a painting—as a sexual invita-
tion.[75]
    But the epistle includes a second telling disjunction that resonates
with the already-established rivalry between the cosmetic and poetic
arts: although the poem represents paintings, the poet debunks all
painting, whether face painting or portrait painting, claiming instead
that only poetry can represent women accurately. Pope famously argues that women's "Characters are not so strongly mark'd as those of
Men, seldom so fixed, and still more inconsistent with themselves" (1,
note). As the poet explains, "Pictures like these"—images of women—
"to design, / Asks no firm hand, and no unerring line" (151–52); thus

the painter's attributes, a "firm hand" and an "unerring line," cannot provide true representations of women. Visual pictures fix an image, but poetry formally reflects the changefulness that women reputedly embody: a Popean couplet encapsulates an image, only to have that image supplemented (in the Derridean sense) by a succeeding one. The poet insists that one must "Chuse a firm Cloud, before it fall, and in it / Catch, ere she change, the Cynthia of this minute" (19–20). "Pictures like these" require the "Cloud" of language and the "sense" of a reader; together these tools of language are the poet's "paint." In the face of women on display, the poet rejects their visual — and implicitly cosmetic — self-presentations to claim that poetry is the only adequate means of representing them.

The final satiric portrait, that of Queen Caroline (181–92), denounces poets and painters who represent her supposed virtues with objects that actually displace those virtues, thereby making them dead metaphors: she is "describ'd by all / With Truth and Goodness, as with Crown and Ball / Poets heap Virtues, Painters Gems at will / . . . and hide their want of skill" (183–85). "Virtues" are only as ornamental as "Gems," thereby corroborating a deflation of moral standards that Pope attributes to the Court. In contrast to these falsifying images, an "Artist" (187), whether poet or painter, finds "true delight" only in drawing the "Naked" (188). Pope does not distinguish between false and true artists, but between those nonartists who do not wish to represent truth, and artists, who, by definition, do. In an action not unlike the application of cosmetics, women who wish to have their deceitful self-conceptions externalized in portraits must sit to nonartists. We expect Pope to strip away the queen's surface pretensions and expose her to public scrutiny, but she is such a cosmetic lie — "a Robe of Quality . . . struts and swells" (189) — that "None see what Parts of Nature it conceals" (190). Although unable to see and thereby represent the queen's "Parts of Nature," which the pun on "quean" forces us to read as "genitalia," Pope is able to transform his inability to represent the naked truth into another kind of truth. He implies that the queen is so layered with disguises that she has no interior and that, therefore, there is nothing else to see. Although her body seems to render the traditional tools of satire ineffectual, her cosmetic surface, paradoxically, is her truth. To represent the queen ekphrastically with "Crown," "Ball," and "Gems" is to capitulate to the terms of her self-representation. By refusing to do this, Pope acknowledges the limits of ekphrasis and uses this apparent failure to sharpen the poem's satire. Pope's reticence or inability to represent the queen through ekphrasis actually marks the poem's crowning satiric censure of publicly displayed femininity in both form and content. The reader learns that she is a surface covering a vacuum not by seeing a picture of the queen, but by reading Pope's poem, the lesson of which confirms that of *The Rape of the Lock*: the reader's sense, not the gazer's eye, ultimately discovers the truth.

Given the poem's sustained critique of public women's self-display, it is not surprising that Pope imagines his idealized female addressee in a domestic context, and specifically in a familial structure: she is the ideal sister, mother, and wife — roles that suggest she safeguards the domestic order and social bonds that the other women threaten. Of course, the historical Martha Blount, upon whom the portrait is modeled, was neither wife nor mother, and satisfied only one of those roles (as sister to Teresa). Ever critical of Pope's longtime friend and companion, William Warburton argued in the 1751 edition of Pope's *Works* that the "Lady" was not Martha Blount, but that she was "created out of the poet's imagination; who therefore feigned those circumstances of a *Husband*, a *Daughter*, and love for a *Sister*, to prevent her being mistaken for any of his acquaintance."[76] Even if one rightly disputes Warburton's erasure of Blount from the history of the poem's production, to describe the lady as a figment of the poet's imagination is telling; as Valerie Rumbold astutely notes, the poem's final portrait is of an ideal woman in "the generic subjunctive."[77] The effect of this mood is to produce a female companion who is an abstraction. She is the famously contradictory "softer Man," Heav'n's "last best work" (271–72). Just as the poet's representation of Belinda's beauty in *The Rape of the Lock* renders her unvisualizable and ultimately denies her the power of an ekphrastic image, the climactic portrait of a "softer Man" not only denies the poet's companion independence, but also a physical presence.

The invisibility of the "softer Man" is an effect of ideology and of Pope's aesthetics. But the aesthetics of management evident in *The Rape of the Lock* changes registers in the later poem. Whereas Belinda's presence is repeatedly figured by metonymy, the ideal woman in *To a Lady* consists of purely abstract qualities and virtues, nouns that are physically intangible. Moreover, these characteristics are identified as either masculine or feminine, an ambiguity that attenuates the abstraction of gender difference. The poet praises the "softer Man" because this third gender is picked "from each sex, to make the Fav'rite blest."

> Your love of Pleasure, our desire of Rest:
> Blends, in exception to all gen'ral rules,
> Your Taste of Follies, with our Scorn of Fools,
> Reserve with Frankness, Art with Truth ally'd
> Courage with Softness, Modesty with Pride,
> Fix'd Principles, with Fancy ever new;
> Shakes all together, and produces — You.
>
> (273–80)

Howard D. Weinbrot tellingly calls this composite image a "cosmic kitchen," a response that literalizes the domestic sphere that Pope himself refuses to describe.[78] The portrait's possessive pronouns—"your" (female) and "our" (male)—not only align most qualities with a gender, but also attempt to represent masculinity and femininity as stable and monolithic categories, even while the portrait threatens to conflate them. One irony in this project, of course, is that this femininity is a "part [of] and counterpart [to]" the poet's masculinity.[79] Unlike the satirized women, and unlike Belinda, this "softer Man" is a composite of characteristics, ranging from "Pleasure" and "Rest" to "Courage," "Softness," "Modesty," and "Pride," and those gendered possessive pronouns eventually fall out of the description. Only nouns remain. The portrait of "You" not only actively resists visualizing its subject, but it also avoids naming her, apart from this ungendered pronoun. The poem opens with the famous couplet, "Nothing so true as what you once let fall, / 'Most Women no Characters at all'" (1–2), but it is not a dialogue; Pope's "softer Man" is the ideal woman because we cannot see her and only rarely hear her. At the end of this gallery tour, we are left with an antiportrait, one that ultimately sheds its pictorial skin and that can exist only in language. Ekphrasis again marks a limit in the representation of femininity, leaving the abstraction of language to privilege Pope's truths.

From *The Rape of the Lock* to *To a Lady* Pope's aesthetic management of women moves from objectification to abstraction, a trajectory that culminates, paradoxically, with the erasure of female embodiment and agency. By using ekphrasis to manage the subject (and subjectivity) of women, Pope reiterates his poetry's status as art and also adopts the topic of female beauty as the occasion to produce an art that supplants women's art. Just as *The Rape of the Lock* concludes with stargazing, *To a Lady* imagines an ideal woman beyond reach and out of view. But *To a Lady* is distanced from *The Rape of the Lock* by its vigorous attempts to supplant the powerful image of femininity that captures the attention of the beau monde with an abstract portrait.

Pope is among the many writers who lambaste women for making themselves up and who fear women's gaining independence, autonomy, and—as Gauden's treatise demonstrates—critical skills. But Pope is distinctive in his perception that the danger was not only social, but also aesthetic; the allure of the cosmetic spectacle and the power of its theatricality had the potential to divert his audience. Pope replicates the cosmetic art in beautiful, glittery images, but only to contain and degrade them. *The Rape of the Lock* and *To a Lady* offer conclusions that similarly subordinate the art of women's self-display to poetry. Just as the poet assures Belinda that she will be remembered because of *The*

Rape of the Lock, *To a Lady* famously concludes that "The gen'rous God" (289) "To you gave Sense, Good-humour, and a Poet" (292). As Felicity Rosslyn notes, Pope implies that "'Sense' and 'Good-humour' notwithstanding, Martha Blount would have vanished anonymously into the Dionysiac stream of life if Apollo and a poet had not converted her, by form, into eternal meaning."[80] Fearing the vulnerability of gazers and the power that beautiful women—even if their beauty is only cosmetic—might hold over them, Pope reifies female beauty into a kind of poetry that promotes itself as a model for understanding: representation by a poet is superior to cosmetic self-fashioning.

The controversies surrounding women's use of cosmetics illuminates the fraught ideological nature of the lady's dressing room. If, as Gauden argues, cosmetics actually allow women to represent their piety and devotion to God while also facilitating the development of their intellects, then we can see what can be at stake in the representation of a woman at her toilet. Just as she has the tools to fashion herself physically, she also has a venue for legitimate knowledge production. In an odd convergence, Gauden and Pope both promulgate the legitimacy of cosmetic surfaces, although the similarity ends there. We have seen that *The Rape of the Lock* and *To a Lady* both institute a rivalry between a woman's cosmetics and a man's poetry, with the intention of displacing the art of face painting with the transcendent qualities of poetic representation. But just as important to Pope is the issue of an audience. As in much of Pope's writing, the alluring spectacle is a fundamentally dangerous and anti-intellectual phenomenon, so much so that the poet offers reading as the more secure means of either representing or apprehending truth. While Pope opens with Belinda at her dressing table, assuming the magical powers of theatricality, he concludes by comforting his companion in *To a Lady* that she has been given a poet who praises her for constituting the wonderfully abstract and wholly untenable "softer Man." Concurrently, Gauden's argument that cosmetics allow women to be self-determining agents is, of course, marked with pitfalls. But the eighteenth-century debate about cosmetics demonstrates that while the arts of beauty may construct a tyranny of the beautiful, they also embody the potential to empower women in some unexpected ways.

5

The Epistemology of the Dressing Room: Experimentation and Swift

What, the D— — look in Closestools instead of the Bible!
And write on poor *Cælia* so dirty a Libel.[1]

Some write of Angels, some of Goddess,
But I of dirty human BODIES.[2]

In this manner, the *opera-glasses* are constructed; with which a gentleman may look at any lady at a distance in the company, and the
lady know nothing of it.[3]

I͏F THE SATIRIC DRESSING ROOM EMBODIES A NEXUS OF CONNOTA-
tions about art and artifice, allowing us to unveil the gender politics of
aesthetics in the eighteenth century, then it likewise foregrounds epistemological concerns that intrigue and plague satirists. As we saw in
chapter 3, writers such as Mary Evelyn, Daniel Defoe, and Elizabeth
Thomas faced the excesses and disorder of the dressing room with an
epistemological resolve to order these spaces into an inventory, but
even these gestures of conceptual housecleaning failed to compress a
woman's material surrogates into neat classificatory systems, underscoring the mayhem and disarray housed in a lady's dressing room. As
readers for hundreds of years have noted, Jonathan Swift's satires take
as their subject this question of disorder and produce the most extreme
version of it—excrement. But his satires likewise accomplish the remarkable feat of making defecation seem simultaneously deviant and
normative. Defecation is exemplary because it horrifies the characters
who encounter it in Swift's texts: Strephon, in "The Lady's Dressing
Room," plunges his hand into his beloved's chamber pot, only to be
trapped into thinking that women's beauty covers excrement. These
same texts suggest that defecation is normal insofar as the reader is encouraged to take the knowing attitude that these characters are naive,
if not downright delusional, for being horrified. Cassinus, of "Cassinus

132

and Peter," looks the fool for his breakdown upon discovering that his Celia shits. To many readers of Swift—and many readers of his brand of eighteenth-century satire—this is merely ironic.[4] Within this understanding, Swift aims to expose the dirty truth behind any shiny exterior, revealing the dark truth beneath civilization. Swift as satirist thus becomes one afflicted with an "excremental vision" of humanity or, alternately, an "excremental reality," condemned to write only "scatological" or "excremental" satires throughout his career.[5]

Eighteenth-century responses regularly presupposed that Swift's satire resulted from his own psychological and sexual inadequacies. In *The Reasons that Induced Dr. S——to write a Poem call'd The Lady's Dressing-room* (1734), Lady Mary Wortley Montagu suggested that impotence with a prostitute led Swift to satiric revenge. In 1752, the Earl of Orrery reflected that, "[Swift's] general want of delicacy and decorum [in "The Lady's Dressing Room"], must not hope even to find the shadow of an excuse. . . . From his early, and repeated disappointments, he became a misanthrope."[6] For Orrery, Swift's "want of delicacy and decorum"—the most extreme example of which must be excrement—supports the claim that Swift hated men and women. Patrick Delany took issue with the characterization of Swift as a misanthrope by arguing that Swift did "more charities, in greater variety of ways . . . than perhaps any other man of his fortune in the world."[7] But Laetitia Pilkington also rebuked Swift's choice of subject matter, explaining that "with all the Reverence I have for the Dean, I really think he sometimes chose Subjects unworthy of his Muse, and which could serve for no other End except that of turning the Reader's Stomach."[8] Sixty years later, Sir Walter Scott repeated Orrery's argument, but added that the lack of delicacy and decorum were ultimately symptoms of Swift's madness, his "incipient disorder of the mind."[9]

In twentieth-century criticism, the conflation of Swift with his satirist has often served an effort to condemn or to recuperate Swift's reputation. Susan Gubar claims that Swift's satire enforces "a mode of imprisonment for the woman reader."[10] On the other side of the contemporary debate, Nora Crow Jaffe's argument is typical; she contends that "the narrator seems to excuse Celia and find Strephon at fault for holding his discoveries against her."[11] Margaret Anne Doody likewise argues that there is a significant difference between the imaginary lover and the distanced satirist, a point that supports her larger claim that Swift satirizes the tradition of satires about women by ridiculing Strephon's voyeurism and by presenting the satirist as supremely ironic and ultimately supportive of women.[12] For Doody, "Swift's kind of teasing is explorative, a challenge to women in the sex war to which they were allowed to respond. The effect of Swift's humour is not to silence the woman but to force her into utterance."[13]

Swift's satires have polarized critics for nearly three hundred years, but the beauty of Swift's strategy is the unyielding tension between horror and acceptance, such that any reading must ultimately account for the plausibility of both; even Swift's attitude to the body is marked, as Carol Houlihan Flynn notes, by both fascination and revulsion.[14] By foregrounding either the positivist or pessimistic in Swiftian satire, readers frequently ensnare themselves within the terms of the satire itself; in other words, to lambaste or to defend Swift's satires is to replicate the binaristic structure of those very same satires. To do so is also to obscure more central questions that Swift's texts demand we consider: Why do these satires return again and again to the dressing room as a *locus amoenus* for excrement? Why is the female body consistently figured as the site and producer of excrement?

Swift's satires, particularly "The Lady's Dressing Room," have long been associated with the production of bodily disorder, whether embodied in the satiric objects who leave their waste behind or in readers or spectators who consume these poetic bits and feel nauseous. Laetitia Pilkington's mother, for example, "instantly threw up her Dinner" after reading "The Lady's Dressing Room."[15] The poet imagines that the sight of Corinna, the Beautiful Young Nymph, causes a similar discharge: "*Corinna* in the Morning dizen'd, / Who sees, will spew; who smells, be poison'd."[16] One could easily argue that physical revulsion is a characteristically Swiftian response to the sight of a grotesque female body. In the *Journal to Stella*, Swift describes a similar encounter:

> I was to see lady— —, who is just up after lying-in; and the ugliest sight I have seen, pale, dead, old and yellow for want of her paint. She has turned my stomach. But she will soon be painted, and a beauty again.[17]

And Gulliver himself records feeling "Horror and Disgust" when he is placed on a dressing table and witnesses the giant Brobdingnagian Maids of Honor naked and freely urinating.[18]

Several critics have considered the topics of order and disorder in Swift's writings about women.[19] Claude Rawson wryly notes that "in the face of life's teeming disorders, the order of art seemed to Swift a falsifying thing."[20] Ever ready to upend the imperative to categorize, Swift's poetry, in particular, documents the inability of cosmetic categories to contain the body, a failure that is so often figured through the excremental. As Rawson reminds us, "reality and artifice . . . are at their usual tug of war" in Swift's poetry, an opposition that is not so easily resolved and which "gives his work its particular urgency and truth."[21]

We learn a valuable lesson from Rawson's reading. The irresolution of the opposition between "reality" and "appearance" suggests that any gesture toward the real is itself constructed: "If truth is painful, and indecorous, like a play in bad taste, it is also 'ridiculous,' funny—and, in some paradoxical ways, just as artificial."[22] Throughout Swift's corpus, there is a decided emphasis on an opposition between idealization and realization, a polarity that inevitably seems to privilege the truth-production of unmasking, but that Swift likewise calls into question.

Rawson's resolution to this binary is to frame it within a reading of Swift's temperament, particularly his "dislike of 'lofty' writing" and aggression toward the reader's "squeamishness, his complacent normality, his shoddy idealisms and self-deceptions, his attachment to the human form divine, and his belief in the rationality of the human mind, in short, against all those serene peaceful states that Swift wants to 'vex' the world out of."[23] But such biographically driven conclusions—readings that are so characteristic of Swift criticism—distract us from the real insight: the kernel of truth that predictably, if uncomfortably, appears in every Swift poem is itself an object of inquiry, largely because of its similarly vexed and even cosmetic nature. If many of these poems "are actually pleas for seeing straight, rather than through a rosy film of false poeticising," then it is incumbent upon us to attempt to see "straight" just exactly what Swift accomplishes in his own poems.[24]

As much as Swift's satires could be said to be designed to nauseate and as grotesque as the female body is made out to be, "The Lady's Dressing Room" famously concludes with an epistemological maxim: "Such Order from Confusion sprung, / Such Gaudy Tulips rais'd from Dung."[25] At the end of the poem, order is instituted, a condition at odds with the potential for disorder that the satire engenders. The "such" in this couplet immediately refers to the character Celia, whose dressing room has been anatomized by her voyeuristic admirer Strephon and who ultimately gains the admiration of the satirist. However, critics have failed to note that the qualities the satirist praises, Celia's "order" and her "gaudy Tulips," are linked by the poem's structure and suggest that the representation of women's dressing rooms speaks to eighteenth-century epistemology. If, as Stephen Shapin and Simon Schaffer argue, "Solutions to the problem of knowledge are solutions to the problem of social order," then the tensions between order and disorder, as well as those between art and nature, belie an endorsement of artifice—evident in Swift's comfort that the postnatal mother "will soon be painted, and a beauty again"—while also reflecting a concern about knowledge acquisition.[26] Through this reading of Swift, we can see that eighteenth-century representations of the dressing room could use the social problem of femininity as a figure for epistemology. Swift's focus on the *objects* of Celia's dressing room assumes the reliability of facticity, which, as Peter Dear explains, "was all about invoking social catego-ries."[27]

In this chapter, I take up the question of how Swift's poetry self-consciously reveals the constructedness and artificiality of its own con-clusions that have for so long been taken as "facts" about women. Laura Brown has shown us that Swift's "misogyny is appropriately under-stood in the context of mercantile capitalism," particularly through the trope of dressing, which "naturalizes the enterprise of mercantile capi-talism, so that all of nature seems to cooperate in decorating the female figure."[28] Reading the dressing room poems in conjunction with Swift's Irish tracts, Brown contends that the figure of a woman takes on re-sponsibility for both economic and imperialist expansion.[29] In spite of Brown's insights, Swift's scatological poetry has drawn a particular sort of commonsensical attention, one that normally takes its bodily residue as a fact. In contrast to this vein of criticism, and drawing on Brown's cultural analysis, I argue that Swift's dressing room satires capitalize on the gap between a woman's body and her public image, not only to wrench apart the artifice that Pope celebrates (as many have noted), but also to theorize the problematics of empirical epistemology. In addi-tion to the ideology that Brown identifies in Swift's writings, this chap-ter contends that Swift's account of the approximation and disorder associated with women, especially in "The Lady's Dressing Room," im-plicitly depends upon an acceptance of empiricism. In this way, to mod-ify Ann Jessie Van Sant's argument about Richardson, Swift produces a "coincidence" between scientific and satiric forms of narrative.[30]

By asserting an explicitly *epistemological* reading of Swift, I am evok-ing Swift's famous contributions to the infamous debates that pitted the wisdom of the Ancients against the innovations of the Moderns. Begin-ning with Sir William Temple's *Upon Ancient and Modern Learning* (1690) — Temple was Swift's longtime patron — and continuing with William Wotton's rebuttal in *Reflections upon Ancient and Modern Learning* (1694), Charles Boyle's critical edition of the *Epistles of Phalaris* (1695), Richard Bentley's *A Dissertation upon the Epistles of Phalaris* (1697), and various other responses, British intellectuals had been arguing over what kinds of knowledge mattered. Trying to assign value to learning, the debate between the Ancients and the Moderns emblematizes not only a culture of personal insult (Temple, for example, was furious with Wotton),[31] but also an intellectual culture living out the implications of the Baconian revolution.[32] As critics have widely noted, Swift enthusi-astically ridiculed the limits of the Moderns' position in *A Tale of a Tub*, *The Battle of the Books*, and the third voyage of *Gulliver's Travels*.[33]

Swift's *poetry* has always been considered outside of this context, pri-

marily because critics have not recognized the extent to which epistemological concerns also inflect Swift's verse productions;[34] too often the
poems are labeled Swift's "most personal works."[35] Instead, I attend to
the hallmarks of empiricism placed throughout Swift's verse satires to
situate them in the context of seventeenth- and eighteenth-century debates about epistemology, specifically the aesthetics and politics of experimentation. Thomas Sprat's *The History of the Royal Society* (1667)
serves as an implicit model for Swift's characterization and satire of
Strephon. Swift's play with experimental knowledge in "The Lady's
Dressing Room" not only points to two particular hobbyhorses of the
satirist—pillorying the Moderns' belief in experimentation and ridiculing naïveté—but it also indicates an important fact about the dressing
room trope's function in eighteenth-century literary culture. Swift acknowledges that there was an epistemological question at the heart of
the dressing room: when a woman's exterior is cosmetic and artificial,
how can one "know" and judge her properly? Strephon's actions suggest a pervading solution—examine the dressing room as a surrogate
for the woman herself. For Swift and his eighteenth-century readers,
the dressing room offers an empiricist blueprint for the transformation
of the observed particulars of the female body into the production of
general knowledge about women. Given that what constitutes a fact or
a piece of evidence explicitly underscores a particular social model or
organization, I contend that the so-called evidence of the dressing room
in Swift's satire makes the denigration of the female body contiguous
with the production of speculative knowledge. Swift's critique of female
embodiment—whether focused on invading the privacy of the dressing
room or on deconstructing a body made-up of prosthetics—is corroborated by a paternalistic hierarchy that imbues the poem's methodology
and its conclusions about epistemology. Gender difference and the ev-
eryday actions of the female body function as a vehicle for the articulation of order in early-eighteenth-century Britain, even as these same
satires belie the contradictions of empiricism.

IN DEEP SH–T: SWIFT'S TOILET

Following convention, one of Swift's solutions to the "problem" of
the dressing room is to employ a dual strategy of exposure and deconstruction. The poems "A Beautiful Young Nymph Going to Bed"
(1734) and "The Progress of Beauty" (1719) use dressing room scenes
to debunk the concept of beauty foregrounded in their titles and to offer
narratives of exposure that reveal women's cosmetic secrets. Both
poems feature a prostitute (or an actress; it is not clear which) suffering

from the effects of syphilis and its eighteenth-century cure, mercury.[36]
Corinna, the "Beautiful Young Nymph," is the "Pride of *Drury-Lane*"
(1). Rather than satirize the sordid venues of her neighborhood's playhouse culture and its marketplace for prostitutes, "A Beautiful Young
Nymph" details the private effects of its reputed sexual economy, beginning with Corinna's return "at the Midnight Hour; / Four Stories
climbing to her Bow'r" (7–8). Corinna's "Bow'r," in this mock-pastoral
context, domesticates the theatrical and erotic economies of the playhouse tiring-room, a context that is reconfirmed by Corinna's elaborate
and grotesque undressing.

Swift's poem satirizes the theatricality of the dressing room with a
narrative that dismembers Corinna in a kind of dressing room autopsy.
Her body is made up of prosthetics, like props in a theater: she "takes
off her artificial hair" (10), picks out a "Crystal Eye" (11), pulls off her
"Eye-Brows [made] from a Mouse's Hyde" (13), removes her "Plumpers" (17) and "Bolsters" (28) and so on before going to bed. This body
of parts suggests that Corinna is a parody of natural women. The morning does not leave her or her prostheses in much better shape; a rat has
stolen her "Plaister" (59), the "Crystal Eye, alas, was miss't" (61), the
cat has "p——st" (62) on her plumpers, a pigeon has pecked at her
"Issue-Peas" (63), and her lapdog's fleas have swarmed in her wig (64).
Corinna is left, at the end of the poem, to "unite" her "Limbs" (66), a
condition that figures the toilet as an act of willful, even painful, construction. The satirist also claims that it is an unnarratable act; even
though the poem has charted her deconstruction, the satirist asks,

> how shall I describe her arts
> To recollect the scatter'd Parts?
> Or shew the Anguish, Toil, and Pain,
> Of gath'ring up herself again?
>
> (67–70)

By offering a conclusion in which nothing is concluded, "A Beautiful
Young Nymph Going to Bed" renders Corinna's "beauty" a very dim
possibility at best. "The Progress of Beauty" satirically reverses the
genre made popular by Bunyan's late-seventeenth-century religious
narrative to chart a similar decomposition. This woman degenerates
into "rotting Celia," for whom "Two Balls of Glass may serve for Eyes, /
White Lead can plaister up a Cleft."[37] Unlike "A Beautiful Young
Nymph," much of this poem's satiric play focuses on the repair of her
diseased face; Celia makes herself beautiful "by help of Pencil, Paint
and Brush" (46), tools that "teach her Cheeks again to blush" (48). The
privacy afforded Corinna and Celia allows them to continue the game

of refashioning themselves for public view, apparently deceiving those who gaze upon them into believing that they are beautiful—and healthy. The satirist's exposure of a woman's private cosmetic rituals therefore disabuses readers.

"The Progress of Beauty" compounds its satire of Celia's beauty by suggesting that her public appearance is actually an effect of her cosmetics being in order. When the satirist identifies the "Three Colours" giving shape to Celia's face—the "Black, Red, and White" (21) from the lyric tradition that metonymically represent a woman's beautiful features—it is to note that each is only "gracefull in their proper Place" (22). This qualification admits the possibility that these colors, when out of their proper place, would reflect a woman who is not beautiful. Predictably enough, the poem literalizes this bathetic possibility by imagining what Celia looks like in the morning; after all, sleeping ruins the order of beauty because that beauty is cosmetic and cosmetics get smudged during the night. When Celia goes to bed, "All her Complexions" (30) are in place, but "when she rose" the next morning, "the black and red / Though still in Sight, had chang'd their Ground" (31–32). Apparently, it is not only sleeping that disorders Celia's face and makes her ugly, but also, in an admittedly twenty-first-century phrase, sleeping around. Celia has not stayed in her "proper Sphear" and the symptoms of syphilis that mark her body prove it. Just as the goddess Diana falls apart—when the moon wanes, "Each Night a bit drops off her Face" (87)—the mortal Celia decomposes. Her "progress" concludes with the utter deterioration of her body and the simultaneous elimination of any possibility that she might create a beautiful facade. The sexually active female body becomes an ugly body, out of place and with no chance to be beautiful.

The satirist's theory about Celia's beauty as an effect of her cosmetics' order is adapted to an argument for this woman to stay in her place, a reading of beauty that exposes its cultural and ideological underpinnings. The poem has already exposed in detail the artificiality and the contingency of Celia's reputedly beautiful face, but the satirist redoubles the poem's satiric censure by advising such women to keep to the "Window" that is their "proper Sphear" (66) and not "let the Beaux approach too near" (68). "The Progress of Beauty" posits that feminine beauty is an effect of aesthetic and social orders, but these orders notably depend upon an absent body, one that has been hidden far away from public view. Rather than merely suggesting that voyeurs not look too closely, the poem gestures toward a private sphere that is inaccessible to outsiders. The proper kind of privacy for women is therefore represented as an idea, ripe for speculation, rather than a physical reality. This is in stark contrast to Swift's unusual celebration of domesticity in

"The First of April" (ca. 1723), in which a mother cannot "spare a *Minute / From Husband, Children, Wheel* or *Spinnet.*"[38] In spite of this "positive" view of female domesticity, however, a woman's public beauty is produced as an effect of order, control, and abstraction. "The Progress of Beauty" even applies this argument about the order of beauty to its promotion of a secluded and isolated private sphere. In this alternative kind of privacy, women are out of public view and subject to the hierarchical asymmetry of gender difference. Swift's satiric verse succinctly represents women as objects in—rather than subjects of— their dressing rooms, a subtle difference of aesthetic and social orders that has the not-so-subtle goal of keeping women subordinate.

"The Lady's Dressing Room" (1732) critiques women's privacy by turning attention from the female body to the space that encompasses this body, the dressing room itself. Unlike "The Progress of Beauty" and "A Beautiful Young Nymph," "The Lady's Dressing Room" does not observe a woman's decomposition at night, but imagines a voyeur sneaking into her private chamber once she has departed for the day. "No Object" (47) in this room of "Litter" (8) "*Strephon's* Eye escapes" (47). However, the conclusion of "The Lady's Dressing Room" is the same: although "The Goddess from her Chamber issues, / Arry'd in Lace, Brocades and Tissues" (3–4) at the beginning of the poem, Celia's reputation for beauty is exposed by the end as fraudulent and as merely a theatrical effect. The curtain of this Celia's beauty is ripped away with Strephon's discovery of the chamber pot, the undisputed climax of the poem. After he sticks his hand inside, "Disgusted *Strephon* stole away / Repeating in his amorous Fits, / Oh! *Celia, Celia, Celia* shits!" (116–18). He flees the dressing room and speaks in the poem for the first time. Corinna and the other Celia decompose before our eyes, but Strephon's Celia is represented through the voyeur's reactions to the things she has left behind, her bodily waste.

Excrement, of course, figures centrally in a range of Swift's writings. Gulliver is pelted with it by the Yahoos in his final voyage and, as Laura Brown has noted, the Yahoos' qualities are analogous to those of Swift's women: "their stench, their fleshiness, their corruption, and their un-controlled sexuality are . . . the essential attributes of the female fig-ure."[39] In Swift's dressing room poems, defecation is a domestic problem, in the broadest sense. "Shit" is not in the faraway land of the Houyhnhnms, but at home in England and Ireland and, as such, is pri-marily identified as a woman's characteristic throughout much of Swift's verse. Even in "Cassinus and Peter" (1734) and "Strephon and Chloe" (1734), excrement originates as a woman's problem that threat-ens to infect men, a condition even more urgent because, as Mary Ellin D'Agostino argues, the domestic chamber pot was a metaphor for female sexuality.[40] Over twenty years before Swift's image, John Oldham and Ned Ward exploit the ornate chamber pot as a simile to indict women. She may have "gay charming looks," Oldham admits, but those looks inevitably encase "a nasty Soul," just "Like T— — —," or turd, "of quality in a gilt Closestool."[41] Ward satirizes the demise of a prostitute, whom he calls a "*Liplicking Lady*," when she transforms into "a Scandalous *Close-Stool* herself, that has nothing to protect her from Publick Contempt, but her being cover'd with Velvet, and when she's strip'd of her disguise, and appears plainly what she is, the World will cry *Foh*, as if she stuck in their Nostrils."[42]

The availability of the chamber pot metaphor for Swift corroborates not only the rich tradition of satires about women, but also the skepticism that underwrites these satires. Women prove, or so claim satirists, that surface and essence are at odds with one another. The appropriation of the chamber pot motif—the object within the dressing room that reputedly holds a woman's secrets—to express this discordance suggests that the female embodiment of allure and horror is not only widespread, but that it is also familiar *and* identifiable. If beautiful women are, indeed, like chamber pots, then everyone should know that they are truly horrific inside, just as everyone ought to be able to identify a chamber pot when they see one, even if it is gilt, even if it is covered with velvet. A beautiful surface can keep an object from turning into an object of communal contempt, but just barely, and everyone is presumed to know that this is exactly what is going on. Celia's chamber pot, like her body, has a beautiful facade, for it is "*Disguise[d]*" (77) with "Rings and Hinges *counterfeit*" (76) to appear like "A Cabinet to vulgar Eyes" (78). Its design can be read as a jest characteristic of this satiric age; Lady Mary Wortley Montagu boasted of a chamber pot lined with portraits of Pope and Swift on the bottom. The text suggests that only those people with "vulgar Eyes" would mistake the chest for a cabinet, while everyone else would get the joke.

But Swift's image is denser than a witticism, and to apprehend its full implication we need to move beyond the interpretive possibilities suggested by the text itself. Eighteenth-century material culture offers an important context for just such a reading: a cabinet in contemporary usage was a locked piece of furniture that held valuable objects. The first exclusively private space in early modern domestic interiors was probably a locked cabinet in a husband's bedroom.[43] Dora Thornton contends that the cabinet denoted private study, and it functioned as a portable desk that "could contain all those objects conventionally associated with the study."[44] As Samuel Johnson defines it in *The Dictionary of the English Language*, a cabinet is "a private box"; secondly, it is "any place in which things of value are hidden." Notably, Johnson quotes

this passage from "The Lady's Dressing Room" to illustrate his definition, further evidence that Swift's satire evoked the "legitimate" cabinet
for contemporary readers. To disguise a woman's chamber pot as a cabinet, even if unsuccessfully, evokes this material context and renders
the anxiety surrounding the cabinet analogous to that of the dressing
room. Celia's cabinet represents, in miniature, the potential for privacy
associated with a woman's dressing room. Readings of Swift's verse,
such as Ellen Pollak's contention that Swift and Pope manipulate a
"myth of passive womanhood" to produce their texts, miss the point.[45]
Celia's privacy and its violation in "The Lady's Dressing Room" represent little to do with passivity, and everything to do with the threat of
women's privacy and the possibly transgressive activities that it could
allow, whether sexual or intellectual. Therefore, the satiric representation of Celia's chamber pot reflects an important regulatory strategy
that attempts to question the legitimacy of the woman's dressing room
and to restrict the potential for privacy, privilege, and autonomy that it
represented.

Swift accomplishes this demotion by making Celia's chamber pot a
false cabinet in its design and use. "The Lady's Dressing Room" suggests a confusion of domestic furniture, while simultaneously implying
that Celia uses her privacy for unsavory ends. The cabinet facade fails,
and its failure emphasizes the illegitimacy of a cabinetlike object that
houses shit. Not only does Strephon easily gain access to the room
when Celia's maid Betty is not looking, but the chamber pot "stand[s]
full in Sight" (73), is not locked (whereas a "real" cabinet probably
would have been), and the smell of her excrement permeates the room.
Strephon's ease of discovery confirms the satire of Celia's space as a
degradation of and parody of a "real" private space—in other words,
one occupied by a gentleman. While the cabinet surface of Celia's
chamber pot could have suggested to the "vulgar Eyes" of an eighteenth-century audience that it contained Celia's valuables, whether
they were physical objects such as books or a figure for her sexuality,
Swift's satiric mode exposes this cabinet as a parodic sign of legitimate
claims to privacy. Not only does the chamber pot hold the most grotesque of bodily materials, but this fact is also verifiable by a voyeur
as naive as Strephon. One can understand more fully that Strephon's
invasion of Celia's space is designed to render the privacy of a woman's
dressing room simultaneously illegitimate and futile. Swift's exposé of
Celia's dressing room and her cabinet within attempts to impose a gender hierarchy through the representation of a woman's private space as
open and necessarily subject to satiric regulation, in implicit contrast to
the gentleman's closet.

SATIRIC EXPERIMENTATION: THE EPISTEMOLOGY
OF "THE LADY'S DRESSING ROOM"

In the previous section, we have taken a thematic approach to Swift's dressing room poems, identifying the means through which the satirist addresses the "problem" of women's cosmetic dissembling. The sustained critique of women's potential for privacy, and the commensurate idealization of a female privacy that itself is left unrelated to the body, situates Swift's approach firmly in a satiric tradition that views women as productive for satire. But my analysis has left an important question unanswered, namely the epistemological implications of Swift's own verse. As we discussed in chapter 3, the satiric appropriation of the dressing room trope introduces a vexing theoretical situation, given the slipperiness of the enclosure a dressing room presupposes. For satirists, the dressing room is a conceptual space that is necessarily neither fully open nor fully closed. The liminal nature of the dressing room thus offers Swift an opportunity to use its exposure as a test case for the limits and strengths of empiricism, an epistemological experiment hidden beneath the veneer of the satiric dressing room tradition.

Many of Swift's dressing room poems teach an apparently simple lesson. We learn that Corinna approximates what beautiful women "really" look like, and we learn this by observing her decouché, at which point the prosthetics that constitute the female body are taken off and put on display. A beautiful young nymph going to bed is anything but a beautiful sight. Only worse is her reconstitution in the morning, that event which is beyond representation. But what is new in Swift's appropriation of the dressing room trope is its explicit alignment with problems of order and society, a preoccupation that allows us to reconsider Swift's dressing room poems not only as commentary on the status of gender roles in the eighteenth century (as most critics have), but also as documents testifying to the interrelation of gender and epistemology in the period. In order to understand the implications of Swift's methodology and the ideological work of a text such as "The Lady's Dressing Room," we must also consider the empirical context that makes available the tactile and materialistic account of feminine beauty upon which Swift's dressing rooms depend.

Few critics have noted the epistemological implications of "The Lady's Dressing Room," save Laura Mandell's brief comment that Swift satirizes empiricism and links it to misogyny by "overdramatizing" the empirical method and Deborah Baker Wyrick's observation that the poem "emphasizes the grim work of discovery and interpretation."[46] The satire opens as an epistemological model for knowledge acquisition. In the poem's first eighteen lines, Swift presents a hypothesis (Celia is a goddess) and an experiment designed to test the veracity of this hypothesis (Strephon's examination of her dressing room). The dressing room becomes a laboratory, a space where the "truth" of a woman may be determined. When Strephon trespasses into Celia's dressing room, fingers her belongings, and "produces" (as the satirist explains on line nineteen) the material for the satire "The Lady's Dressing Room," Swift conjoins the principles of experimental knowledge with the production of satire. In effect, Swift implicitly supports the position that Thomas Sprat advocates in *The History of the Royal Society*: "The *Wit* that is founded on the *Arts* of Mens Hands is masculine and durable: It consists of *Images* that are generally observ'd, and such visible Things which are familiar to Mens Minds."[47] One cannot say with certainty that Swift is responding to Sprat, who was recruited to provide a comprehensive response to the Society's earliest critics and, in so doing, outlined the methodological and epistemological principles of experimentation.[48] Even so, the *History* embodies the empirical idealization that Swift satirizes. Sprat's celebration of the masculine hand feeling up the natural world finds its alter ego in the figure of the young and naive Strephon feeling up Celia's dressing room. If the New Scientist is meant to discover heretofore hidden truths about the natural world, then Strephon merely discovers the so-called truth about women that Swift's satires endorse all along—they are stinky, yucky, and probably fake.

To understand Strephon's adventure in Celia's dressing room as a mode of satiric experimentation, consider that Sprat defines experimentation as dependent upon the facts that members collect through "their *own Touch* and *Sight*" (83). It is a *"fundamental Law"* of the Royal Society that members produce data from experience—"whenever they could possibly get to *handle* the Subject, the *Experiment* was still perform'd by some of the *Members* themselves" (83)—for *"Truth"* is produced by the *"Contentions* of Hands, and Eyes; as it is commonly injur'd by those of Tongues" (100). Strephon, like the experimental philosopher, "handles" the materials of Celia's dressing room through sight and touch and through a third sense, smell. These are the bodily sensations that form the basis for "facts," the kind of knowledge that the New Science privileges.[49] Sprat's belief in facticity is in line with a shift in seventeenth-century notions of evidence that conceived of facts as stable truths to be discovered, rather than manufactured.[50] Strephon's first fact in his "Survey" (7) is Celia's smock. It is introduced through the passive voice—"a dirty Smock appear'd" (11)—but its magic of appearance is quickly displaced by Strephon's own tactile examination of it. He "display'd it wide, / And turn'd it round on every Side" (13–14). The acts of picking up the armpit-stained smock, pulling it wide open, and rotating it for examination suggest the methodology of experimentation, as Sprat would have it. Strephon's sensory experiment is even framed within the language of the New Science. Soon after Strephon sneaks into Celia's dressing room, he begins to produce a "strict Survey" (7) of its contents and Strephon's exclamation that Celia shits concludes his "grand Survey" (115). A survey, as Sprat implicitly notes, is made up of *"Particulars"* (103), namely particular observations and particular facts, and forms the foundation for experimental knowledge. Strephon's observations focus on the details of Celia's consumeristic accumulation of material goods, objects that are all designed to make her beautiful. As we noted in chapter 3, Swift's catalogue differs somewhat from the satiric dressing room inventories of Mary Evelyn, Daniel Defoe, and Elizabeth Thomas; these earlier satires limit their use of adjectives to describe women's possessions, except to indicate that the items are broken and no longer useful.[51]

But Strephon is a fool, and the poem's narrative of exploration and learning point to the poem's status as a case study for satiric experimentation. Through the figure of Strephon, we witness a voyeur following the principles of the New Science; he handles Celia's belongings, sees the "truth" in them, and privileges things over words by presenting item after item and speaking only twice, to swear "how damnably the Men lie, / In calling *Celia* sweet and cleanly" (17–18) and then to moan "Oh! *Celia, Celia, Celia* shits!" (118). From the perspective of the satirist, the spirit of the idiot scientist is aptly captured by the naïveté of Strephon, who ridiculously plunges his hand into Celia's chamber pot to feel what it contains. He seems to be another of the self-deluded projectors whom Gulliver meets, which is why the narrator begs for the suspension of language: "On such a Point few Words are best, / And *Strephon* bids us guess the rest" (15–16). The appeal that "few words are best" is ostensibly made by the satirist for reasons of politeness, supposing that the dirty secrets of a beautiful woman ought not to be exposed to public view. In the context of Strephon's acquisition of experimental knowledge, Swift's claim that "few Words are best" seems more aptly a parody of the antifigural stance held by Sprat and the New Scientists.[52] The satirist and Strephon may well allude to descriptive restraint, but these are hollow gestures, especially insofar as Celia's dirty smock has already been logged in the poem's inventory. More notably, the appeal for discursive economy points to the empirical hope that facts, those observed particulars that the poem inventories, speak for themselves. Strephon, like those philosophers lugging objects on their backs, believes that the meaning of an object is unequivocal and stable. Only if the materials in Celia's dressing room are transparent signifiers will

Strephon's request that we "guess the rest" succeed. In the world of Strephon's experiment, the evidence of a dirty smock leads to the reputedly incontrovertible conclusion that its owner is likewise dirty.

One could argue that with every object Strephon examines, the link to Celia and her undesirability is replicated in an apparent capitulation to the New Science's requirement for confirmation; Sprat explicitly notes the Royal Society's provision for secondary testing in front of the assembled society or by other natural philosophers as the primary means of ensuring certainty (99).[53] This might explain why the satire proceeds undaunted through Celia's possessions, one by one, as Strephon fingers and examines them all, producing a list of "things" to prove his overall point—and implicitly satisfying Sprat's mandate for a catalogue of things and for secondary testing. One could just as easily argue that Strephon does not learn from his experiment in the dressing room, while the reader and the satirist know all too well what the conclusion will inevitably be. If, indeed, Strephon were attempting a thoughtful experiment, the satire suggests that Celia's beauty, or even her reputation for beauty, is not a proper topic. His conclusion, in this sense, is too obvious, and the following 126 lines only confirm what the reader already learns from the dirty smock. This latter view is supported by the satirist's gentle reprimand of Strephon, a reprimand that includes the satirist's bemusement at his own participation in this experiment:

> The Stockings, why shou'd I expose,
> Stain'd with the Marks of her stinking Toes;
> Or greasy Coifs and Pinners reeking,
> Which *Celia* slept at least a Week in?
>
> (51–54)

The point, then, is that Strephon himself, the taker of this "grand Survey" (115), is obsessed with the production of experimental knowledge.

Strephon's error, however, is also methodological: his whole system of knowledge production not only depends upon experimentation, but also upon speculation. In other words, the material objects that Strephon catalogues gain meaning in relation to Celia *only* through the process of speculation. The dirty smock is just a dirty smock unless one such as Strephon makes a link between its filth and Celia's—and this link is an act of cognition, which should be at odds with the empirical program of optical and tactile observation. Through the figure of Strephon, Swift exposes the tension between materialism and speculation that lies at the heart of experimental knowledge.

Although the term "speculation" has ties to the eighteenth-century financial market, the speculation that is relevant to Swift's satire comes from the empirical tradition, precisely because experimentation in the Royal Society depended on it.[54] Sprat insists that empirical observations are true, but notes that the Royal Society utilizes its own mechanism of confirmation, an effort that depends upon an explicitly theoretical construction: consensus. Lorraine Daston reminds us that "very few of the facts retailed by seventeenth-century civil and natural histories were the fruit of the author's personal observation. Hearsay was unavoidable."[55] The double-checking institutionalized into the Society's procedures underlines its investment in a stable and socially acceptable standard of facticity that would avoid the charge of "hearsay," but the possibility of dissension exposes the limits of Sprat's more common and optimistic charge that rational methods will necessarily and inevitably produce true results. Robert Markley argues that the concept of experimentation in the Royal Society recognized intellectual disagreements but attempted to use them to "jerry-rig a broad ideological consensus."[56] Sprat's account also indicates that the very category of scientific interpretation itself is implicitly constructed, rather than transparent, though he attempts to paper over the messy issue of interpretation — and the theoretical principles that guide it — throughout the *History*.

Swift critiques the possibility of consensus by compounding it with the epistemology of speculation. In the context of the dressing room, Strephon sees things and produces conclusions from these observations, but a careful reading indicates the extent to which this relation itself is dependent upon the viewer's interpretation. Reading Strephon's examination of Celia's dressing room, we quickly note that his survey uses speculation to render the material objects of Celia's dressing rooms signifiers for her body. The cataloguing of belongings is a typical enough scenario of dressing room satires, one that we have seen replicated in verses by Evelyn, Defoe, and Thomas. But Swift's "The Lady's Dressing Room" pauses its inventory with a glance into the looking glass of Celia's dressing table, an act that reflects the satire's productive use of speculation:

> When frighted *Strephon* cast his Eye on't
> It shew'd the Visage of a Gyant.
> A Glass that can to Sight disclose,
> The smallest Worm in *Celia's* Nose,
> And faithfully direct her Nail
> To squeeze it out from Head to Tail;
> For catch it nicely by the Head,
> It must come out alive or dead.

(61–68)

The magnification of the mirror replicates the satire's general aim to reflect—or claim to reflect—the smallest details in Celia's dressing room for the public's view. This is why some have identified this passage as emblematic of Swift's satiric technique; the glass appears to hold the satire's objects up for inspection.[57] The example of "the smallest Worm in *Celia's* Nose," upon which such a claim necessarily depends, is a detail that *only* appears to be descriptive, just as Celia *only* seems to be present in the dressing room. The rhetoric of the text challenges the reader to remember that Celia is not there. Only by noticing the subjective mood of the phrase can one see that this image of a worm reflects the poem's speculation about Celia rather than a reflection of her face: this is "A Glass that *can* to Sight disclose" (emphasis added). The speculative view available at this moment in the dressing table mirror allows the poet to imagine what Celia would do if there *were* a worm. By depending on that initial subjunctive "can," the description continues to suggest that such a mirror "can"—and therefore *does*—"faithfully direct her Nail / To squeeze it out from Head to Tail," without ever clarifying that this is only a possibility. Since the image of a worm in Celia's nose is not descriptive, the glass functions as a vehicle not for mimesis or reflection, but for speculation—producing an image for the mind's eye, rather than the optical sense privileged by the New Science. Some readers too easily accept this system of logic, suggesting that "the poem asks us to imagine such a woman, and the point is made."[58] But what point is made? To answer this fully, we must consider just *how* the poem asks us to imagine such a woman.

Speculation is not only key to empiricism; it is also central in Swift's famous description of satire. The convergence of speculation and mirroring takes us back to Swift's claim that satire is "*a sort of* Glass, *wherein Beholders do generally discover everybody's Face but their Own.*"[59] Indeed, "The Lady's Dressing Room" imagines Celia's face while the only image actually visible in the mirror is the "Visage of a Gyant" that is presumably a distortion of Strephon's own face, although it is never identified as such. As a figure through which the poem's use of speculation is reflected, Swift's glass—be it the satire or the dressing table mirror—functions not to confirm identification, but to make a difference. Speculation in turn has the potential for mimesis, although this *potential* for similarity and reflection inevitably leads to the production of difference, as Mikkel Borch-Jacobsen has shown. By making theories out of visual observations, the threat of "similarity" inherent in the occasion of the mirror "leads to disagreement and the claim of difference; mimesis of the other leads to propriation."[60] Strephon's moment of potential self-reflection results in a vision of Celia that is both derogatory *and* speculative. If Strephon's peering has the possibility of merging his identity with Celia's—or at least evincing some sympathy—then Swift's satire abruptly undercuts this option and uses the speculative moment to reflect instead Strephon's sense of difference and, by extension, superiority, reminding us again of Fredric V. Bogel's contention that satire makes the differences that it reports to discover.[61]

The moment in the glass also allows us to understand the epistemological contradiction in Strephon's fact-finding mission. Strephon, at one and the same time, must handle and observe Celia's belongings, as well as speculate about each item's function and its relation to Celia's status as a goddess. Laura Brown contends that Celia's body is present metonymically in the dressing room (and by extension, in the poem), but we ought to remember that she is undeniably absent.[62] This, of course, is the main difference between "The Lady's Dressing Room" and Swift's other poems that similarly deconstruct the category of female beauty, with figures such as Celia in "The Progress of Beauty" and Corinna in "A Beautiful Young Nymph" falling apart before our very eyes. Strephon's experimental speculations participate in the wider cultural problematic of—in the words of Barbara Maria Stafford— imaging the unseen. The promise of enlightenment through scopic apprehension was coupled with the undeniable limitations of the empirical method; as Stafford notes, "optical demonstration and visualization were central to the processes of enlightening. Yet from a conceptual standpoint, images, paradoxically, were reduced to misleading illusions without the guidance of discourse."[63] Through a narrative that attenuates the prosthetics featured in these other poems, Strephon views Celia's body only through its association with the objects in the dressing room, objects that themselves become "misleading illusions" in Strephon's hands.

Although marked with the signs of empirical discovery, "The Lady's Dressing Room" imbues an anxiety about semblance, focusing much cultural weight on the power to unmask the truth, expose dissemblers, and dispel the power of images in a world dominated by those masks that Norbert Elias associates with the modern consciousness.[64] Unmasking Celia's subterfuge presents a specific challenge, one that extends the project of enlightenment that Stafford describes. Remarkably, Swift presents an abundance of seemingly tactile evidence, but both Strephon and the poem can offer only an *image* of Celia's body—just the type of phantasm that the normative strain in the satire critiques.

The body of the poem speculates about individual objects in the dressing room to generate its truth about Celia. There are, in fact, two steps in this process of association, moving from object to use and from use to Celia. Early in the poem, the satirist enjoins us to listen to Strephon's "survey" of the objects in Celia's dressing room that includes combs clogged with "Sweat, Dandriff, Powder, Lead and Hair" (24), a facecloth "with Oyl upon't" (25), vials filled with "Ointments good for scabby Chops" (36), a basin "Fowl'd with the Scouring of her Hands" (38) and "The Scrapings of her Teeth and Gums" (40), towels "Begumm'd, bematter'd, and beslim'd" (45), handkerchiefs "varnish'd o'er with Snuff and Snot" (50), and stockings "Stain'd with the Marks of stinking Toes" (52). One could claim that Swift's satire "presents us not so much with a woman as with her *disjecta membra*."[65] Yet these scattered remains instead correlate in specific ways to Celia's body. Each item is speculated to be associated with a particular body part, and even comes to represent a substitute for that part. In order, the comb stands for her hair, the cloth her face, the ointments her jaw, the basin her hands and mouth, the handkerchiefs her nose, and the stockings her feet. Strephon abstracts a picture of Celia from her toilet. With this rhetorical sleight of hand, Celia's body is literally absent—she has left the room, after all—but speculatively present. Strephon holds up Celia's things and thinks he knows her.

Strephon discovers Celia's bodily waste when he invades her privacy, but the chamber pot is only the climax of a survey that links the dirt in the dressing room to Celia herself. By listing each item and the particular kind of filth that covers it, the text enacts an additional chain of speculative signification: the sweat, dandruff, dirt, and cosmetics on the comb stand for her *dirty* hair, the oil on the cloth for her *greasy* face, the grime in the basin for her *filthy* hands and mouth, the mucus evident on her handkerchiefs for her *snotty* nose, and a mixture of sweat and dirt on her stockings for her *stinky* feet. All of these items reduce Celia to a composite of cosmetics and accessories, and all the dirt and excrement satirically reverse the assumed function of the dressing room, much as the rain in "A Description of a City Shower" (1710) brings out London's filth. For Strephon, he is faced with an indecent body and can only swear that everyone lies about Celia's beauty. The "Litter" of the dressing room can produce an interpretation of Celia because Strephon consistently speculates about its relation to her body. Without speculation, all we have is a dirty room. But the poem's representation of Celia's body by signs of its waste functions as a Derridean supplement that "adds only to replace."[66] By presenting dirt, sweat, dandruff, powder, lead, hair, "Scrapings," and finally feces as signs of her body, the poem substitutes the bodily waste that covers Celia's accessories in the dressing room for the comb, the cloth, the basin, the handkerchiefs, and the stockings. Such slippery rhetoric paints a picture of Celia's body by associating a residue of waste with it; the text generates *theoretical* knowledge about Celia from the *physical* evidence of her dressing room. Strephon's acquisition of experimental knowledge in the dressing room demonstrates that material evidence is actually filtered through a theoretical grid as meanings are assigned to it. We quickly see that such speculation does not even need its real object of inquiry to occasion the production of theory—and that this is fundamentally at odds with the apparently empirical modus operandi of the poem. Figures such as Strephon and the New Scientists hope that facts are self-evident, but Swift's satire exposes a reality in which facts, these physical objects, are not transparent and, instead, require a theoretical context for meaning.

The means through which Strephon's conclusion about Celia and all women is generated reveals the epistemological terms of Swift's satire: while Strephon is certainly portrayed as a satiric boob, bumbling about naively in a woman's inner sanctum, the sharpest critique resides in Swift's censure of his empirical method. Experimental knowledge, as Swift's satire indicates, equally depends upon theoretical constructs, and as theoretically dubious as speculation proves to be, it is also a sign for Swift of the Moderns' fallibility. The speculation machine in the third voyage of *Gulliver's Travels* promises that with a "little bodily Labor"—which can be taken as the labor of handling Celia's things— "the most ignorant Person" may produce works of speculation.[67] Swift's parody of the debate sparked by Wotton's rebuttal of Temple, *A Full and True Account of the Battel Fought last Friday, Between the Antient and the Modern Books in St. James's Library* (1697), also provides apt coverage of the demerits of speculation. In particular, speculation for Swift is aligned with the material object that sullies Strephon himself— excrement. No wonder that the speculative scientists in the Royal Academy of Lagado also work to turn shit back into food.

For Swift, the Moderns exhibit a prejudice for speculation, even though the paradigm of experimental knowledge presupposes tactile and optical experience. Speaking to their aspirations, Swift's satirist in *A Battel* soberly contends that "being light-headed, they have in Speculation, a wonderful Agility, and conceive nothing too high for them to mount" (145). The interlude between the bee and the spider provides an allegory for the differences between those who support the superiority of ancient knowledge (the bee) and those who support modern accomplishments (the spider). The Moderns are hubristic posers in the most literal of senses. As Joseph M. Levine notes, Swift considered the Moderns ridiculous because "their facts were trivial and irrelevant to any larger matter and their posture was arrogant and pretentious."[68] Their light-headedness, Swift's text implies, produces theories of knowledge that have little value and the faults of the Moderns are explicitly identified as the pairing of speculation and excrement. Whereas the bee "*visit[s] all the Flowers and Blossoms of the Field and the Garden, but . . . enriches [himself] without the least Injury to their Beauty, their Smell, or their Taste"* (149), the spider, *"by an overweening Pride, which feeding and engendering on it self, turns all into Excrement or Venom"* (150). The spider's web, the proverbial net that ensnares its victims, is in fact a flimsy mixture of defecation and poison. Speculation is thereby likened to excretory productions, an analogy seconded by a resentful "Aesop," who furthers the image to contend that Moderns spin shit out of their own brains. The question of scientific method, "Aesop" argues, is moot when experimental knowledge itself is false: *"Erect your Schemes with as much Method and Skill as you please,"* he tells the Moderns, *"yet, if the materials be nothing but Dirt, spun out of your own Entrails (the Guts of* Modern *Brains) the Edifice will conclude at last in a* Cobweb" (151). The Ancients make honey, the Moderns excrement.

Given Swift's conjunction of excrement with the speculative in experimentation, Strephon's punishment by "Vengeance" (119) makes more sense. "Vengeance" condemns the voyeur for his transgression by confining him to a cognitive model of speculation, namely the process by which two attributes are associated in the *mind's* eye, not the physical eye. After the dressing room experiment, Strephon is forced to view every woman he sees as defined by the olfactory category of "Stinks" (122), while every putrid odor he smells will remind him of women. "By vicious Fancy," these two ideas are "coupled fast" (127), and such a dialectic between women and filth promises to sustain Strephon's simple, yet totalizing, theory of gender difference: women are smelly and he, as a man, finds them noxious. His association between odor and women is strictly figured as theoretical, for it is a product of his "Imagination," "foul" (121) as it may be. Strephon's fulfillment of Sprat's epistemological promise ironically precludes heterosexual desire. The coupling "by vicious Fancy" of smell and femininity is not merely Strephon's punishment, but also part and parcel of experimentation more generally. In other words, "Vengeance" merely traps Strephon into the tyranny of speculation that he has used all along, a punishment aptly in line with the methodology and spirit of Strephon's empirical project.

Following my analysis of Strephon's epistemological liabilities, it is tempting to emphasize the extent to which the satirist's attitude toward Strephon is generally one of distance, a strategy of distinction that is designed to render Strephon's conclusions additionally dubious. For hundreds of years, critics have adopted this very viewpoint to defend Swift. The satirist's disavowal manifests itself through regular asides that themselves litter the poem's account of Strephon's experiment. Strephon is a "rogue" (13) and "wretched" (129) and he exhibits little restraint and great naïveté, particularly with the turn to Celia's chamber pot: "Why *Strephon* would you tell the rest? / And must you needs describe the Chest?" (69–70) begs the satirist. And the poem famously concludes with the satirist's claim of difference, stipulating that Strephon's error is to designate sensory perception as a legitimate means to acquire knowledge. In other words, if Strephon were only to look at women as they present themselves in public and only to admire them optically, rather than olfactorily or tactilely, then Strephon would learn "to think like me" (141) and desire women just as they present themselves. It is at this place that the satire veers to voice the alignment between a notion of order and a category of beauty, as the satirist's concluding couplet opines. If Strephon were to appreciate the effect of desirability, rather than be pressed to verify its authenticity, he could enjoy women as performances of "Glory" (135) that "ravisht" (142) a beholder's eyes. For the satirist, the experimental knowledge that Strephon acquires by examining Celia's dressing room is entirely irrelevant to the issue at hand—whether Celia can be an object of masculine desire. Her material condition may very well be that of a disgusting body, but to the satirist, her effect, the analogy with those "gaudy Tulips," is the realm of meaning that matters. Swift's satirist accomplishes a typical Swiftian posture, that of the knowing admirer, the one who is willing—as Strephon and Chloe are in the poem of the same name—to call a "Spade, a Spade" and leave it at that.[69] The idiotic stance is Strephon's, the person who believed the image and feels betrayed by learning that it is only a simulacrum.

But for all of this labor to distinguish the satirist from Strephon, an important and difficult question remains: how different are they? Tellingly, Laura Brown suggests that the satirist offers Strephon "mock-advice."[70] When the satirist asks "should I expose" (51) Celia's private belongings, in an apparent moment of criticism, the satirist reveals that the poem itself is also inextricably complicit in Strephon's project by detailing just the sorts of "facts" that capture Strephon's eyes. The satirist says that Celia ought to be admired and Strephon surmises that she ought to be despised, but one must pause to wonder how opposed these responses really are. Given the same material from which each may draw conclusions, Strephon is repulsed by women and the satirist is knowingly entranced by them. If we suspend their apparent opposition for a moment, we can realize that their reactions are actually more similar than different. Both Strephon and the satirist use this occasion to generate a binaristic and totalizing theory of femininity. Their reactions are, so to speak, two sides of the same coin; as Christine Rees argues, "The speaker implicitly condemns both Strephon's original illusion and his violent disillusion as ferments of a diseased imagination, but his own insinuating answer is no less ironic, and no more tenable."[71] Together these responses replicate a binary of femininity that constrained the eighteenth century, namely that women are sex objects or loathsome objects (another version of this opposition takes the view that women are whores or fine ladies).[72] In this light, the satirist and Strephon begin to seem not so different.

If Strephon's and the satirist's reactions are two versions of the same thing, then so, too, are their means of arriving at these conclusions. To return to Sprat momentarily: near the conclusion of the *History*, Sprat creates a category of wit, which he describes as the "Arts of Mens Hands" (415). Using the language of a common cause, Sprat suggests that writers "may behold that their Interest is united with that of the *Royal Society*; and that if they shall decry the promoting of *Experiments*, they will deprive themselves of the most fertil Subject of *Fancy*" (417).[73] Sprat attempts to gain the good will of the wits, all the while acknowledging their influence, and compounds his efforts by contending that laughter in and of itself is merely a cheap trick, the "easiest and the slendrest Fruit of *Wit*" (418). To move beyond this limited notion of wit, Sprat urges commentators to focus not on the "*Deformity* of things," which inevitably leads to easy humor, but to understand that "there is a nobler and more masculine Pleasure, which is rais'd from beholding their *Order* and *Beauty*" (ibid).

If the literary voice of the New Scientist is meant to derive its inspiration from an examination of the world and ultimately to behold its order and beauty, then "The Lady's Dressing Room" seems to fit the bill almost perfectly when the satirist famously concludes: "Such Order from Confusion sprung, / Such gaudy Tulips rais'd from Dung" (143–44). Because Swift's poem ultimately embodies the empirical drive of experimentation that the New Science endorses, it also beholds the order and beauty of the observed world, perhaps ironically following Sprat's aesthetic extrapolation, but following it nonetheless. The similarity between the satirist and Strephon permeates not just their universalizing conclusions, but also, even more significantly, their methods of knowledge acquisition, for the poem's final couplet reflects Strephon's and the satirist's epistemological similarity. As any reader can observe, the satirist explicitly rebukes Strephon for seeing women as disgusting. However, if the satirist's point of view is the correct one and Strephon should instead enjoy the appearance of beauty, then this maxim results in direct contradiction to the evidence "produced" in the poem. Nowhere does the description of Celia's dressing room support the view that she is a "Beauty." After the "Goddess" issues forth from her chamber in lines three and four, we only see Celia through a speculative lens that renders her increasingly abstracted and increasingly disgusting. For 140 lines, there are no hints of those "Tulips" (144), and even in the lines leading up to this famous conclusion, the text digresses: "If

Strephon would but stop his Nose" (136), claims the satirist, "He soon would learn to think like me" (141). But this contention is interrupted by a detailed, parenthetical account of Strephon "Who now so impiously blasphemes" (137) all the material objects from Celia's dressing room that he believes confirm her disgusting physicality. At precisely the moment the satirist praises the appearance of beauty, readers are reminded of the grotesque body that they have been told to imagine all along.

While the satirist explicitly condemns Strephon's claims and encourages him to look at Celia with more sympathy, his own answer employs the same speculative logic as Strephon's reading of Celia's dressing room: the poem's concluding couplet draws general principles about women and epistemology from the material evidence of the dressing room. The final couplet is not merely an ironic claim for order, as critical convention would have it, nor is it a testament to the satirist's difference. The poem's famous conclusion reminds readers of the impossibility of "real" beautiful women, and also renders this failure a feature of eighteenth-century epistemology. Vengeance's punishment encapsulates both Strephon and the satirist by forcing them to interpret women in terms of a general principle, whether it is about their overriding monstrosity or their universal desirability. Strephon and the satirist are more similar than different because their conclusions utilize and naturalize an epistemology that depends upon the denigration of the female body to produce general knowledge. Whether they are disparaged or idealized, women are still objectified and subject to the order of theories and epistemologies that promulgate an asymmetrical model of gender difference. The figure of the female body stands as the occasion for both the satirist and Strephon to exhibit the problems with knowledge. In other words, the satirist's fantasy of optical seduction itself depends upon the same logic of association that Strephon uses. The satirist comes to look more like the figure whom Sprat envisages, the wit who enjoys a "nobler and more masculine Pleasure" of "beholding . . . *Order* and *Beauty*" (418). That is, as much as Swift is known to pillory the methodology of the Moderns, both the satirist and the satiric figure (Strephon) utilize and ultimately promulgate a theory of speculation that underwrites the production of experimental knowledge — and is key to "The Lady's Dressing Room."

The epistemology of "The Lady's Dressing Room" endorses an empirical model of knowledge acquisition that has the added effect of subordinating women. The implication of my reading is that Swift introduced, but did not explore, the possibility that the deconstruction of female beauty in "The Lady's Dressing Room" allows one also to deconstruct claims of general knowledge. Speculation is prevalent, but also suspect, within Swift's satiric mode and this opens the way for my critique of the production of general knowledge and its dependence, here in particular, on the objectification and subjugation of women. To return to Sprat's warning that those who "decry the promoting of *Experiments* . . . will deprive themselves of the most fertile Subject of *Fancy*"—it seems that Swift ably manages to have his cake and eat it, too: satiric experimentation in Celia's dressing room allows Swift a most fertile subject of fancy, but one that reveals a profoundly misogynistic order of things.

III
Domestic Novels, Education, and Motherhood

6

Richardson's Closet Novels:
Virtue, Education, and the Genres of Privacy

> It is only by seeing women in their own homes,
> among their own set, just as they always are, that
> you can form any just judgment.
>
> —Jane Austen, *Emma*

IN THE PREVIOUS THREE CHAPTERS, WE CONSIDERED SATIRISTS' USES
of the dressing room trope during the late seventeenth and early eighteenth centuries. While always suggesting a connection to the "real
world," satiric dressing rooms maintain a curious in-between status that
renders them rich imaginative spaces for writers and repositories of social, aesthetic, or epistemological anxieties. The dressing room introduces a set of literary "problems" that relate to theatricality and artifice
and offers a conceptual solution to the question of privacy. Instituting
at one and the same time a boundary and a means to violate that boundary, satiric dressing rooms embody the dialectic of autonomy and obedi-
ence that characterizes eighteenth-century definitions of femininity. In
so doing, they also refer beyond their *own* apparent boundaries into the
realms of aesthetic classification and knowledge acquisition.

In the following two chapters, we shall see how domestic novelists
inherit these literary, aesthetic, and epistemological preoccupations. Beginning with the novels of Samuel Richardson, I trace the emergence
of a generic distinction between satire and the novel that is powerfully
expressed through the trope of the dressing room. With the focus in
Pamela (1740) and *Clarissa* (1747–48) on a heroine's ability to establish
modes of integrity—physical, psychological, and, in the case of Clarissa,
spiritual—Richardson redefines the dressing room as virtuous, thereby
establishing an architectural analogue for the production of virtue, epistolarity, and interiority. Following Richardson's separation of satire and
the dressing room, domestic novelists—including Charlotte Lennox,
Oliver Goldsmith, Frances Burney, Maria Edgeworth, and Jane Aus-

ten—continue to use the dressing room trope as a measure for a heroine's virtue and character, but notably reincorporate the trope's satiric
legacy and the commensurate concern with artifice and epistemology.
The dressing room in these novels is a figure for women both before
and after marriage, as both maidens and mothers. Over the course of
the eighteenth century, the dressing room trope transforms from a metaphor for aristocratic and reputedly lascivious women and actresses
into a vehicle for the representation of an apparently transparent model
of female domesticity and virtuous maternity. Within a one-hundred-
year span, the dressing room trope reformulates the question of female
sexuality and desire into an implicit celebration of sexual reproduction.
Concluding with an extended reading of Edgeworth's *Belinda*, I demonstrate the dressing room's centrality to the maturation of novelistic heroines, the recuperation of fallen mothers, and the articulation of
novelistic hierarchies.

To think about the importance of the dressing room in Richardson's
two novels, we need to begin at the beginning: Pamela's very first letter
is penned in her mistress's dressing room. This letter is a document that
not only describes Mrs. B's death and her son's rise to the head of the
household, but also recounts Pamela's first dramatic and sexually
charged encounter with her new master, Mr. B. Second, the focus of
Clarissa's days throughout her novel is on securing the privacy necessary to pen her own letters of resistance, an effort that reflects a desire
to secure the physical and psychological seclusion available in her
closet. Admittedly, this is a term distinct from the "dressing room," but
we need to be mindful of the fact that "closet" and "dressing room"
were used interchangeably by the middle of the eighteenth century; as
evidence of this, Clarissa's "closet" performs the functions of her dressing room insofar as this is where she stores her clothing, dresses for the
day, and reads and writes.[1] Finally, remember that near the end of *Clarissa*, Richardson goes to great effort to associate the *literary* legacy of the
dressing room trope with satire through a vivid return to Mrs. Sinclair's
house, which exposes the prostitutes for the horrific, Swiftian bodies
that they are. I will return to discuss all of these features of Richardson's novels in greater detail, but mention them here as a way of introducing the centrality of the dressing room trope to Richardson's works.
Perhaps most significantly, the dressing room can help us to reformulate the conundrum that has plagued readers of Richardson's novels
from the start and that continues to shape criticism of his novels: are
the heroines Pamela and Clarissa authentic or duplicitous?
    Responses to Richardson's novels generally fall along the lines of de-

fending the heroine's virtue or challenging it. Perhaps the most famous readings of *Clarissa* focus on the question of which character's "discourse" wins and is "true." William Beatty Warner interprets the novel as a struggle for supremacy between Clarissa and Lovelace, where they, "their respective allies, and the two ways of interpreting the world they embody, collide."[2] For Warner, Clarissa manipulates a rhetoric of the natural, exposing her as a dissembler who is self-centered and attempts to "hide her weaving fingers."[3] Terry Castle responds that the power differential between Clarissa and Lovelace predetermines Lovelace's success, for he is supported by political power. Clarissa's language "remains a fragmentary, futile utterance subject to the potent collective rhetoric — the patriarchal discourse of the Harlowes and Lovelace."[4] For Castle, Clarissa's language reflects the truly shattered nature of her existence and approximates a political truth about the lives of women; Clarissa herself is a cypher and "an exemplary victim of hermeneutic violence," whose "'Story' . . . is doomed to suppression, interruption, incompletion."[5] Clarissa's textual productions, therefore, are not projects of dissembling, but of authenticity.

Readings that concentrate on the heroine's behavior, rather than her language, come up against a similar bifurcation, what Caroline Gonda calls the Catch-22s that characterize *Clarissa*'s rendering of the heroine's heart and will.[6] Patricia Meyer Spacks borrows Richardson's language when she describes Clarissa as perfect but not impeccable.[7] In a later reading of Richardson, William B. Warner interprets the "difficulty" of controlling novel readers' opinions in the 1740s as the reason behind Richardson's development "of the novel author as proprietor of the book."[8] Through a reading of *Pamela*, Tassie Gwilliam contends that while the female body itself is duplicitous, Richardson's heroine is simultaneously duplicitous *and* honest.[9] For Liz Bellamy, the mid-eighteenth century was a time when the culture was unsure how individuals should act and Richardson was fully aware of the instability of the meanings — or, more precisely, the character assessments — that might be placed on his heroines.[10] Michael McKeon also acknowledges the tension in the character of Pamela, contending that there is a "subversive potentiality in Pamela" because her "progressive social character is a complex compound composed at the intersection of her two identities as a common servant and a woman."[11]

Even critics who bring cultural forces such as commerce to bear on Richardson's novels read his characters as defined by opposing values. Rita Goldberg conceptualizes the conflict of *Clarissa* as the opposition between a Christian life and commercial values; Catherine Ingrassia reads Pamela's subjectivity "firmly in a material culture preoccupied with credit, speculation, and intangible forms of property," thereby instituting a tension between domestic and commercial spheres.[12] If, as Deidre Shauna Lynch contends, the social quality of interiority and literariness derives from the newly developing practices surrounding money and credit, then Richardson is left in a double bind.[13] James Cruise understands this conflict as being shaped by Richardson's attempts to control Pamela's characterization through the employment of a moral typology, and his inability to succeed because of the novel's commercial progress.[14] More recently, Scott Paul Gordon has suggested that we read Richardson's novels through the trope of passivity in order to reshape the debate about each heroine's authenticity into a debate about the opposition between self-interest and disinterest, demonstrating, ultimately, that Richardson's heroines assume the posture of ethical disinterest.[15]

These readings of Richardson underscore the prevalence of a particular way of reading Richardson's novels and the extensive critical investment in either defending or attacking a heroine's authenticity. To my mind, it is no coincidence that a pair of novels that weave the structure of the dressing room into their plots and characterizations would elicit efforts to celebrate their heroines' worthiness or to confirm their disrepute: we should remember that Pope's *The Rape of the Lock* has produced similarly bifurcated responses to Belinda, as readers vigorously defend and attack her. While these readings provide us with plenty of insight, I believe that this dynamic of success and failure itself warrants our special consideration. As Richardson's focus seems more often on the "sensations he is eliciting than with the moral he is drawing," it is more productive to remember that Clarissa's status is immediately problematic: she has power, wants to give it away, but cannot.[16] If we instead use the trope of the dressing room as our means of interpreting Richardson's novels, then we can reformulate this question to see how Pamela and Clarissa are constituted by the *tension* between failing and succeeding. Two decades ago, Christina Marsden Gillis devoted a book-length study to matters of physical space and epistolary form in *Clarissa* and, more recently, Ruth Bernard Yeazell showed us that authenticity in *Pamela* was determined through obliquity and indirection and suggested that Richardson strives to imagine a space of female freedom.[17] Developing these insights, I argue that reading Richardson's novels, through the trope of the dressing room, will help us to overcome the binaristic interpretive options that the question of a heroine's veracity inherently presupposes. Although Richardson was, at times, infuriated by the negative readings of his heroines—going to great lengths to limit possible negative interpretations of them—he continued to depend upon a trope that foregrounded the potential for moral, sexual, and ethical dubiousness.

This chapter is concerned with a double problematic facing Richardson: the need to mark the satirically rendered dressing room dubious in
moral, epistemological, and literary terms, as well as the imperative to
advance the cause of female privacy in the dressing room by rendering
it an analogue to a heroine's virtue. To accomplish this simultaneously
generic, sexual, and ideological transformation, Richardson explicitly
associates satire with the erotic and theatrical dressing room. An opening discussion of satire illuminates the ways in which Richardson re-
vises what good satire is, voicing this aesthetic model through Clarissa
herself. The dressing room in its virtuous sense is a site for knowledge
production of the highest kind — relating to a woman's morals, modesty,
and virtue — and alludes to the pedagogical tradition that envisaged
women's intellectual potential as valuable and admirable. Satirists consistently sidelined this potential, but educationalists looked to the dressing room as a figure for the beautification of the female body and
intellect, suggesting that what results is not a duplicitous performance,
but a woman who has adorned her mind as well as her body. Ultimately, the incorporation of the dressing room trope into the domestic
novel reveals to us the mechanism by which Richardsonian narrative
consolidates an early modern psychologized novel, while simultaneously instituting moral and generic instabilities.

"UNPREPARED FOR BEING SEEN": DRESSING ROOMS AND RICHARDSON'S CRITIQUE OF SATIRE

First, we must consider the terms through which Richardson explicitly broaches the topic of his — and the dressing room's — satiric heritage. Near the very end of the monumental *Clarissa*, the novel takes the
reader back to the brothel where Lovelace imprisoned and raped the
heroine. We return through the eyes of the reformed rake Belford to
witness not only the painful deathbed of the bawd Mrs. Sinclair, but
also a belated exposé of the brothel. The brothel has always been a
place of performance, a commercial zone for the acting out of sex. During Clarissa's residence, it appeared to her to be a respectable lodging,
particularly in the inner house she rented, even though business remained vibrant in the forehouse. Once Clarissa dies, Belford is left in
the awkward rhetorical position of making the prostitutes' vice materially evident, peeling away the facade and going backstage, as it were,
to describe them in yet another letter designed to convince Lovelace to
mend his ways.

Belford's task is awkward because he must convey in persuasive, if
not graphic, terms how horrible the prostitutes are; the remarkable as-

pect of this interlude is not so much his efforts to convert Lovelace, as he has tried many times, but the editorial commentary that annotates Belford's characterization of the prostitutes: "Whoever has seen Dean Swift's *Lady's Dressing Room* will think this description of Mr Belford not only more natural but more decent painting, as well as better justi- fied by the design, and by the use that may be made of it."[18] For Jocelyn Harris, Richardson's allusion to Swift here reflects Lovelace's failed at- tempts to render the heroine pornographic, while for Brenda Bean, "Richardson's most significant change in revising the dressing room scene is to align physical decay and filthiness with moral corruption and to preserve a space both physically clean (even 'elegant') and morally pure for his exemplary woman, Clarissa."[19] To extend their arguments, consider the placement of Belford's letter within the structure of the narrative. It appears when the crisis of Clarissa's reputation must be resolved for her coffin to return to Harlowe Place in the following let- ter; Jones DeRitter reads Mrs. Sinclair's deathbed, surrounded by these prostitutes, as the bawd's "final submersion into bodily dys-ap- pearance can be read as a displacement of the whole weight of both Clarissa's physical experience and her own onto the figure of a single corrupt individual."[20] The sight of the prostitutes confirms that Clarissa is better than they are—and this is clearly the conclusion that we are meant to draw as well. Belford tells Lovelace that "as a neat and clean woman must be an angel of a creature, so a sluttish one is the impurest animal in nature" (1388). Ever anxious that his novel be interpreted "correctly" (and that it avoid the suggestion of impropriety that plagued the reception of *Pamela*), Richardson labors to distinguish Clarissa from the prostitutes who surround her for a third of the novel. Though she lived in a brothel and was raped by Lovelace, Richardson insists that Clarissa was always pure and virtuous, and that she never once ran the risk of joining the ranks of the prostitutes. Clarissa's closet, as we shall see, is exclusively a site of virtue, while the prostitutes—associated with both the dressing room and with the satiric mode—are necessarily de- bauched and perverted imitations. Even in death, Clarissa cannot re- turn to her father's house to lie in state until the novel confirms that she is free from the theatricality and eroticism associated with the dressing room and with these prostitutes. Because of Belford's language and subject matter, Richardson must identify the description as both satiric and in the tradition of Swift.

But Richardson's use of the satiric dressing room introduces addi- tional issues that we need to pursue, namely how Richardson represents the brothel in a light that confirms its degeneracy (in the interest of defending Clarissa before she returns home for good) without falling into linguistic indiscretion. In his correspondence, Richardson worries about the particular generic and moral concerns that shape the return to Mrs. Sinclair's house and the novel's use of satiric discourse: "I hope, at worst, there will be nothing either in the language or sentiments, that may be so very censurable as may be found in the works of some very high names, who have, uncalled for by their subjects, given us specimens of their wit at the expense of their modesty, and even of common decency—nay, sometimes to the dishonour of human nature."[21] Does Belford give us a specimen of his wit at the expense of his modesty and common decency? The question becomes more pressing if we believe, as Madeleine Kahn argues, that Belford is a voice for Richardson himself.[22]

Critics have long noted Richardson's vexed attitude toward satire and satirists. John Carroll argues that Richardson did not criticize satire as a genre when discussing Pope and Swift, but "frequently objected to their methods as satirists and deplored the hearts capable of conceiving the animosity which pervaded their writings."[23] When Richardson claims that Belford's text is more natural, more decent, better justified by design and use, he attempts to draw aesthetic and implicitly ideological distinctions between his narrative and satire. It is clear that Richardson regards satire with suspicion, beginning with the list of characters in *Clarissa*. By naming the "haughty, vindictive, [and] humorously vain" (preface, 37) protagonist Lovelace, the novelist explicitly evokes a range of satiric connotations both to mark this character as undesirable and to critique satire more generally. "Lovelace," of course, specifically alludes to the seventeenth-century poet and rake, although the life and works of Rochester also inspired Richardson.[24] Living up to his literary namesake, Lovelace refers to satiric texts several times.[25] Even the sound of the name suggests that he is less than desirable: as one character puts it, he is truly "Luveless" (984).[26]

In spite of these negative versions of satire, Richardson still uses it, prompting Ronald Paulson to call Richardson a "satiro-novelist."[27] Paulson devotes attention to Anna Howe's satire, arguing that it is necessary "to give distance and suggest certain hidden truths, such as Clarissa's attraction to Lovelace" and "to keep Clarissa on an even keel," but the role of satire in the novel's characterization of Clarissa, particularly as a model for feminine virtue, has received little critical attention.[28] Through the voices of his heroine and later the reformed rake Belford, Richardson explicates a theory of satiric method and context that struggles to harness the parodic power of the satiric mode for admirable (at least in Richardson's eyes) ends; *Clarissa* redefines what good satire is and how it should function. Clarissa devotes the most attention to the form of satire that is appropriate and, in Richardson's terms, "decent" and "natural" in two episodes, one in an early letter to Anna

Howe and the second in her own brothel scene. Writing to Anna, Clarissa reprimands her friend for the young woman's raillery of her own suitor, Hickman. Anna, according to Clarissa, is a satirist, "too cruel, too *ungenerous* . . . in [her] behaviour to a man who loves [her] so dearly, and is so worthy and so sincere a man" (280). The occasion of Anna's abuse prompts Clarissa to articulate the situations in which satire is not only permissible, but also useful. Satire:

> is intended to instruct; and though it bites, it pleases at the same time: no fear of a wound's rankling or festering by so delicate a point as you carry; not envenomed by *personality*, not intending to expose, or ridicule, or exasperate. The most admired of our moderns know nothing of this art. Why? Because it must be founded in good nature, and directed by a right heart. The *man*, not the *fault*, is the subject of *their* satire: and were it to be *just*, how should it be *useful*? How would it answer any good purpose? When every gash (for their weapon is a broadsword, not a lancet) lets in the air of public ridicule, and exasperates where it should heal. Spare me not therefore, because I am your *friend*. For *that* very reason spare me not. I may *feel* your edge, fine as it is; I may be pained: you would lose your end if I were not: but after the first sensibility (as I have said more than once before), I will love you the better, and my amended heart shall be all yours; and it will then be more worthy to be yours. (280)

Clarissa's point is just the distinction that Swift's speaker ridicules in the preface to *A Tale of a Tub* (1704). Swift argues that "you may securely display your utmost *Rhetorick* against Mankind, in the Face of the World. . . . And when you have done, the whole Audience, far from being offended, shall return you thanks as a Deliverer of precious and useful Truths."[29] But if the critique is personal or, in the language of Clarissa, of the man (rather than the fault), Swift warns that the satirist "must expect to be imprisoned for *Scandalum Magnatum*: to have *Challenges* sent him; to be sued for *Defamation*; and to be *brought before the Bar of the House*."[30] The Swiftian echo here illuminates Richardson's efforts to narrow the scope of Swift's satire. Rather than demolish or question, Richardson envisages good satire upholding moral hierarchies.

Clarissa argues that satire is not useful if it is personal, but this claim raises several problems, especially in her analysis of Anna's satire. Here Richardson articulates a satiric structure that is entirely pedagogic, but the nature of that pedagogy depends upon some amount of the shame that Clarissa derides. As she explains, Anna's satire "bites" and "pleases" at the same time. Indeed, the pleasure derived from a satiric attack is open to question, for Richardson here appears to endorse a model of shaming that is limited only by the "good nature" of the satirist. The satiric object must experience the pain of humiliation, but not too much of it. Clarissa contends that the sharp wounds of good satire ultimately heal the satiric object and conceptualizes good satire through the metaphor of the lancet, as opposed to the destructive effects of a broadsword. The subject envisaged by this model of satire is one who experiences pain, followed by gratitude and moral transformation. But this sequence of experience is as tenuous as its founding assumption that pain leads to gain. In Clarissa's analysis of good satire, Richardson attempts to stabilize a mode of rhetoric that is not only invested in constructing its own authority, but that also inevitably betrays the impossibility of doing so. By focusing on the effects of satire, Richardson is able to distance his heroine—and his novelistic model—from the difficulties that we have seen associated with satiric discourse in chapter 3. It also allows Richardson to establish a generic rivalry between the narrative penned by Clarissa and her admirers, and the satiric mode that informed so many of the popular representations of female subjectivity and privacy that we have seen in previous chapters.

When one turns to Clarissa's treatment of a rhetorical sibling of satire, wit, Richardson's emphasis on the pedagogical importance of satire coincides with the effect of Clarissa's language on those around her—and this takes place, appropriately enough, in the novel's brothel. Belford recalls to Lovelace the evening Clarissa spent with Lovelace's friends and the prostitutes: "We talked of *wit*, and of *wit*, and aimed at it, bandying it like a ball from one to another of us, and resting it chiefly with thee," the man whom Richardson describes elsewhere as "the daring, learned, witty, and thence dangerous Libertine Lovelace" (711).[31] Belford's memory alludes to Swift's characterization of satire in the preface to *A Tale of a Tub*. Satire, writes Swift, "'tis but a *Ball*, bandied to and fro, and every Man carries a *Racket* about Him to strike it from himself among the rest of the Company."[32] The allusion aligns Swiftian satire with the degenerate figures who ape it in the brothel. To them, it seems to be a harmless game of rhetorical hot potato, and a means through which the most successful gain popularity and renown. But to Clarissa, wit is an entirely more serious affair, and its use must be different for men and for women.

Clarissa's disquisition on wit enables Richardson to articulate the moral paradigm in which satire ought to operate, and she refashions it in the place where words are merely signs of performance. Clarissa draws her definitions from two Abraham Cowley poems, "Ode of Wit" and "On the Death of Mrs. Philips." Clarissa recites verse paragraphs from Cowley's poetry to define wit not through its formal structure, but by its association with decency. She renounces immodest language— wit ought not make "a virgin hide her face"—and argues that wit must be joined with virtue; if not, it is like a vine "deform'd, and rotting on the ground" (712). Belford describes her recitation as so good that it "would have made bad poetry delightful" (711). And it seems she does, or at least her performance makes sense of Cowley. Richardson admired the metaphysical (he "has great merit with me"), but others were more critical; as Morris Corbyn argues in 1744, Cowley "had no clear Idea of *Wit*."[33] Clarissa's delivery—her own form—provides as much persuasion as the selection of her illustrative passages, for her reading leaves the motley audience quiet in their shame, until Lovelace follows up her reading with his own definition of wit, mostly so that he would "not seem to be surprised into silent modesty" (712). Clarissa performs satire in the brothel, redefining the stance that satirists for generations have used to objectify, censure, and ridicule women, and enacting this reformation in a dressing-room-like space. Her performance and Belford's commentary about its effect suggest the elements of wit, and by extension, satiric discourse that Richardson valued: support of established moral codes and the power to compel readers to adhere to those codes.

To return to the scene at Mrs. Sinclair's house: reformation of the prostitutes clearly seems out of the question. Reformation of Lovelace is, however, Belford's ostensible motive: "Oh Lovelace! I have a scene to paint in relation to the wretched Sinclair, that if I do it justice will make thee seriously ponder and reflect, or nothing can" (1386). As a reformed rake satirizing the evil Mrs. Sinclair and her prostitutes, Belford is practically guaranteed of using the satiric mode appropriately—at least, within this narrative's logic. Just a few paragraphs later, Belford uses Pope's *To a Lady* to critique the viewpoint that he thinks it espouses. Belford writes, "We rakes, indeed, are bold enough to suppose that women in general are as much rakes in their *hearts*, as the libertines some of themselves to be taken with are in their *practice*" (1393). Richardson insists upon the redefinition of satiric discourse throughout Belford's letter. The language must avoid the risk of delving into the immodest and indecent, and it must be adopted for specifically moral ends.

As to the language, Belford's description borrows from typical satiric dressing room scenes. He offers an image of greasy, ugly women, with "slipshod" clothing "hanging trollopy" (1387). They are likewise "(unpadded, shoulder-bent, pallid-lipped, feeble-jointed wretches) appearing from a blooming nineteen or twenty perhaps overnight, haggard well-worn strumpets of thirty-eight or forty" (1387–88). In the midst of this kind of description, Belford puts the prostitutes in an explicitly satiric context in order to suggest that the sight of them would disgust any spectator and would lead naturally to moral reprobation. As he explains to Lovelace:

I am the more particular in describing to thee the appearance these creatures made in my eyes when I came into the room, because I believe thou
never sawest any of them, much less a group of them, thus unprepared for
being seen. . . . If thou *hadst*, I believe thou wouldst hate a profligate woman
as one of Swift's Yahoos, or Virgil's obscene Harpies squirting their ordure
upon the Trojan trenchers; since the persons of such in their retirements are
as filthy as their minds. (1388)

Some have suggested that Belford is constructed as another
Strephon, rifling through the underclothes of women to prove their
falseness, but Belford's conclusions are methodologically different from
Strephon's.[34] As we saw in chapter 5, Strephon's satiric experimentation in Celia's dressing room produces a general truth that women — all
women — are disgusting, a perspective that leaves the voyeur simultaneously obsessive and repulsed. In contrast, Belford's complaint begins in
the realm of physical decay and uses this trope to advance the hypothesis that these specific women, not all women, are unappealing not because they are physically disgusting, but because they are *morally*
reprobate.

As to the use of satire here, the passage is ostensibly designed to convert Lovelace and to be an example of satire producing self-controlled
subjects. But the novelist's claim that a single description could finally
provoke a change of heart in Lovelace with regard to the prostitutes
and Clarissa is rather suspect, given that Belford has been reprimanding his friend for several hundred pages already, to no avail. In a seemingly self-conscious moment, the editor adds an awkward explanation
for the visit to the novel's otherwise conventional chapter summary,
claiming that Mrs. Sinclair's house has never been fully condemned.[35]
Any reader knows by this point that the house is a house of evil and
treachery. Clarissa is dead and we are, after all, near the end of the
novel. In short, Lovelace is not ready to reform and the reader already
knows the brothel is bad.

In the absence of an explicit moral use, Belford's description of Mrs.
Sinclair's house runs the risk of obscenity: these passages could very
well make an eighteenth-century virgin hide her face because they are
not necessarily joined with virtue. The issue of narrative decency, the
issue that Fielding exploits in *Shamela*, is particularly tricky for Richardson, insofar as this account of Mrs. Sinclair's house threatens to
upset the novel's strict attention to decorum. Belford's letter may be
more "decent" than Swift's poetry (there are no chamber pots, after
all), but his phrases and descriptions imitate dressing room satires by
focusing on the degenerating bodies of sexually and morally dubious
women. Richardson's text seems to be open to the same criticisms that

he himself lodges: Belford uses satiric voyeurism to "give us specimens of [his] wit at the expense of [his] modesty, and even of common decency," to quote Richardson's letter again. The central aesthetic and ideological reason for the Dover House letter, therefore, concerns the effect of this experience on Belford himself and the conclusions *he* draws from it, suggesting, in the end, an uneasy reliance on the satiric strategies of objectification and denunciation deeply associated with the satiric dressing room. Richardson uses Belford's letter to indict the lewd, to idealize the virtuous, and to present all this material as serving the conversion of a reader (here Lovelace), even though the most dramatic effect is on Belford, our surrogate. Whether ultimately successful or not, Belford's letter, the last on this subject before Clarissa returns home, is designed to expunge any hint of impropriety from Clarissa and her virtuous narrative by associating theatricality, sexuality, and the Swiftian satiric mode with both libertinism and prostitution, and by reserving moralistic satire for his heroine and her surrogates.

"THE BEAUTIES OF THE MIND": WOMEN'S LEARNING AND THE PEDAGOGY OF THE CLOSET

With the artifice and sexuality of the satiric dressing room explicitly—if not necessarily successfully—denounced through Belford's exposé of the brothel, we must now consider how Richardson sets about providing an alternative mode of privacy for women. It will depend, in large part, on the evocation of the dressing room as a site for learning, alluding to its predecessor, the gentleman's closet. The goal of assigning "bad" satire to the realm of sexual indiscretion is concomitant with Richardson's reconfiguration of the dressing room as a closet and its particular association with the production of intellectual and moral virtue. As we saw in chapter 2, the dressing room did not solely connote theatricality and eroticism, but was also deeply implicated in the practice of study, and it is this alternate genealogy that Richardson foregrounds in both *Pamela* and in *Clarissa*.

The topic of women's education in the eighteenth century was controversial. Lady Mary Wortley Montagu's complaint in 1753 illustrates the conundrum: "I think it the highest Injustice to be debarr'd the Entertainment of my Closet, and that the same Studies which raise the character of a Man should hurt that of a Woman."[36] From its entrance into the English figurative vocabulary, the language of the dressing room, especially the association with cosmetics that we explored in chapter 4, shaped discussions of pedagogical reform and theory. Harriet Guest notes in another context that "feminine learning is perceived with increasing insistence in the mid- to late century in a parallel relation to fashionable elegance," but we shall see that the convergence between a woman being beautifully adorned and a woman being intellectually appealing was evident earlier.[37]

Henry Care's *The Female Secretary: or, Choice New Letters* (1671) voices a debate about the merits and dangers of women's education and employs the rhetoric of the dressing room to support both viewpoints. One correspondent conflates a bad makeup job with superficial education: "Womens smattering in Learning only adds *Confidence* to their *natural impertinence*, and does no less mischief to their Souls, than *Painting* to their Faces, the one destroying their *native Colour*, the other enfeebling that small portion of *common sense* they are born to."[38] Care's advocate for women's education reverses this analogy to argue that learning will render women desirable, even if they are not necessarily physically attractive:

> I hereby design to fortify our selves with *new Arms* for the support of our *Empire*, wherein all the *homely Girls*, and *Reverend Matrons* at least are obliged in point of Interest to joyn, that so when Age or Sickness have blasted the *Roses* and *Lillies* of our Cheeks, plundred our Eyes of their *Killing Artillery*, and banished the Aery inviting Spirits thence, we may still have some Charms left to detain the fleeting hearts of votaries to the *Wit* and *Learning* of our age, no less than to the springing *Beauty* of our Youth.[39]

To support women's education is not to threaten to institute "the *Salique Law* in Schools, and make the Muses forswear their Sex, and put on Breeches."[40] Care assures readers that teaching women will not make them into men, just the provision that Richard A. Barney argues is characteristic of women educationalists during this period.[41] Mary Astell's proposal for a women's school offers a more famous example adopted to advance the cause of female learning. For Astell, learning is merely another facet of the toilet, and it will make women better wives and mothers, an outcome designed ultimately to support a patriarchal social structure.[42] Her design is to "improve your Charms and heighten your Value. . . . Its aim is to fix that Beauty, to make it lasting and permanent, which Nature with all the helps of Art cannot secure" and education will "procure you such Ornaments as all the Treasures of the Indies are not able to purchase."[43] Astell utilizes language of empire to persuade her readers; she also alludes to the traditional function of a young woman's dressing room—to make her beautiful for the marriage market, and to raise her value—even while critiquing this same function.[44]

Pedagogical writers likewise discussed women's education in the context of the superficial values of theatricality and cosmetic beauty that had been historically linked to the dressing room. James Burgh's *Thoughts on Education* (1747) is particularly critical of the pedagogical emphasis on women's beauty, and suggests that if there is no "inner" beauty, then an appealing surface only emphasizes this absence: "ornaments or trappings . . . serve only to make the defect of real inward worth the more conspicuous."[45] A late-eighteenth-century conduct book, *The Female Ægis; or, The Duties of Women from Childhood to Old Age* (1798), concurs that women's appearances are overvalued, arguing in similar language that "Ornamental accomplishments too frequently occupy the rank and estimation which ought to have been assigned to objects of infinitely higher importance."[46]

The point for these educational theorists and conduct book writers is that, in Burgh's words, "accomplishments of the mind" last longer than physical beauty.[47] Burgh utilizes the dressing room trope to encourage a program of self-improvement, writing that "When a handsom young woman views herself in a glass, instead of being puffed up with pride and self-admiration,"

> it is her business to take care that her mind be as well adorned with the Christian graces and virtues as her face is by the exquisite hand of Nature with a just mixture of the lily and the rose; to consider the superficial beauty she and others admire is every day drawing nearer to old age, wrinkles, and corruption; but that the beauties of her mind will still be improving to all eternity; to remember, that however amiable and delicate any human form may appear to the eye, there is nothing more mortifying than the consideration of the gross substances our bodies consist of, and the many nauseous and disagreeable properties of them; and that if beauty is really in any degree valuable, it ought to fill the person possessed of it with gratitude to Him, who bestowed it, and inspire her with the ambition of improving her mind suitably, and so become an object the most completely amiable that the eye of man can behold, which I believe every one will own is, A woman whose person is adorned with affected beauty, and her mind with Good-nature, Prudence, Virtue, and Religion.[48]

Rather than pursing the amusements available in town, young women ought to be encouraged to develop a love of reading; "I don't mean plays, romance, or love-poetry," writes Burgh, since they "all tend to give their minds a wrong cast," but "books on moral and divine subjects," "History, and Biography or the Lives of eminent men."[49] Many conduct books respond to the concern Burgh articulates and explicitly address the question of what women ought to think about in their dressing rooms, a preoccupation reflected in titles such as *The Ladies Cabinet, or a Companion for the Toilet* (1743) and *The Young Ladies*

Companion, or, Beauty's Looking-Glass (1740). Such books frequently include essays, sermons, and model letters, both religious and practical. But more importantly, for all of these writers, the dressing room ought to be a site of *reflection* for women, not just of their physical appearance, but also of their moral and intellectual development. While the emancipatory potential of the dressing room as a study is confined to the rubric of a woman's desirability—the "reasonable Creatures" whom Addison and Steele admire within the pages of the *Spectator* for "join[ing] all the Beauties of the Mind to the Ornaments of Dress, and inspire a kind of Awe and Respect, as well as Love, into their Male-Beholders"[50]—this constitution of the dressing room nonetheless makes room for women to develop themselves as legitimate, active learners.

DESPERATELY SEEKING VIRTUE:
THE POLITICS OF PRIVACY IN *PAMELA*

In thinking about Richardson's appropriation of the dressing room trope, we have noted the novelist's efforts to render the satiric dressing room a signifier of debauchery. But as the previous section indicates, Richardson had at his disposal an alternative to the theatrical and erotic dressing room, that of the space for virtuous and valuable intellectual production. In what follows, I argue that this tension between the two competing meanings of female privacy in the dressing room structures Richardson's first novel, *Pamela*. As mentioned earlier, Pamela's opening letter is set in the recently deceased Mrs. B's dressing room where Mr. B, the surviving son and heir, praises Pamela for being a "good Girl" and promises that he will be "a Friend" (26) to her. The dead mother's dressing room is a space of refuge for Pamela, a place where she composes and hides the letters that come to document her virtue. William B. Warner reminds us that there are two narrative trajectories possible in *Pamela*, based on the novel's "intertexts" of "the conduct-book guide tradition and the novel of amorous intrigue," and that they are both unacceptable, forcing Richardson to develop a hybrid form.[51] However, rather than "steer its characters between the Scylla of virtuous withdrawal and the Charybdis of complaint seduction," the novel insistently holds the two plots in tension by idealizing the virtuous narrative through the pressure of its possible failure.[52] Therefore, when Mr. B plucks a letter that Pamela begins to hide in her "Bosom" and warns her to "do as [she] *should* do" (26), the dressing room also underscores the sexual and social potential of her relationship with Mr. B, a potential that threatens to make Pamela more like the prostitutes Richardson satirizes late in *Clarissa* than a virtuous heroine.

Readers since Fielding have taken this second viewpoint and suggested that the novel *Pamela* tells not a tale of virtue rewarded, but of sexual virtue commodified. Following Allen Michie's observation that "it seems to have always been, and to always be, almost impossible to read [Richardson and Fielding] free from the horizon of the other," I offer Fielding's *Shamela* (1741) as an example of the nascent eroticism in Richardson's text.[53] Shamela and Mr. Booby speak of her "vartue" for hours on end, hours that are explicitly figured as foreplay. As Shamela admits to her mother, "I thought once of making a little fortune by my person. I now intend to make a great one by my vartue."[54] Shamela's "vartue" is actually a vice (Mr. Booby thinks she's a virgin, but Shamela had a child the previous year), and Fielding's Parson Tickletext is there to remind us of the voyeuristic pleasure readers get from this kind of titillating epistolary tale. The author of *Pamela Censured* (1741) likewise argues that the novel contains "such Scenes of Love, and such lewd Ideas, as must fill the Youth that read them with Sentiments and Desires worse than Rochester can."[55] These responses mark a central difficulty for Richardson: while he adopts the dressing room metaphor to represent Pamela's virtue, alluding to the pedagogical tradition that valued women's intellectual and moral beautification, the trope likewise conjures up the image of a woman's sexuality. Contemporary responses highlight this bifurcation. At one and the same time, *Pamela* was recommended reading by one Reverend Benjamin Slocock, from his pulpit of St. Saviour's Church, Southwark, while it was pilloried by others for representing "one low, private, strumpet's shame."[56] When Richardson "invokes duplicity and hypocrisy in his representation of Pamela," he does it explicitly through the trope of the dressing room.[57] The central critical response to *Pamela*—is she a virtuous or a fallen woman?—begins in the novel's opening pages, in the space of the dressing room. And it is compounded by the novel's other great use of the dressing room, the scene in which Pamela prepares for her departure and dresses in clothes appropriate to her station. With a torrent of detail, Pamela describes every feature of her outfit, only to conclude that she "look'd about me in the Glass, as proud as any thing.—To say Truth, I never lik'd myself so well in my Life" (60). The mirror not only "blinds her to the social controls that create and define her," but it also reflects the novel's tension between theatricality and authenticity.[58]

Consider the opening letter at greater length: soon after Pamela completes the first letter to her parents, Mr. B bursts into the dressing room and finds her "scribbling." The body of Pamela's letter both details and obscures her precarious position within the household now that Mrs. B has died, particularly the fact that she has been singled out by Mr. B for special attention, but her postscript describing their encounter in the dressing room throws this delicate balance into crisis. When Mr. B enters the dressing room, Pamela's reaction suggests that she interprets his behavior as an invasion not only of her private space, but also of her private thoughts and writing, a conflation that firmly links architecture and psychology throughout the novel. But this scene inaugurates another, equally important, conflation: the figural substitution of Pamela's virtuous body with her ability to claim physical privacy. Pamela's "frightned" reaction shows that she knows "that however kind, this is her master's first attack."[59]

The dressing room in *Pamela* is vulnerable to "attack" because any and all private spaces are defined by their vulnerability to violation, as discussed in chapter 1. But the dressing room in *Pamela* underscores this vulnerability, for it is only a tenuously private space for the young servant girl. The dressing room that stages the novel's first scene is the recently absented dressing room of Mr. B's dead mother. It is owned by no one, but *open* to Pamela, Mrs. Jervis, and Mr. B. Within these admittedly fragile boundaries, Pamela overcomes Mr. B's attempts at seduction. When Pamela describes feeling "sham'd" and "frightned," and asks for Mr. B's forgiveness—"yet I know not for what" (26)—she subtly acknowledges the extent to which her virtue is under attack as well as her problematic status in the household—not fully a servant and yet certainly not a member of the family. In return, Mr. B asserts his role as a master by alluding to Pamela's sense of duty to him, rather than to her parents, and by commanding her to "Be faithful, and diligent; and do as you should do" (ibid.). The threat behind Mr. B's command highlights Pamela's dilemma; allegiance to her parents and her sexual virtue, or duty to her master and his sexual will. Pamela is marked as different because of her reading and writing; indeed, although she acquires the rather comical responsibility of caring for Mr. B's linen, she also gains assurances from him that she may continue to use Mrs. B's library, so long as she takes care of the books. Two things shock Mr. B: Pamela's insistence that she is not his property, much less his sexual property, and the fact that she writes letters.[60] Her handwriting is admirable, her learning surprising. The space of the dressing room allows Pamela a certain intellectual freedom in which she may read from Mrs. B's library, compose her letters, and textually construct herself, but it also encloses Pamela within the confines of Mr. B's regulation and the threat of his censure and encroachment, within the snare of his designs.

Richardson's novel uses the dressing room to institute a foundational difficulty that mirrors Pamela's own struggle to protect her sexual virtue, namely the architectural possibility for Pamela to claim privacy and the constraints on this potential instituted by Mr. B's machinations.

While simultaneously arranging to have her letters delivered to him before they are sent to her parents, Mr. B also arranges to have some of
Pamela's letters snatched outright. Pamela does not know she is under
surveillance, but she does sense that something is not quite right. She
writes of her unease to her parents: "And when I had finish'd my Letter,
I put it under the Toilet, in my late Lady's Dressing-room, where nobody comes but myself and Mrs. *Jervis*, besides my Master; but when I
came up again to seal it up, to my great Concern it was gone" (37). This
"great Concern," in turn, eventually prompts Pamela to hide the letters
on her body, among other places, and the sign of Pamela's bosom carries the weight of this transformation. From the opening letter, which
Pamela tries to hide in her bosom, to Mr. B's groping—Pamela "found
[Mr. B's] Hand in my Bosom" (67), after he hid in Mrs. Jervis's
closet—the space of the dressing room emblematizes the eroticized female body and the agent of that body registering violation.

Mr. B waits several hundred pages to undress Pamela at his Lincolnshire estate (under the pretense of untacking her journal from her clothing), but he begins this process metonymically, appropriately enough,
in his mother's dressing room. He gives the young heroine pieces of
clothing from his mother's wardrobe, which he fingers as he prepares
to give them away. The objects he hands over are of the intimate kind
and bring Pamela's own sexual knowledge to the surface, highlighting,
too, her embarrassment for even possessing such knowledge. Mr. B's
gifts include "Four Pair of fine white Cotton Stockens, and Three Pair
of fine Silk ones; and Two Pair of rich Stays, and a Pair of rich Silver
Buckles in one Pair of the Shoes" (31). Ever excited by items of luxury,
Pamela cautiously adds, "I was inwardly asham'd to take the Stockens"
(ibid.). Pamela is inwardly ashamed because she knows that her private
parts are supposed to remain private and these stockings lead right up
to them. In response, Mr. B makes the erotic potential of underclothing
explicit by asking of her, "Dost think I don't know pretty Maids wear
Shoes and Stockens?" (ibid.). Both Pamela (through her blush) and
Mr. B (through his question) associate this clothing with a sexualized
female body. Richardson uses the power of metonymy to color both of
his characters, but the metonymy has a specific referent: sex. Jean-Jacques Rousseau adapts Richardson's strategy of erotic substitution to a
seduction scene in his novel *La Nouvelle Héloïse* (1761). The scene in
question features the lover Saint-Preux surreptitiously gaining access
to his beloved's dressing room when she is absent. Nevertheless, he
searches for traces of Julie's presence in the material objects that she
has left behind, especially her clothing. Each object prompts the lover
to speculate that he feels his mistress nearby: "I imagine that I hear the
pleasing sound of your voice. All the parts of your scattered dress pres-

ent to my ardent imagination those of your body that they conceal."[61] Julie's clothing, like those stockings that embarrass Pamela, does not serve its conventional purpose of clothing the female body. Instead, Saint-Preux handles each article of clothing as if he were taking it off Julie's body, and it is by this means that Rousseau creates a narrative that metonymically undresses the heroine in absentia. Moving from her headdress, to her bodice shawl, to her gown, to her slippers, and finally to her stays, Saint-Preux acts out a fanciful seduction of his mistress in anticipation of the consummation of their relationship in the following letter.

The example of Rousseau points to the real source of shame for Pamela: hers is a narrative of seduction. Richardson's novel charts the sense of violation that the young heroine feels as a result of the association between her body and her privacy.[62] As Mr. B's advances become more explicit, and as Pamela's ability to secure privacy becomes more compromised, her attitude toward the dressing room changes. No longer a refuge, its seclusion houses danger, treachery, and duplicity: "the Closet, which was my good Lady's Dressing-room, [was] a Room I once lov'd, but then as much hated" (43). Not coincidentally, Pamela's sharp rebukes to Mr. B point to the dressing room as a space of sexual opportunism (followed by his advances in other places throughout the Bedfordshire, and later the Lincolnshire, estates) when she reminds the young son "That my good Lady did not desire your Care to extend to the Summer-house and her Dressing-room" (63).

For Richardson to place a virtuous heroine inside of a dressing room (one not even hers to claim) only makes his goal of representing a paragon of virtue that much more difficult. But for Richardson, this is a necessary move. This is not to replicate Ruth Bernard Yeazell's contention that "modesty is the resistance that enables courtship," but to argue that the very thin line between virtue and vice — between an admirable woman and a fallen woman — is drawn throughout Richardson's first novel and becomes part of the narrative's moral.[63] If Mr. B were to succeed in his attempts to "Dressing-room" Pamela, as she describes it, Richardson's tale could mutate into a harlot's progress. That Pamela avoids this fate makes her virtuous. Indeed, in Richardson's third novel, *Sir Charles Grandison*, the abducted heroine Harriet Byron is confirmed unseduced by the fact that she spent no more than six minutes alone with her kidnapper Sir Hargrave Pollexfen, but this point of reputation must be confirmed by three separate accounts. In Richardson's logic, the fact that neither heroine falls just proves how virtuous each is. Richardson's constitutive association between violation and virtue reveals its performativity: virtue is defined by being constantly under attack, just as the privacy of the dressing room is articulated through the threat of

its violation.[64] The *OED*'s definition emphasizes that "virtue" is a concept to be protected, and it is this process of defending virtue that, paradoxically, generates its meaning. Virtue is "conformity of life and
conduct with the principles of morality; voluntary observance of the
recognized moral laws or standards of right conduct; abstention on
moral grounds from any form of wrong-doing or vice." Since virtue is
a behavior that avoids transgression of norms that themselves may be
fluid, it is a category of identity that must be maintained and proven,
over and over again. This dependence upon reiteration, however, exposes the cracks in virtue, for, as Judith Butler has shown us, each of
these reiterations suggests that this category of identity "runs the risk
of being *de*-instituted at every interval."[65]

Richardson regularly places his heroines in danger to prove their virtue, but he is certainly not unique. Richard Allestree's conduct manual
The Ladies Calling (1676) spends twenty-seven pages explaining only the
ways that women's modesty may be violated, not *what* it is.[66] The quality
cannot be defined in positive terms, only relationally: "the Vertue of
Modesty . . . may be considered in a double notion, the one as it is opposed to Boldness and Indecency, the other to Lightness and Wantonness."[67] Allestree's primary message is that modesty is defined by being
defended: "the best way therefore to countermine those Stratagems of
men, is for women to be suspiciously vigilant even of the first approaches. He that means to defend a Fort, must not abandon the Out-
works, and she that will secure her Chastity, must never let it come too
close a siege, but repel the very first and most remote insinuations of a
Temter."[68] These observations read like a road map for Richardson's
Pamela, as well as a template for *Clarissa*: Richardson observes that
"Like pure Gold, tried by the Fire of Affliction, [Clarissa] is found
pure," while Lovelace argues that virtue is not worthwhile unless tested
and that if Clarissa fails, then no woman is virtuous.[69] Paradoxically, as
Tassie Gwilliam suggests, conduct books such as *The Ladies Calling* police "both male and female gender roles, . . . but women are held responsible for initiating the dislocation."[70] The significant difference between
Richardson and Allestree is that the former pens a narrative structure
that depends upon the dialectic of encroachment and resistance to move
forward. Therefore, Pamela is placed in situation after situation in
which her virtue must be tested in order to be validated, a circumstance
that opens up the possibility that her virtue is "*de*-instituted" and almost
seamlessly gives rise to contemporaries' accusations of lewdness. The
fundamental instability of the dressing room trope, as rendered in *Pamela*, demonstrates that Richardson adopts a metaphor whose meanings
allow the novelist to develop a narrative preoccupied with the active
production of virtue. But his appropriation of the dressing room simul-

taneously and problematically introduces the possibility that Pamela is, indeed, Shamela.

"HER CLOSET HER PARADISE": *CLARISSA*

As we have seen, Richardson's first novel appropriates the dressing room to inculcate a model of virtuous femininity, but in so doing likewise introduces the means through which this claim to virtue might be challenged. *Pamela* holds a fragile grip on the educational strain of the dressing room's contemporary associations, meanings that Richardson did not fully appropriate until he composed his second novel. *Clarissa* embraces the dressing room trope to draw a model for female education that facilitates women's intellectual and moral independence, rendering her the ideal "modest Lady" who views "her Closet [as] her Paradise."[71] But, as we shall see, Clarissa's claims to privacy and authenticity come under a certain amount of pressure, limitations that are ultimately inherent to the trope of the dressing room and that produce the critical question that has plagued the novel from its original publication — is Clarissa an emblem of true, uncompromised virtue? Or is she an embodiment of flaws that call this virtue into question? In the pages that follow, I offer two accounts of the novel that prove Richardson's heroine may very well be considered both of these.

In this first mode of reading the novel as a testament to a heroine's virtue, one notes that Richardson follows the general principles that an advocate such as James Burgh outlines and so envisages a heroine with critical skills. Clarissa Harlowe is a self-consciously educated and knowledgeable heroine — and rightfully so. Part of Richardson's efforts in *Clarissa* can certainly be traced to his concern that this novel forestall, at least implicitly, the criticism engendered by Pamela's sexuality. In its most obvious acknowledgment of the conflicted meanings of the dressing room, *Clarissa* uses the period's alternate word for the dressing room, the closet. Although "dressing room" and "closet" designate a similar space by this point, Richardson's choice of terminology can be read as a preliminary attempt to evict any association with eroticism or performance from the representation of Clarissa's privacy. Richardson's second, and more notable, alteration is to change his heroine's status and thereby to forestall the question of duplicity that plagued the reception of *Pamela*: Clarissa is no eroticized housemaid in her mistress's dressing room, subject to the advances of the young son, and anxious to rise in class and status. To provide a moral model of privacy, one that is free from the suggestion of theatricality or sexuality, Richardson creates a heroine who has a fortune and a room of her own.

Following this pattern of feminine propriety, Clarissa's closet holds her library, her papers, and her clothing, the traditional setup of the eighteenth-century dressing room. From her perspective, privacy is the ability to maintain sexual, intellectual, and spiritual integrity. Before the novel begins, this is the place where she spends at least three hours a day devoted to "closet-duties" (1470) — reading and writing about being a virtuous young woman. It is also where she produces her correspondence with Anna Howe, who reflects that their letters are "domestic and sedentary" and "innocent" (75), just the sort of behavior that Richardson advocates in his correspondence with Sophia Westcomb: "I have taken care to make my Clarissa . . . inculcate this doctrine — that all the intellectual pleasures a lady can give herself, not neglecting the necessary employments that shall make her shine in her domestic duties, should be given."[72] If Clarissa uses her closet properly, insists her tyrannical brother James Harlowe, Jr., then it is a space for "*private devotions*" (119) where she is schooled for her future as a Lady Bountiful, the role her grandfather envisaged for her by bequeathing the dairy house to her.[73]

Clarissa clearly has spent time reading in her closet, and her letters and library prove it. Once her family begins to insist that Clarissa marry the odious Solmes, she spends even more time writing in her closet, composing impassioned letters. Her Uncle John Harlowe criticizes Clarissa for swaying everyone's opinion but her own, which, he argues, makes the family stand together more firmly (253); Mrs. Harlowe insists to her daughter that "reading was more to the purpose, at present, than writing: that by the one, I might be taught my duty; that the other, considering whom I was believed to write to, only stiffened my will" (328). Clarissa also engages in an interpretive battle with her brother over the correct meaning of Virgil's *Georgics*; she reprimands him for suggesting that she consult Dryden's translation, both indicting James, Jr. for his lack of humanity (this, in spite of his humanistic university education) and showing off her own classical learning by quoting Juvenal XV (218–19). In the will she drafts in her lodgings above Mr. Smith's glove shop in London, Clarissa bequeaths this library to her cousin Dolly Hervey with the observation that they are "not ill chosen for a woman's library," and that the volumes contain Clarissa's marginalia as well as "some very judicious" (1415) observations written by Dr. Lewen, the family's preacher.[74] Through these gifts, Clarissa signals that Dolly is marked as her heir apparent, another young, virtuous woman who shall be trained in the closet-duties that have shaped Clarissa's own virtuous character.

Clarissa, like *Pamela*, depends upon the narrative dialectic of encroachment and resistance; therefore the potential of Clarissa's closet for intellectual independence is challenged in many ways by her family because her behavior threatens the family's plans and they respond by struggling to take control of her. Tom Keymer argues that "the case at Harlowe Place could not have been more finely balanced or more highly charged" for eighteenth-century readers, but the critical commonplace is to note that the Harlowes imprison their youngest daughter.[75] While Lovelace's entrapment of Clarissa produces "scenes of her isolation that dominate the vast central portion of the novel," the strategy of enforcing isolation — or solitude without privacy — begins earlier in the Harlowes' treatment of Clarissa.[76] The Harlowes force Clarissa into isolation as their primary form of punishment. Even though Clarissa attempts to withdraw from *them*, the family undercuts her agency by locking her out of their conversations and by confiscating her keys. After Mrs. Harlowe and Arabella trick Clarissa into meeting with Solmes, Clarissa edges away from their machinations, and her desire to take refuge in her closet is interpreted (by both Clarissa and her mother) as resistance to the family's will. Clarissa writes, "I was moving to go up — " when, by her mother's response, it becomes clear that her behavior is interpreted as insubordination: "And *will* you go up, Clary?" (116). Clarissa desires privacy in her closet, only to hear the silence of the family's own retreat from her and to have "the keys of everything . . . taken away from me" (ibid.). Two letters later, James, Jr. explains the family's strategy for objectifying her: she is not allowed to correspond with anyone (particularly Anna Howe and Lovelace), she is prohibited from coming into her parents' or uncles' presence, and she must remain confined in her chamber apart from her daily airings in the garden, which she must access by way of the back stairs, "that the sight of so perverse a young creature may not add to the pain you have given everybody" (121). Clarissa herself calls her chamber a "prison" (352), a thought that can be seen as justifying her meditations about escaping through the same back door that James insists she use. And in the face of an increasingly defiant daughter, the Harlowes contemplate sending her to her uncle's moated house, a plan that confirms their attempts to isolate and control her (215).

By planning to stage a private wedding to Solmes in Clarissa's closet, with a clergyman willing to marry an unwilling daughter, Richardson shows how the Harlowes threaten to erase the intellectual and moral potential of Clarissa's privacy and to reduce her to a pawn in their plans for financial and social aggrandizement. While Clarissa equates her privacy with her virtue, her family equates controlling their daughter's privacy with objectifying and possessing her sexuality. Richardson's novel specifically critiques the Harlowes because they come to view this favorite daughter as a sexual pawn, as their sexual commodity to be exchanged as they please—even if the proposed transaction is morally vacuous. The Harlowes' behavior belies an attitude that evokes both Leon Battista Alberti's fifteenth-century notion that the sexualized female body was a prized family possession, as analyzed in chapter 2, and the structure of exogamy that Gayle Rubin associates with the traffic in women.[77] Appropriating the gendered consumerism associated with the dressing room, Clarissa's mother attempts to persuade her daughter with promises of clothing, jewels, and money, objects that only emphasize the daughter's commodification by her family. Clarissa is offered luxurious goods in exchange for her virtue, items ranging from the "richest silks," to "six suits (three of them dressed)," a "set of jewels" from Solmes (to add to those of her own and from her grandmother), a "very round sum—which will be given in full property to yourself," and a "fine annual allowance for pin-money" (188). John Zomchick's argument that commerce and market forces determine how "intimate relations" function in the novel is apparent in the family's preparations for Clarissa's marriage to Solmes, but rather than holding out for the best deal, Clarissa struggles vainly to change the terms of exchange and remove herself from the forms of objectification and commodification that her family perpetuates.[78]

Even after Clarissa escapes to London with Lovelace, her family continues to read her closet as a metonymy for her sexuality and her rebellion, rather than for her spiritual and sexual virtue, and they metaphorically punish her by shutting it up. Arabella Harlowe writes to her sister: "Your drawings and your pieces are all taken down; as is also your own whole-length picture in the Vandyke taste, from your late parlour: they are taken down and thrown into your closet, which will be nailed up as if it were not a part of the house; there to perish together: for who can bear to see them?" (509). Alison Conway persuasively reads this scene as an indication of Clarissa's status as a young woman of privilege, focusing in particular on the banishment of her portrait and the commensurate loss of status.[79] But Arabella's report of the family's punishment also falls on the heels of a sexual accusation: Arabella angrily conflates Clarissa's sexuality and her closet. The family fears that Clarissa is now a harlot—"Clarissa, *what?—Harlowe*, no doubt!" (ibid.). Even though Clarissa's closet will be nailed shut, this violent, crass boundary only reminds the family that they never really had control of Clarissa and this in itself is infuriating.

If the first portion of the novel is shaped by the family's profound misunderstanding of Clarissa's privacy, then their error is confirmed by Clarissa's continued efforts to safeguard that very privacy following her escape, and Richardson highlights Clarissa's pious behavior by placing his heroine in morally dubious settings. The new territory of London topography "*seem[s]* to give the option of freedom to Clarissa," but she has not left behind her desire for physical privacy.[80] The features of Mrs. Sinclair's house in London that attract Clarissa are its "inner house" that she will occupy and its "light closet" (470), which she says (twice) that she will put to good use if she stays there long. Once there, Clarissa thinks better of Mrs. Sinclair's "daughters" after she examines the library they leave behind in her closet, a collection that includes a dozen pieces of devotional writing (525–26).[81] Clarissa's closet is the space where she contemplates Lovelace's various proposals; in her words, she "retires" (533) to her closet and her pen. It is also where she hides her letters and papers; after Lovelace tries to snatch a letter from her in the dining room, Clarissa vows never to use a room for reading or writing if she cannot lock the door (571, 572, 576). It is, too, the place where she drafts notes in her book of memoranda—another text that Lovelace manages to acquire (926). No wonder that her rape produces disordered texts, composed in what Clarissa by then considers the prison of Mrs. Sinclair's inner-house, for the violation of body and space is likewise felt in her mind (see 890ff.).

Clarissa's efforts to create a zone of privacy impervious to the commercial and sexual demands of her family and Lovelace fail through two-thirds of the novel, but she finally achieves success when she reaches her apartments above Mr. Smith's glove shop (with two light closets), her final resting place in London (1075). She hovers, dramatically, above the consumerism and mercantilism that we will see ensnare heroines of later domestic novels; as Elizabeth Kowaleski-Wallace observes, "while the selling process goes on directly below her, Clarissa remains entirely immune to the commodification process to which both her family—and her society—would subject her."[82] Commerce of any sort is beyond the range of Clarissa's cares, and the novel highlights the heroine's focus on the immaterial through Mrs. Sinclair's plot to have her arrested for back rent; when the justices arrive, they find her praying in private, a scene that Belford describes with great pathos (1065). The transitory nature of women's physical attractiveness—the beauty that Pope's Clarissa threatens will fade in *The Rape of the Lock*—is made literal when Clarissa's coffin becomes a writing desk where she pens letters of forgiveness and advice to nearly everyone she knows.

In a dramatic act of self-definition, Clarissa's coffin is her final closet, her final dressing room, and she seals its perimeter with the demand that only women touch her body and her clothing (kept in her trunks and boxes) after death. All Clarissa can leave behind is language, and she leaves that language in the locked drawer of her dressing table. Shortly before her death, Clarissa removes a book of meditations from the drawer and replaces it with her sealed posthumous letters, an inventory of her belongings, and the keys to her clothes trunk (1329). She locks the dressing table drawer and hands the key to her executor, the reformed rake and confidant of Lovelace, Belford. In her will, Clarissa stipulates that these letters must remain locked in her dressing table drawer if they cannot be delivered (ibid.). This command serves as Clarissa's final gesture of self-determination in the novel; she has addressed her various audiences and has ensured a distributor. With only meditations to read, Clarissa now ceases her textual production and waits to die, ever a symbol of moral superiority and respectability. And Clarissa's dressing table is now the repository of her good works and good words, a resolution that firmly displaces the dressing room's potential for theatricality and sexuality. The dressing table at last is a signifier for the beautiful female soul.

As the above account of *Clarissa* suggests, one can move through Richardson's plot identifying the various ways in which Clarissa feels that the ability to claim privacy is synonymous with keeping her virtue intact. Clarissa's closet is figured either as liberatory, especially as an emblem for (as well as material space to facilitate) intellectual and spiritual discretion and independence, or as a prison, in which the family and Lovelace reduce her subjectivity to that of sexual commodity. But even the threats that Clarissa resists function, in this sense, to enhance her virtuous characterization. This way of reading *Clarissa* requires that we suppose a certain amount of transparency and authenticity in these moments of resistance, that we believe that Clarissa is telling the truth. For this reason, critics have fiercely defended Clarissa, in the tradition of viewing the heroine as authentic; for example, Scott Paul Gordon argues that Clarissa "resolutely resists entering an economy in which she must make herself up for the eyes she imagines watch her."[83]

However, while these readings are certainly available in the novel, they do not foreclose the other option—that Clarissa's characterization also invites speculation about whether her claims to virtue are also a duplicitous performance. By reading the novel through the trope of the dressing room, we can see that the meanings of Clarissa's privacy are not as stable as the summary of the novel provided in the previous pages might suggest. If, as I contend in chapter 1, the dressing room underscores the conceptual problematics of exposure, then we need to remember that every instance of opening or transparency does not necessarily lead to illumination and explication. Instead, "coming out" can produce opacity that masquerades as transparency; Pepys writes his journal in a straightforward and truth-telling manner, writing only to himself, but manages to keep secrets out of the text nonetheless. Access to Clarissa's private spaces does not necessarily produce moments of the genuine and the novel explicitly dramatizes this theoretical possibility. One could just as easily argue that Clarissa *does* make herself up for the eyes she imagines watch her.

Now consider an alternate telling of the novel's plot that focuses on the various ways in which Richardson documents Clarissa *staging* scenes of transparency in order to resist her family and later Lovelace, such that the closet becomes a means to express misgivings about Clarissa herself. While some have noted that Clarissa's willingness to resort to violence is the decision that saves her, I believe that the novel forces us, instead, to consider that it is Clarissa's willingness to perform that enables her survival, as problematic as this strategy ultimately is.[84]

While thinking of and presenting herself as frank and honest, Clarissa simultaneously adopts strategies of deception to keep things private and she begins to act this way early on in the novel. While fighting with her sister, Clarissa retreats to her closet and shuts its sash door and then the silk curtain to block Arabella's view inside, refusing to submit to her sister's authoritarian gaze (229). As her family's behavior becomes increasingly outrageous, Clarissa's behavior takes increasingly deceptive turns: she sets up a secret correspondence, first with Lovelace and later with Anna Howe; she hides pens and papers before her family confiscates her writing materials (66) and refers to her "private pen" (341); she locks herself in her closet when she writes, to avoid being surprised (324, 325); she lies to her family members (366–67); she plants essays—"such of my hidden stores as I intend they shall find" (365)—for her family. Clarissa also begins to "leave" her keys in her closet door, her cabinet, and escritoire as a gesture suggesting that she has nothing to hide, even though she clearly does (281). Clarissa's encounter with her Aunt Hervey, at one point the family's surrogate inspector, is equally artful: "I thought myself very lucky to be so well prepared by my cousin Dolly's means for this search: But yet I artfully made some scruples, and not a few complaints of this treatment: after which, I not only gave her the keys of all; but even officiously emptied my pockets before her, and invited her to put her fingers in my stays, that she might be sure I had no papers there" (366). And she admits to Anna Howe that she continues to dress every day, in spite of her confinement to her chamber, not only to appear neat (as every woman should), but also to be ready in case she needs to escape her father's house (282). Clarissa repeatedly performs moments of transparency. The novel's narrative suggests that these performances are justified responses to the encroachment of others, but Clarissa's artfulness is deceptive nonetheless.

The contradiction written into the character of Clarissa is amplified when she finds herself housed in Mrs. Sinclair's brothel, a change in locale that actually necessitates additional performances. In fact, it is only Clarissa's willingness to dissemble that ultimately allows her to escape the brothel. Clarissa's departure from Harlowe Place and her arrival at the brothel solidify the fact that she now moves through a world of "misrepresentations" (93), to borrow the word that Clarissa uses to describe her siblings' efforts to discredit her. While at home, there is always the chance that things may be put right and that Clarissa may once again inhabit her closet with impunity. But once she leaves her father's house, Clarissa is subject to the "libertine style" (467) of Lovelace, whom Anna Howe labels a *"dissembler"* (451). She has such difficulty managing Lovelace because of the playacting that surrounds her; nothing is as it should be, and though Clarissa is uneasy, she cannot imagine that she comes to live in a brothel. That "light closet" Clarissa admires, in no small part because of its library of good works, is manufactured by Lovelace, who even has the names of Mrs. Sinclair and her two "daughters" (prostitutes) inscribed inside the covers (525–26).[85] The closet's former inhabitants (Sally and Polly) and its presumed former use (for sex) leave a residue of meaning that cannot be erased. The proverbial fresh coat of paint—transforming it into a room that Clarissa considers legitimate and safe, however mistakenly—does not cover over the fact that any kind of private space in Mrs. Sinclair's house is, first and foremost, a site for eroticism, theatricality, and commerce.

It is not just the context of the brothel that undercuts Clarissa's authenticity and credibility as a virtuous heroine, but also her reliance on strategies of deception. Her attempts to reason and to argue fail, such that it is only when she takes up the mantle of performance that the heroine may escape the house. She slips out of the house by slipping on the clothing of a maid (967). Once safely at the Smith's, she again takes up the mode of dissembling when she misleads Lovelace with her claim that she is returning to her father's house (1233). Clarissa knows full well that Lovelace will interpret her letter as precipitating her return to Harlowe Place in Berkshire, while Clarissa means, instead, that she is dying and going to heaven. Again, as with Clarissa's deception of her family, the novel *Clarissa* positions the heroine's deceptions as necessary tools in a world of misrepresentations. Truth, honor, and virtue have no sway with Lovelace, Mrs. Sinclair, or the prostitutes. After she is raped, feeling broken and betrayed, Clarissa adopts their own methods of misrepresentation. Just as at Harlowe Place, Clarissa gives up trying to reconstruct the walls of privacy, escaping at last by admitting a gap between how she represents herself and what she means.

Richardson again and again places Clarissa in situations where her natural recourse is to evoke the privileges of domestic life that a young lady of her means ought to be accorded and, when this fails, to institute a pattern of dissembling and theatricality that has been associated with the feminized dressing room from its inception. Rita Goldberg suggests that Clarissa is trapped between two models of female virtue, both of which threaten the heroine with annihilation: "one which sees disobedience, any exercise of individuality or will, as a loss of grace" and the other "as a weapon against an individual [and] the values of a society."[86] If so, then it is also true that Clarissa is trapped between two competing models of the dressing room, neither one of which offers her any rest or resolution—until death.

PRIVATE I'S: PEERING INTO THE DRESSING ROOM AND RICHARDSON'S EPISTOLARY NOVEL

As we have seen throughout this chapter, Richardson provocatively folds the trope of the dressing room into his novels, redefines the appropriate form and context for satire, and privileges the educational potential of women's privacy. But in all of these efforts, his novels return to the critical bind that has shaped interpretations of his novels from the start—whether a heroine is true or false. In this final section, I want to suggest that Richardson's novels explicitly produce these oppositional readings as a by-product of their narrative mode. Richardson certainly adapts the dressing room to his novels for the range of reasons I have suggested, particularly as a means of representing the possibility that feminine virtue may be cultivated in private. But Richardson also uses the dressing room in these novels to produce a specific form of narrative mode—the epistolary novel that produces the effect of a character's interiority.

Particularly in our accounts of Pamela and Clarissa, we have seen that both women are at pains to *be* authentic, but that both novels likewise subject them to the accusation of dissembling and put them into situations where they actively dissemble. But these limitations also resonate with the vexed nature of privacy: while gaining access to a dressing room might seem to guarantee epistemological transparency, it is just as likely to produce opacity and mere signifiers of authenticity. This problematic boundary assumes a more visible presence in the domestic novel, as Margaret Anne Doody reminds us: "the private is always public in the Novel."[87] Nevertheless, it has become a commonplace in studies of eighteenth-century domestic novels to argue, as Ian Watt does, that "the delineation of the domestic life and the private experience of the characters who belong to it . . . go together—we get inside their minds as well as inside their houses."[88] Watt and others make reference to Francis Jeffrey's 1804 review that praises Richardson's novels for allowing readers to "slip invisible, into the domestic privacy of [their] characters, and hear and see everything that is said and done."[89] A "Sonnet to the Author of Clarissa" (1810) uses spatial metaphors to praise Richardson for his ability to get inside the mind of his heroine: "O master of the heart! Whose magic skill / The close recesses of the soul can find."[90] Mr. B, the Harlowes, and Lovelace all act under this supposition, believing that if they can gain access to a woman's private space, then certainly they have access to her thoughts. *Pamela* and *Clarissa* both dramatize, however, that this strategy of knowledge acquisition is itself open to manipulation and misreading.

It is no coincidence that Richardson's chosen form of narrative is the epistolary mode; privacy and epistolarity are intimately bound up with one another.[91] The very act of getting access to another person's thoughts structures Richardson's narratives, whether in the figure of Pamela fending off Mr. B's advances or in Clarissa retreating to her closet to resist paternal (and later Lovelace's) will. Critics following Watt presume that letters, even fictive letters, unproblematically *reflect* their subjects, but this is a misreading of Richardson's narrative, a misreading that plagues Lovelace and various other readers.[92] In *Clarissa*, Lovelace says that he enjoys writing familiar letters because this is "writing from the heart (without the fetters prescribed by method or study)" (3rd ed., 4: 269). Contemporary responses to *Clarissa* perpetuate this point of view. The Rev. Philip Skelton contends that *Clarissa* is a "new Species of Novel" not only because it is filled with "natural Incidents," but also because it exposes "the Workings of *private* and *domestic* Passions" (emphasis added).[93] And Joseph Spence argues that the "best way" to "give a plain and natural Account of an Affair that happened in a private Family . . . was to carry the Story . . . by making them write their own Thoughts to Friends."[94] Richardson self-consciously chose to write in the form of letters because, as he explains in the preface to volume 1 of *Clarissa*, "the Letters on both Sides are written while the Hearts of the Writers must be supposed to be wholly engaged in their Subjects. . . . So that they abound, not only with critical Situations; but with what may be called *instantaneous* Descriptions and Reflections."[95]

If, as some have suggested, we assume the libertine's view when we *look* at Clarissa, then we might very well be trapped into reading like one, too.[96] Lovelace's praise obscures the fact that the eighteenth-century familiar letter was conceived of as a performance.[97] In a famous letter to Sophia Westcomb, Richardson reveals that he views the epistolary as a particularly manufactured form of exchange:

> While I read [your letter], I have you before me in person: I converse with you, and your dear Anna, as arm-in-arm you traverse the happy terrace:

kept myself at humble distance, more by my own true respect for you both, than by your swimming robes: I would say hoops, but that I love not the mechanic word! — I see you, I sit with you, I talk with you, I read to you, I stop to hear your sentiments, in the summer-house: your smiling obliging-ness, your polite and easy expression, even your undue diffidence, are all in my eye and my ear as I read. — Who then shall decline the converse of the pen? The pen that makes distance, presence; and brings back to sweet re-membrance all the delights of presence; which makes even presence but body, while absence becomes the soul; and leaves no room for the intrusion of breakfast-calls, or dinner or supper direction, which often broke in upon us.[98]

Richardson's admiration hinges on a model of access that is superior to physical presence because it allows the reader to "rewrite" his sub-ject: Westcomb's "mechanical" hoops transform into "swimming robes" and their "conversation" remains safeguarded from the interruptions or indignities of daily life. The "converse of the pen" that Richardson praises gains its power from the sense of intimacy it produces. Letters produce closeness without the potential complications of physical prox-imity — Sophia might not be listening to him or might be called to a meal. Letters also produce a sense of closeness because they allow Rich-ardson to believe he knows what Sophia is thinking, a knowledge claim that predates the innovation of free indirect discourse. But letters like-wise allow Richardson to choose whether to be in communicative ex-change with Westcomb ("I converse with you," he tells her) or indulge in his own scopophilic pleasure (I "kept myself at humble distance" from you).

Considering Richardson's description of the familiar letter allows us to understand the feature of the epistolary novel that renders it the ideal formal corollary for the dressing room trope: epistolary novels produce a tension between intimacy and spectacle. Several critics have made this connection, but no one has understood that this opposition replicates the tension that readers experience between the urge to praise the hero-ines and to lambaste them.[99] The epistolary novel not only invites the reader "inside," but also leaves the reader in the position of a voyeur, at one remove from the subject in question.[100] Metaphors of space — the dressing room in particular — corroborate the structure of Richardson's novelistic form. Therefore, when critics emphasize the extent to which Clarissa's and Pamela's spaces are violated by other characters, they miss the extent to which the Richardsonian heroine's desire for privacy contributes to the text's production of her characterization through the tool of epistolarity. A character's interiority begins with the fact of inte-rior space and ends with writing that structurally replicates the expo-sure of that space. "Character," as Deidre Shauna Lynch has recently argued, is central to the eighteenth-century novel, particularly the idea that characters in novels have inner selves.[101] This is the reason why Pamela and Clarissa have been subject to the critical discourse of praise and blame. Lynch questions whether the epistolary form produces the effect of psychology and contends, instead, that "character" developed as the result of an emergent market culture, but my analysis suggests that the formal and architectural technologies of privacy that Richardson utilizes are at the core of the eighteenth-century domestic novel's production of subjectivity.[102]

For Richardson, the doubled position of the reader is a necessary one, though frequently neglected by critical commentaries on the epistolary novel.[103] Richardson's model of epistolarity features a binary of apprehension, the tension between intimacy and distance, in order to eliminate the limitations of each, leaving only the "sweet remembrance [of] all the delights of presence," rather than presence itself. Perhaps the most telling eighteenth-century commentary comes from Sarah Fielding, whose response confirms the success of Richardson's design. When Fielding reads *Clarissa*, "I am all sensation; my heart glows; I am overwhelmed; my only vent is tears; and unless tears could mark my thoughts as legibly as ink, I cannot speak half I feel. I become like the Harlowe's servant, when he spoke not; he could not speak; he looked, he bowed, and withdrew."[104] Letters have the power to make readers feel as if they were there. Fielding becomes silent and shamed, patterning her reaction on the Harlowe's servant, and can have these feelings because the epistolary novel allows readers to experience, simultaneously, the effects of intimacy and distance. Reading letters is a process that produces an illusion of intimacy, susceptible to the conflation of time, thought, and action. When Richardson tells Sophia Westcomb, "I see you, I sit with you, I talk with you, I read to you, I stop to hear your sentiments," we see that this subject, too, is rendered an object, ever serviceable to the needs and desires of a reader. This is the "sweet remembrance" of "presence" that hangs so uneasily between the poles of the intimate and the spectacle.

Ultimately, Richardson takes on the potential liabilities of the dressing room trope and the satiric mode in order to develop and privilege his own mode of "virtuous" narrative. This aesthetic rivalry goes to the heart of the novel itself and to our understanding of its literary history. If the eighteenth-century domestic novel depends upon the representation of femininity, as many have argued, then there are two reasons to suggest that the satiric mode and the rise of the novel are not as disparate literary phenomena as most literary critics would suggest. Not only do the writers discussed throughout this study adopt the metaphor of the dressing room, but also the midcentury Richardsonian novel uses this point of convergence to demarcate its difference from other kinds of writing about women, specifically the tradition of satires about women. Critics who study the relationship of satire and the novel are quick to disclaim that the novel arose from satire, and suggest that this is a commonplace of generic understanding.[105] But as my analysis suggests, the trope of the dressing room and its claims to material accuracy, as provisional as they ultimately are, show that the two kinds of writing share a structure that, by its nature, produces an effect of the "real." I want to make the case that Richardson's *Clarissa*, at least, is evidence of a tension between the development of narrative form and the influence of satire. Although Richardson initially uses Clarissa to promulgate a theory of the virtuous and just use of satire, and separates the mode of satire from the trope of the dressing room, this redemption is overshadowed by Belford's grotesque duplication of Swift's poem "The Lady's Dressing Room" and, more notably, by the suggestion that heroines such as Clarissa and Pamela are dissemblers. If we remember the interrelationship of satire and the dressing room analyzed in part II, we can see that Richardson struggles throughout this opus to mark satire as the mode of the degenerate and the dressing room as the site of virtue as a means of codifying his own form of interior, closet narrative. The dressing room trope in the epistolary novel facilitates a form of writing in which "Characters sink deeper into the mind of the Reader."[106]

7

From Maiden to Mother:
Dressing Rooms and the Domestic Novel

IN CHAPTER 6 WE SAW THAT RICHARDSON'S FICTION ACTIVELY APPRO-
priated the dressing room trope from its satiric context, short-circuited
the trope's doubled legacy to promulgate his heroines' virtuous learning
and his style of novel, and denigrated female sexuality and those who
would write about it. In this chapter, we shall see that domestic novelists following Richardson return to the dressing room trope's satiric legacy as a site of female self-construction and sexuality, while also
introducing the possibility of its reformulation into a virtuous and maternal space.

The opening two sections of this chapter argue that the dressing
room retains its founding tension between legitimacy and transgression
precisely because it functions as a narrative hurdle for heroines to overcome. The dressing room represents the possibility that a heroine in a
domestic novel may, indeed, "fall" during the course of her transition
from daughter to wife. To educate young women, domestic novels regularly incorporate warnings styled after the trope's satiric heritage, particularly its use of ridicule, shame, and mortification. However,
departing from the satiric assumption that women are naturally debauched and impervious to reformation, domestic novelists enjoin heroines to improve themselves by resisting the temptations of fashion and
the commensurate possibility for self-fashioning. Domestic novels are
thus engineered to entertain and simultaneously to foreclose the possibility of sexual misadventure as these heroines are en route to the
classic ending of the English bildungsroman—a happily-ever-after marriage.

The final three sections of this chapter are devoted to the trope's
transformation into a metaphor for maternity. As much as daughters
are educated to renounce the allure of the dressing room, these same
domestic novels regularly imagine that their mothers or mother figures
are ensnared by them. One can trace the transformation of the dressing
room trope into a maternal space to the sequel of *Pamela* that Richard-

son published in 1741, the story after Pamela and Mr. B marry. *Pamela
II* still has a closet, but the novel reconfigures the heroine into a mother.
She is embodied through her maternity and given a certain amount of
authority by means of this new role, but Richardson's extension of
Pamela's story produces an important and influential side effect: the
representation of maternity in the domestic novel through the dressing
room trope. As counterpoints to a heroine's development, "bad" and
selfish mothers likewise populate domestic narratives and only sometimes are they able to realize their mistakes. In this alternative use of
the trope, we also find the idealization of maternity, namely transparent
virtue and selfless devotion to one's children, represented vis-à-vis the
dressing room.

Through its simultaneous use to represent young heroines and maternal figures, the trope of the dressing room reveals the important ways
in which feminine domesticity was constructed novelistically in the later
eighteenth century. While Nancy Armstrong and others call our attention to the "rise of the domestic woman" in British culture and its contribution to the rise of the novel, this analysis focuses exclusively on
the desexualization of domestic novels' heroines as figures for a new
bourgeois subjectivity.[1] Indeed, as Armstrong notes, "the feminized
household was already a familiar field of information" by the time of
Richardson, but Armstrong's exclusion of the path of feminine maturation implicitly emplotted in these novels—the transition from daughter
to wife to mother—neglects the dialectical nature of a heroine's education, as well as the domestication of maternity that cast shadows over
these texts.[2] The dressing room figures centrally in the "developmental
narratives" of the English domestic novel.[3] Just as the "successful" heroine resists the possibility of deviating from her prescribed role, even
though novel after novel places such heroines in contexts where they
are always at risk of transgression, this same heroine's success is
scripted to culminate in an explicitly transparent model of maternity. A
good mother in these domestic novels transforms herself into the abstracted, idealized, and submissive angel of the house, that figure celebrated by the now infamous Coventry Patmore in the nineteenth
century.

The plots considered throughout this chapter utilize the dressing
room trope in a variety of ways, underscoring the extent to which the
dressing room is part of what Margaret Anne Doody calls the novel's
"deep rhetoric."[4] As the range of readings will indicate, sometimes writers draw a full-blown dressing room scene in the room itself. But others,
just as notably and even more profoundly, *assume* the dressing room by
representing the dangers and pleasures of a woman's fascination with
her dress, cosmetics, and its associated objects, and by pointing out the

rewards and failures this attention produces. In this sense, dressing rooms "operate on the experiential level" of the domestic novel.[5] The novels are selected for the ways in which they imbibe the spirit of the dressing room trope and use its associations to shape the narrative possibilities for each woman: for an unmarried woman, the dressing room trope is designed, ultimately, to school her into a socially sanctioned marriage; for a married woman, it becomes a litmus test for her maternity. In the readings that follow, the emphasis on physical appearance that domestic novels place on their heroines, whether maidens or mothers, can suggest female agency and autonomy, albeit of a limited kind. But this potential also leads heroines, again, whether maidens or mothers, into trouble, such that many novels chart a narrative of shame in order to reform these heroines into their proper roles. The chapter concludes with an extended reading of Maria Edgeworth's *Belinda* that brings together the generic, aesthetic, and ideological attributes of the dressing room trope at the dawn of the nineteenth century.

"DRESS, DRESS, IS THE ORDER OF THE DAY": DRESSING ROOMS AND THEORIES OF THE FEMALE BILDUNGSROMAN

Plot "shapes and conveys meaning," as Patricia Meyer Spacks reminds us, and the marriage plots of many domestic novels take their heroines through the precipitous transition from daughter to wife.[6] This is the model of eighteenth-century female novelistic development, or bildungsroman, which Eve Tavor Bannet explains is a journey "through a series of social and familial relationships, meeting a variety of . . . 'helpers' and 'opponents,' and overcoming all those features of characters and manners which each novel defined as constituting obstacles."[7] Although the bildungsroman is predominantly associated with young men, prompting some to ask whether there is a bildungsroman for women, the female bildungsroman also moves its subjects from innocence to experience and from ignorance to knowledge.[8] However, with marriage the end point, as Rachel Blau DuPlessis notes, the "female *Bildung* tends to get stuck in the bedroom."[9] Young women in domestic novels "grow up" in the course of these narratives only to become wives, a convention that has understandably frustrated feminist critics.[10] As we shall see, stories of these heroines are told through the dialectic of danger and reward, and their narrative fate is determined by their handling of the dressing room, itself marked by a series of contradictory imperatives.

The domestic novel imagines a young heroine's development to begin with marriageability and to conclude with marriage, but this trajectory is fraught with conflict. The work of Franco Moretti, although grounded in the nineteenth-century novel and not specifically shaped to explain the plots available to women, gives us a way to see that the contradictions inherent to the bildungsroman are analogous to and exacerbated by those of the dressing room:

> Even though the concept of the *Bildungsroman* has become ever more approximate, it is still clear that we seek to indicate with it one of the most harmonious solutions ever offered to a dilemma conterminous with modern bourgeois civilization: the conflict between the ideal of *self-determination* and the equally imperious demands of *socialization*. . . . How can the tendency towards *individuality*, which is the necessary fruit of a culture of self-determination, be made to coexist with the opposing tendency to *normality*, the offspring, equally inevitable, of the mechanism of socialization?[11]

To translate Moretti's dichotomy of "normality" and "individuality" into eighteenth-century terms, the domestic novel forms its subjects in two potentially contradictory ways: the genre privileges the Lockean model of cooperation and the social contract, while also allowing for the valuation of personal liberty.[12] The tensions in these plots—whether called bildungsroman or domestic—between what is "normal" and "individual" and what is "socialization" and "self-determined" correlate to the contradictory imperatives that the domestic novel inculcates for women. As Mary Poovey has shown, romance promised women a fantasy of autonomy and power, allowing them to design their futures, but marriage legally foreclosed these possibilities.[13]

The novelistic dressing room expresses this paradox by suggesting that women can self-fashion themselves, even though their success on the marriage market depends on a subordination of the desire for autonomy that this process may produce. For young women to develop *successfully* in the terms of the domestic novel's agenda is to marry wisely, which is read as "normal," the result of proper "socialization," and another manifestation of the Lockean social contract. To accomplish this goal, however, young women must actively make themselves attractive in the widest sense of the term—the belle of the ball, as it were—and viable on the marriage market, thereby foregrounding a woman's potential for self-determination, individuality, and personal freedom, precisely the characteristics that satirists attacked earlier in the century.

The balancing act between these two poles is precarious, for the heroine needs to embrace and reject the allure of the dressing room at one and the same time. As an aesthetic to be admired and imitated, the dressing room produces female beauty and promises a heroine social visibility, key to landing a husband. But as an object or set of values to be rejected, the dressing room stands as the potential for seduction by a spectrum of vices, from dressing "inappropriately" to taking sexual advantage of the temporary independence such a space and time allows, from self-fashioning to self-determination. Ruth Bernard Yeazell has shown us the ambiguous nature of female modesty in relation to these plots; "neither a prude nor a coquette, as the conduct books never tired of repeating, the modest woman occupies a mystified space between, a space largely defined by the repudiation of those imagined opposites."[14] In terms of our concerns, the dressing room precisely embodies the contradiction that constitutes these female subjects: they must present themselves as desirable objects, but they must also train themselves to be *reasonable* subjects and emblems of "natural virtue," which actually means that they will shape their own desires to fit their husbands'.[15]

Samuel Richardson imagines just such an idealized heroine in his third novel, *Sir Charles Grandison* (1753–54). Harriet Byron is a long-suffering young woman in love with a man of virtue who has, famously, a heart divided by his affections for her and for an Italian, Clementina. In Harriet's actions we can see the way that domestic heroines *ought* to behave, a model of propriety that emblematizes a heroine's successful negotiation of the domestic novel's narrative demands. Notably, Richardson removes the barriers that brought difficulty to his two earlier heroines, Pamela and Clarissa: Harriet is orphaned, has a fortune of £10,000 to £15,000, and is free to choose her own husband. She is beautiful and properly—not overly—educated: "I am *not* learned," Harriet insists, but "a *Bible* scholar."[16] Harriet's dressing room stages one of her most important revelations about the romance that challenges Sir Charles's virtue, her admission to Sir Charles's sisters that she loves him. But Harriet's confession and her able handling of this "trial of that frankness of heart" serve to consolidate the sororal bond among these three women, as both Grandison sisters, Charlotte and Caroline (Lady L), "embraced [Harriet], and assured [her] of their united interest."[17] Although the sisters artfully tease Harriet into a confession, Harriet's dressing room is a site of authenticity and frankness, rather than theatricality and secrecy. Harriet's dressing room also emphasizes the comparatively secret behavior of Sir Charles and his ill-fated love affair with Clementina, a young woman whom Harriet comes to pity and eventually befriends—the perfect sign of the subordination of her desires to her then husband's.

In Harriet Byron, we have a seemingly perfect heroine. But the very theatricality of the dressing room demands that we interrogate the assumed naturalness of this developmental paradigm. The several dressing room scenes in Maria Edgeworth's *The Absentee* (1812) foreground the dialectic of authenticity and pretension characteristic of the trope and are fundamental to the novel's conflict between the urbanity of London society and the pastoral Irish world of the resident landowner. (Even though Edgeworth apparently liked *The Absentee* best out of her "Irish tales" and it made her reputation, the novel has received comparatively little critical attention.)[18] Through the examples of Grace Nugent and Miss Broadhurst, *The Absentee* envisages a model of femininity that successfully thwarts the dangers of the beau monde—the gossip, the desire, the social climbing that preoccupy Grace's aunt, Lady Clonbrony—without renouncing it wholesale. In one of the novel's foundational scenes, Grace Nugent and Miss Broadhurst have a heart-to-heart in Grace's dressing room, as the former prepares for an evening's concert. In this space, ripe with the potential for female dissembling, these young women cement a bond of female friendship and a commitment to authenticity. They rationally discuss the sudden departure of Lord Colambre to Ireland and his implicit abandonment of any claim to Miss Broadhurst's affections; Miss Broadhurst in turn discerns that Grace herself is impossibly in love with him herself. Then the heiress tells her friend that the subject is closed: "We have subjects enough of conversation; we need not have recourse to pernicious sentimental gossipings. There is great difference between wanting a *confidante*, and treating a friend with confidence. My confidence you possess; all that ought, all that is to be known of my mind, you know."[19] Grace Nugent concurs: "I entirely agree with you about *confidantes* and sentimental gossipings: I love you for not loving them" (77). The women who gossip in *The Absentee* are, instead, older women and their maids.

It is important, however, that Grace Nugent and Miss Broadhurst, clearly the models of female propriety in the novel, do not eschew the dressing room aesthetic altogether—and that they understand that this is hard work. They know how to play the part of a fashionable lady without being vain and know that this behavior is expected of them. Their scene of revelation is staged in the dressing room itself, with Grace poised in front of her dressing table, and their conversation concludes with both acknowledging the labor of feminine beauty:

> A loud knock at the door announced the arrival of company.
> "Think no more of love, but as much as you please of admiration—dress yourself as fast as you can," said miss Broadhurst. "Dress, dress, is the order of the day."
> "Order of the day and order of the night, and all for people I don't care for in the least," said Grace. "So life passes!" (77)

Grace's attitudes toward the life of fashion represented by the dressing room demonstrate that she has managed to walk the conceptual tightrope between self-determination and socialization, between "love" and "admiration." Following Mr. Spectator's advice to his female readers, Grace seems to "join all the Beauties of the Mind to the Ornaments of Dress, and inspire a kind of Awe and Respect, as well as Love, into their Male-Beholders," an ideal that combines women's physical and intellectual beauty.[20] The goal, as Mr. Spectator articulates it, is to render women aesthetically pleasing in both body and mind and to make them symbols of the harmoniously supportive (for their husbands, at least) domestic sphere. Even though the artifice of Grace and Miss Broadhurst is deemed natural in the world of the novel, Edgeworth reminds us, by way of the playful repetition of "Dress, dress, is the order of the day," that the requirements of the dressing room aesthetic—and those of being properly feminine—are never ending. Being a heroine in a domestic novel and a young lady in polite society presupposes a certain amount of theatricality, but not too much; another young woman is lampooned for her efforts to gain Lord Colambre's favor: "Lady Isabel appeared to suffer so exquisitely and so naturally from this persecution, that lord Colambre said to himself, 'If this be acting, it is the best acting I ever saw. If this be art, it deserves to be nature'" (98). Thus, when the uncle of Grace Nugent visits his niece's dressing room to return the £5,000 he has borrowed, and he boldly remarks, "Ready! . . . ay, always ready—so I said" (210), we know that his observation primarily reflects the constant work of hiding the labor that being a woman requires.

If figures such as Harriet Byron, Grace Nugent, and Miss Broadhurst represent what domestic novelists consider "good girls," then their opposites are aptly embodied by Sarah Fielding's "fine ladies" in her novel *The Adventures of David Simple* (1744/1753). The reformed wit Cynthia explains such women are vain: "My Lady *Wish-for't* at her Toilette is a perfect picture of them, where she insults over, and thinks herself *witty* on a poor ignorant Wench."[21] To Fielding, these women have lost themselves by having fallen into the snares of the dressing room aesthetic; they "have no *Minds of their own*, [and] they have no *Idea of other Sensations*."[22] The indictment of female vanity and its association with cognitive delusion is certainly not new to Fielding; Thomas Browne contended in 1705 that "the Predominant Passion of Women" is "Self-Love," "which may be term'd an *Evil*, that contains all others; since there is no *Disorder* in the World, which does not acknowledge that *Passion* to be its Principle."[23] If the dressing room occupies a central position in this kind of critique, then it likewise embodies its potential for imitation. Fielding imagines that the even more pressing danger of the dressing room is that it encourages all sorts of women to act vainly and in a self-interested, improper manner. Just as Hogarth's plates in *The Harlot's Progress* are preoccupied with social aping (plate 2 features a well-heeled harlot decked out with a telltale monkey at the edge of the engraving),[24] Fielding's Cynthia warns that the mimicry inherent to the dressing room is prevalent and undesirable: "They are not confined to any Station; for I have known, while the Lady has been insulting her Waiting-woman in the Dressing-Room, the Chamber-Maid has been playing just the same Part below stairs, with the Person she thought her inferior, only with a small Variation of Terms."[25] Women with pretensions to be "fine ladies" are bad enough on their own, in this sense, but their transgressive power is heightened by the imitation they implicitly encourage. This message, reminiscent of satirists' voices a generation earlier, is precisely the one that young heroines in their own bildungsromans ought not to follow.

Domestic novels, however, rarely emplot heroines who are baldly virtuous and well-developed or already fully seduced by the narcissistic pleasures of the dressing room. Nearly every young heroine, out of cultural and narrative necessity, passes "through" the pleasures and dangers of the dressing room in one way or another on her way to marriage. It is the test of the female bildungsroman, and most novels represent their heroines actively learning these lessons. As Kristina Straub reminds us, "rising and falling are among the repertoire of romantic tropes that eighteenth-century novels incorporated in a variety of ways," and many novelists seal a young woman's fate and narrative according to her success negotiating the double bind of the dressing room.[26] Therefore, the path leading to the female bildungsroman's ideal of marriage, even in the scripted world of domestic narratives, is a treacherous one, ready to tempt self-willed young women to fail to transform themselves into dutiful wives at any moment.

MAIDEN VOYAGES: PLOTS OF MORTIFICATION AND REFORMATION

Domestic novelists refer with greater frequency to the dressing room's association with theatricality and eroticism than to its connection with learning. Unlike Richardson, many domestic novelists also use ridicule, shame, and mortification to *educate* heroines; the dressing room's legacy with satire is one way that these texts can accomplish this. Unlike the satirists of an earlier generation, however, many of these novelists imagine that young women, while susceptible to the pleasures of the dressing room, may also be *trained* out of this weakness. The possibility for reformation is at the heart of the domestic novel's adaptation of the satiric dressing room. A complex generic picture begins to emerge. On the one hand, mid- and later-eighteenth-century novels distance themselves from their satiric forbearers in that the dressing room is not solely a vehicle for the indictment of women, but a naturalized condition of femininity that may, ultimately, serve a pedagogical purpose. On the other, many domestic novels utilize strategies of ridicule, mortification, and shame from this earlier tradition in order to change their heroines. In other words, satirists generally conceive of women in their dressing rooms as irrevocably dissolute, but domestic novelists see many of these same women as open to development and change.

Because the dressing room allows heroines a certain amount of cosmetic agency, domestic novels regularly imagine young women who misuse its tools of self-fashioning, as in the case of Oliver Goldsmith's *The Vicar of Wakefield* (1766), a novel notable for its appropriation of the dressing room trope and its commensurate critique of female domesticity.[27] There can be no dressing room for the daughters once Primrose loses the family's fortune, which shrinks from £14,000 to £400 overnight, but the conflicts of the dressing room aesthetic determine both the expectations and experiences of these young women, and emblematize what Peter M. Briggs calls Goldsmith's "muse of disjunction."[28] When Goldsmith appropriates the trope as a measure of the daughters' and the family's social and moral descent, the dressing room becomes part of the novel's "deep rhetoric," to evoke Margaret Anne Doody again.[29] For example, in the family's newfound poverty, the dress of the Primrose women horrifies the vicar. They assume a mode of dress appropriate for their *former* fortune and status when they plan to attend Sunday services with "their hair plaistered up with pomatum, their faces patched to taste, their trains bundled up into an heap behind, and rustling at every motion."[30] The Primrose women are made-up into figures of vanity, ready to impress their new community with their finery.

But the inappropriateness of their self-fashioning allows the father to voice a response that indicates how his family's situation — and the dress allowable for them to assume — has changed, linking the trope of the dressing room to a concern about rank and reputation. If the dressing room historically referenced both actresses and the wealthy elite, then Primrose well knows that the continued adoption of fashion by his daughters — no longer women of relative wealth and status — would only convey moral impropriety. Primrose first shames his wife and daughters by ridiculing them when he responds to their dress by calling for the coach that their appearance suggests the family owns, even though there is not one (the mother and daughters attempt to ride their workhorses to church on another Sunday). Then he lectures them by pointing to the cultural claims of the sartorial — and the dangers of the dressing room. If his daughters dress finely, then only a coach will confirm that they have wealth. Since there is no coach, and since they are all walking to church, the only interpretive option available would be that they are "streetwalkers." When Mrs. Primrose defends her daughters (and herself) by arguing that they merely look "neat" and "handsome" to honor him, Primrose interrupts his wife: "this is not neatness, but frippery" (34). Though this is, indeed, their "former splendour," Dr. Primrose calls it instead "rufflings, and pinkings, and patchings" (ibid.).

The vicar's second form of ridicule comes with his prediction that the neighborhood children would "hoot after us" (ibid.) because his wife's and Olivia's and Sophia's dress would be a sign not only of pretension, but also of sexual license. While these unnamed, unseen "children in the parish" (ibid.) would be the most audible of the dissenters, the malicious gossip of neighborhood wives would turn the Primrose women into figures of indecency. These arbiters of morality, warns Primrose, would condemn the young women solely because of what they wear. Goldsmith offers a scene of humiliation and ridicule, as well as a scene of *imagined* humiliation and ridicule, a warning that dressing out of place may *make* one out of place. Fashion threatens to transgress the bounds of decency, even when a family is preparing to go to church on a Sunday morning. Fashion also positions daughters and wives at odds with their fathers and husbands, when the women take their ability for self-determination too far; later in the novel, Primrose responds to the news that his wife and daughters are making "a *wash* for the face" (41) by knocking the whole mixture over.[31]

On a basic level, a paternalistic figure such as Primrose ridicules his wife and daughters so that they will change—and they do, to an extent, or at least they change their clothing on that day, but they do not completely eradicate their desire for female self-fashioning, which continues to take form in a dressing room aesthetic. The plot of *The Vicar of Wakefield* consistently satirizes these women's attempts at self-fashioning and self-determination and concludes its schooling of them through an almost farcical turn of events that threatens to toss them firmly into indecency at any moment. The allure of looking better than their station regularly plagues these young women: when they meet "women of very great distinction and fashion from town" (53), they fail to realize that these are prostitutes whom their rakish landlord, Squire Thornhill, has hired to lure them unprotected to London. Primrose complains that the "finery" of "Lady Blarney" and "Miss Carolina Wilelmina Amelia Skeegs," "threw a veil over any grossness in their conversation. My daughters seemed to regard their superior accomplishments with envy; and what appeared amiss was ascribed to tip-top quality breeding" (53–54). The women's lavish clothing and sophisticated airs give them license, and Sophia and Olivia accept the ladies' behavior as fashionable and fine, though the narration clearly undercuts the masquerade with Primrose's skepticism and ridicule. Most notably, however, the social connotations of clothing—the very issue at the heart of Primrose's satire of his daughters' Sunday splendor—play upon the young women's naïveté. The dressing room aesthetic blinds them: because these women from town *look* fashionable and fine, they are taken to *be* fashionable and fine, and seem to promise Olivia and Sophia the possibility of being the same.

But the risks that Goldsmith imagines are ultimately contained by the novel's conclusion, which marks the classificatory closure par excellence of the English bildungsroman, as Moretti reminds us, that shapes the tradition: all three eligible children, the two daughters and son, are married in the closing pages.[32] Yet these marriages depend upon a whole-scale renunciation of all the pleasures of the dressing room aesthetic. The marriages are only *possible* because of the family's humiliations, shame that results from a father's naïveté and the daughters' and mother's pretensions and delusions of grandeur. Of course, Primrose himself is not immune from the charge of egotism (he is duped at the market by a con pretending to admire Primrose's theological work), but Goldsmith explicitly structures the narrative of *The Vicar of Wakefield* through the temptations of fashion and living beyond oneself. Were it not for the mechanism of a fairy-tale denouement, the plot of the Primroses would not be so rosy. The improbable resolution shows us the domestic novel's investment in safeguarding the lines of decency that render women of fashion objects of satire and machinations, as well as the domestic novel's absorption of the dressing room trope as a narrative device.

With a father and mother in the picture, much less a father who is a man of the cloth, and the narrative safety that Goldsmith ultimately provides, the Primrose daughters run little risk of *actually* falling into danger. The dressing room for them highlights their character flaws more than it underscores the vulnerability of their position. In a much more serious sense, Frances Burney's *Evelina* (1778) examines deeply just how precipitous the female bildungsroman is and stages several episodes that constitute a violent schooling of its heroine, who is always at risk of falling into indecency and becoming anything from a kept woman or high-class mistress to a streetwalker. In other words, Burney understands that the dressing room trope, while seemingly necessary for a young woman's maturation, simultaneously introduces profound dangers. When Evelina goes to London and becomes a heroine who, by narrative necessity, negotiates the temptations of self-fashioning, Burney aptly represents the importance of public presentation as the cognate of gaining status in the marriage market. The crux of the novel's conflict resides in Evelina's inability to claim a proper family name for herself and the resulting ambiguity of her status within the world of London. She is the legitimate daughter of a baronet who refuses to acknowledge her and this problem gains a material presence through her assumption of the dressing room aesthetic in the opening pages of the text. Quite succinctly, Evelina's toilet coincides with her entrance into society *and* the commensurate crisis of her status.

In a classic bildungsroman move, the novel takes the young heroine on a journey from her home in the country to visit London with family friends, the Howards, who introduce her to all of the consumerism and society that the metropolis has to offer, activities that are regularly associated with the values of the dressing room—shopping, balls, and pleasure gardens. In this way, the novel documents a heroine's indoctrination into the aesthetic of the dressing room and challenges her to negotiate its benefits and dangers. The consumerism evident in Burney's novel is famous—she coined the phrase "Londonize"—but it also vividly captures the cosmetic transformation that Evelina undergoes.[33] At Berry-Hill, Evelina is a retired beauty, but in the city she is a decked-out toast after going "*a shopping* . . . to buy silks, caps, gauzes, and so forth" (27) and entering a "full-blown commodity culture."[34] Burney fails to detail Evelina's shopping expedition, but we can garner a sense of what her experience would have been like from accounts provided by foreign visitors. In 1786, Sophie von la Roche wrote:

> Behind the great glass windows absolutely everything one can think of is neatly, attractively displayed, in such abundance of choice as almost to make one greedy. Now large slipper and shoe shops for anything from adults down to dolls, can be seen. . . . There is a cunning device for showing women's materials. Whether they are silks, chintzes, or muslins, they hang down in folds behind the fine, high windows so that the effect of this or that material, as it would be in the ordinary folds of a woman's dress, can be studied.[35]

Shopping in London, the emporium of Europe, opened women to the public sphere of the marketplace and enabled them to assume the mantle of fashionability; as Neil McKendrick wryly observes, "this was the fantasy land of the rich and the ultra fashionable."[36]

If, as Catherine Gallagher contends, *Evelina* functions as "a book for and about Everybody," then it is precisely because of Evelina's toilet that she is considered anybody at all.[37] Her morning of consumerism facilitates her eighteenth-century makeover, which renders her an object of men's sexual desire when she enters society:

> I have just had my hair dressed. You can't think how oddly my head feels; full of powder and black pins, and a great *cushion* on the top of it. I believe

you would hardly know me, for my face looks quite different to what it did before my hair was dressed. When I shall be able to make use of a comb for myself I cannot tell, for my hair so much entangled, *frizled* they call it, that I fear it will be very difficult. (27–28)

Evelina's toilet produces a concoction of artifice for her head not atypical for the time. McKendrick describes the range of extravagant hairstyles popular in the 1770s and 1780s: "live flowers—with concealed bottles of water to keep them fresh—large butterflies, baskets of fruit, caterpillars in blown glass, even models of coaches and horses sprouted from, or galloped across, or merely inhabited the mountainous hairstyles then in vogue."[38] With this fashion came the professionalization of hairstylists. One Alexander Stewart published a handbook for fashionable ladies to give to their maids, *The Art of Hair Dressing; or The Ladies Director* (1788), which details elaborate instructions for combing out, curling, and powdering hair, and even stipulates where the maid should stand.[39]

The remarkable aspect of Evelina's toilet is that Burney presents it as not only a necessary feature of urbanization, but also as a *natural* rite of passage for any young woman of quality who enters into polite society. Some read Burney's narrative as asserting "the authority of private identity with a public discourse that denies it," but Evelina's transformation strains this logic: the dressing room produces an Evelina prepared for the marriage market.[40] Even though the dressing room makeover threatens to make her alien to herself and to Mr. Villars, and even though it produces an Evelina over which she does not seem to have control, with hair that she cannot comb, Evelina's toilet paradoxically renders her appearance naturally beautiful and, to her admirers, brings forth the "real" woman.[41] At the first ball she attends, Evelina is received as an "angel" with "an elegant face [that] can never be so vile a mask" (35) and a "Helen" (36). Moreover, her beauty as a marker of authenticity is enhanced when she, in turn, responds to the foppish dress and manner (and ugliness) of Mr. Lovel. Evelina, the ostensibly natural beauty, has a natural rejoinder to ridiculousness: she laughs, proving that she is "a rational, ordinary girl."[42] But Evelina's ill-timed laugh also breaks the rules of polite behavior and so marks the beginning of her tortured, and at times dangerous, path toward marriage, regularly tormented by the pretentious and jilted Sir Clement Willoughby.

The dressing room aesthetic makes Evelina visible in London society, but it also exposes her to scenes of embarrassment, humiliation, and danger, and literalizes Evelina's "social marginality" and lack of a proper surname.[43] Although some critics have noted that there is often "a limit to the risks Evelina runs," some of her moments of shame are especially pointed, and potentially very dangerous.[44] Evelina's cosmetics are perceived as natural and appropriate in some contexts, namely among the social elite, but Burney's novel likewise imagines scenarios in which the heroine is out of place and in danger precisely because her made-up appearance can mean *other* things. Evelina's status is dangerously in question when in the company of her natural relatives, Madame Duval and the merchant-class Branghtons. The cosmetically enhanced Evelina always runs the risk that the Vicar of Wakefield fears for his own family—to be taken as a streetwalker. The potential for children "hooting" in the countryside is realized in the much more threatening urban context of the London pleasure garden, one of several public spaces that Steven J. Gores argues form the backdrop for Evelina's self-construction.[45] Twice Evelina finds herself out of place in a public setting, both times in the company of her grandmother and cousins (these excursions take place during Evelina's second visit to London, a time when she sees the city as a riotous space and labors to avoid her earlier, more genteel and titled acquaintances).

A riotous, carnivalesque atmosphere is the feature of Vauxhall Gardens, the twelve-acre pleasure garden in Lambeth famous for its mixing of social classes, that disturbs Evelina's sense of decorum and feminine delicacy—and that introduces the possibility of her made-up appearance being misinterpreted.[46] Evelina's feelings of propriety are strained when her two female cousins lead her down an allegorically laden dark path, "a long alley, in which there was hardly any light" (195), which spills out into a group of drunk young men who take them for streetwalkers. The young women scream, men encircle them, and Evelina breaks free, only to run into another party of men. Now alone, they paw at her as she insists, "'No,—no,—no,—' I *panted* out, 'I am no actress,— pray let me go,—pray let me pass—'" (196). Although Evelina is magically rescued by the untrustworthy Sir Clement Willoughby, she momentarily suffers from the context of her made-up body: dressed and only in the company of her female cousins, she looks like an "actress" or, at the very best, a lowborn woman to these pleasure-seekers. It is worse, in a sense, that she *knows* it. The Londonization that Evelina undergoes prepares her for polite society and makes her sexually available in the marriage market. But in a different context, it threatens to render her a woman of the sexual underclass. If this lesson were not enough to illustrate the fine line between appearing genteel and seeming vulgar, then Burney places Evelina in a second crowd scene during an excursion to Marybone Gardens when she finds herself alone surrounded by strangers, subject to "bold and unfeeling" men and finally groped by an officer who says, "I enlist you in my service" (233); panicked, Evelina

inadvertently turns to prostitutes for help. The novel *Evelina* regularly
and powerfully places its heroine in situations that result in social mortification, but these trials are only metonymies for the moral turpitude
around every corner for a young woman with no name, but with a beautiful face. As this scene emblematizes only too well, however, the potential for a woman's mortification is much graver than mere
embarrassment: a young woman such as Evelina is all too likely to fall
prey to the trap of prostitution when her feet touch the streets of
London.[47]

If the trope's associations with cosmetics and sexuality offer novelists
a seemingly obvious source of critique, then even its seemingly "legitimate" connotations with the study, which Richardson emphasized in
his novels, produces the opportunity for a female bildungsroman. Published only a few years after *Clarissa*, Charlotte Lennox's *The Female
Quixote* (1752) vibrantly entertains the pedagogical possibilities of the
dressing room. In Clarissa-like fashion, Arabella also uses her dressing
room as a study and occupies it nearly all day, "where Reading and the
Labours of the Toilet employ'd her Time till Dinner: Tho' it must be
confess'd to her Honour, that the latter engross'd but a very small Part
of it."[48] Arabella studiously reads her library of seventeenth-century
French romances, her maternal inheritance, and even bases her toilet
on the styles described in them. Her appearance—out of date, out of
country, and out of fiction—is described as "singular," though "far from
being unbecoming" (8); she also wears a veil to protect her modesty
when in public. But the dressing room shapes her experiences in the
novel in a more profound way because the romances tutor Arabella and
shape her self-determination.[49] Arabella is a powerful reader who ex-
pects the world to behave according to the morals, principles, and narrative possibilities of French romances.[50]

If Arabella's dressing room is the originary space for her body and
mind, then some contend that she exemplifies "unwitting self-deceit"
and quixotism, or "differences of mind."[51] Arabella could be the young
woman Mary Molesworth Monck critiques in "On a Romantic Lady"
(1716) for believing the world of courtship in contemporary England
to be like that in the French romances: "Nor are you one of the Seven
Wonders, / But a young damsel very pretty, / And your true name is
Mistress Betty."[52] Nevertheless, Arabella secures seclusion and autonomy in her dressing room, which allows this young woman to fashion
herself and the world as she pleases. From Janet Todd's perspective,
Arabella "knows that one tool of self-creation is literary depiction. She
wishes to be the heroine of a romantic history, the subject of a narrative
of which she can be the auditor."[53] The comedy and, more importantly,
the narrative and ideological strife of Lennox's text emerge from the

disjunction between the world of chivalrous adventures in which she stars and authors, and the world of English gentry in which Arabella finds herself held accountable. Outside of her dressing room, she is no longer in control and her agency is represented as dangerous and undesirable, ultimately an impediment to her narrative's conclusion.

The mortification that Lennox plots is designed to train Arabella *out* of this fantasy of self-determination and to school her into a model of behavior that will ensure her safe arrival at a relation of marriage in which she subordinates her desires to those of her husband. Arabella meets a maternal surrogate who has already renounced her own self-determination (and passion for reading romances), a model whom Arabella is meant to imitate. The Countess of — — is a model of the self-transformation that both the domestic novel and the marriage plot require of young women. Hers is the story that must constitute the rest of Arabella's narrative, not the terms of adventure celebrated in the romance tradition; as the countess explains, "I was born and christen'd, had a useful and proper Education, receiv'd the Addresses of my Lord—through the Recommendation of my Parents, and marry'd him with their Consents and my own Inclination, and that since we have liv'd in great Harmony together" (327). From the countess's point of view, her marriage plot successfully combines the imperatives of socialization (her parents' "Consents") and her individualized desire ("my own Inclination"), conflating what Moretti designates as "normal" with "individual."[54] Lennox's resilient (and stubborn) heroine, however, does not capitulate that easily. This encounter does not change Arabella's point of view, nor does it precipitate a renunciation of all that she learned in her dressing room; the countess's "nominalist, unsentimental arguments cannot sway the essentialist, absolutist Arabella":[55] thus our heroine was "surpriz'd, embarrass'd, perplex'd, but not convinc'd" (329). Faced with a maternal figure who scolds her, Arabella is ashamed but not reformed.

Renouncing all that she learned in her dressing room, namely the efficacy and veracity of romances, is key to Arabella's absorption into the role her father and suitor desire for her and evidence that her "misbehavior is a threat to political stability."[56] While Arabella's life in her dressing room gives her tools for self-determination, this attribute is increasingly figured as delusional and dangerous, and Arabella's repudiation of intellectual self-fashioning is integral to her reformation. A woman with autonomy in her dressing room is socially acceptable as long as she follows the prescribed narrative; any deviation renders her mad. There has been long critical debate that the chapter in which the doctor in Richmond "argues" Arabella into being an appropriate young woman was actually penned by Samuel Johnson.[57] The novel's conclu-

sion is famously vexed: "the novel ends as it must; but it does not leave
all readers confident that this is a fine way of closing a novel."[58] Regardless, its result is unquestionable. Catherine Gallagher notes that Arabella's reformation pivots on her understanding the "true" nature of
fiction, but this exchange also requires Arabella to renounce the intellectual freedom she so enjoyed in her dressing room and to believe, in
retrospect, that all she has learned there is unreliable.[59] Arabella thus
reflects, "I begin to perceive that I have hitherto at least trifled away
my Time, and fear that I have already made some Approaches to the
Crime of encouraging Violence and Revenge" (381). In the penultimate
chapter of the novel, Lennox's heroine must surrender the intellectual
prerogative that her dressing room had given her if she is to be incorporated successfully into the role of wife. If, as Julie Shaffer suggests,
"her reward for repudiating her desire to exercise power . . . is the continued love of her suitor and his hand in marriage," then *The Female
Quixote* makes painfully clear that this surrender results from mortification and humiliation, ultimately a result of the heroine's shame, and a
disavowal of women's learning.[60]

These domestic novels are ultimately designed to control a young
woman's *sexual* transition from maiden to wife, whether by means of
the trope's association with eroticism and theatricality or with learning.
The dressing room does not merely enable women to feel they have a
self-determination that they do not; it also introduces the possibility of
sexual knowledge and experience that is outside of the realm of propriety. In the context of *The Vicar of Wakefield*, for example, Timothy Dykstal argues that the weakness in the vicar's political—and implicitly
domestic—theory is its "failure to account for the power of sexuality
(specifically of woman's sexuality)."[61] The vicar's failure to understand
female sexuality leads to several more instances of mis-self-representa-
tion, as evidenced in the family's ridiculous portrait that cannot fit
through the door and in their son Moses's own toilet when he goes to
sell their horse at a market, only to return fleeced. Evelina's danger
throughout her novel, of course, is that she will acquire sexual knowledge outside of marriage, a distinct possibility not only because she is
in the transitional stage between maid and wife, but also because of the
ambiguity of her social status. The scene in which she is enveloped by
prostitutes only foregrounds this possibility. The countess in *The Female
Quixote* makes very clear to Arabella that the rhetoric of romances suggests a sexual freedom at odds with English gentility. When Arabella,
"in the Style of Romance, intreated the countess to favour her with the
Recital of her Adventures," the countess responds in such a way as to
highlight the fundamentally inappropriate nature of Arabella's discourse: "The Word Adventures carries in it so free and licentious a

Sound in the Apprehensions of People at this Period of Time, that it can hardly with Propriety be apply'd to those few and natural Incidents which compose the History of a Woman of Honour" (327). The challenge for domestic novelists is to get their heroines out of the dressing room and safely into the marriage bed.

With every young heroine, the trope of the dressing room becomes an obstacle to surmount. The dressing room offers various manifestations of women's independence that are all sharply curtailed in the domestic novel's pattern of reformation, even though its dangers and its pleasures threaten to derail the path of a heroine's journey to marriage. Domestic novel after domestic novel envisages a repudiation of the dressing room aesthetic primarily through the tools of mortification and a pedagogy of shame. The dressing room is too dangerous a place to stay, it leads too often to mistakes; it must be used and then renounced in some form or another for the heroine to find her resolution and get married. As we shall see in the remainder of this chapter, however, the ultimately conservative course of the dressing room trope as a rhetoric for the bildungsroman is countered in these same novels by portrayals of adult women—some married, some single—who clearly have not given up their right to the dressing room and its privileges. The marriage plot of the female bildungsroman suggests that these young women will live happily ever after, but they are regularly paired with women who have not learned these lessons. And it is to this topic, the mothers and mother figures who parallel these heroines, that we shall now turn.

"Entitled to take liberties"? Bad Mothers and the Domestic Novel

If a young woman's dressing room implicitly foregrounds her sexuality, then the question of female sexuality returns in a different register once these young women marry. Again Samuel Richardson's work signals an important moment of transition in the trope's history when *Pamela II* (1741) opens with his heroine married and surveying her home with Mr. B. In the novel's opening letter, Pamela describes standing in the window of their bedchamber for two hours, listening to the nightingales singing outside, and mentions, notably, that there is a "little room he intends for my use."[62] The married Pamela will still have her closet and will still compose letters, many addressed to her reformed sister-in-law, Lady Davers. But the plot of this second novel focuses on Pamela as a mother.

Pregnant seven times in the course of the narrative, the rise of Pamela's domesticity *after* marriage is inextricably linked to her motherhood. Richardson's sequel does a bait and switch with female sexuality: as Toni Bowers explains, "motherhood becomes the crucible that virginity had been before: the contested object, the authority Pamela and B. compete to define and claim, the site where violent struggles over autonomy and agency are waged."[63] Pamela's original claim to sexual virtue and the threat of sexual misadventure (B raping Pamela) are transformed in her sequel into *maternal* virtue and the danger of wifely insubordination. Debates about maternity—what mothers should do and how they ought to behave—not only began in the early modern period, but maternity was "continuously invented and re-invented. What remained constant was the enormous popularity of the image of the mother—the consistency with which it was invoked and adjusted for a range of political concerns."[64] In particular, Augustan conduct literature for mothers provided women an authority to rival their husbands', specifically by advocating breast-feeding.[65] This is the conflict in *Pamela II*: Pamela desperately wants to nurse her baby, following the advice of the conduct manuals, while Mr. B vehemently objects.

The point to draw from this convergence of maternity and domesticity is that, by midcentury, motherhood and the dressing room were both figures for female sexuality, and both likewise offered women the potential for autonomy. Questions of virtue would seem to be irrelevant after the conclusion of the marriage plot, but domestic novels from this period return again and again to questions of maternity, often conceptualizing mothers according to their penchant for Juvenalian misrule or their well-trained Richardsonian self-management. In this way, the dressing room trope opens up the possibility of representing the dangers of maternal embodiment, without threatening the boundaries of decency. The dressing room keeps in tension the "representational paradox" that Carolyn Dever identifies in the nineteenth-century "bourgeois mother of bodily excess and cultural ideal."[66] The issue for us, therefore, is how the domestic novel utilizes the dressing room trope to evaluate women's character not only before marriage, as we have seen, but also after it.

The trope's applicability to women *after* marriage, as well as its continued associations with transgressive fantasy, is illustrated in a dressing room scene in eighteenth-century erotic ephemera. An epistle signed by "TOM IN THE SECRET" in *The Covent-Garden Repository: Or, Ranger's Pack of Whim, Frolick, And Amusement* confesses to an erotic episode in a young widow's dressing room, a scenario that serves as inspiration for the volume's frontispiece.[67] The servant Tom is called to his mistress's dressing room while "the ceremonies of the Toilette have been going forward."[68] As the widow returns her attention to a novel,

Tom catches a glimpse of her cleavage because her robe de chambre was not "so closely fastened as some prudes might have deemed necessary," a sight that arouses his sexual desire.[69] "Not daring to attack my Lady herself," Tom instead directs his attention toward Lucy the maid, a woman who is "as full of frolic as myself," but Lucy, surprised by his kisses, accidentally burns her mistress with the curling irons.[70] Upon discovering them, Mrs. Sporter dismisses Lucy for her indiscrete behavior and, to Tom's amazement, initiates a sexual relationship with him. The plot of "TOM IN THE SECRET" underscores the sexual license that continues to be associated with the eighteenth-century dressing room and features a free and enfranchised woman "who upon the presumption of knowing life, thinks herself entitled to take liberties."[71]

Mrs. Sporter is not so different from the "bad" mothers in domestic novels, for they are women who likewise think themselves entitled to take liberties; novelists regularly represent this transgressive independence through the conjunction of the dressing room trope with some form of satiric comeuppance. Consider Burney's Madame Duval, maternal grandmother of Evelina, who began life as an English barmaid. Owned by no one, Evelina needs a family, but the ridiculous and scheming Madame Duval is explicitly the *wrong* family member to adopt her—at least from the perspectives of Evelina, her guardian Mr. Villars, and the novelist. For starters, Madame Duval plans to force Sir John Belmont to acknowledge Evelina as his daughter and hatches a plot to take them to Paris. This "supposed foreigner" (52) lays claim to Evelina, much to the horror of Evelina and her surrogate family, the Mirvans.

If, as Kristina Straub explains, Madame Duval is censured throughout the novel because she "possesses a kind of renegade female strength," then this critique is sharply expressed through her misuse of the dressing room aesthetic.[72] Open to the stereotypically antifeminist charge that she attempts to look younger than she is, Madame Duval's toilet facilitates her desires for self-aggrandizement. The heroine holds the perspective of the novel's status quo: fashioning oneself through dressing room accessories is natural for heroines entering the marriage market, but transgressive and, ultimately, pathetic, for older women. Evelina's first characterization of her grandmother focuses on the garishness of her appearance: "She dresses very gaily, paints very high, and the traces of former beauty are still very visible in her face" (53). Given the fact that Evelina herself utilizes the toilet, the heroine's contention that Madame Duval "dresses very gaily, paints very high" is grounded in ageism; Evelina later writes, "I should have thought it impossible for a woman at her time of life to be so very difficult in regard to dress. What she may have in view, I cannot imagine, but the labour of the toilette seems the chief business of [Madame Duval's] life" (155). Jill Campbell's argument that such an older woman "epitomizes for her male viewers the horrific persistence of the female body after it has been declared socially dead at the end of its reign of beauty" suggests that Evelina takes up the male gaze.[73] Campbell focuses on Lady Mary Wortley Montagu and one need only remember Horace Walpole's withering description of Lady Mary from 1740, when they became acquainted in Florence, to see the correlation between the notion of appropriate female beauty and its illegitimate, aged imitation. Although his accounts of her later in life are decidedly kinder, Walpole describes Lady Mary with repeated reference to cosmetics and accessories that emphasize her body as grotesque: she "wears a foul mob, that does not cover her greasy black locks, that hang loose, never combed or curled. . . . Her face swelled violently on one side with the remains of a — —, partly covered with a plaister, and partly with white paint, which for cheapness she has bought so coarse, that you would not use it to wash a chimney."[74]

Walpole's and Evelina's comments make clear that if aging women are subject to scorn, then the dressing room trope makes this indictment all the more explicit and visible. "What [Madame Duval] may have in view" with her toilet, of course, also references Evelina's quiet condemnation of her grandmother's inappropriate flaunting of her sexuality with her lover, Monsieur Du Bois. Young women such as Evelina and her peers are expected to spend hours ensuring that they are properly "Londonized," though their own (and their maid's) labor is forgotten. But a Madame Duval-like figure carries traces of cosmetic construction about her. Moreover, there emerges a new distinction between the appropriate amount of cosmetic application and an inappropriate amount. Even though Evelina cannot recognize her own image after her urban makeover, her critique of Madame Duval "paint[ing] very high" assumes the ridiculousness of an aging woman who has pretensions of being young once again. Madame Duval is another "Lydia" from Lady Mary Wortley Montagu and John Gay's "The Toilette. A Town Eclogue," waiting vainly in her dressing room for admirers to attend her. Madame Duval is also a Francophile Lady Wishfort who wants her face to be painted just like a portrait taken years ago.

Out of the hands of the comparatively mild Evelina, the issue of Duval's appearance becomes a focal point of the novel's satire, carried out by Captain Mirvan. The captain's "highway robbers" bind Madame Duval's feet together, tie her to a tree, and leave her stranded in a ditch, all a cruel practical joke orchestrated to humiliate her. But the scene also underscores her already parodic and grotesque toilet; when Evelina rescues her grandmother, she reflects that "so forlorn, so miserable a figure, I never before saw" (148). At the best of times, Madame Duval's toilet leaves her open to mockery. This, however, is the worst of times:

> Her head-dress had fallen off; her linen was torn; her negligee had not a pin left in it; her petticoats she was obliged to hold on; and her shoes were perpetually slipping off. She was covered with dirt, weeds, and filth, and her face was really horrible, for the pomatum and powder from her head, and the dust from the road, were quite *pasted* on her skin by her tears, which, with her *rouge*, made so frightful a mixture, that she hardly looked human. (ibid.)

Madame Duval embodies the antidressing room, the woman whose makeup does not cover her physical deformities but emphasizes them. In the spirit of the dressing room trope's satiric heritage, this violent transformation renders Madame Duval comic and even Evelina knows it.[75] "The servants were ready to die with laughter" (148), she writes; Evelina does not call the footman to assist her with the rope, "being very unwilling to add to his mirth, by the sight of Madame Duval's situation" (147). But the most notable result of this assault is its silencing effect. Evelina is astonished that her grandmother would take back her wig, such "a great quantity of hair, in such a nasty condition," but its loss signifies to Madame Duval that she cannot be seen in public: "Why, I can't see nobody without them:—only look at me,—I was never so bad off in my life before. *Pardie*, if I'd know'd as much, I'd have brought two or three sets with me: but I'd never a thought of such a thing as this" (149). Without the wig, she cannot call on the justice of the peace, and she spends the night figuring out a way to hide her disarray from the captain; at last she contrives a solution, "which was, having a large gauze handkerchief pinned on her head as a hood, and saying she had the tooth-ach" (154). The very tools of beautification that render Evelina a universal object of speculation and desire produce in Madame Duval a carnivalesque misappropriation. But life without them is worse, for Duval feels silenced and erased: she cannot make a public appearance without the labors of the toilet.

The critique through the dressing room trope of flawed mother figures does not always focus on appearance, as in the case of Madame Duval, but may foreground, instead, behavior patterns borne from the self-delusion associated with the trope. Jane Austen borrows the dressing room trope to indict a maternal character in *Pride and Prejudice* (1813) by extending the potential for the abuses associated with "bad" mothers and their dressing rooms to implicate domesticity more generally. Within a domestic space permeated by Mrs. Bennet's clumsy machinations to marry off her five daughters, Austen's novel represents the father's study not as an emblem of paternal authority, but as a small space of dissension within a larger sphere of domestic effeminization. Characterized as an ineffective satirist, Mr. Bennet ridicules his wife "with no intention of reforming" her when Mrs. Bennet anxiously plays to any eligible bachelor's ego.[76] Prone to somber conversation or to reading quietly, Mr. Bennet frequently retreats to his sanctum: "In his library he had been always sure of leisure and tranquillity; and though prepared, as he told Elizabeth, to meet with folly and conceit in every other room in the house, he was used to be free from them there."[77] Although Mr. Bennet's study is only a residue of paternalistic privilege, it is a space for honesty, where the heroine Elizabeth may speak frankly to her father and explain that she loves Darcy and wants to accept his marriage proposal.

Austen explicitly juxtaposes the paternal study with the maternal dressing room, so as to denigrate the latter and its occupant. After Elizabeth announces her engagement in her mother's dressing room (the only scene to take place there), Mrs. Bennet is shocked into momentary silence, but then quickly regains her excitement and articulates it in precociously material terms. A marriage for a daughter is an all-too-desirable thing, and a union with Darcy (and his £10,000 a year) precipitates a rush to celebrate the very fine life that Mrs. Bennet envisages. Her reaction consists of short, exclamatory sentences focused on the material advantages such a match will produce, a combination of bewilderment and pride: "Who would have thought it! And is it really true? Oh! my sweetest Lizzy! how rich and how great you will be! What pinmoney, what jewels, what carriages you will have!"[78] If Pride and Prejudice is, as Claudia L. Johnson suggests, "almost shamelessly wish fulfilling," then part of its resolution fulfills Elizabeth's wish to refashion her family and to forget her flawed mother.[79] Elizabeth is the proper kind of novelistic heroine, who knows that looking nice is necessary, but who forgoes any mention of appearance (like her predecessors Grace Nugent, Miss Broadhurst, and even Clarissa); her mother is a blatant example of the dangers of frivolity long associated with the dressing room. Mrs. Bennet's dressing room monologue seals her fate in Austen's narrative, for the narrator follows this outburst with a description of the heroine's disappointment and shame: "Elizabeth, rejoicing that such an effusion was heard only by herself, soon went away."[80] Given a moment to reflect, Elizabeth "found, that though in the certain possession of [Darcy's] warmest affection, and secure of her relations' consent, there was still something to be wished for" in her own family, a desire that sets up the erasure of the Bennets in the novel's final paragraph.[81]

In the examples of Madame Duval and Mrs. Bennet—and one could easily add The Vicar of Wakefield's Mrs. Primrose—it is clear that the "problem" of the dressing room does not go away after the marriage plot concludes. Instead, domestic novels actively portray the continued snares that threaten to derail women throughout their maturation, even rendering them unfit role models upon whom novelists heap critique and ridicule and then eventually discard. These women stand as counterexamples in the bildungsromans that describe them, another set of implicit warnings to young heroines (and readers alike) that the potential of the dressing room for autonomy must be tempered and, ultimately, repressed. Conflict arises because, of course, these women are out of the marriage market (at least its traditional form, though Madame Duval clearly enjoys Monsieur Du Bois) and have comparatively little to lose. What they suffer, then, is novelistic ridicule and erasure. Madame Duval not only enacts social aping—seeming to forget, even, that she is not actually French—but also is an emblem of the dangers that mismothering can cause; for this reason, the novel's marriage plot must dispose of the threat that she embodies, ultimately displacing her misrule with the rule of the father, Sir John Belmont, who finally acknowledges his daughter. In line with the older satiric tradition of ridicule and censure, both Burney and Austen, famous for their subtle and often brutal use of the mode, level these deviant mother figures into inconsequentiality.[82]

The examples considered so far contain these maternal figures by satirizing them and making them fundamentally powerless; however, domestic novels may also suggest precisely the opposite: some bad mothers are in desperate need of reformation because they have the potential to wreck both social and economic havoc on their families. The mother in Belinda Edgeworth's *The Absentee*, Lady Clonbrony, is an Anglo-Irish woman seduced by the frosty airs of London society and ever anxious to ingratiate herself among the finest set. After learning of his parents' debts taken to present themselves in this fashionable milieu, her son, Lord Colambre, openly lectures his mother; although his father was close to forfeiting the son's inheritance secretly to pay the current debts, it is Lady Clonbrony who receives the brunt of her son's—and the novel's—scorn: "And at what expence [*sic*] have we done all this? For a single season, the last winter (I will go no farther), at the expence of a great part of your timber, the growth of a century—swallowed in the entertainments of one winter in London!" (200). A family's lavish lifestyle is blamed solely on the maternal will, such that Lord Colambre contends that it is his mother's responsibility to save them all and to "restore my father to himself!" (201). Ironically, Lady Clonbrony has the power to "ruin" the family and serves as a scapegoat for both father and son, but is herself "tricked" back to Ireland with the promise of living the same kind of life there, one filled with social importance *and* elegance. She is convinced to return to the family's estate when given the chance to redecorate the castle's interior—"if any body could conceive, how I detest the sight, the thoughts of that old yellow damask furniture, in the drawing-room at Clonbrony Castle—" (202). Lady Clonbrony's distaste for her pastoral life in Ireland narrows to the fabric on her chairs and, by appealing to her vanity without ultimately questioning it, the family may once again take up their position as landlords in residence.

The son blames and manipulates his mother, and the novel justifies his behavior through an explicitly carnivalesque dressing room scene in Lady Clonbrony's abandoned Irish estate. The novel artfully counterpoints Lady Clonbrony's London excesses with a mercantilist insurrection staged in her dressing room in Clonbrony Castle in Ireland; the episode richly emblematizes what Anne K. Mellor identifies as Edgeworth's association between successful egalitarian domestic arrangements and the practices of good government.[83] But the scene also emphasizes a lack of aristocratic propriety that produces a desire for the traditional terms of distinction to be restored, as they are by the novel's end. The novel contrives this exposé by constructing a journey to Ireland for the young heir, both to avoid the company of his beloved but unattainable Grace Nugent and to see his family's holdings for himself. To apprehend the true nature of the estate's health, he decides to travel incognito. Apparent immediately is the misrule that has taken root in the family estate. Not only does the castle bear an "air of desertion and melancholy" with its "broken piers," "mossy gravel and loose steps at the hall-door," and formerly forested lands turned to "white stumps . . . to make up the last remittances" (167); it has also been overrun by Lord Clonbrony's agent, Nicholas Garraghty, and his associates. On this particular day, with the son and heir in attendance incognito, Nicholas takes his meetings in Lady Clonbrony's dressing room, claiming that his office is too damp. Tenants and business visitors are directed up the grand staircase of the castle, "through the magnificent apartments, hung with pictures of great value, spoiling with damp" (168). A crush of people clamor to get the attention of Nicholas and his brother Dennis.

> There was a full levee, and fine smell of great coats.—"O, would you put your hats on the silk cushions?" said the widow to some men in the doorway, who were throwing off their greasy hats on a damask sofa.
> "Why not? where else?"
> "If the lady was in it, you wouldn't," said she, sighing.
> "No, to be sure, I wouldn't: great news! would I make no *differ* in the presence of old Nick and my lady?" said he, in Irish. "Have I no sense or

manners, good woman, think ye?" added he, as he shook the ink out of the pen on the Wilton carpet, when he had finished signing his name to a paper on his knee.

(ibid.)

In this mock dressing room scene, greasy hats, inky pens, agents, and the "Irish" language are signs of aristocratic abdication: Lady Clonbrony has inappropriately *absented* herself from her estate and responsibilities, replaced by the principle of self-advancement. Aristocratic benevolence is displaced by this "perfect picture of an insolent, petty tyrant in office" (168), who takes "compliment" (169) money into his private purse moments before refusing to renew the widow's leases and to return her house key. This is not the playful, temporary indiscretion of the carnivalesque, but, from the novelist's point of view, a dangerous shift from the governance of hierarchical rule to a freewheeling and corrupt marketplace. Transformed from a place for a Lady Bountiful to act out her charitable designs to a setting for one "Mr. Nicholas Garraghty, seated in state" to steal money, the dressing room serves as a moral thermometer to measure the damage of negligent landowners, locating the origin of this lapse in the desires of women. The memory of the Lord and Lady Clonbrony's goodness haunts the scene (and their community), highlighting the cost of Lady Clonbrony's desire to ascend to the highest spheres of London society. Left in their wake is a set of agents who take great profits at the expense of the poor tenants *and* of the landowners. The dangerous pleasures of the dressing room exemplify and facilitate, on a local level, the vanity that motivates Lady Clonbrony in nearly everything she does. But Edgeworth's novel also moralizes that the dangers of the dressing room extend far beyond the character of a mother to the familial unit and its place in society; if Lady Clonbrony has the power to restore the father to himself, as her son pleads, then she also has the power to secure her son's inheritance and the well-being of her tenants. Extending from the boundaries of this family romance, Edgeworth's narrative warns that the mother's selfishness and vanity also threaten the livelihood and well-being of an estate and those who depend upon its economy.

The "perfection of motherhood": Domesticity and Maternal Virtue

It is no surprise that bad mothers in the domestic novel are represented through the trope of the dressing room, given its satiric heritage and persistent associations with illicit female agency. But the cases of

Madame Duval, Mrs. Bennet, and Lady Clonbrony raise two important questions: What makes a *good* mother? Can a woman be a good mother and have a dressing room, too? Just as heroines are configured through the dichotomy of the dressing room, maternal figures are likewise subject to the trope's idealizing powers. A famous portrait of Queen Charlotte suggests that the dressing room may also be a site for maternal order, if not redemption. The German painter Johann Zoffany, who had gained the admiration of George III and was nominated by him to the Royal Academy in 1769, painted a royal conversation piece, *Queen Charlotte with her Two Eldest Sons* around 1766. The queen is painted in her dressing room on the first floor of Buckingham Palace, flanked by her sons the Prince of Wales and Prince Frederick and a dog, on whose head the queen rests her hand. The boys are dressed, respectively, in a "Telemachus Dress" and in a "Turk's," while Charlotte wears a rich ivory gown.[84] Charles Saumarez Smith notes that Zoffany took liberties with the decoration of the dressing room, but the portrait is notable for

Johann Zoffany, *Queen Charlotte with her Two Eldest Sons*, ca. 1766. The Royal Collection © 2004, Her Majesty Queen Elizabeth II.

its detailed representation of this interior space.[85] The portrait fore-grounds a meticulously rendered dressing table with extravagant lace-work and an elaborate toilet service made up of gold plate containers and crystal bottles. Charlotte, here figured as mother to the two young princes, turns her back on the toilet, leaving her profile reflected in its peering glass. Clearly, the labors of the toilet have ceased: is she always ready, as Grace Nugent is? Frances Burney's letters from court, where she served as Second Keeper of the Robes to Queen Charlotte from 1786–91, would suggest otherwise, as her accounts detail the rigors and time-consuming nature of attending the queen's toilet throughout the day; Burney was in attendance from six in the morning until midnight.[86] But in this public display of Zoffany's portrait, the ease of motherhood surrounds the queen in her dressing room. With the children in fancy dress, a toy drum cast on a side chair, and a family pet in attendance, this portrait "cleans up" the dressing room by making it familial. This is not an enclosed, secretive space: the large window looks out broadly onto the garden front of the palace, the door into the corridor is thrown wide open, and a large mirror behind the queen's head reflects another image of the opened door. The corridor itself is light and broad, with only a hint of something hidden in the reflected face of a waiting woman down the hall. The focus of the portrait, the maternal dressing room, is open to view and publicly memorialized. Its emphasis on transparency, manifested in the windows, mirrors, and passageways, functions to den-igrate the potential for autonomy and independence with which the dressing room had been associated. Here, with the brush of Johann Zoffany, the lady's dressing room is transformed into a private and *ma-ternal* space, paradoxically ready for public display, inspection, and cel-ebration.

Just as "bad" maternal figures are represented through their dressing rooms, the iconography of Zoffany's portrait suggests that there may be a productive convergence of "proper" maternity and the dressing room trope and, additionally, that the two may also be fundamentally inter-twined. In the tradition of readings produced for women to consume in private, Lady Sydney Owenson Morgan published *The Book of the Bou-doir* (1829), an instructional manual with essays on topics ranging from "Egoism and Egotism," "Eternity," and "Doctrine of Causation" to "Love in Idleness," "Foreign Visiters" [*sic*], and "Fêtes, Parties, and Soirées." While Lady Morgan's explanation of her book haphazardly finding its way into print was duly mocked by reviewers, she explains that *The Book of the Boudoir* is the result of nightly entries composed in private.[87] Speaking to its title, Lady Morgan writes,

All who have the supreme felicity of haunting great houses, are aware, that those odd books, which are thrown on round tables, or in the recesses of windows, to amuse the lounger of the moment, and are not in the catalogue of the library, are frequently stamped, in gold letters, with the name of the room to which they are destined: as thus; — "Elegant Extracts, Drawing-room;" "Spirit of the Journals, Saloon," &c. &c. As my Book of the Boudoir kept its place in the little room which bore that title, and was never admitted into my bureau of official authorship, it took the name of its *locale*. (v)

The locale suggests that women may not only consume reading materials, but also produce them.

Relevant to this discussion is the essay entitled "Wonderful Children, and Good Mothers," in which Lady Morgan's conceptualization of maternity points to its potentially contradictory nature, and the extent to which the *assumption* of maternity resonates with the domestic novel's imperative to reform the dressing room and its occupant. She argues that "the more or less powerful instinct of maternity is an affair of temperament, nurtured or modified by other instincts or passions, and by circumstances favourable or unfavourable to its existence" (243–44). Lady Morgan insists that this "instinct of maternity" is not an "abstraction" or a natural attribute, but that it instead requires vigilant socialization and education to be realized: "The perfection of motherhood lies, therefore, in the harmonious blending of a happy instinct, with those qualities which make the good members of general society — with good sense and information — with subdued or regulated passions, and that abnegation, which lays every selfish consideration at the feet of duty" (245). Motherhood, argues Lady Morgan, is produced simultaneously by nature and nurture, a woman's individual makeup and her socialization. Good women turn into good mothers, primarily because they are attuned to the necessities of socialization and subjection. This precarious situation parallels the young heroine's development in the domestic novel — she must both *be* naturally good and *learn* to live a good life in the ways available in and expected by her milieu.

After articulating the ideals of maternity, maternal role models, and the maternal instruction necessary to produce good mothers, Lady Morgan turns her attention to the novelist Maria Edgeworth. While Edgeworth produced educational texts for youth, *Practical Education* (1798), Lady Morgan, also a novelist (*The Wild Irish Girl*), reprimands her fellow Irishwoman for a wholesale neglect of motherhood as an instructional category: "Clever and truth-telling Miss Edgeworth — you who have written such rational and charming books for children — why have you not written some *easy lessons* for their mothers? Why have you not composed an easy manual for their use, to teach them a few elementary facts in physics and in morals; and, above all, to teach them that nature, in all things, is the sole basis of right thinking and right acting,

under all circumstances, and in all times?" (247).[88] Lady Morgan's indictment of Edgeworth's textual production is telling, particularly when
one turns to Edgeworth's novel *Belinda*. This novel does not include
pedagogical tracts, but it does feature a powerful mother who is in dras-
tic need of reformation. As we shall see, in *Belinda*, Edgeworth uniquely
uses the trope of the dressing room first as a measure of this mother's
failures and then as a site for her redemption as a matriarch.

"A Romance called the Mysterious Boudoir": Maternal Reformation, *Belinda*, and the Genres of the Novel

Following the pattern of domestic novels in the latter part of the eighteenth century, Maria Edgeworth's *Belinda* (1801) depends upon the
trope of the dressing room to produce a narrative that features character development and reformation in explicitly maternalistic terms. As
evident through the reading of Edgeworth's *Belinda* that follows, the
dressing room trope by the end of the eighteenth century is associated
with motherhood and the potential for maternal reformation. Unlike the
portrayals of unsuitable mothers in Burney and Austen, Edgeworth
uniquely conjoins the trope of the dressing room not to the satiric mode,
but to the question of romance and narrative form. This generic mobil-
ity allows for a relation with an entirely new set of literary concerns.
Within Edgeworth's narrative, the dressing room trope is inserted into
a generic debate about the relative value of "romance" in opposition to
moralistic stories, a debate that compounds Richardson's preoccupation
with creating a virtuous narrative form and that reorients it from an
opposition between satire and the novel to one between *romance* and the
novel.

Lady Delacour, the fashionable and wealthy socialite and temporary
guardian of the novel's heroine, Belinda Portman, initiates the young
woman into the pleasures of polite society—balls, masquerades, and
gossip. But from the start, Lady Delacour's demeanor is far too like that
of a "spoiled actress off the stage."[89] As a fashionable and aristocratic
woman, Lady Delacour's independence, taste, and activities all go
against the grain of the kind of harmonious domestic setting implicitly
idealized throughout the novel. Rather than acting as a wise maternal
figure to Belinda, much less as a mother to her own daughter Helena,
Lady Delacour's likeness to an actress manifests itself in her being
"over stimulated by applause, and exhausted by the exertions of supporting a fictitious character" (10–11). The novel's early narration indicates a disjunction between Lady Delacour's public and private

performances, a gap exploited by the novel's sustained use of the dressing room trope.

Our introduction to Lady Delacour's dressing room comes through the figure of Marriott, her trusted servant. In the second chapter, with the none-too-subtle title "Masks," Marriott appears on the dressing room's threshold holding costumes for Belinda and Lady Delacour to wear to a masquerade. The theatricality of that evening's form of entertainment, Lady Delacour's conversation about how to dress, and the dressing room itself imbue the conversation and narration: Lady Delacour observes to Belinda, " 'But whilst we are making speeches to one another, poor Marriott is standing in distress like Garrick, between tragedy and comedy.' Lady Delacour opened her dressing-room door, and pointed to [Marriott] as she stood with the dress of the comic muse on one arm, and the tragic muse on the other" (19). The explicit references to players and drama resonate with the dressing room trope's seventeenth-century antecedent, the tiring-room.

The sight of Marriott, the dresses, and the forbidden, secret room prompt Belinda into a whirl of speculation, demonstrating the continued imaginative effect of the dressing room. The sequence of explanations for what Lady Delacour's dressing room contains — or, more appropriately, hides — rehearses the connotations that we have seen persist throughout the late seventeenth and eighteenth centuries. Predictably, the first possibility relates to Lady Delacour's physical appearance: "Miss Portman at first imagined that lady Delacour dreaded the discovery of her cosmetic secrets, but her ladyship's rouge was so glaring, and her pearl powder was so obvious, that Belinda was convinced there must be some other cause of this toilette secrecy" (20–21). Lady Delacour has the garishness of a Madame Duval or a Lydia or a Lady Wishfort, an older woman painting herself into ridiculousness. But she is certainly hiding something related to her toilet. In the following scene at Lady Singleton's house, Lady Delacour and Belinda exchange dresses and Lady Delacour conspicuously dons hers alone in a bolted closet, which distresses Lady Singleton's maid: "Lord bless and forgive me, . . . but, if your la'ship has not been dressing all this time in that den, without any thing in the shape of a looking glass — and not to let me help! I that should have been so proud" (22). Lady Delacour's response is trifling; she gives the maid a half-guinea and "laughed affectedly at her own *whimsicalities*, and declared, that she could always dress herself better without a glass than with one" (22). It is because of this that Belinda wonders whether the secrecy derives from Lady Delacour's selfishness with regard to Marriott, the only servant allowed to wait on her.

The second kind of explanation that Belinda considers borrows from the tradition of skepticism for the autonomy provided women on their own. Unlike the tiring-room, a space of relatively *open* and even self-conscious theatricality, however, Lady Delacour's dressing room evokes the context of privacy, a relation that we have seen regularly associated with illicit models of femininity, when the narrator reflects that "there had always been some mystery about her ladyship's toilette; at certain hours doors were bolted, and it was impossible for any body but Marriott to obtain admission" (20). Sensitive to the fact that the room is off limits to everyone save Marriott and that it has a private entrance "by a back stair-case" (21), Belinda's speculations implicitly suggest that the room is analogous to the fundamentally uncontrollable female body, a body implicitly sexualized. Later in the novel, Lord Delacour admits a suspicion that realizes this association when he fears that his wife hides a lover inside, a conclusion that others are only too ready to believe (128). Even later, a nosy and gossipy servant tries to pry her way inside after hearing footsteps behind the door (295). The novel's inaugural dressing room scene anticipates these interpretations by moving swiftly from an explicit critique of artificial female beauty to the vexed nature of women's privacy.

Deviating from the typical structure of suspense, Edgeworth explicitly introduces the tension of the lady's dressing room only to release it pages later near the same chapter's conclusion. Lady Delacour repeatedly demands the key to the boudoir from Marriott and frantically beckons Belinda to follow her inside:

> The room was rather dark, as there was no light in it, except what came from one candle, which lady Delacour held in her hand, and which burned but dimly. Belinda, as she looked round, saw nothing but a confusion of linen rags — vials, some empty, some full — and she perceived that there was a strong smell of medicines.
>
> Lady Delacour, whose motions were all precipitate, like those of a person whose mind is in great agitation, looked from side to side of the room, without seeming to know what she was in search of. She then, with a species of fury, wiped the paint from her face, and returning to Belinda, held the candle so as to throw the light full upon her livid features. Her eyes were sunk, her cheeks hollow — no trace of youth or beauty remained on her deathlike countenance, which formed a horrid contrast with her gay fantastic dress. (31)

In a Bertha Mason moment, Lady Delacour embodies the contradictions visualized by such pictorial representations as Robert Dighton's *Life and Death Contrasted* (1784), where one half of the figure displays the accoutrements of fashionable life and the other half is a skeleton. Images such as these were commonly read as representing the "transitory vanities of society which conceal human mortality," but they are particularly associated with older women inappropriately using the materials of the dressing room.[90]

But Lady Delacour reveals herself to be a gothic specter amid a *medicinal* landscape. We can remember Edgeworth's own appreciation for the dressing room she uses at the Strutts, which is beautifully furnished with a toilet and a writing desk.[91] Unlike any of the dressing rooms I have discussed, Edgeworth's *Belinda* draws a space of female privacy that sequesters illness, and it is the very nature of this ailment that sets the stage not only to express the depravity of Lady Delacour's condition, but also to lay the groundwork for her recuperation and reformation in the novel. The dressing room hides the secret of Lady Delacour's diseased breast, which she exposes to Belinda: "You are shocked," Lady Delacour says to Belinda, "'but as yet you have seen nothing— look here—' and baring one half of her bosom, she revealed a hideous spectacle" (32). Lady Delacour is haunted by her own failings, sensitive to her lack of cooperation with what Elizabeth Kowaleski-Wallace calls a "new-style patriarchy."[92] But this type of social arrangement demands the internalization of its imperatives—in this case, the "sense of maternal guilt and obligation."[93] To Lady Delacour, her infected—which she believes to be cancerous—breast is a symptom of her maternal guilt and obligation; she confesses in desperation that "I have sacrificed reputation, happiness—every thing, to the love of frolic" (30), a passion that now necessitates the "horrid business of my toilette" (33). The particular form of frolic to which she alludes is her relationship with the sexually androgynous Harriet Freke. Although the connotation of "freak" as "monster" was not available until the mid-nineteenth century, Freke's name nevertheless marks her as a signifier of difference, and it quickly becomes apparent that this difference is sexual.[94] Given to cross-dressing, and sporting "bold masculine arms" (49), Harriet Freke had "a wild oddity in her countenance which made one stare at her"— and Lady Delacour desire her (43). Although Belinda steps in as Lady Delacour's confidant early in the novel, Harriet Freke returns again and again, and several critics have commented on Harriet Freke's homoerotic status in the novel. Emma Donoghue calls Harriet "one of the most memorable of fictional lesbians" and Lisa L. Moore astutely notes Harriet's role in the novel's domestication of its heroine: "her several reappearances work to expose the political and moral ruin threatening young ladies who trust too much to intimacy with other women, as well as the grave consequences for society of such relationships."[95]

Lady Delacour attributes her physical, moral, and social problems to her intimacy with Harriet. In her competition with Mrs. Luttridge for social supremacy, Lady Delacour finds herself ensnared with Harriet in

the duel. When Lady Delacour discharges her pistol, it recoils and damages her breast; her injury is compounded when a local mob assembles
to taunt and harass the women. Following these events, Lady Delacour's guilt is complex. It obviously relates to the secret of her ill-health,
causing her an abundant amount of pain and discomfort and isolating
her from her family. But it also renders her dressing room a figure for
illicit female sexuality in a new way. With the emphasis on a breast,
Edgeworth's novel suggests a correlation between the female body and
female private space that we have not seen up to this point. The injury
to Lady Delacour's breast actively suggests an Amazonian independence and eroticism and Lady Delacour refers to herself as an Amazon
twice in the novel; Kathryn Schwarz reminds us that Amazons were
constituted in the early modern era "out of an inappropriate relationship between sexed bodies and gendered acts, constructing an identity
defined by the agency of sexual choice and by a perception of that
choice as inherently perverse."[96] For one of the first times in the history
of the dressing room metaphor, we have the potential for illicit sex between two women. The novel's punitive end for Harriet Freke confirms
her deviance and renders it in suggestively phallic terms. The day before Lady Delacour is "cured," Harriet is scarred when she steps into a
gardener's trap, mutilating her leg and eliminating the possibility that
she might "appear to advantage dressed in man's apparel" (312). The
man-woman Harriet Freke pulls Lady Delacour into a torpor of female
sexuality and indiscretion; thus, Lady Delacour interprets her own
wounded breast as the cost of transgressing the bounds of (hetero)sexu-
ality.

While the homoerotic potential of Lady Delacour's dressing room remains in place—underscored through the almost unexplainable closeness between Marriott and Lady Delacour that Belinda pries apart by
taking over part of Lady Delacour's toilet[97]—the novel jettisons the
question of transgressive sexual independence with the imagery of maternity. In this context, the breast is also a sign of maternal health, and
Lady Delacour's pain and infection are the most visible sign of her failure as a mother. As Susan C. Greenfield argues, "new commercialism
and old aristocratic values conspire to objectify" Lady Delacour's maternity.[98] No wonder, then, that Lady Delacour fails the domestic ideal,
particularly as a mother. Her first child died. The second she nursed, as
it was the fashion to breast-feed, but this one died, too. Her third, Helena, was sent to the country and adopted a surrogate family in the Per-
civals. If the loss of the breast is Edgeworth's way of representing
improper female independence and eroticism, then its recovery signals
the reconstitution of maternity.

Even the prospect of recovery is tempered, as Lady Delacour's ability to mother her surviving child is measured by the health of her breast. While Helena is long past breast-feeding, the narrative stages a crucial scene in which Lady Delacour desires—for the first time—to be a good mother, but does not have the capacity to be one. During a temporary reunion between mother and daughter, Lady Delacour compliments Helena by saying that she is "one of the sweetest little girls in the world" and begs her to "Kiss me, my child" (173). Helena's enthusiasm is desperate, but inadvertently highlights the provisional nature of Lady Delacour's recovery as a mother: "The little girl sprang forwards, and threw her arms around her mother, exclaiming, 'Oh, mamma! are you in earnest?' and she pressed close to her mother's bosom, clasping her with all her force" (ibid.). This scene of affection, however, is quickly aborted when Lady Delacour screams in pain and pushes her daughter away. The diseased maternal breast, the mother's bosom against which the lonely daughter presses herself, cannot withstand "all the force" of a child and, ultimately, cannot function properly. The pain of her breast tests Lady Delacour's relationship with her daughter, but its exposure quickly reestablishes that with her husband. Though an aristocratic degenerate in his own right—a gambler and an alcoholic—Lord Delacour immediately reforms his ways when Lady Delacour finally shows him her injury during an unnarrated scene in the boudoir (268–69). This is the first time she has shown her body to him in years, a revelation that prompts Lord Delacour's profession of love.

In a multitude of ways, Lady Delacour's status as a fashionable, aristocratic woman explicitly threatens the ideals of domesticity.[99] But good mothers do not threaten domesticity, they embody it—often literally. The good mother in the novel turns out to be Helena's foster mother, Lady Anne Percival, and the narrative reiterates this ideal by focusing on the two women's *physical* differences. If Edgeworth presents Lady Delacour as a highly painted, fabricated lady of fashion, then she likewise presents Lady Anne as the antithesis in character and affect. In a passage that could very well be considered another kind of antidressing room scene, we see the ideal mother through the eyes of one of Lady Delacour's gallants (and eventual suitor to Belinda):

> Clarence Hervey was so much struck with the expression of happiness in lady Anne's countenance, that he absolutely forgot to compare her beauty with lady Delacour's. Whether her eyes were large or small, blue or hazel, he could not tell; nay, he might have been puzzled if he had been asked the colour of her hair. Whether she were handsome by rules of art, he knew not; but he felt that she had the essential charm of beauty, the power of prepossessing the heart immediately in her favour. The effect of her manners, like that of her beauty, was rather to be felt than described. (98)

A literary descendent of Richardson's Clarissa, Lady Anne Percival fills a room, but not with her physical beauty, which is left undescribed. Her presence is *felt* but not registered; she brings the best out in those around her, but she herself is rendered an intangible entity, embodying the ideal domestic woman whose value far exceeds her surface appeal.[100] The novel *Belinda* institutes a powerful corrective to the rakishness and errors of Lady Delacour in the figure of Lady Anne Percival, and does it by revising the rhetoric of the dressing room. Clarence Hervey's narration evokes the anatomization of the dressing room trope, only to displace it with sentiment. Though Lady Anne is certainly not the heroine of the novel nor the center of readerly identification, she strongly anticipates the angel in the house whom Coventry Patmore so idealizes in the nineteenth century and against whom Virginia Woolf rails in the twentieth. Watching Lady Anne Percival, young Belinda Portman realizes that "domestic life was that which could alone make her really and permanently happy" (217), a feminized domestic ideal that subsequently haunts the nineteenth-century novel.

If the opening chapters of the novel *Belinda* establish both the problem that afflicts Lady Delacour and implicitly chart the terms of her restoration, then why do we return for a second exposure of the same space one hundred pages later? In other words, Edgeworth establishes and reveals the mystery of Lady Delacour's boudoir just pages into the novel, but returns to the question of its status as a space in chapter 10, entitled "The Mysterious Boudoir." Why open its doors again?

The first reason is epistemological. When Belinda takes the initiative to find adequate medical help, Lady Delacour resists calling a physician to attend her for fear of the secret getting out; she is particularly concerned that the suggested Dr. X— — would expose her to Clarence Hervey.[101] Finally gaining her ladyship's permission, Belinda recruits the services of Dr. X— —, but he must decide whether to take on the case of Lady Delacour. To convince him, Belinda offers to take the doctor into Lady Delacour's private space (by way of the back staircase) to explain to him the nature of Lady Delacour's ailments, "to give positive proofs of my speaking truth" (132). It is the matter of Dr. X— —'s conditions that are of particular interest; he agrees to enter the room, but with the following caveat: "As a polite man . . . I believe that I should absolutely refuse to take any external evidence of a lady's truth; but demonstration is unanswerable even by enemies" (ibid.). Dr. X— —'s concern is the suspicion of the household, namely that Lady Delacour hides a lover in her dressing room. But Belinda's exposé, unlocking the room to reveal its horrific medicinal furnishings, will serve as evidence of Lady Delacour's sickness rather than moral depravity. Beneath Dr. X— —'s response is an assumption that the tools of empiricism produce secure and stable facts. The novel's second examination of Lady Delacour's dressing room corroborates the epistemology that, paradoxically, Swift's Strephon uses throughout "The Lady's Dressing Room." Looking through her belongings, Dr. X— — comes to this re- cuperative conclusion: "this cabinet was the retirement of disease, and not of pleasure" (133). The introduction of Dr. X— — and his reason- able diagnosis of Lady Delacour reinforces the novel's endorsement of empirical principles echoed elsewhere through Lady Anne Percival and her household management. Dr. X— — pronounces that Lady Dela- cour suffers, but not from her injury; instead, her quack has gotten her addicted to "terrible quantities of laudanum" (313), a drug used to "weaken the sentient power of the nerves."[102] Lady Delacour does not need a mastectomy or any other kind of surgery. She has the potential to heal herself into a proper matriarch.

Edgeworth uses this second dressing room scene for another reason: to draw an equally vital generic distinction, a move that illuminates the adaptability of the dressing room trope to a range of literary debates. Several critics have astutely noted the two narratives in the novel, the first dealing with Lady Delacour's maternity and the second with the British colonies.[103] Indeed, as Felicity A. Nussbaum has shown, mater- nity and empire were deeply implicated in one another through the course of the eighteenth and nineteenth centuries, for "the domestic monogamous Englishwoman, who personifies chaste maternal woman- hood, frequently contrasts to the wanton polygamous Other."[104] But I argue that *Belinda* also incorporates a generic shift of significance at this point. As we recall, Samuel Richardson productively appropriated the dressing room trope, in part, to distinguish the satiric mode from his novelistic style, concluding with a form of narrative theory that pro- moted his heroines' virtuous narratives at the expense of satire. This is not to say that Edgeworth does not use satire, for the novel is filled with a range of satiric moments.[105] But satire is not the focus of Edgeworth's generic anxiety. In *Belinda* we have a different, but equally significant, set of generic claims made through the trope of the dressing room. In addition to providing a rational explanation for Lady Delacour's suffer- ing, the surgeon voices Edgeworth's literary agenda. The doctor tells Belinda, "my dear miss Portman, you will put a stop to a number of charming stories by this prudence of yours—a romance called the Mys- terious Boudoir, of nine volumes at least, might be written on this sub- ject, if you would only condescend to act like almost all other heroines, that is to say, without common sense" (132–33). Belinda's actions, which change the course of the narrative, also change the *type* of narra- tive that novel produces. She assumes the mantle of common sense and precipitates a generic reversal.

Through this renunciation, Edgeworth expresses dissatisfaction with the terminology of literary classification available to her. The now accepted divide between novel and romance was instituted in the eighteenth century—some would say codified by 1785 in Clara Reeve's usage—though the terms could be used interchangeably up through the early part of the century.[106] In his long review article of Jane Austen in 1815–16, Sir Walter Scott posits romance as the novel's predecessor, writing that "the novel was the legitimate child of the romance . . . and the manners and general turn of the composition were altered so as to suit modern times."[107] But even this classification was not adequate to Edgeworth's literary sense; the novelist hoped for a term to differentiate "philosophical novels" ("written both to reveal and to extend that inner life of continuous discrimination and ethical choice") from "trifling silly productions."[108] Her rejection of the term "romance" puts her at odds with what Jane Spencer identifies as the "feminocentric" novelistic tradition that used "romance" to refer to "a certain attitude to women" that valued their concerns and desires.[109] Edgeworth's novels do not repudiate the aristocratic notions of honor and love long associated with the romance, nor this sense of women's value, but they do demote the moral freedom implied in a heroine's adventures, just as Lennox's countess warns nearly half a century earlier. Rather than finishing *Belinda* as a romance "of nine volumes at least," Edgeworth explicitly identifies it in the "Advertisement" as "a Moral Tale—the author not wishing to acknowledge a Novel. . . . so much folly, errour, and vice are disseminated in books classed under this denomination, that it is hoped the wish to assume another title will be attributed to feelings that are laudable, and not fastidious." Edgeworth's *Belinda* redeploys the dialectic within romance that Michael McKeon identifies with the formation of the novel, particularly insofar as "romance" in its historical sense was a genre preoccupied with (McKeon implies) female chastity and constancy.[110] The "romance called the Mysterious Boudoir" would undoubtedly conceptualize Lady Delacour in transgressively sexual terms, so its denigration ushers in the generic possibility of moralistic, if imperialistic, narrative.[111]

The opening of Lady Delacour's secret boudoir ensures the production of a "Moral Tale" rather than a "romance," and simultaneously allows Edgeworth to endorse a particular model of aristocratic propriety and maternity. As Mitzi Myers argues, "*Belinda* is a reparative mythology romancing the abandonment of daughters and making their fate come out right."[112] But it is not just daughters who "come out right." Against the background of Zoffany's portrait of Queen Charlotte in her dressing room, we can identify the importance that opening up Lady Delacour's secret boudoir bears on her transformation from a fashionable woman into a proper matriarch. In fact, what follows in the narrative are the tumultuous reformation of Lady Delacour and her subsequent social maneuverings, which are designed to ensure so-called proper courtships; this is a "Moral Tale" insofar as these alignments are designed to ensure the prosperity of the British empire. Belinda ultimately does not marry the Creole Vincent, who, it is revealed, gambles and disdains reason, and Lady Delacour arranges the events that lead to Virginia St. Pierre's attachment to Captain Sunderland, a union that leaves Hervey free for Belinda. In the latter part of the novel Lady Delacour is interested in aligning British "reproductive purity with colonial ambition."[113] When Lady Delacour rejects her fashionable lifestyle and develops into a proper mother, her coming out of the dressing room promises the world of *Belinda* clarity and order, even though these are attributes ultimately figured as contributing to conservative efforts designed to institute an imperialistic model of matriarchy — the matchmaker who ensures through her actions the persistence of the British status quo.

Edgeworth's novel structures its narrative through a recuperation and redefinition of the dressing room. From the novel's beginning to its end, the text utilizes the dressing room trope as a metonymy for the dangerous effects of female embodiment and as an occasion for the production of narrative — at first, a romance, and finally a moral tale. This "romance of the Mysterious Boudoir" is the literary analogue to Lady Delacour's fear she has breast cancer, an ailment that forecloses the possibility of her being a proper mother, unable as she is to hug her estranged daughter without great pain. Edgeworth's narrative focuses on questions that include the generic and ideological differences between "romances" and "Moral Tales," as well as the domestic roles and education of women. What Edgeworth's novel accomplishes is a double transformation: within the terms of the novel, this revelation facilitates the proper education of the young Belinda Portman and the recuperation of Lady Delacour as a mother; it also justifies Edgeworth's narrative form. We can therefore see in *Belinda* the convergence of the two uses to which the domestic novel puts the dressing room trope: as an obstacle that must be negotiated for a young woman to develop and to find success on the marriage market and as a means for maternal figures to realize their errors. To these occasions for character development, Edgeworth adds a new means of negotiating generic difference — using the trope of the dressing room to debate the merits of moral tales over romances.

Coda: "Vanity Knows No Limits in a Woman's Dressing Room"

IN SOME WAYS CHARACTERISTIC OF HIS AGE, SHAFTESBURY COMPLAINS that the eighteenth-century female world was defined by "rich stuffs, and coloured silks," a reference that materially identifies theatricality and artifice as feminine attributes.[1] As we have seen throughout this book, femininity in the eighteenth century was regularly and insistently figured through the trope of the dressing room, a strategy that could likewise produce a range of unexpected connotations, including the possibility for women to fashion themselves physically as well as intellectually. The metaphor of the dressing room could also offer writers a vehicle to express a range of other issues, particularly about aesthetics, epistemology, education, and motherhood, and to naturalize their opinions. Beginning with satires and concluding with domestic novels, this book charts a conceptual and generic history of eighteenth-century literary culture that underscores the richly vexed relations between kinds of literary writing, as well as a literary text's uneasy relationship to its contexts of cultural production.

Perhaps not surprisingly, Shaftesbury's complaint about women finds telling parallels in twenty-first-century representations of female identity that indicate the widespread legacy of the dressing room trope, ranging from home decoration to clothing stores. A fascination with "feminine" interior decoration shapes recent discussions of contemporary dressing rooms. In the March 2002 issue of the magazine *House Beautiful*, two decorators describe what they view as the best designs, features, and uses for a woman's dressing room in language that eerily adopts the rhetoric of adornment and of the eroticized female body that characterizes the eighteenth-century dressing room. When one decorator suggests that she prefers "an understated, glamorous 1940s-style oasis, all mirrors and painted trim" with a chair that has "a very girly shape with painted legs and plain fabric," she describes a decorative mode that conflates a sensual female body with a sensual decor.[2] These are rooms with several mirrors, soft lighting, and vanity tables, material objects that both facilitate the production of female beauty and stand as surrogates for it. *House Beautiful*'s "All Dolled Up" is presented as a guidebook for decorating that very special, very feminine domestic space of the dressing room, where a woman can "be herself." But it reads as a formula for female performance and for the objectification of women, not as a template for feminine authenticity. The professional advice offered to contemporary women in *House Beautiful* is not an anomaly: Hilary Robertson's interior design book, *Boudoir: Creating the Bedroom of Your Dreams*, conceptualizes the dressing room as a woman's personal expression, offering the objectification that "All Dolled Up" posits as a kind of feminine *agency*. Readers may select the kind of woman they want to *be*. Under the three headings "Romantic," "Sexy," and "Exotic," Robertson imagines interior decoration as a manifestation of feminine stereotypes, including "material girl," "ice queen," "fashionista," "starlet," "orientalist modernist," and "china girl."[3] The dressing room and the woman not only reflect each other, but Robertson's manual also implies that a woman cannot *be* one of these figures *without* the dressing room. This modern-day decoration book doubles as a conduct manual, instructing readers on just what these various women "want" out of life and how their boudoirs measure up.

The strategy of transforming the tools of objectification into a vehicle for autonomy informs the widespread commercialization of the most famous dressing room in contemporary American culture: the ubiquitous Victoria's Secret that populates nearly every mall. Decorated in reds, pinks, and gold, with princess furniture (merchandise for sale is often in "underwear" drawers), ornate peering glasses, and heavy curtains, Victoria's Secret transforms signifiers of private female sexuality into mass consumerism specifically aimed at women. Victoria's Secret is designed to attract female consumers by freeing the lingerie industry from its earlier associations with illicit sexuality, particularly the sex trade and pornography. This endeavor is big business: Victoria's Secret's parent company, The Limited, reported June 2003 sales of $832.8 million. As the store's name attests, the explicit reference is to the nineteenth-century corset and the interior decoration of many of its stores, as well as the style of its lingerie lines in the 1990s, highlight the connection.[4] But the historical antecedent is also eighteenth century. The contradictory imperative built into the store's message—buy that sexy lingerie and be yourself—trades on the eighteenth-century dressing room's associations with female sexuality, privilege, secrecy, and consumerism. The company's annual runway shows on network television and the Web feature supermodels walking the catwalk in their underwear. If sex sells, then Victoria's Secret has managed to sell it openly and publicly. Current collections of lingerie—"Such a Flirt™: Playfully Seductive," "Very Sexy™: Very Provocative," and "Glamour by Victoria's Secret™"—likewise cash in on the commodification of femininity under the guise of giving women a way to be independent and "themselves."[5] The marketing of Victoria's Secret sends this message: play this role (and buy this product) and you will be a real woman, the woman you always wanted to be. Part of the modern-day shopping experience also includes the cosmetic counter that opens nearly every large department store, each corporate brand reaching out to the female consumer by offering a personalized "makeover" right there in the store.

My thumbnail sketch of contemporary manifestations of the eighteenth-century dressing room could continue by looking at voyeurism on the Internet or to a variety of fashion magazines. But I hope my point is clear: the issues that the lady's dressing room foregrounds continue to shape representations of gender, sexuality, privacy, consumerism, agency, and autonomy. What we have now is a dead metaphor; dressing rooms do not necessarily exist as they did in the eighteenth century, but their powers of figuration linger.

In this book, my argument has been twofold. The first is a chronological claim that the dressing room trope's connotations within satire, and then later in the novel, reflect changing notions of gender and genre in the eighteenth century. The eighteenth-century dressing room originally connoted a sense of female lasciviousness and sexuality, and was consistently allied with the satiric mode. Only later did the dressing room come to be a figure for female virtue and maternity in domestic novels. The second argument of this book posits that the dressing room trope in eighteenth-century literary culture speaks to *more* than gender and genre, and that this is particularly evident in the trope's centrality to debates about aesthetics, epistemology, virtue, education, and maternity. Within this simultaneously conceptual and chronological narrative about gender and genre in the eighteenth century is the paradox built into the dressing room itself: peering into the dressing room objectifies women within now predictable terms of sexuality and theatricality, while also promising them tools for independence and agency. As such, the dressing room is a study in fascination, home to powerful connotations central to the problems of literary culture and of gender.

Notes

PREFACE

1. Samuel Richardson, *Pamela; or, Virtue Rewarded*, ed. T. C. Duncan Eaves and Ben D. Kimpel (Boston: Houghton Mifflin, 1971), 27, 28. Subsequent references are cited parenthetically within the text.

CHAPTER 1. WOMEN'S PRIVATE PARTS

1. *A Court Lady's Curiosity; or, the Virgin Undress'd. Curiously surveying herself in her Glass, with one Leg upon her Toilet* (London, 1741). Subsequent references are cited parenthetically within the text.

2. Ian Watt briefly makes this point about the closet. Ian Watt, *The Rise of the Novel: Studies in Defoe, Richardson, and Fielding* (Berkeley and Los Angeles: University of California Press, 1957), 188.

3. The first usage of "boudoir" cited in the *Oxford English Dictionary (OED)* is from 1781. The *OED* implies that a boudoir is distinct from a dressing room, for it is a "small elegantly-furnished room, where a lady may retire to be alone, or to receive her intimate friends." I argue that the earlier dressing room provided the same functions.

4. Mark Girouard, *Life in the English Country House: A Social and Architectural History* (New Haven and London: Yale University Press, 1978), 123; and John Fowler and John Cornforth, *English Decoration in the 18th Century* (London: Barrie & Jenkins, 1974), 56–60, 78–81.

5. Orest Ranum, "The Refuges of Intimacy," in *Passions of the Renaissance*, ed. Roger Chartier, vol. 3 of *A History of Private Life*, ed. Philippe Ariès and Georges Duby (Cambridge: Harvard University Press, 1989), 210–29.

6. Simon Varey, *Space and the Eighteenth-Century English Novel* (Cambridge: Cambridge University Press, 1990), 4.

7. Ibid., 200.

8. Philippa Tristram, *Living Space in Fact and Fiction* (London and New York: Routledge, 1989), 2. Tristram writes: "Every new-built house or freshly furnished room is a fiction of the life intended to be lived there. Every inhabited building or interior tells a different story, of how life is or was. . . . Moreover, a house, like a novel, is a small world defined against, but also reflecting, a larger one" (1).

9. Ibid., 13.

10. Lee Morrissey, *From the Temple to the Castle: An Architectural History of British Literature, 1660–1760* (Charlottesville and London: University Press of Virginia, 1999), 9.

11. In each case, Morrissey draws structural and ideological links between the text and its architectural context, framing *Paradise Lost* with an analysis of Renaissance architectural theory, *The Provok'd Wife* with Vanbrugh's Queen's/Haymarket Theatre, *An*

Essay on Man with Palladianism, "Elegy Written in a Country Churchyard" with Stonehenge and the discourse of archaeology, and *The Castle of Otranto* with Strawberry Hill. Moreover, Morrissey's framings allow him to distill a central principle that determines each figure's notion of form: for Milton, it is proportion; Vanbrugh, variation; Pope, uniformity; Gray, rudeness and simplicity; and Walpole, historical forgery.

12. William B. Warner, *Licensing Entertainment: The Elevation of Novel Reading in Britain, 1684–1750* (Berkeley and Los Angeles: University of California Press, 1998), 133.

13. J. Paul Hunter, *Before Novels: The Cultural Contexts of Eighteenth-Century English Fiction* (New York and London: W. W. Norton, 1990), 157.

14. Patricia Meyer Spacks, *Privacy: Concealing the Eighteenth-Century Self* (Chicago and London: University of Chicago Press, 2003), 27–54.

15. William Wycherley, *The Country Wife*, in *The Complete Works of William Wycherley*, ed. Montague Summers, 4 vols. (New York: Russell & Russell, 1964), 4:3.

16. Peter Cryle, *Geometry in the Boudoir: Configurations of French Erotic Narrative* (Ithaca and London: Cornell University Press, 1994), 1–31; and Michel Delon, *L'invention du boudoir* (Paris: Zulma, 1999), 24–25.

17. See, for example, Edmund Waller's "Of her Chamber" in *Poems, &c. Written by Mr. Ed. Waller* (London, 1645) and, of course, Dryden's Virgil and Pope's Homer.

18. Mary Molesworth Monck, "On *Marinda's* Toilette," in *Marinda, Poems and Translations upon Several Occasions* (London, 1716), 1–2.

19. Jeremy Collier, *A Short View of the Immorality, and Profaneness of the English Stage* (1698), ed. Arthur Freeman, reprint (New York and London: Garland Publishing, 1972), 13.

20. Kristina Straub, *Sexual Suspects: Eighteenth-Century Players and Sexual Ideology* (Princeton: Princeton University Press, 1992), 3–23. See also, Barbara Freeman, *Staging the Gaze: Postmodernism, Psychoanalysis, and Shakespearean Comedy* (Ithaca and London: Cornell University Press, 1991), 7–46.

21. Catherine B. Burroughs, *Closet Stages: Joanna Baillie and the Theater Theory of British Romantic Women Writers* (Philadelphia: University of Pennsylvania Press, 1997), 12, 105–6.

22. Ibid., 8.

23. Felicity Nussbaum, *The Brink of All We Hate: English Satires on Women, 1660–1750* (Lexington: University Press of Kentucky, 1984), 6.

24. Ibid., 93.

25. Ellen Pollak, *The Poetics of Sexual Myth: Gender Ideology in the Verse of Swift and Pope* (Chicago: University of Chicago Press, 1985), 13–14.

26. Ibid., 15.

27. Ibid., 20.

28. Pollak argues that "Neither the political reality of masculine privilege nor the predominant cultural inscription of woman as inferior to man disappeared with the social and epistemological revolutions of the seventeenth and early eighteenth centuries that produced the conditions under which the novel flourished and that, in many respects, can be thought of as marking the transition from the ancient to the modern world" (ibid., 1). If novelists such as Defoe and Richardson are especially committed to "the values of interiority, personal psychology, and individual voice," then Pope and Swift are somewhat more ambivalent, if still aware of these "problems" of modernity. Pollak situates Swift and Pope in the novelistic tradition, insofar as they engage the "formal and epistemological dilemmas of their age" and are not merely nostalgic for a lost classicism (8).

29. Nussbaum's analysis, in particular, depends upon Dryden's notion of satire.

30. Margaret Ezell, *Writing Women's Literary History* (Baltimore and London: Johns Hopkins University Press, 1993), 133.

31. Patricia Meyer Spacks, "Some Reflections on Satire," *Genre* 1 (1968): 13–20.

32. Alexander Pope, *Correspondence of Alexander Pope*, ed. George Sherburn, 5 vols. (Oxford: Oxford University Press, 1956), 1:211.

33. Laura Brown, *The Ends of Empire: Women and Ideology in Early Eighteenth-Century English Literature* (Cornell and Ithaca: Cornell University Press, 1993), 3.

34. Laura Mandell, *Misogynous Economies: The Business of Literature in Eighteenth-Century Britain* (Lexington: University Press of Kentucky, 1999), 1.

35. Nancy Armstrong, *Desire and Domestic Fiction: A Political History of the Novel* (New York and Oxford: Oxford University Press, 1987), 4.

36. Ibid., 14.

37. Ibid., 63–69. A generic approach to the question left unanswered by Armstrong's study may be found in Helene Moglen's *The Trauma of Gender: A Feminist Theory of the English Novel*. Moglen likewise contends that the eighteenth-century novel was particularly focused on modern sexual and gender difference, but produced different results through its two narrative modes — realism and fantasy. For Moglen, the eighteenth-century novel's "fantastic and realistic narratives interact to form composite texts that function to manage gender relations even as they reveal the precariousness of selfhood and identity." Helene Moglen, *The Trauma of Gender: A Feminist Theory of the English Novel* (Berkeley and Los Angeles: University of California Press, 2001), 14.

38. Michael McKeon, *The Origins of the English Novel, 1600–1740* (Baltimore and London: Johns Hopkins University Press, 1987), 268–69, 341.

39. Mikhail Bakhtin, *Problems of Dostoevsky's Poetics*, ed. and trans. Caryl Emerson (Minneapolis and London: University of Minnesota Press, 1984), 109.

40. Ronald Paulson, *Satire and the Novel in Eighteenth-Century England* (New Haven and London: Yale University Press, 1967), 11–23.

41. G. S. Rousseau, "From Swift to Smollet: The Satirical Tradition in Prose Narrative," in *The Columbia History of the British Novel*, ed. John Richetti (New York: Columbia University Press, 1994), 129.

42. Paulson, *Satire and the Novel*, 10.

43. Ibid., 211, 126.

44. Ibid., 310.

45. Philippe Ariès, introduction, in *Passions of the Renaissance*, ed. Roger Chartier, vol. 3 of *A History of Private Life*, ed. Philippe Ariès and Georges Duby (Cambridge: Harvard University Press, 1989), 5.

46. Lawrence Stone, *The Family, Sex, and Marriage In England, 1500–1800* (New York: Harper & Row, 1979), 169. Raffaella Sarti makes a similar point about the development of domestic privacy in early modern Europe. Raffaella Sarti, *Europe at Home: Family and Material Culture, 1500–1800*, trans. Allan Cameron (New Haven and London: Yale University Press, 2002), 142–47.

47. Ibid., 171.

48. Ibid., 253–56.

49. Lena Cowen Orlin, *Private Matters and Public Culture in Post-Reformation England* (Ithaca and London: Cornell University Press, 1994), 8.

50. Ibid., 17.

51. Joseph Addison and Richard Steele, *The Spectator*, ed. Donald F. Bond, 3 vols. (Oxford: Oxford University Press, 1965), no. 10, 12 March 1711.

52. Terry Eagleton, *The Function of Criticism from* The Spectator *to Post-Structuralism* (London: Verso, 1987), 9–27.

53. The domestic woman wielded "authority over the household, leisure time, courtship procedures, and kinship relations, and under her jurisdiction the most basic qualities of human identity were supposed to develop" (Armstrong, *Desire and Domestic Fiction*, 3).

54. Ibid., 5. Conduct books contribute to the politicization of the domestic sphere: "By developing a language strictly for relations within the home, conduct books for women inadvertently provided the terms for rethinking relationships in the political world, for this language enabled authors to articulate both worlds while they appeared to represent only one" (75).

55. Lawrence E. Klein, "Gender and the Public/Private Distinction in the Eighteenth Century," *Eighteenth-Century Studies* 29, 1 (1995): 99–100.

56. Amanda Vickery, *The Gentleman's Daughter: Women's Lives in Georgian England* (New Haven and London: Yale University Press, 1998), 7, 9.

57. Ibid., 9.

58. Ibid., 10.

59. *The Spectator*, no. 10, 12 March 1711.

60. Neil McKendrick, introduction, in Neil McKendrick, John Brewer, and J. H. Plumb, *The Birth of a Consumer Society: The Commercialization of Eighteenth-Century England* (Bloomington: Indiana University Press, 1982), 1; and Elizabeth Kowaleski-Wallace, *Consuming Subjects: Women, Shopping, and Business in the Eighteenth Century* (New York: Columbia University Press, 1997), 11. See also Colin Campbell, *The Romantic Ethic and the Spirit of Modern Consumerism* (Oxford: Basil Blackwell, 1987), 17–35.

61. Ibid., 1–2. See also Hoh-Cheung Mui and Lorna H. Mui, *Shops and Shopkeeping in Eighteenth-Century England* (Kingston, Montreal, London: McGill Queen's University Press; London: Routledge, 1989).

62. G. J. Barker-Benfield, *The Culture of Sensibility: Sex and Society in Eighteenth-Century Britain* (Chicago and London: University of Chicago Press, 1992), 174.

63. McKendrick, "Commercialization and the Economy," in *The Birth of a Consumer Society*, 21–22.

64. Ibid., 43. See also 52.

65. Jan de Vries suggests that McKendrick's thesis depends "on a studied vagueness in definitional statements and a careful removal of most of the concepts from the economic to the cultural sphere" (Jan de Vries, "Between Purchasing Power and the World of Goods: Understanding the Household Economy in Early Modern Europe," in *Consumption and the World of Goods*, ed. John Brewer and Roy Porter [London and New York: Routledge, 1993], 89).

66. McKendrick, "Commercialization and the Economy," in *The Birth of a Consumer Society*, 21. See also John Styles, "Custom or Consumption? Plebeian Fashion in Eighteenth-Century England," in *Luxury in the Eighteenth Century: Debates, Desires and Delectable Goods*, ed. Maxine Berg and Elizabeth Eger (New York: Palgrave Macmillan, 2003), 103–15.

67. Harriet Guest, *Small Change: Women, Learning, Patriotism, 1750–1810* (Chicago and London: University of Chicago Press, 2000), 74.

68. Brewer and Porter, introduction, in *Consumption and the World of Goods*, 4.

69. Kowaleski-Wallace, *Consuming Subjects*, 60.

70. Ibid., 5.

71. Vivien Jones, "Luxury, Satire and Prostitute Narratives," in *Luxury in the Eighteenth Century: Debates, Desires and Delectable Goods*, ed. Maxine Berg and Elizabeth Eger (New York: Palgrave Macmillan, 2003), 178–89.

72. Yves Castan, "Politics and Private Life," in *Passions of the Renaissance*, ed. Roger Chartier, vol. 3 of *A History of Private Life*, ed. Philippe Ariès and Georges Duby (Cambridge: Harvard University Press, 1989), 61.

73. Peter Brooks, *Body Work: Objects of Desire in Modern Narrative* (Cambridge and London: Harvard University Press, 1993), 49.

74. *Dictionary of the English Language*, s.v. "dressingroom."

75. Norbert Elias, *The Court Society*, trans. Edmund Jephcott (New York: Pantheon Books, 1983), 245–46, 250.

76. "Urbanization, monetarization, commericialization and courtization are parts of a comprehensive transformation that leads people at this time to experience 'Nature' as something standing opposed to them, as landscape, as the world of 'objects', as something to be explored and known" (ibid., 242).

77. Ibid., 243.

78. Philippe Ariès introduces the third volume of *A History of Private Life* by arguing for a dialectical methodology for the analysis of privacy's emergence in this period: "One approach should focus on the opposition between the public servant and the private individual and the relations between the state and what would ultimately become the domestic preserve. The other should focus on the transition from an anonymous form of sociability, in which notions of public and private were confounded, to a more fragmented sociability that combines remnants of the old anonymous form with relations based on professional affinities and with the equally private relations born of domestic life" (Ariès, introduction, 11). More widely appropriated (and critiqued) is Jürgen Habermas's model of the public sphere, in which he famously—if controversially—argues that "the line between private and public sphere extended right through the home. The privatized individuals stepped out of the intimacy of their living rooms into the public sphere of the *salon*, but the one was strictly complementary to the other" (Jürgen Habermas, *The Structural Transformation of the Public Sphere: An Inquiry into a Category of Bourgeois Society*, trans. Thomas Burger [Cambridge: MIT Press, 1989], 45). Along with Elias (if only implicitly), Habermas makes a connection between the conceptual demarcations of social space and subjectivity, arguing that this privatization precipitated psychological emancipation more broadly (46.).

79. Spacks, *Privacy*, 5.

80. Francis Barker, *The Tremulous Private Body: Essays on Subjection*, 2nd ed. (Ann Arbor: University of Michigan Press, 1998), 8–9.

81. Thus, for Barker, Pepys is a mad, self-censuring subject, "A bourgeois man. Riven by guilt, silence and textuality. Forbidden to speak and yet incited to discourse, and therefore speaking obliquely in another place" (ibid., 53, 7).

82. Eve Kosofsky Sedgwick, *Epistemology of the Closet* (Berkeley and Los Angeles: University of California Press, 1990), 67.

83. Ibid., 70.

84. Ibid., 73.

85. Ibid., 68–69.

86. Ibid., 71.

87. Ibid., 72.

88. See Richard Rambuss, *Spenser's Secret Career* (Cambridge: Cambridge University Press, 1993) and *Closet Devotions* (Durham and London: Duke University Press, 1998); Alan Stewart, "The Early Modern Closet Discovered," *Representations* 50 (Spring 1995): 76–100; and Mark Wigley, "Untitled: The Housing of Gender," in *Sexuality & Space*, ed. Beatriz Colomina (New York: Princeton Architectural Press, 1992), 327–89. I discuss Wigley's work at length in the following chapter.

89. Sedgwick, *Epistemology of the Closet*, 16.

90. Carolyn Dever, *Skeptical Feminism: Activist Theory, Activist Practice* (Minneapolis: University of Minnesota Press, 2004), 156.

91. Eve Kosofsky Sedgwick, *Between Men: English Literature and Male Homosocial Desire* (New York: Columbia University Press, 1985), 18; see also 1–5.

92. For work that richly analyzes Sapphic and lesbian iconography in eighteenth-century literature, see Emma Donoghue's *Passions Between Women: British Lesbian Cul-*

ture, 1668–1801 (New York: HarperCollins, 1993) and Lisa L. Moore's *Dangerous Intimacies: Toward a Sapphic History of the British Novel* (Durham and London: Duke University Press, 1997).

93. Randolph Trumbach, *Sex and the Gender Revolution: Heterosexuality and the Third Gender in Enlightenment London* (Chicago and London: University of Chicago Press, 1998), 4, 9–10.

94. Susan Staves, *Married Women's Separate Property in England, 1660–1833* (Cambridge and London: Harvard University Press, 1990), 1–26, 222–28.

95. Thomas Laqueur, *Making Sex: Body and Gender from the Greeks to Freud* (Cambridge and London: Harvard University Press, 1994), 149.

96. Ibid., 150. Through readings of eighteenth-century science, Ruth Salvaggio offers another means of understanding this claim of the female body's incommensurability: fluidity. See Ruth Salvaggio, *Enlightened Absence: Neoclassical Configurations of the Feminine* (Urbana and Chicago: University of Illinois Press, 1988), 14, 26.

CHAPTER 2. "THE ART OF KNOWING WOMEN"

The chapter title comes from François Bruys's *The Art of Knowing Women; Or, The Female Sex Dissected* (London, 1730).

1. Francis Lenygon, *The Decoration and Furniture of English Mansions During the Seventeenth and Eighteenth Centuries* (London: T. Werner Laurie, 1949), 18.

2. Lorna Weatherhill, *Consumer Behavior and Material Culture, 1660–1760* (London: Routledge, 1988).

3. From a deposition by John Alleyn given in 1592. Quoted in E. K. Chambers, *The Elizabethan Stage* (Oxford: Clarendon Press, 1923), 2:392.

4. James Mabbe, "To the Memory of Master William Shakespeare," in *The Complete Works of William Shakespeare*, ed. Stanley Wells and Gary Taylor (Oxford: Clarendon Press, 1989), xlvi.

5. William Shakespeare, *A Midsummer Night's Dream*, in *The Riverside Shakespeare*, ed. G. Blakemore Evans et al. (Boston: Houghton Mifflin, 1974), 3.1.3–6.

6. Andrew Gurr, *Playgoing in Shakespeare's London* (Cambridge: Cambridge University Press, 1994), 19.

7. Ibid.

8. T. Fairman Ordish, *Early London Theatres* (London: Elliot Stock, 1894), 156. Richard Leacroft speculates that this space above the tiring-room could have functioned either as seating or as a balcony for the drama itself (*The Development of the English Playhouse* [Ithaca: Cornell University Press, 1973], 33).

9. Quoted in Montague Summers, *The Restoration Theatre* (New York: Macmillan, 1934), 59.

10. Ibid.

11. "It is thought fitt that some one or two be appoynted to stand at the Tyring house Dore till the House is discharged" (quoted in John Allardyce Nicoll, *Restoration Drama, 1660–1700*, vol. 1 of *A History of English Drama, 1660–1900* [Cambridge: Cambridge University Press, 1952], 324).

12. Colley Cibber, *An Apology for the Life of Colley Cibber* (London: Dent, 1976), 52.

13. Samuel Pepys, *The Diary of Samuel Pepys: A New and Complete Transcription*, ed. Robert Latham and William Matthews, 11 vols. (Berkeley: University of California Press, 1970–83), 29 September 1662. Subsequent references are cited parenthetically in the text.

14. For discussions of the erotics of boy actors playing women's roles on the Re-

naissance stage, see Lisa Jardine, *Still Harping on Daughters: Women and Drama in the Age of Shakespeare* (Sussex: Harvester Press; Totowa, N.J.: Barnes and Noble Books, 1983); Phyllis Rackin, "Androgyny, Mimesis, and the Marriage of the Boy Heroine on the English Renaissance Stage," *PMLA* 102 (1987): 29–41; Marjorie Garber, *Vested Interests: Cross-Dressing and Cultural Anxiety* (New York: HarperCollins, 1993), 84–92; Jean E. Howard, *The Stage and Social Struggle in Early Modern England* (London and New York: Routledge, 1994), 93–128; and Laura Levine, *Men in Women's Clothing: Anti-Theatricality and Effeminization, 1579–1642* (Cambridge: Cambridge University Press, 1994), 10–25.

15. John Harold Wilson, *All the King's Ladies: Actresses of the Restoration* (Chicago: University of Chicago Press, 1958), 67–86.

16. William Wycherley, *The Plain Dealer*, in *The Complete Works of William Wycherley*, ed. Montague Summers, 4 vols. (New York: Russell & Russell, 1964), 4.2. sd 379.

17. John Evelyn, *The Diary of John Evelyn*, ed. Guy de la Bédoyère (Dorchester, England: Dorchester Press, 1994), 18 October 1666.

18. Richard W. Bevis, *English Drama: Restoration and Eighteenth Century, 1660–1789* (London and New York: Longman, 1988), 35.

19. Elizabeth Howe, *The First English Actresses: Women and Drama, 1660–1700* (Cambridge: Cambridge University Press, 1992), 32; see also 32–36.

20. Ibid., 32.

21. For this controversy, see Straub, *Sexual Suspects*; Thomas A. King, " 'As if (she) were made on purpose to put the whole world into good Humour': Reconstructing the First English Actresses," *The Drama Review* 36 (Fall 1992): 78–102; Laura J. Rosenthal, " 'Counterfeit Scrubbado': Women Actors in the Restoration," *The Eighteenth Century: Theory and Interpretation* 34, 1 (1993): 3–22; and Deborah C. Payne, "Reified Object or Emergent Professional? Retheorizing the Restoration Actress," in *Cultural Readings of Restoration and Eighteenth-Century Theater*, ed. J. Douglas Canfield and Deborah C. Payne (Athens and London: University of Georgia Press, 1995), 13–38.

22. [James Wright], *Historia Histrionica: An Historical Account of the English-Stage* (1699), facsimile reprint (New York and London: Garland Publishing, 1974), 5–6.

23. Katharine Eisaman Maus, " 'Playhouse Flesh and Blood': Sexual Ideology and the Restoration Actress," *English Literary History* 46 (1979): 601.

24. See especially the entry for 6 August 1666.

25. Pegg was probably Margaret Hughes, later Prince Rupert's mistress (*The Diary of Samuel Pepys*, 9:198n3).

26. John Dryden, *Tyrannick Love; or, The Royal Martyr*, in *The Works of John Dryden*, ed. Maximillian E. Novak, vol. 10 (Berkeley and Los Angeles: University of California Press, 1970), epilogue, 27–30.

27. *A Pleasant Battle Between Two Lap Dogs of the Utopian Court* (London, 1681). Gwyn left the stage a short time after performing this role in June 1669 to become Charles II's mistress (Howe, *The First English Actresses*, 74).

28. Wycherley, "The Epistle Dedicatory," in *The Plain Dealer*.

29. Howe, *The First English Actresses*, 98–101.

30. [Charles Gildon?], *A Comparison between the Two Stages* (1702), in *The English Stage: Attack and Defense, 1577–1730*, gen. ed. Arthur Freeman, facsimile reprint (New York: Garland Press, 1973), 17.

31. Cibber, *Apology*, 91.

32. Ibid., 92.

33. James Boswell, *The Life of Johnson* (Oxford: Oxford University Press, 1980), 143.

34. Simon Thurley and Anna Keay, "Charles II, Louis XIV, and the English Royal Bedchamber," lecture at the Newberry Library, 12 March 2002.

35. Mark Girouard, *Life in the English Country House*, 149.

36. Fowler and Cornforth, *English Decoration in the 18th Century*, 78, 79.

37. Julius Bryant, *Marble Hill House, Twickenham* (London: English Heritage, 1988), 3.

38. Colin Campbell, *Vitruvius Britannicus; or, The British Architect*, 1715–25, vol. 1, facsimile reprint (New York: Benjamin Blom, 1967), C. 3, PL. 93.

39. Bryant, *Marble Hill House*, 14.

40. Ibid., 15.

41. Addison and Steele, *The Spectator*, no. 10, 12 March 1711.

42. Ibid., no. 45, 21 April 1711.

43. William Hogarth, *Marriage à la Mode*, plate 4, in *Engravings by Hogarth*, ed. Sean Shesgreen (New York: Dover Publications, 1973), 54.

44. *The Diary of John Evelyn*, 10 September 1676.

45. Ibid., 4 October 1683.

46. Wycherley, *The Country Wife*, 4:3.

47. Lenygon, *The Decoration and Furniture of English Mansions*, 29, 56.

48. Charles Saumarez Smith, *Eighteenth-Century Decoration: Design and the Domestic Interior in England* (New York: Harry N. Abrams, 1993), 19, 46.

49. Lorna Weatherhill, "The meaning of consumer behaviour in late seventeenth- and early eighteenth-century England," in *Consumption and the World of Goods*, ed. John Brewer and Roy Porter (London and New York: Routledge, 1993), 208. See also Maxine Berg, "New commodities, luxuries and their consumers in eighteenth-century England," in *Consumers and Luxury: Consumer Culture in Europe, 1650–1850*, ed. Maxine Berg and Helen Clifford (Manchester and New York: Manchester University Press, 1999), 63–85.

50. *A Catalogue of the Household Furniture Of Mrs. Masters, Deceas'd* (1760), 4.

51. *A Catalogue of All the Genuine Household Furniture of John Trevor, Esq.; At his House, in Castle-Street, Canterbury* (1766), 3; and *A Catalogue of the Household Furniture, And Effects of the Hon. Col. John Mercer, Late of Demark-Street, Soho; And Nicholas Hawskmoor, Esq; Both Deceased* (1740), 16.

52. *A Catalogue of the Superb and Elegant Household Furniture . . . Late Property of Monsieur de Calonne* (1793), 3.

53. Thomas Sheraton, *The Cabinet-Maker and Upholsterer's Drawing-Book* (1802), ed. Charles F. Montgomery and Wilfred P. Cole (New York: Praeger Publishers, 1970), 397.

54. William Ince and John Mayhew, *The Universal System of Household Furniture* (London, 1762), plate 38; *Gillow Furniture Designs, 1760–1800*, ed. Lindsay Boynton (United Kingdom: Bloomfield Press, 1995), monochrome figures 29–34.

55. Sheraton, *The Cabinet-Maker and Upholsterer's Drawing-Book*, 398.

56. Ince and Mayhew, *The Universal System of Household Furniture*, plates 40 and 41.

57. Sheraton, *The Cabinet-Maker and Upholsterer's Drawing-Book*, 406.

58. Ince and Mayhew, *The Universal System of Household Furniture*, plates 34 and 35.

59. Ibid., plates 36 and 37.

60. *Catalogue of all the Houshold [sic] Furniture And Other valuable Effects of Edgeley Hewer, Esq.; (Deceas'd) Brought from his Seat at Clapham, to his House in Buckingham-street, York-Buildings* (1729), 9.

61. Sheraton, *The Cabinet-Maker and Upholsterer's Drawing-Book*, 405.

62. Neville Williams, *Powder and Paint: A History of the Englishwoman's Toilet, Elizabeth I–Elizabeth II* (London: Longmans, Green, 1957), 54.

63. *The Diary of John Evelyn*, 31 July 1662.

64. *Edgeley Hewer, Esq.*, 14.

65. The National Trust, *Ham House* (London: Balding + Mansell for National Trust Enterprises, 1995), 5.

66. Ibid., 32.

67. Gervase Jackson-Stops and James Pipkin, *The English Country House: A Grand Tour* (Boston: Little, Brown and Company, 1985), 189; The National Trust, *Ham House*, 33.

68. *A Catalogue of the Rich Household Furniture, &c. of Edward Lisle, Esq.* (1739), 4, 5; *A Catalogue of the Genuine Houshold [sic] Goods, Pictures, fine old China, Fire-Arms, &c. of his Excellency Don Thomas Geraldino* (1740), 10; *The Particular and Inventory of Sir Harcourt Master, Knt.* (1721), 8; and *Edgeley Hewer, Esq.*, 9, 14.

69. Hon. Col. John Mercer [and] Nicholas Hawskmoor, Esq., 21.

70. *The Particular and Inventory of the Estate of Sir John Lambert, Bart.* (1721), 1.

71. Kowaleski-Wallace, *Consuming Subjects*, 58; see 52–69.

72. Addison and Steele, *The Spectator*, no. 69, 19 May 1711.

73. Laura Brown makes this argument in a reading of Belinda's toilet scene from *The Rape of the Lock*. See Brown, *Ends of Empire*, 103–34.

74. Celia Fiennes, *Through England on a Side Saddle In the Time of William and Mary* (London: Field & Tuer, Leadenhall Press, 1888), 53.

75. *Harcourt Master, Knt.*, 8, and *The Particular Inventory of Richard Wooley* (1732), 8.

76. Jackson-Stops and Pipkin, *The English Country House*, 237.

77. *A Catalogue of the Rich Household Furniture and valuable Cabinet of Curiosities of the Right Honourable the Countess Dowager of Gainsborough, Deceased* (1739–40), 14.

78. Christopher Hussey, *English Country Houses: Early Georgian, 1715–1760* (London: Country Life Limited, 1965), 72, 83–84.

79. Ibid., 134.

80. Ibid., 61–64.

81. See chapter 1, note 2.

82. Jackson-Stops and Pipkin, *The English Country House*, 197.

83. Ibid., 193, 236.

84. William Congreve, *The Way of the World*, in *The Complete Works of William Congreve*, ed. Montague Summers, vol. 3 (New York: Russell & Russell, 1964), 3.

85. *The Trial, with the whole of the evidence, between the Right Hon. Sir Richard Worsley and George Maurice Bissett, Esq. defendant, for Criminal Conversation with the Plaintiff's Wife* (London, 1782), 13, 14.

86. Ibid., 20.

87. Ibid., 13.

88. Ibid., 14.

89. A chambermaid reports that one Francis William Sykes and one Mrs. Parslow must have shared a bed because "there was only one made up for them." *Trial for adultery, in Westminster Hall, on Wednesday, December 9, 1789, before Lord Kenyon, John Parslow, Esq. plaintiff, and Francis William Sykes, Esq. defendant, for Criminal Conversation with the Plaintiff's Wife* (Dublin, 1790), 21. In Henry Frederick, the Duke of Cumberland's Criminal Conversation case from 1770, a maid reports that "the lady and gentleman were then sitting on a couch, close to one another" and did so regularly, testimony that is interpreted as evidence of sexual infidelity. *The Trial of His R. H. the D. of C. July 5th, 1770 for Criminal conversation with Lady Harriet G— — — — — — — — — —r* (London, 1770), 45.

90. *Adultery. The Trial of Mr. William Atkinson, Linen-Draper of Cheapside, For Criminal Conversation with Mrs. Conner, Wife of Mr. Conner, late of the Mitre, at Barney* (London, 1789), 11.

91. Orlin, *Private Matters and Public Culture*, 17.

92. Leon Battista Alberti, *On the Art of Building in Ten Books*, trans. Joseph Rykwert, Neil Leach, and Robert Tavernor (Cambridge and London: MIT Press, 1994), 144; and Ranum, "The Refuges of Intimacy," 225–26.

93. Charles Hoole, *Joh. Amos Commenii Orbis Sensualium Pictus* (London, 1672), 200.

94. Mary Poovey, *A History of the Modern Fact: Problems of Knowledge in the Sciences of Wealth and Society* (Chicago and London: University of Chicago Press, 1998), 37.

95. Wigley, "Untitled: The Housing of Gender," 348, 347.

96. Stephanie H. Jed, *Chaste Thinking: The Rape of Lucretia and the Birth of Humanism* (Bloomington and Indianapolis: Indiana University Press, 1989), 81–86.

97. Alberti, *On the Art of Building*, 149.

98. Leon Battista Alberti, *The Family in Renaissance Florence*, trans. Renée New Watkins (Prospect Heights, Ill.: Waveland Press, 1994), 79.

99. Stewart, "The Early Modern Closet Discovered," 81.

100. Ibid., 87–89.

101. Poovey, *A History of the Modern Fact*, 34–36.

102. Henry Wotton, *The Elements of Architecture* (London, 1624).

103. Roger North, *Of Building: Roger North's Writings on Architecture*, ed. Howard Colvin and John Newman (Oxford: Clarendon Press, 1981), 134.

104. Laura J. Rosenthal, *Playwrights and Plagiarists in Early Modern England: Gender, Authorship, Literary Property* (Ithaca and London: Cornell University Press, 1996), 23, 29. For a detailed response to Locke's ideal of liberal individualism, see Carole Pateman, *The Sexual Contract* (Stanford, Calif.: Stanford University Press, 1988).

105. James Dallaway observes that the opulence and luxury of English country houses are unique insofar as the European nobles built their palaces in urban environs (James Dallaway, *Observations on English Architecture* [London, 1806], 229–30).

106. Campbell, *Vitruvius Britannicus*, C. 1, PL. 56.

107. Dallaway, *Observations on English Architecture*, 214, 208.

108. Sir John Vanbrugh, *The Letters*, vol. 4 of *The Complete Works of Sir John Vanbrugh*, ed. Geoffrey Webb (Bloomsbury, England: Nonesuch Press, 1927), 45 (30 September 1710).

109. Sir Christopher Wren, "Tract I." Quoted in James Elmes, *Memoirs of the Life and Works of Sir Christopher Wren* (London: Priestly and Weale, 1823), appendix, 118 (reprinted from *Parentalia*).

110. Vanbrugh, *The Letters*, 35 (18 July 1709).

111. Dallaway, *Observations on English Architecture*, 231.

112. Geoffrey Webb, introduction, in *The Letters*, vol. 4 of *The Complete Works of Sir John Vanbrugh*, ed. Geoffrey Webb (Bloomsbury, England: Nonesuch Press, 1927), xvii.

113. Sacheverell Sitwell, *British Architects and Craftsmen: A Survey of Taste, Design, and Style during Three Centuries, 1600–1830* (New York: Charles Scribner's Sons, 1946), 92.

114. Girouard, *Life in the English Country House*, 135.

115. Letter from John, Lord Hervey to George II, 6 July 1742; quoted in Edward Raymond Turner and Gaudens Megaro, "The King's Closet in the Eighteenth Century," *The American Historical Review* 45, 4 (July 1940): 763.

116. Turner and Megaro, "The King's Closet in the Eighteenth Century," 767–68.

117. *Memoirs of Sarah, Duchess of Marlborough*, ed. William King (London: George Routledge & Sons, 1930), 128–34.

118. Vanbrugh, *The Letters*, 48–49 (3 October 1710). Elsewhere in their correspondence, the duchess claims that the same workman charges four to five times the amount for the same masonry, figuring that the Royal Treasury is footing the bill: "stone and that article commonly at 18 or 20 in the Queens accounts I dare say may be computed at four or five shillings by the same man" (70 [16 June 1716]).

119. Fiennes, *Through England on a Side Saddle*, 287.

120. Jackson-Stops and Pipkin, *The English Country House*, 232.

121. Ibid., 197.

122. Barbara Coulton, *A Shropshire Squire: Noel Hill, first Lord Berwick, 1745–1789* (Shrewsbury, England: Swan Hill Press, 1989), 74.

123. Fiennes, *Through England on a Side Saddle*, 52–53.

124. For a discussion of the development of doors and doorways in British domestic architecture, see James Ayers, *Domestic Interiors: The British Tradition, 1500–1850* (New Haven and London: Yale University Press, 2003), 61–68.

125. Fiennes, *Through England on a Side Saddle*, 18.

126. Congreve, *The Way of the World*, 3:55.

127. Ibid., 3:56.

128. Ibid.

129. Ibid.

130. *Wren Society*, 20 vols. (Oxford: Oxford University Press, 1924–43), 7:136.

131. Frances Burney, *Journals and Letters*, ed. Peter Sabor and Lars E. Troide (London: Penguin Books, 2001), 240.

132. Ibid., 241–42.

133. Ibid., 242–43.

134. Smith, *Eighteenth-Century Decoration*, 234–36.

135. Lucy Phillimore, *Sir Christopher Wren: His Family and His Times* (London: Kegan Paul, Trench, & Co., 1883), 267–68; Elmes, *Memoirs of the Life and Works of Sir Christopher Wren*, 454; Christopher Wren, *Life and Works of Sir Christopher Wren, From the Parentalia or Memoirs by His Son Christopher*, ed. Ernest J. Enthoven (London: Arnold, 1903), 204.

136. Sitwell, *British Architects and Craftsmen*, 59.

137. Simon Thurley, *Hampton Court Palace* (Great Britain: Historic Royal Palaces 2000, 1996), 40.

138. Elmes, *Memoirs of the Life and Works of Sir Christopher Wren*, 456; Sitwell, *British Architects and Craftsmen* 59.

139. Girouard, *Life in the English Country House*, 144.

140. Thurley, *Hampton Court Palace*, 41.

141. John Soane, *Sketches in Architecture. Containing Plans and Elevations of Cottages, Villages, and Other Useful Buildings* (London, 1793), plate 15. See also plate 25.

142. *Sir Harcourt Master, Knt.*, 8.

143. Ibid., 8.

144. Ibid., 5.

145. *Sir John Lambert, Bart.*, 1.

146. Ince and Mayhew, *The Universal System of Household Furniture*, plate 65.

147. *The Inventory and Particular of All and Singular the Lands, Tenements, and Hereditaments, Goods, Chattels, Debts, and Personal Estate whatsoever of Stephen Child, Esq.* (1721), 2.

148. The National Trust, *Ham House*, 41.

149. Jackson-Stops and Pipkin, *The English Country House*, 184.

150. The National Trust, *Ham House*, 41.

151. *Countess Dowager of Gainsborough*, 19.

152. *Monsieur de Calonne*, 12, 22.

153. *An Inventory of the Household Goods and other Effects of Edward Dennis, lately seiz'd by Virtue of a Warrant under the Hands and Seals of the Commissions of the Land-Tax, for the Year 1726* (1726), 3, 4.

154. *The Particulars and Inventory of Sir John Blunt, Bart.* (1721), 43.

155. Maria Edgeworth, *Letters from England, 1813–1844*, ed. Christina Colvin (Oxford: Clarendon Press, 1971), 25.

156. Ralph Dutton, *The English Interior* (London: B. T. Batsford Limited, 1949), 79–80; and Christopher Simon Sykes, *Country House Album* (Boston: Bulfinch Press, 1989), 20.

157. *The Particular and Inventory of Richard Houlditch, Esq.* (1721), 6.

158. *Mrs. Masters*, 5, 8, 9.

159. The "Green Room" had a "dressing glass in a gilt frame" and a "wainscot dressing-table with a drawer," while the "best Chamber" featured a "dressing-table, with a drawer" and a "dressing-glass" (*A Catalogue of All the Household Goods, &c. &c. of Miss Lampreys In St. Alphage, Canterbury* [1764], 3, 4).

160. *A Catalogue of all the Entire Live and Dead Stock. Implements in husbandry, Dairy and Brewing Utensils, and Household Furniture, of Mr. Thoˢ. Laugher, the Younger, at Aldington, in the Parish of Badsey, and County of Worcester* (1782), 11, 12.

CHAPTER 3. "A PAINTED WOMAN IS A DANG'ROUS THING"

1. *On the author of a dialogue concerning women, pretended to be writ in Defence of the Sex* (ca. 1690). Manuscript X.d. 194. Folger Shakespeare Library. The satire is directed at Dryden.

2. [John Breval], *The Art of Dress: An Heroi-Comical Poem*, 2nd ed. (London, 1717), 15.

3. *The Original of Apparel: Or, the Ornaments of Dress* (London, 1732), 2.

4. Daniel Defoe, *The London Ladies Dressing-Room: Or, the Shop-keepers Wives Inventory* (London, 1705), 4.

5. William Wycherley, "The Epistle Dedicatory," in *The Plain Dealer*.

6. Bruys, *The Art of Knowing Women*, 113–14.

7. Breval, *The Art of Dress*, 8.

8. Ibid., 14.

9. Ibid., 15.

10. Ibid.

11. Nussbaum, *The Brink of All We Hate*, 105–6.

12. Ibid., 19.

13. Ibid., 105.

14. Dustin Griffin, *Satire: A Critical Reintroduction* (Lexington: University Press of Kentucky, 1995), 119–20.

15. Pollak, *The Poetics of Sexual Myth*, 22–76.

16. Nussbaum, *The Brink of All We Hate*, 9–16.

17. Ibid., 9.

18. Rose Zimbardo, "The Semiotics of Restoration Satire," in *Cutting Edges: Postmodern Critical Essays on Eighteenth-Century Satire*, ed. James E. Gill (Knoxville: University of Tennessee Press, 1995), 33, 35. Zimbardo contends that satiric texts, especially those from the Restoration, are "designed not to attack 'real' persons, or to ridicule 'real' circumstances or behavior, but to attack our fatal tendency to believe that the empty fictions which govern and shape our consciousness are real" (36).

19. Fredric V. Bogel, *The Difference Satire Makes: Rhetoric and Reading from Jonson to Byron* (Ithaca: Cornell University Press, 2001), 11; see also 5–6.

20. Griffin, *Satire: A Critical Reintroduction*, 123; see also 115–32.

21. Angela J. Wheeler, *English Verse Satire from Donne to Dryden: Imitation of Classical Models* (Heidelberg: Carl Winter Universitätsverlag, 1992), 311; and Nussbaum, *The Brink of All We Hate*, 92.

22. Mary Evelyn, *Mundus Muliebris; or, The Ladies Dressing-Room Unlock'd And her Toilette Spread* (London, 1690), title page.

23. William Kupersmith, *Roman Satirists in Seventeenth-Century England* (Lincoln and London: University of Nebraska Press, 1985), 69; and Wheeler, *English Verse Satire from Donne to Dryden*, 199. Susanna Morton Braund argues that Dryden's "distaste for what he sees as Juvenal's unfair criticisms of women leads him to sanitize his published translation." Susanna Morton Braund, "Safe Sex? Dryden's Translation of Juvenal's Sixth Satire," in *John Dryden (1631–1700): His Politics, His Plays, and His Poets*, ed. Claude Rawson and Aaron Santesso (Newark: University of Delaware Press, 2004), 139.

24. "The Sixth Satyr of Juvenal," in *Juvenal's Sixteen Satyrs, or, a Survey of the Manners and Actions of Mankind*, trans. Sir Robert Stapylton (London, 1673), 83, marginalia. Stapylton's first version was published in 1644, followed by five more editions over the next thirty years. See Kupersmith, *Roman Satirists*, 64–69.

25. Ibid., 499, 501–2.

26. Ibid., 509–10.

27. "The Sixth Satire of Juvenal," in *The Works of John Dryden*, ed. Edward Niles Hooker, H. T. Swedenberg et al., vol. 4 (Berkeley and Los Angeles: University of California Press, 1970), 625–26.

28. Stapylton, "The Sixth Satyr of Juvenal," 98, note x; and Dryden, "The Sixth Satire of Juvenal," 202n33.

29. Stapylton, "The Sixth Satyr of Juvenal," 84, marginalia.

30. Ibid., 517–18.

31. Bruys, *The Art of Knowing Women*, 117.

32. Dryden explains that in *Satire Six* Juvenal "has run himself into his old declamatory way." John Dryden, "Discourse concerning the Original and Progress of Satire," in *The Works of John Dryden*, ed. Edward Niles Hooker, H. T. Swedenberg et al., vol. 4 (Berkeley and Los Angeles: University of California Press, 1970), 80.

33. Bruys, *The Art of Knowing Women*, 114.

34. *Female Taste: A Satire* (London, 1745), 26.

35. Ibid.

36. Bruys, *The Art of Knowing Women*, 112.

37. Ibid., 112–13.

38. Dryden, "Argument of the Sixth Satire," in *The Works of John Dryden*, ed. Edward Niles Hooker, H. T. Swedenberg et al., vol. 4 (Berkeley and Los Angeles: University of California Press, 1970), 145.

39. Michael Seidel, *Satiric Inheritance: Rabelais to Sterne* (Princeton: Princeton University Press, 1979), 12.

40. Harry M. Solomon categorizes these poems as "toilette pastorals" and notes that Waller's works were reprinted in folio the year before Swift wrote "The Lady's Dressing Room" ("'Difficult Beauty': Tom D'Urfey and the Context of Swift's 'The Lady's Dressing Room,'" *SEL* 19 [1979]: 433–34).

41. Waller, "Of her Chamber," 43.

42. Ibid., 44.

43. John Oldham, "A Satyr Upon a Woman, who by her Falshood and Scorn was the Death of my Friend," in *The Poems of John Oldham*, ed. Harold F. Brooks and Raman Selden (Oxford: Clarendon Press, 1987), 80–84. The speaker argues that his friend died because of his lover's indifference, a so-called fact reiterated by Oldham's twentieth-century editor. Harold F. Brooks, introduction, in *The Poems of John Oldham* (Oxford: Clarendon Press, 1987), lix.

44. Ibid., 6–7.

45. Ibid., 69, 72.

46. Ibid., 32, 33.

47. Judith Butler, *Excitable Speech: A Politics of the Performative* (New York and London: Routledge, 1997), 20.

48. Oldham, "A Satyr Upon a Woman," 42–45.

49. The *OED* provides two instances for this third definition, the first from 1609 and the second from 1702.

50. Trumbach, *Sex and the Gender Revolution*, 24–29. Trumbach argues that most disputes centered around money. However, to attack a woman for being a woman in the pejorative sense of the word (as sexually dangerous and fundamentally duplicitous) served any number of functions and provided one of the central strategies for legally attacking women. Trumbach's conclusions are based on cases heard in the London Consistory Court throughout the eighteenth century. Significantly, he notes that nearly 70 percent of the cases heard in the London Consistory Court from 1700–1709 were for defamation and constituted an important forum for the legal vindication of a person's reputation.

51. Oldham, "A Satyr Upon a Woman," 41.

52. Ibid., 31.

53. Ann Van Sant, "Satire and Law: The 'Case' against Women," *REAL: The Yearbook of Research in English and American Literature* 18 (2002): 40.

54. Thomas D'Urfey, "Paid for Peeping," in *New Poems, Consisting of Satyrs, Elegies, and Odes* (London, 1690), 68.

55. Joseph Thurston, *The Toilette; In Three Books* (London, 1730), 36.

56. Allan Ramsay, "The Morning Interview" (1721), in *The Poems of Allan Ramsay*, 2 vols. (London, 1800), 2:208, 209.

57. Ibid., 2:208.

58. "Signior Dildo," in *The Complete Poems of John Wilmot, Earl of Rochester*, ed. David M. Vieth (New Haven and London: Yale University Press, 1968). Noting the numerous courtiers mentioned in the satire, Dustin Griffin argues that the satire was "probably intended as scandalous amusement for the Court" (Dustin Griffin, *Satires Against Man: The Poems of Rochester* [Berkeley, Los Angeles, and London: University of California Press, 1973], 88).

59. Donald Posner, "The Lady and her Dog," in *Watteau: A Lady at her Toilet* (London: Allen Lane of Penguin Books, 1973), 77–84.

60. Ames, *The Folly of Love*, 8.

61. Ramsay, "The Morning Interview," 2:211.

62. Ibid.

63. *Woman in Miniature. A Satire* (London, 1742), 4, 5.

64. Ibid., 8.

65. Ibid., 8, 9.

66. Ibid., 8.

67. Andrew Marvell, *The Garden*, in *The Complete Poems*, ed. George deF. Lord (New York: Knopf, 1993), 57–58.

68. Ames, *The Folly of Love* 27.

69. Breval, *The Art of Dress*, 16.

70. E. Ann Kaplan, "Is the Gaze Male?" in *Powers of Desire*, ed. Ann Snitow (New York: Monthly Review Press, 1983), 311.

71. Stapylton, "The Sixth Satyr of Juvenal," 529.

72. Ibid., 530.

73. Dryden, "The Sixth Satire of Juvenal," 660–65.

74. Andrew Marvell, "The last Instructions to a Painter," in *The Complete Poems*, ed. George deF. Lord (New York: Knopf, 1993), 93.

75. Ibid., 95.

76. "The Toilette. A Town Eclogue. Lydia," in *The Poetical, Dramatic, and Miscellaneous Works of John Gay* (1795), 6 vols., facsimile reprint (New York: AMS Press, 1970), 3:86, 85. The poem was originally circulated in manuscript. Robert Halsband, *The Life of Lady Mary Wortley Montagu* (Oxford: Clarendon Press, 1956), 49. Regarding authorship and the various versions of the poem, Robert Halsband and Isobel Grundy argue that "Gay's version of it, printed among his *Poems on Several Occasions*, 1720, really amounts to a different poem" from Lady Mary Wortley Montagu's (*Essays and Poems and* Simplicity. A Comedy, ed. Robert Halsband and Isobel Grundy [Oxford: Oxford University Press, 1977], 182). For the purposes of this discussion, I refer to Gay's version of the poem.

77. Jonathan Crary, *Techniques of the Observer: On Vision and Modernity in the Nineteenth Century* (Cambridge and London: MIT Press, 1996), 39.

78. Ibid., 41.

79. Ronald Paulson, *The Fictions of Satire* (Baltimore: Johns Hopkins University Press, 1967), 5.

80. Penelope Wilson, "Feminism and the Augustans: Some Readings and Problems," *Critical Quarterly* 28, 1, 2 (Spring, Summer 1986): 82.

81. Bogel, *The Difference Satire Makes*, 12.

82. Ibid., 32.

83. Robert Gould, *Love given o're; or, a Satyr against the Pride, Lust, and Inconstancy, &c. of Woman* (1682), 5.

84. Nussbaum, *The Brink of All We Hate*, 30.

85. *Oxford English Dictionary*, s.v. "reflect."

86. Gould, *Love given o're*, 2.

87. Kaplan, "Is the Gaze Male?" 319.

88. Zimbardo, "The Semiotics of Restoration Satire," 35.

89. Judith Butler, "Imitation and Gender Insubordination," in *The Gay and Lesbian Studies Reader*, ed. Henry Abelove, Michèle Aina Barale, David M. Halperin (New York: Routledge, 1993), 309.

90. Jean Marie Goulemot, "Literary Practices: Publicizing the Private," in vol. 3 of *A History of Private Life*, ed. Philippe Ariès and Georges Duby (Cambridge: Harvard University Press, 1989), 387.

91. Butler, "Imitation and Gender Insubordination," 308, 309–10.

92. Elizabeth Thomas, "An Inventory of a Lady's Dressing-Room," in *The Metamorphoses of the Town: or, A View of the Present Fashions*, 4th edition (London, 1738), 55.

93. Ibid., 54.

94. Defoe, *The London Ladies Dressing-Room*, 2.

95. Evelyn, *Mundus Muliebris*, 9.

96. Ibid., 9, 10, 11.

97. Thomas, "An Inventory of a Lady's Dressing-Room," 58.

98. Ibid., 55, 56.

99. Ibid., 54.

100. Ibid.

101. Ibid., 57.

102. Evelyn, *Mundus Muliebris*, 10.

103. Ibid., 12.

104. Defoe, *The London Ladies Dressing-Room*, 7.

105. Addison and Steele, *The Spectator*, no. 15, 17 March 1711.

CHAPTER 4. THE ARTS OF BEAUTY

1. Oldham, "A Satyr Upon a Woman," 71.

2. [John Wilmot, Earl of Rochester or Robert Gould?], "A General Satyr on Woman," in *Female Excellence; or, Woman Displayed, In Several Satyrick Poems* (London, 1679), 4.

3. Statute 26, George II, cap. 49; quoted in Williams, *Powder and Paint*, 65.

4. Williams, *Powder and Paint*, 25–67. See also Sharon Romm, *The Changing Face of Beauty* (St. Louis, Mo.: Mosby Year Book, 1992), 69–82; Lydia Ben Ytzhak, *Petite Histoire du Maquillage* (Paris: Éditions Stock, 2000), 59–71; and Max Wykes-Joyce, *Cosmetics and Adornment: Ancient and Contemporary Usage* (New York: Philosophical Library, 1961), 49–78.

5. Louis A. Landa, "Pope's Belinda, The General Emporie of the World, and the Wondrous Worm," in *Essays in Eighteenth-Century English Literature* (Princeton: Princeton University Press, 1980), 186, 189. This essay was originally published in *South Atlantic Quarterly: Essays in Eighteenth-Century Literature in Honor of Benjamin Boyce* 70 (1971): 215–35.

6. Kowaleski-Wallace, *Consuming Subjects*, 52–69.

7. Oldham, "A Satyr Upon a Woman," 6–7.

8. Alexander Pope, *The Rape of the Lock and Other Poems*, ed. Geoffrey Tillotson, vol. 2 of *The Twickenham Edition of the Poems of Alexander Pope*, gen. ed. John Butt (New Haven: Yale University Press, 1954), 5.7n5. Subsequent references are cited parenthetically within the main text.

9. Nussbaum, *The Brink of All We Hate*, 137.

10. Pollak, *The Poetics of Sexual Myth*, 77–107. Deborah C. Payne argues that Belinda's objectification is rendered in optical terms ("Pope and the War Against Coquettes; Or, Feminism and *The Rape of the Lock* Reconsidered — Yet Again," *The Eighteenth Century: Theory and Interpretation* 32, 1 [1991]: 11). For an insightful, though brief, treatment of the ways in which the boundary between subject and object collapse in the poem, see Rebecca Ferguson's "'Quick as her Eyes, and as unfix'd as those': Objectification and Seeing in Pope's *Rape of the Lock*," *Critical Survey* 4, 2 (1992): 140–46.

11. Christa Knellwolf, *A Contradiction Still: Representations of Women in the Poetry of Alexander Pope* (Manchester and New York: Manchester University Press, 1998), 3.

12. Ibid., 5.

13. Ibid., 179.

14. Brown, *Ends of Empire*, 119.

15. Ibid., 121–34.

16. Robert W. Jones, *Gender and the Formation of Taste in Eighteenth-Century Britain: The Analysis of Beauty* (Cambridge: Cambridge University Press, 1998), 1.

17. Jones does not discuss face painting or cosmetics and focuses primarily on texts after 1750. Neville Williams treats the topic in *Powder and Paint*, 33–92. More recently Tassie Gwilliam has analyzed two later eighteenth-century texts in "Cosmetic Poetics: Coloring Faces in the Eighteenth Century," in *Body and Text in the Eighteenth Century*, ed. Veronica Kelly and Dorothea von Mücke (Stanford, Calif.: Stanford University Press, 1994), 144–59.

18. Marvell, "The last Instructions to a Painter," 79–80.

19. Congreve, *The Way of the World*, 3.

20. Addison and Steele, *The Spectator*, no. 523, 30 October 1712; *The Correspondence of Alexander Pope*, ed. George Sherburn, 5 vols. (Oxford: Oxford University Press,

1956), 1:214; and Maynard Mack, *Alexander Pope: A Life* (New York: W. W. Norton, 1988), 331; see also, 248–57.

21. [Nicholas Amhurst and James Welton], *The Art of Beauty: A Poem. Humbly addressʼd to the Oxford Toasts* (London, 1719), v–vi. Subsequent references are cited parenthetically within the text. "J.B.," who signs the epistle dedicatory, may be the publisher J. Bettenham. See D. F. Foxon, *English Verse, 1701–1750: A Catalogue of Separately Printed Poems*, 2 vols. (Cambridge: Cambridge University Press, 1975), 1:30.

22. Nancy J. Vickers, "Diana Described: Scattered Woman and Scattered Rhyme," in *Writing and Sexual Difference*, ed. Elizabeth Abel (Chicago: University of Chicago Press, 1982), 97.

23. Addison and Steele, *The Spectator*, no. 41, 17 April 1711. Subsequent citations in this paragraph are from this number.

24. *A Wonder of Wonders; or, A Metamorphosis of Fair Faces voluntarily transformed into foul Visages* (London, 1662), 9.

25. Originally published in 1656 as *A Discourse of Auxiliary Beauty*, reprinted as *A Discourse of Artificial Beauty* in 1662 and 1692: the last of these is used in this chapter. Subsequent references are cited parenthetically within the text. Although *A Discourse* has been attributed to both Jeremy Taylor and Obadiah Walker, it is generally attributed to Gauden. Williams, *Powder and Paint*, 51.

26. For such prefaces, see Johann Jacob Wecker, *Cosmeticks; or, The Beautifying Part of Physick* (London, 1660); *Beauties Treasury: or, the Ladies 'Vade Mecum'* (London, 1705); and *The Art of Beauty, or, A Companion for the Toilet* (London, 1760).

27. *A Wonder of Wonders*, 24.

28. Ibid., 29.

29. Gauden's proxy provides a multitude of ways to critique paternalistic voices. See, for example, 5, 19, 51, 76–77, 79, 81, 113, and 132.

30. Will Pritchard, "Masks and Faces: Female Legibility in the Restoration Era," *Eighteenth-Century Life* 24, 3 (2000): 41.

31. *A Wonder of Wonders*, 22.

32. *The Correspondence of Alexander Pope*, 1:151.

33. Ibid., 1:207

34. Edmund Burke, *A Philosophical Enquiry into the Origin of our Ideas of the Sublime and Beautiful*, ed. James T. Boulton (Notre Dame: University of Notre Dame Press, 1986), 113.

35. It is not clear whether Pope ever saw Fermor in person (his correspondence mentions leaving a "pacquet at her lodgeing" when she was out of town), but he wrote to her and knew about her activities through mutual acquaintances (*The Correspondence of Alexander Pope*, 1:142, 269, and 271–72).

36. See Robert Halsband's *The Rape of the Lock and its Illustrations, 1714–1890* (Oxford: Clarendon Press, 1980).

37. Foxon, *English Verse, 1701–1750*.

38. Alexander Pope, *Poetical Works* (1776), frontispiece.

39. Brown, *The Ends of Empire*, 107.

40. For discussions of this connection in relation to other literary texts, see Gwilliam, "Cosmetic Poetics," 144; and Frances E. Dolan, "Taking the Pencil out of God's Hand: Art, Nature, and the Face-Painting Debate in Early Modern England," *PMLA* 108, 2 (March 1993): 224.

41. *Polygraphice; or, The Arts of Drawing, Engraving, Etching, Limning, Painting, Washing, Varnishing, Gilding, Colouring, Dying, Beautifying and Perfuming* (London, 1673), 288–93.

42. Jean Hagstrum classifies the poem as ekphrastic and argues that *The Rape of the Lock* moves from "visual scene to visual scene" like a "picture gallery with supporting

comment and some narrative links." Jean Hagstrum, *The Sister Arts: The Tradition of Literary Pictorialism and English Poetry from Dryden to Gray* (Chicago and London: University of Chicago Press, 1958), 222.

43. William Christie, "'To Advantage Drest': Poetics and Cosmetics in *The Rape of the Lock*," in *Imperfect Apprehensions: Essays in English Literature in Honour of G. A. Wilkes*, ed. Geoffrey Little (Sydney: Challis, 1996), 138.

44. Ibid., 140.

45. Hagstrum, *The Sister Arts*, 18n34; and Murray Krieger, *Ekphrasis: The Illusion of the Natural Sign* (Baltimore and London: Johns Hopkins University Press, 1992), 284.

46. James A. W. Heffernan, *Museum of Words: The Poetics of Ekphrasis from Homer to Ashbery* (Chicago and London: University of Chicago Press, 1993), 3.

47. Ibid., 7.

48. Ibid., 6.

49. Laura Claridge similarly argues that "Woman's art threatens male artistry," but identifies Belinda's art as sexual and Pope's as a "substitute for the creative act of bearing a child" ("Pope's Rape of Excess," in *Perspectives on Pornography: Sexuality in Film and Literature*, ed. Gary Day and Clive Bloom [New York: St. Martin's Press, 1988], 131).

50. Heffernan, *Museum of Words*, 7.

51. See Mack, viii, and passim. See, also, Helen Deutsch's argument that deformity became a kind of poetics for Pope in *Alexander Pope and the Deformation of Culture* (Cambridge and London: Harvard University Press, 1996).

52. John Dennis, *A True Character of Mr. Pope and His Writings* (1716), facsimile reprint (New York: Garland Publishing, 1975), title page. Ned Ward, *Apollo's Maggots in his Cups, or the Whimsical Creation of a Little Satyrical Poet* (1729), in *Pamphlet Attacks on Alexander Pope 1711–1744: A Descriptive Bibliography*, ed. J. V. Guerinot (London: Methuen, 1969), 178. Steve Clark argues that Pope's body provoked scorn and ridicule in "'Let Blood and Body bear the fault': Pope and misogyny," in *Pope: New Contexts*, ed. David Fairer (London: Harvester Wheatsheaf, 1990), 81–101.

53. Colley Cibber, *A Letter From Mr. Cibber to Mr. Pope, Inquiring into the Motives that might induce him in his Satyrical Works, to be so frequently fond of Mr. Cibber's name* (1742), facsimile reprint (Los Angeles: William Andrews Clark Memorial Library, University of California, 1978), 47.

54. *Sawney and Colley* (1742), ed. W. Powell Jones, facsimile reprint (Los Angeles: William Andrews Clark Memorial Library, University of California, 1960), 7.

55. *The Correspondence of Alexander Pope*, 1:120, 25 June 1711.

56. Carolyn D. Williams, *Pope, Homer, and Manliness: Some Aspects of Eighteenth-Century Classical Learning* (London and New York: Routledge, 1993).

57. *The Correspondence of Alexander Pope*, 1:114, 25 January 1710/11.

58. Edward Young, "Conjectures on Original Composition," in *The Complete Works*, ed. James Nichols, vol. 2 (London, 1854), 566.

59. "Preface to the *Iliad*," in *Selected Prose of Alexander Pope*, ed. Paul Hammond (Cambridge: Cambridge University Press, 1987), 109.

60. *The Iliad of Homer*, ed. Maynard Mack, vol. 8 of *The Twickenham Edition of the Poems of Alexander Pope*, gen. ed. John Butt (New Haven: Yale University, 1967), 358–70.

61. Heffernan, *Museum of Words*, 14.

62. *The Iliad of Homer*, 362–63.

63. Heffernan, *Museum of Words*, 7.

64. Deutsch, *Resemblance and Disgrace*, 52–53.

65. Knellwolf, *A Contradiction Still*, 172.

66. *The Iliad of Homer*, 19.23.

67. Ibid., 19.17–18.

68. Cleanth Brooks, "The Case of Miss Arabella Fermor," in *The Well-Wrought Urn: Studies in the Structure of Poetry* (New York: Harcourt, Brace & World, 1947), 96; and Pollak, *The Poetics of Sexual Myth*, 83. For a rigorous analysis of how the poem as a whole is interpreted much as Belinda has been (i.e., prompting either praise or blame), see Christopher Norris, "Pope among the Formalists: Textual Politics and 'The Rape of the Lock,'" in *Post-Structuralist Readings of English Poetry*, ed. Richard Machin and Christopher Norris (Cambridge: Cambridge University Press, 1987), 134–61.

69. On satire's epideictic lineage, see Griffin, *Satire: A Critical Reintroduction*, 71ff. For examples of Pope criticism that replicates the epideictic tradition of praise and blame, see Valerie Rumbold, *Women's Place in Pope's World* (Cambridge: Cambridge University Press, 1989), and Nussbaum, *The Brink of All We Hate*, 137–58.

70. "Ideal representations of woman are inherently violent in the same way that satires of woman are violent. Both chop up women's bodies, as is suggested by the fact that the name 'anatomy' has been applied to both" (Mandell, *Misogynous Economies*, 23).

71. *The Correspondence of Alexander Pope*, 1:211.

72. Alexander Pope, *Imitations of Horace and An Epistle to Dr Arbuthnot and The Epilogue to the Satires*, ed. John Butt, vol. 4 of *The Twickenham Edition of the Poems of Alexander Pope*, gen. ed. John Butt (New Haven: Yale University Press, 1953), 350–51.

73. Alexander Pope, *Epistles to Several Persons*, ed. F. W. Bateson, vol. 3, pt. 2 of *The Twickenham Edition of the Poems of Alexander Pope*, gen. ed. John Butt (New Haven: Yale University Press, 1951), 25. Subsequent references are cited parenthetically within the text.

74. Alison Conway, *Private Interests: Women, Portraiture, and the Visual Culture of the English Novel, 1709–1791* (Toronto, Buffalo, and London: University of Toronto Press, 2001), 20.

75. In *The Rover*, a prostitute named Angellica Bianca displays a provocative portrait of herself to attract customers. *The Rover; or, The Banished Cavaliers*, in *The Works of Aphra Behn: Volume 5, The Plays, 1671–1677*, ed. Janet Todd (London: William Pickering, 1996). In *Memoirs Of the Extraordinary Life, Works, and Discoveries of Martinus Scriblerus*, a publicly displayed "pourtrait of two Bohemian Damsales"—prostitutes who are Siamese twins—lures Martinus into their brothel (*Memoirs Of the Extraordinary Life, Works, and Discoveries of Martinus Scriblerus*, ed. Charles Kerby-Miller [Oxford: Oxford University Press, 1988], 86).

76. *The Works of Alexander Pope Esq.*, ed. William Warburton (London, 1751), 3:142 n269.

77. Rumbold, *Women's Place in Pope's World*, 277.

78. "Even God is viewed with domestic spectacles in this familial vision, as 'Blends' and 'Shakes' suggest God the chef following a recipe in the cosmic kitchen" (Howard Weinbrot, *Alexander Pope and the Traditions of Formal Verse Satire* [Princeton: Princeton University Press, 1982], 197).

79. Pollak, *The Poetics of Sexual Myth*, 108–27.

80. Felicity Rosslyn, "'Dipt in the rainbow': Pope on Women," in *The Enduring Legacy: Alexander Pope Tercentenary Essays*, ed. G. S. Rousseau and Pat Rogers (Cambridge: Cambridge University Press, 1988), 61.

CHAPTER 5. THE EPISTEMOLOGY OF THE DRESSING ROOM

1. "An Epigram upon the Lady's Dressing-Room," in *Chloe Surprized; Or, The Second Part of the Lady's Dressing-Room* (London, 1732), 8.

2. *The Gentleman's Study in Answer to the Lady's Dressing-Room* (London and Dublin, 1732).

3. James Ferguson, *Lectures on Select Subjects in Mechanics, Pneumatics, Hydrostatics, and Optics* (London, 1764), 148.

4. F. R. Leavis, "The Irony of Swift," in *Determinations: Critical Essays* (London: Chatto and Windus, 1934), 79–108.

5. Carole Fabricant, *Swift's Landscape* (Baltimore and London: Johns Hopkins University Press, 1982), 30; Donald Greene, "On Swift's 'Scatological' Poems," *The Sewanee Review* 75, 4 (Autumn 1967): 673; John M. Aden, "Those Gaudy Tulips: Swift's 'Unprintables,'" in *Quick Springs of Sense: Studies in the Eighteenth Century*, ed. Larry S. Champion (Athens: University of Georgia Press, 1974), 15–32; Jae Num Lee, *Swift and Scatological Satire* (Albuquerque: University of New Mexico Press, 1974); Thomas B. Gilmore, Jr., "The Comedy of Swift's Scatological Poems," *PMLA* 91, 1 (January 1976): 33; and Donald T. Siebert, "Swift's *Fiat Odor*: The Excremental Re-Vision," *Eighteenth-Century Studies* 19, 1 (Fall 1985): 21.

6. John, Earl of Orrery, *Remarks on the Life and Writings of Dr. Jonathan Swift, Dean of St. Patrick's, Dublin* (1752), facsimile reprint (New York and London: Garland Publishing, 1974), 122–23.

7. Patrick Delany, *Observations Upon Lord Orrery's Remarks On The Life And Writings of Dr. Jonathan Swift* (Dublin, 1754), 5–6.

8. Laetitia Pilkington, *Memoirs of Mrs. Laetitia Pilkington, Written by Herself* (1754), in *Memoirs With Anecdotes of Dean Swift, 1748–1754*, vol. 19, facsimile reprint (New York and London: Garland Publishing, 1975), 121.

9. Sir Walter Scott, *Life of Swift*, vol. 1, *The Works of Jonathan Swift, D. D., Dean of St. Patrick's Dublin*, ed. Sir Walter Scott, 12 vols. (London, 1814), 387.

10. Susan Gubar, "Reply to Pollak," *Signs* 3 (1978): 733. See also Gubar, "The Female Monster in Augustan Satire," *Signs* 3 (1977): 380–94.

11. Nora Crow Jaffe, *The Poet Swift* (Hanover, N.H.: University Press of New England, 1977), 117.

12. Margaret Anne Doody, "Swift among the Women," in *Critical Essays on Jonathan Swift*, ed. Frank Palmeri (New York: G. K. Hall, 1993), 13–37.

13. Ibid., 17.

14. Carol Houlihan Flynn, *The Body in Swift and Defoe* (Cambridge: Cambridge University Press, 1990), 89.

15. Pilkington, *Memoirs*, 161.

16. Jonathan Swift, "A Beautiful Young Nymph Going to Bed," in *The Poems of Jonathan Swift*, ed. Harold Williams, vol. 2, 2nd ed. (Oxford: Oxford University Press, 1958), 73–74. Subsequent references are cited parenthetically within the text.

17. Jonathan Swift, *Journal to Stella*, ed. Harold Williams, 2 vols. (Oxford: Oxford University Press, 1948), 443.

18. Jonathan Swift, *Gulliver's Travels* (1726), in *The Prose Works of Jonathan Swift*, ed. Herbert Davis et al., vol. 11 (Oxford: Oxford University Press, 1939–68), 119 (book 2, chapter 5).

19. Carol Houlihan Flynn's particular focus is on the body, often the female body; she argues that "with pains the matter of the body can be made literary material, but the transformation is of necessity costly and often ironic, taking account of a metamorphosis that cannot occur without a struggle." In the case of "The Lady's Dressing Room," Flynn contends that its frame is ultimately ironic, even though voyeurs such as Strephon and Gulliver are ultimately threatened by a model of female sexuality that is profoundly overwhelming (Flynn, *Body*, 4, 92–93).

20. Claude Rawson, *Order from Confusion Sprung: Studies in Eighteenth-Century Litera-*

ture from Swift to Cowper (London: George Allen & Unwin, 1985), 159. This material was originally published as C. J. Rawson, "The Nightmares of Strephon: Nymphs of the City in the Poems of Swift, Baudelaire, Eliot," in *English Literature in the Age of Disguise*, ed. Maximillian E. Novak (Berkeley, Los Angeles, and London: University of California Press, 1977), 57–100.

21. Ibid., 165.

22. Ibid., 167. Rawson continues: "appearance and reality . . . are locked in an unnatural embrace, and Swift finally knows . . . that he cannot separate them. Still less can he decide which to prefer, for Appearance is not only 'false Lights' but 'Decency,' and Reality is frank 'unmasking' *and* the Yahoo beast" (167).

23. Ibid., 177.

24. Ibid., 178.

25. Jonathan Swift, "The Lady's Dressing Room," in *The Poems of Jonathan Swift*, ed. Harold Williams, vol. 2, 2nd ed. (Oxford: Oxford University Press, 1958), 143–44. Subsequent references are cited parenthetically within the text.

26. Steven Shapin and Simon Schaffer, *Leviathan and the Air-Pump: Hobbes, Boyle, and the Experimental Life* (Princeton: Princeton University Press, 1985), 332.

27. Peter Dear, "From Truth to Disinterestedness in the Seventeenth Century," *Social Studies of Science* 22 (1992): 627. See also Poovey, *A History of the Modern Fact*, 1–7.

28. Brown, *Ends of Empire*, 199, 178.

29. Ibid., 181.

30. Ann Jessie Van Sant, *Eighteenth-Century Sensibility and the Novel: The Senses in Social Context* (Cambridge: Cambridge University Press, 1993), 71.

31. Jonathan Swift, *An Apology For the, etc.* (London, 1704), 18.

32. Barbara J. Shapiro, *A Culture of Fact: England, 1550–1720* (Ithaca and London: Cornell University Press, 2000),107–12.

33. See A. Guthkelch, *The Battle of the Books* (London: Chatto and Windus, 1908), ix–lvi; Richard Foster Jones, *Ancients and Moderns: A Study of the Background of the* Battle of the Books (St. Louis: Washington University Studies, 1936); Miriam Kosh Starkman, *Swift's Satire on Learning in* A Tale of a Tub (Princeton: Princeton University Press, 1950); and Anne Elizabeth Burlingame, The Battle of the Books *in its Historical Setting* (New York: Biblo and Tannen, 1969).

34. Frank Boyle is an exception, although he studies Swift's *Ode to the Athenian Society*, a verse that explicitly responds to the Royal Society (Frank Boyle, *Swift as Nemesis: Modernity and Its Satirist* [Stanford, Calif.: Stanford University Press, 2000], 78–103).

35. Rawson, *Order from Confusion Sprung*, 148.

36. Irvin Ehrenpreis, *The Personality of Jonathan Swift* (Cambridge: Harvard University Press, 1958), 39.

37. Jonathan Swift, "The Progress of Beauty," in *The Poems of Jonathan Swift*, ed. Harold Williams, vol. 1, 2nd ed. (Oxford: Oxford University Press, 1958), 103, 113–14. Subsequent references are cited parenthetically within the text.

38. Jonathan Swift, "The First of April," in *The Poems of Jonathan Swift*, ed. Harold Williams, vol. 1, 2nd ed. (Oxford: Oxford University Press, 1958), 41–42.

39. Brown, *Ends of Empire*, 184.

40. Mary Ellin D'Agostino, "Privy Business: Chamber Pots and Sexpots in Colonial Life," *Archaeology* 53, 4 (July/August 2000): 32–37.

41. Oldham, "A Satyr Upon a Woman," 72–73.

42. Ned Ward, *The London Terræfilius; Or, The Satyrical Reformer*, no. 2 (1707), 21.

43. Ranum, "The Refuges of Intimacy," 225–26.

44. Dora Thornton, *The Scholar in His Study: Ownership and Experience in Renaissance Italy* (New Haven: Yale University Press, 1997), 72.

45. Pollak, *The Poetics of Sexual Myth*, 22–76, 160.

46. Mandell, *Misogynous Economies*, 90; and Deborah Baker Wyrick, *Jonathan Swift and the Vested Word* (Chapel Hill and London: University of North Carolina Press, 1988), 148.

47. Thomas Sprat, *The History of the Royal Society of London, For the Improving of Natural Knowledge*, 3rd ed. (London, 1722), 415. Subsequent references are cited parenthetically within the text.

48. Jones, *Ancients and Moderns*, 231–46.

49. Sprat explains that the New Scientists use their senses to *"judge* and *resolve* upon the Matter of *Fact"* (99).

50. Shapin and Schaffer, *Leviathan and the Air-Pump*, 67. See also Lorraine Daston, "Baconian Facts, Academic Civility, and the Prehistory of Objectivity," *Annals of Scholarship* 8, 3/4 (1991): 337–63; Lorraine Daston, "Objectivity and the Escape from Perspective," *Social Studies of Science* 22 (1992): 597–618; and Dear, "From Truth to Disinterestedness," 619–31.

51. Evelyn, *Mundus Muliebris*; Defoe, *The London Ladies Dressing-Room*; and Thomas, "An Inventory of a Lady's Dressing-Room." See especially Thomas, 55–56.

52. Sprat contends that the disinterested observer will see truth unclouded by the prejudice of language and theory. The Society's goal is to "separate Knowledge of *Nature,* from the Colours of *Rhetorick,* the Devices of *Fancy* or the delightful Deceit of *Fables"* (62). This separation of knowledge from forms of thinking that distort truth is achieved not through theory (the model of knowledge acquisition that Sprat associates with Descartes, the individual thinker, and the Ancients), but through "solid Practice and Examples; not by a glorious Pomp of Words; but by the silent, effectual, and unanswerable Arguments of real Productions" (62).

53. In their discussion of Robert Boyle, Shapin and Schaffer underscore the importance of witnessing to the New Science:

> Matters of fact were the outcome of the process of having an empirical experience, warranting it to oneself, and assuring others that grounds for their belief were adequate. In that process a multiplication of the witnessing experience was fundamental. An experience, even of a rigidly controlled experimental performance, that one man alone witnessed was not adequate to make a matter of fact. If that experience could be extended to many, and in principle to all men, then the result could be constituted as a matter of fact. In this way, the matter of fact is to be seen as both an epistemological and a social category. (Shapin and Schaffer, *Leviathan and the Air-Pump,* 25)

54. Shapiro, *A Culture of Fact*, 117–21. In a now famous phrase, P. G. M. Dickson contends that the late seventeenth century staged a "financial revolution in England" designed to make money "cheap"—that is, more widely available through the mechanisms of credit. One of the key outgrowths of this revolution, of course, was the possibility of speculative investment, a form of money making that required paper credit, banks, and joint-stock companies. The rise of consumerism, so aptly captured by the stereotypical dressing room scene, was possible in large part due to the increase in what we call "disposable income" today, even though the prime mechanism for making this kind of money—a securities market in London—was, as Dickson notes, "denounced [by contemporaries] as inherently wicked and against the public interest. The phrase 'stock-jobbing,' freely used to denote every kind of activity in the market, had clear overtones of self-interest and corruption." See P. G. M. Dickson, *The Financial Revolution in England: A Study in the Development of Public Credit, 1688–1756* (London: Macmillan; New York: St. Martin's Press, 1967), 3–14, 33; Larry Neal, "The Finance of Business during the Industrial Revolution," in *The Economic History of Britain Since 1700, vol. 1,*

1700–1860, ed. Roderick Floud and Donald McCloskey, 2nd ed. (Cambridge: Cambridge University Press, 1994), 151; and Catherine Ingrassia, *Authorship, Commerce, and Gender in Early Eighteenth-Century England: A Culture of Paper Credit* (Cambridge: Cambridge University Press, 1998), 5.

55. Daston, "Baconian Facts," 339.

56. Robert Markley, *Fallen Languages: Crises of Representation in Newtonian England, 1660–1740* (Ithaca and London: Cornell University Press, 1993), 97.

57. Denis Donoghue, *Jonathan Swift: A Critical Introduction* (Cambridge: Cambridge University Press, 1971), 204.

58. Claude Rawson, *Gulliver and the Gentle Reader: Studies in Swift and Our Time* (London: Routledge & Kegan Paul, 1973), 34.

59. Jonathan Swift, *A Full and True Account of the Battel Fought last Friday, Between the Antient and the Modern Books in St. James's Library* in *A Tale of a Tub with Other Early Works, 1696–1701*, ed. Herbert Davis, vol. 1 of *The Prose Works of Jonathan Swift* (Oxford: Basil Blackwell, 1965), 140. Subsequent references are cited parenthetically in the text.

60. Mikkel Borch-Jacobsen, *The Freudian Subject*, trans. Catherine Porter (Stanford, Calif.: Stanford University Press, 1988), 69.

61. Bogel, *The Difference Satire Makes*, 12.

62. Brown, *Ends of Empire*, 180.

63. Barbara Maria Stafford, *Body Criticism: Imaging the Unseen in Enlightenment Art and Medicine* (Cambridge: MIT Press, 1991), 2. Stafford continues, "Detecting pervasive human forgeries was comparable to the cognate activity of unmasking phony antiquities. Such artificial persons, who carefully constructed their social appearance, were judged to be all optical effect, magic lantern projection without solid foundation" (10).

64. Elias, *The Court Society*, 242–50.

65. Gilmore, "The Comedy of Swift's Scatological Poems," 36.

66. Jacques Derrida, *Of Grammatology*, trans. Gayatri Chakravorty Spivak (Baltimore and London: Johns Hopkins University Press, 1976), 145.

67. Swift, *Gulliver's Travels*, book 3, chapter 5.

68. Joseph M. Levine, *The Battle of the Books: History and Literature in the Augustan Age* (Ithaca and London: Cornell University Press, 1991), 116.

69. Jonathan Swift, "Strephon and Chloe," in *The Poems of Jonathan Swift*, ed. Harold Williams, vol. 2, 2nd ed. (Oxford: Oxford University Press, 1958), 204.

70. Brown, *Ends of Empire*, 176.

71. Christine Rees, "Gay, Swift, and the Nymphs of Drury-Lane," *Essays in Criticism* 23, 1 (January 1973): 15.

72. Laura Mandell makes a similar point in a different context (Mandell, *Misogynous Economies*, 23).

73. The anxiety surrounding Sprat's courtship of the wits betrays the power of critique that they hold. They are, Sprat hastily notes, "terrible men": "I acknowledge that we ought to have a great Dread of their Power: I confess I believe that *new Philosophy* need not (as *Cæsar*) fear the pale, or the melancholy, as much as the humorous, and the merry: For they perhaps by making it ridiculous, becaus [*sic*] it is *new*, and becaus [*sic*] they themselves are unwilling to take pains about it, may do it more injury than all the Arguments of our severe and frowning and dogmatical *Adversaries*" (417).

Chapter 6. Richardson's Closet Novels

1. Pamela slides between the two words, describing "the Closet, which was my good Lady's Dressing-room." Richardson, *Pamela; or, Virtue Rewarded*, 43. Subsequent

references are cited parenthetically within the text. See also my discussion of "dressing room" and "closet" in chapters 1 and 2.

2. William Beatty Warner, *Reading Clarissa: The Struggles of Interpretation* (New Haven and London: Yale University Press, 1979), viii.

3. Ibid., 26; see 1–27.

4. Terry Castle, *Clarissa's Cyphers: Meaning and Disruption in Richardson's "Clarissa"* (Ithaca and London: Cornell University Press, 1982), 25.

5. Ibid., 22.

6. Caroline Gonda, *Reading Daughters' Fictions, 1709–1834: Novels and Society from Manley to Edgeworth* (Cambridge: Cambridge University Press, 1996), 75, 77.

7. Patricia Meyer Spacks, *Desire and Truth: Functions of Plot in Eighteenth-Century English Novels* (Chicago and London: University of Chicago Press, 1990), 85. Richardson explains in the introduction to the 1751 edition that Clarissa is not "impeccable."

8. Warner, *Licensing Entertainment*, 180.

9. Tassie Gwilliam, *Samuel Richardson's Fictions of Gender* (Stanford, Calif.: Stanford University Press, 1993), 31.

10. Liz Bellamy, *Commerce, Morality and the Eighteenth-Century Novel* (Cambridge: Cambridge University Press, 1998) 7, 79.

11. McKeon elaborates: "there is an inherent tension between the dynamic form in which Pamela's personal merit is manifested—the plastic powers of her mind—and the progressive ideal of meritocracy, which envisions the replacement of arbitrary aristo-cratic culture by a rigorous consistency of moral and social success, not by the ethically uncertain force of persuasive self-creation" (McKeon, *The Origins of the English Novel, 1600–1740*, 378).

12. Rita Goldberg, *Sex and Enlightenment: Women in Richardson and Diderot* (Cam-bridge: Cambridge University Press, 1984), 29; and Ingrassia, *Authorship, Commerce, and Gender in Early Eighteenth-Century England*, 139.

13. Deidre Shauna Lynch, *The Economy of Character: Novels, Market Culture, and the Business of Inner Meaning* (Chicago: University of Chicago Press, 1998), 9, 41.

14. James Cruise, *Governing Consumption: Needs and Wants, Suspended Characters, and the "Origins" of Eighteenth-Century English Novels* (Lewisburg, Pa.: Bucknell University Press, 1999), 134.

15. Scott Paul Gordon, *The Power of the Passive Self in English Literature, 1640–1770* (Cambridge: Cambridge University Press, 2002), 192.

16. Carol Houlihan Flynn, *Samuel Richardson: A Man of Letters* (Princeton: Princeton University Press, 1982), 51; and John P. Zomchick, *Family and the Law in Eighteenth-Century Fiction: The Public Conscience in the Private Sphere* (Cambridge: Cambridge Univer-sity Press, 1993), 97.

17. Christina Marsden Gillis, *The Paradox of Privacy: Epistolary Form in* Clarissa (Gainesville: University Presses of Florida, 1984); and Ruth Bernard Yeazell, *Fictions of Modesty: Women and Courtship in the English Novel* (Chicago: University of Chicago Press, 1991), 97, 98.

18. Samuel Richardson, *Clarissa; or, the History of a Young Lady*, ed. Angus Ross (New York: Penguin, 1985), 1388, note a. Subsequent references are cited parentheti-cally within the text.

19. Joceyln Harris, "Grotesque, Classical and Pornographic Bodies in *Clarissa*," in *New Essays on Samuel Richardson*, ed. Albert J. Rivero (New York: St. Martin's Press, 1996), 114; and Brenda Bean, "Sight and Self-Disclosure: Richardson's Revision of Swift's 'The Lady's Dressing Room,'" *Eighteenth-Century Life* 14, 1 (February 1990): 9.

20. Jones DeRitter, *The Embodiment of Characters: The Representation of Physical Expe-rience on Stage and in Print, 1728–1749* (Philadelphia: University of Pennsylvania Press,

1994), 113. Terry Castle uses this scene to emphasize the fragmentation of Clarissa's story (*Clarissa's Cyphers*, 32–37).

21. *The Correspondence of Samuel Richardson*, ed. Anna Laetitia Barbauld, 6 vols. (London, 1804), 2:24.

22. Madeleine Kahn, *Narrative Transvestism: Rhetoric and Gender in the Eighteenth-Century English Novel* (Ithaca and London: Cornell University Press, 1991), 153.

23. John Carroll, "Richardson on Pope and Swift," *University of Toronto Quarterly* 33, 1 (October 1963): 22.

24. Margaret Anne Doody, *A Natural Passion: A Study of the Novels of Samuel Richardson* (Oxford: Oxford University Press, 1974), 373–74n1; John Traugott, "Clarissa's Richardson: An Essay to Find the Reader," in *English Literature in the Age of Disguise*, ed. Maximillian E. Novak (Berkeley: University of California Press, 1987), 157–208; James Grantham Turner, "Lovelace and the Paradoxes of Libertinism," in *Samuel Richardson: Tercentenary Essays*, ed. Margaret Anne Doody and Peter Sabor (Cambridge: Cambridge University Press, 1989), 70–88; and Jocelyn Harris, "Protean Lovelace," *Eighteenth-Century Fiction* 2, 4 (July 1990): 327–46.

25. Carroll, "Richardson on Pope and Swift," 26; and Paulson, *Satire and the Novel in Eighteenth-Century England*, 213. Lovelace's allusions range from the maxim from *Hudibras* that "*the woman was made for the man, not the man for the woman*" (429) to a bit from Swift's *A Tale of the Tub* (700). When Lovelace complains about the Harlowes, he refers to the machinery from Pope's *The Rape of the Lock*: "Why, Belford, the lady must fall, if every hair of her head were a guardian angel, unless they were to make a visible appearance for her, or, snatching her from me at unawares, would draw her after them into the starry regions" (440).

26. Richardson makes the link between libertinism and satire even more explicit in his third novel, *Sir Charles Grandison*, when the Grandison sisters tell the story of their father's debauchery: "thus are wickedness and libertinism called a knowledge of the world, a knowledge of human nature. Swift, for often painting a dunghil, and for his abominable Yahoo story, was complimented with this knowledge: But I hope, that the character of human nature, the character of creatures made in the image of the Deity, is not to be taken from the overflowings of such dirty imaginations." Samuel Richardson, *The History of Sir Charles Grandison*, vol. 2 (pt. 1) (Oxford: Oxford University Press, 1972), 348.

27. Paulson, *Satire and the Novel*, 211.

28. Ibid., 212, 214.

29. Jonathan Swift, *A Tale of a Tub* in *A Tale of a Tub with Other Early Works, 1696–1701*, ed. Herbert Davis, vol. 1 of *The Prose Works of Jonathan Swift* (Oxford: Basil Blackwell, 1965), preface.

30. Ibid.

31. Samuel Richardson, "Hints of Prefaces for Clarissa," in *Clarissa: Preface, Hints of Prefaces and Postscript*, intro. R. F. Brissenden, Augustan Reprint Society (Los Angeles: University of California Press, William Andrews Clark Memorial Library, 1964), 13.

32. Swift, preface, in *Tale of a Tub*.

33. *The Correspondence of Samuel Richardson*, 2:229; and Morris Corbyn, *An Essay Towards Fixing the True Standards of Wit, Humour, Raillery, Satire, and Ridicule* (London, 1744), vi.

34. Bean, "Sight and Self-Disclosure," 1. Moreover, Bean's interpretation follows the traditional pattern of identifying the satirist as sympathetic to women, a reading that I argued in chapter 5 obscures the structural similarities between Strephon's conclusions and the views of the satirist.

35. Richardson writes: "*As the bad house is often mentioned in this work, without any other*

stigma than what arises from the wicked principles and actions occasionally given of the wretches who inhabit it; Mr. Belford here enters into the secret retirements of these creatures, and exposes them in the appearances they are supposed to make, before they are tricked out to ensnare weak and inconsiderate minds." Samuel Richardson, *Clarissa, or the History of a Young Lady*, 3rd ed. 8 vols. (London, 1751), 8:305. Subsequent references are cited parenthetically within the text.

36. *The Complete Letters of Lady Mary Wortley Montagu*, ed. Robert Halsband, 3 vols. (Oxford: Oxford University Press, 1960), 3:40 (10 October 1753).

37. Guest, *Small Change*, 73.

38. Henry Care, *The Female Secretary: or, Choice New Letters* (London, 1671), 89.

39. Ibid., 86.

40. Ibid.

41. Richard A. Barney, *Plots of Enlightenment: Education and the Novel in Eighteenth-Century England* (Stanford, Calif.: Stanford University Press, 1999), 79.

42. Mary Astell, *A Serious Proposal to the Ladies for the Advancement of their True and Greatest Interest*, part 1, 1694, in *The First English Feminist*: Reflections Upon Marriage *and Other Writings by Mary Astell*, ed. Bridget Hill (New York: St. Martin's Press, 1986), 167.

43. Ibid., 139.

44. Barney, *Plots of Enlightenment*, 76.

45. James Burgh, *Thoughts on Education* (London, 1747), 53.

46. *The Female Ægis; or, The Duties of Women from Childhood to Old Age, and in most Situations of Life Exemplified* (London, 1798), 22–23.

47. Burgh, *Thoughts on Education*, 53.

48. Ibid.

49. Ibid., 56.

50. Addison and Steele, *The Spectator*, no. 10, 12 March 1711.

51. Warner, *Licensing Entertainment*, 192.

52. Ibid.

53. Allen Michie, *Richardson and Fielding: The Dynamics of a Critical Rivalry* (Lewisburg, Pa.: Bucknell University Press, 1999), 26.

54. Henry Fielding, *Shamela*, ed. Martin C. Battestin (Boston: Houghton Mifflin, 1961), 325.

55. *Pamela Censured* (London, 1741), 24.

56. Bernard Kreissman, "Pamela-Shamela: A Study of the Criticism, Burlesques, Parodies, and Adaptations of Richardson's 'Pamela,'" *University of Nebraska Studies*, 22 (May 1960): 7, 18.

57. Gwilliam, *Samuel Richardson's Fictions of Gender*, 31.

58. Kristina Straub, "Reconstructing the Gaze: Voyeurism in Richardson's *Pamela*," *Studies in Eighteenth-Century Culture* 18 (1988): 427.

59. Jocelyn Harris, *Samuel Richardson* (Cambridge: Cambridge University Press, 1987), 9.

60. Homer Obed Brown, *Institutions of the English Novel: From Defoe to Scott* (Philadelphia: University of Pennsylvania Press, 1997), 34.

61. Jean-Jacques Rousseau, *La Nouvelle Héloïse (Julie, or the New Eloise)*, trans. Judith H. McDowell (University Park: Pennsylvania State University Press, 1968): 122.

62. Eva Maria Stadler, "Defining the Female Body within Social Space: The Function of Clothes in Some Early Eighteenth-Century Novels," in *Proceedings of the XIIth Congress of the International Comparative Literature Association*, ed. Roger Bauer and Douwe Fokkem (München: Iudicium Verlag, 1990), 3:472. Lennard J. Davis notes

that the strip scene tightly parallels the attempted rape, constructing a metonymy of "private letters in relation to private parts" (Lennard J. Davis, *Factual Fictions: The Origins of the English Novel* [New York: Columbia University Press, 1983], 185).

63. Yeazell, *Fictions of Modesty*, 83.

64. Carolyn Dever, *Death and the Mother from Dickens to Freud: Victorian Fiction and the Anxiety of Origins* (Cambridge: Cambridge University Press, 1998), 20–22.

65. Butler, "Imitation and Gender Insubordination," 315.

66. Richard Allestree, *The Ladies Calling*, 4th ed. (London, 1676), 1–27.

67. Ibid., 5.

68. Ibid., 17.

69. Richardson, "Hints of Prefaces," 1.

70. Gwilliam, *Samuel Richardson's Fictions of Gender*, 25.

71. This phrase comes from a letter Richardson sent to Sophia Westcomb, *Selected Letters of Samuel Richardson*, ed. John Carroll (Oxford: Oxford University Press, 1964), 68 (15 September 1746).

72. *The Correspondence of Samuel Richardson*, 3:244.

73. In the novel's second letter, Clarissa recounts that she had been visiting her grandfather's (and now her) dairy house, where she was "busied in the accounts relating to the estate which my grandfather had the goodness to bequeath me" (41). Clarissa later remembers that her grandfather had called her his "housekeeper" (1414), a title that anticipates what role she should have taken as she matured. The importance of good works is so prevalent in Clarissa's mind that she thinks to include a provision for charity in the draft of a response to Lovelace's marriage proposal; she requests £200 a year for specific groups (655). A ballad based on the novel, set to music by John Moulds, elaborates Clarissa's good works at the dairy house; there one may find her in "Her Morn of Happiness," "Spreading blessings all around / To the needy and distrest / Tasting joy that's only found / In a humble virtuous heart" [*Clarissa Harlow; or the History of a Young Lady, consisting of Four Ballads in different periods of her Life, namely Her Morn of Happiness, Her Noon of Uneasiness, Her Eve of Brighter Prospects, Her Night of Death* (London, n.d.) (n.p. second page). Written by "the Author of the Suffering Negro"].

74. Clarissa gives Dolly several articles of clothing as well as her "harpsichord, [her] chamber-organ, and all [her] music books" (1415).

75. Tom Keymer, *Richardson's 'Clarissa' and the Eighteenth-Century Reader* (Cambridge: Cambridge University Press, 1992), 97. See, for example, Varey, *Space and the Eighteenth-Century English Novel*, 181–99); Doody, *A Natural Passion*, 188; and Gillis, *The Paradox of Privacy*. Cynthia Wall suggests that Clarissa works to carve a private space for herself, but claims that the dining room is the most significant for the heroine. Cynthia Wall, "Gendering Rooms: Domestic Architecture and Literary Acts," *Eighteenth-Century Fiction* 5, 4 (July 1993): 350–51.

76. Jerry C. Beasley, "Richardson's Girls: The Daughters of Patriarchy in *Pamela*, *Clarissa*, and *Sir Charles Grandison*," in *New Essays on Samuel Richardson*, ed. Albert J. Rivero (New York: St. Martin's Press, 1996), 43.

77. Alberti, *On the Art of Building in Ten Books*, and *The Family in Renaissance Florence*; and Gayle S. Rubin, "The Traffic in Women: Notes on the Political Economy of Sex," in *Toward an Anthropology of Women*, ed. Rayna P. Reiter (New York: Monthly Review Press, 1975), 157–77.

78. Zomchick, *Family and the Law*, 64.

79. Conway, *Private Interests*, 81–90.

80. Edward Copeland, "Remapping London: *Clarissa* and the Woman in the Window," in *Samuel Richardson: Tercentenary Essays*, ed. Margaret Anne Doody and Peter Sabor (Cambridge: Cambridge University Press, 1989), 68.

81. Clarissa proceeds to list the books:

Stanhope's *Gospels*; Sharp's, Tillotson's and South's *Sermons*; Nelson's *Feasts and Fasts*; a sacramental piece of the Bishop of Man, and another of Dr Gauden, Bishop of Exeter; and Inett's *Devotions*; are among the devout books; and among those of a lighter turn, these not ill-chosen ones; a *Telemachus* in French, another in English; Steele's, Rowe's, and Shakespeare's plays; that genteel comedy of Mr Cibber, *The Careless Husband*, and others of the same author; Dryden's *Miscellanies*; the *Tatlers*, *Spectators*, and *Guardians*; Pope's, and Swift's, and Addison's works. (525–26)

82. Kowaleski-Wallace, *Consuming Subjects*, 89.
83. Gordon, *The Power of the Passive Self*, 191.
84. Conway, *Private Interests*, 100.
85. The prostitutes also act as Lovelace's amanuenses, for Dorcas, Sally, and Polly surreptitiously transcribe Clarissa's correspondence with Anna Howe and Clarissa's drafts once while Lovelace takes Clarissa to a play and another time when they all (save Dorcas) go for an "airing" (632ff. and 675). Lovelace employs the prostitutes even when Clarissa is in the house. At one point Dorcas needs additional time to transcribe a particularly significant letter and signals that Lovelace needs to keep Clarissa occupied even longer (651). Dorcas, Sally, and Polly not only prostitute their bodies, but also their literacy. These women have the potential for learning, the potential to transform *their* dressing rooms into closets, but they use their skills poorly, helping advance Lovelace's plots against Clarissa.
86. Goldberg, *Sex and Enlightenment*, 84, 85.
87. Margaret Anne Doody, *The True Story of the Novel* (New Brunswick: Rutgers University Press, 1997), 278.
88. Watt, *The Rise of the Novel*, 175.
89. Francis Jeffrey's review of *The Correspondence of Samuel Richardson* (ed. Anna Laetitia Barbauld), printed in the *Edinburgh Review* in 1804 and reprinted in Jeffrey, *Contributions to the Edinburgh Review* (New York: Appleton, 1879), 128.
90. "Sonnet to the Author of *Clarissa*," in Anna Laetita Barbauld, *The British Novelists; with an Essay; and Prefaces, Biographical and Critical*, vol. 1 (London, 1810), n.p. (the sonnet is right after the second title page).
91. Spacks, *Privacy*, 224; Brown, *Institutions of the English Novel*, 27, 32–33; Julia Genster, "Belforded Over: The Reader in *Clarissa*," in *Clarissa and Her Readers: New Essay for The* Clarissa *Project*, ed. Carol Houlihan Flynn and Edward Copeland (New York: AMS Press, 1999), 144; and Goulemot, "Literary Practices: Publicizing the Private," 383, 386. Christina Marsden Gillis notes that Clarissa's "private" letters are actually produced for public consumption and therefore hang uneasily between public and private. Gillis, *The Paradox of Privacy*, 2.
92. Watt, *The Rise of the Novel*, 191, 195.
93. Rev. Mr. Skelton, "Hints of Prefaces for Clarissa," in *Clarissa: Preface, Hints of Prefaces, and Postscript*, intro. R. F. Brissenden, Augustan Reprint Society (Los Angeles: University of California Press, William Andrews Clark Memorial Library, 1964), 8.
94. Mr. Spence, "Hints of Prefaces for Clarissa," in *Clarissa: Preface, Hints of Prefaces, and Postscript*, intro. R. F. Brissenden, Augustan Reprint Society (Los Angeles: University of California Press, William Andrews Clark Memorial Library, 1964), 9.
95. Samuel Richardson, *Clarissa*, vol. 1 (London, 1748), preface, v.
96. Van Sant, *Eighteenth-Century Sensibility and the Novel*, 79; Conway, *Private Interests*, 94.
97. Bruce Redford, *The Converse of the Pen: Acts of Intimacy in the Eighteenth-Century Familiar Letter* (Chicago and London: University of Chicago Press, 1986), 2.

98. *The Correspondence of Samuel Richardson*, 3:246.
99. Christopher Flint makes a somewhat different, but related point: Richardson's "epistolary method . . . relies on a narrative model of relation, immediacy, and imminent conflict." Christopher Flint, *Family Fictions: Narrative and Domestic Relations in Britain, 1688–1798* (Stanford, Calif.: Stanford University Press, 1998), 165.
100. Ibid., 170. My understanding of this dynamic is likewise indebted to feminist film theory. See Laura Mulvey, "Visual Pleasure and Narrative Cinema" (1975), in *Feminisms*, ed. Robyn Warhol and Diane Price Herndl (New Brunswick: Rutgers University Press, 1997), 438–48.
101. Lynch, *The Economy of Character*, 1–20. See also Lisa A. Freeman's consideration of identity in eighteenth-century drama, *Character's Theater: Genre and Identity on the Eighteenth-Century Stage* (Philadelphia: University of Pennsylvania Press, 2002).
102. Ibid., 43, 13.
103. Janet Gurkin Altman briefly notes the voyeurism inherent to reading the epistolary novel, only to drop this line of inquiry. Jane Gurkin Altman, *Epistolarity: Approaches to a Form* (Columbus: Ohio State University Press, 1982), 111.
104. *The Correspondence of Samuel Richardson*, 2:60–61.
105. Paulson, *Satire and the Novel in Eighteenth-Century England*, 10; and G. S. Rousseau, "From Swift to Smollet," 129.
106. Richardson, "Hints of Prefaces," 13.

CHAPTER 7. FROM MAIDEN TO MOTHER

1. Armstrong, *Desire and Domestic Fiction*, 59–95. See also Barker-Benfield, *The Culture of Sensibility*.
2. Armstrong, 87.
3. Susan Fraiman, *Unbecoming Women: British Women Writers and the Novel of Development* (New York: Columbia University Press, 1993), 12.
4. Doody, *The True Story of the Novel*, 304.
5. Ibid., 305.
6. Patricia Meyer Spacks, *Desire and Truth*, 3. In a work that itemizes the roles available to women, "courtship" receives its own chapter, thus signaling the various labors involved in this transition; Elizabeth Bergen Brophy, *Women's Lives and the 18th-Century English Novel* (Tampa: University of South Florida Press, 1991), 94–138. See also Trumbach, *Sex and the Gender Revolution*, 25–48.
7. Eve Tavor Bannet, "Rewriting the Social Text: The Female Bildungsroman in Eighteenth-Century England," in *Reflection and Action: Essays on the Bildungsroman*, ed. James Hardin (Columbia: University of South Carolina Press, 1991), 201. Bannet amplifies some of this work in *The Domestic Revolution: Enlightenment Feminism and the Novel* (Baltimore and London: Johns Hopkins University Press, 2000).
8. Fraiman, *Unbecoming Women*, 1–31; and Nancy K. Miller, "Gender and Narrative Possibilities," in *Sade and the Narrative of Transgression*, ed. David B. Allison, Mark S. Roberts, and Allen S. Weiss (Cambridge: Cambridge University Press, 1995), 213. Margaret Anne Doody argues that a "*Bildungsroman* about a woman is still relatively rare in the eighteenth century." Margaret Anne Doody, *Frances Burney: The Life in the Works* (New Brunswick: Rutgers University Press, 1988), 45. Bannet argues that these heroines are "allowed only one flaw—ignorance of the ways of the world" (*Domestic Revolution*, 73).
9. Rachel Blau DuPlessis, *Writing Beyond the Ending* (Bloomington: Indiana University Press, 1984), 4.

10. Julie Shaffer suggests instead that "one might better view the genre as a site for some women novelists to participate in constructing and disseminating an ideology that granted women greater autonomy and respectability than that which viewed them as subordinate and inferior creatures." Julie Shaffer, "Not Subordinate: Empowering Women in the Marriage Plot—The Novels of Frances Burney, Maria Edgeworth, and Jane Austen," *Criticism* 34, 1 (1992): 52. See also Julie Shaffer, "Romance, Finance, and the Marketable Woman: The Economics of Femininity in Late Eighteenth- and Early Nineteenth-Century English Novels," in *Bodily Discursions: Genders, Representations, Technologies*, ed. Deborah S. Wilson and Christine Moneera Laennec (Albany: State University of New York Press, 1997), 39–56.

11. Franco Moretti, *The Way of the World: The* Bildungsroman *in European Culture* (London: Verso, 1987), 15–16.

12. Flint, *Family Fictions*, 17.

13. Mary Poovey, *The Proper Lady and the Woman Writer: Ideology as Style in the Works of Mary Wollstonecraft, Mary Shelley, and Jane Austen* (Chicago and London: University of Chicago Press, 1984), 237–39.

14. Yeazell, *Fictions of Modesty*, 6.

15. Gonda, *Reading Daughters' Fictions, 1709–1834*, 29; see also 21–34.

16. Richardson, *The History of Sir Charles Grandison*, vol. 1 (pt. 1), 53. Though abducted by the dangerous Sir Hargrave Pollexfen in the novel's opening volume, she maintains her (sexual) reputation and gains respect for her frankness, even though she sometimes struggles between "virgin-modesty and openness of heart" when it comes to falling in love with Sir Charles (1:302).

17. Ibid., 1:419, 1:422.

18. Marilyn Butler, *Maria Edgeworth: A Literary Biography* (Oxford: Oxford University Press, 1972), 350. Much Edgeworth criticism, particularly that which addresses *The Absentee*, considers her novels in terms of Irish nationalism; none of it addresses the dressing room scenes. See, for example, Butler, *Maria Edgeworth*, 374–80; Brian Hollingworth, *Maria Edgeworth's Irish Writing: Language, History, Politics* (London: Macmillan Press; New York: St. Martin's Press, 1997), 148–81; Esther Wohlgemut, "Maria Edgeworth and the Question of National Identity," *SEL* 39, 4 (Autumn 1999): 645–58; and Julia Anne Miller, "Acts of Union: Family Violence and National Courtship in Maria Edgeworth's *The Absentee* and Sydney Owenson's *The Wild Irish Girl*," in *Border Crossings: Irish Women Writers and National Identities*, ed. Kathryn Kirkpatrick (Tuscaloosa and London: University of Alabama Press, 2000), 13–37.

19. Maria Edgeworth, *The Absentee*, ed. W. J. McCormack and Kim Walker (Oxford: Oxford University Press, 1988), 77. Subsequent references are cited parenthetically within the text.

20. Addison and Steele, *The Spectator*, no. 45, 21 April 1711.

21. Sarah Fielding, *The Adventures of David Simple*, ed. Malcolm Kelsall (Oxford: Oxford University Press, 1987), 114.

22. Ibid.

23. Thomas Browne, *A Legacy for the Ladies, or, Characters of Women of the Age* (London, 1705), 94–95.

24. Hogarth, *The Harlot's Progress*, plate 2, 19.

25. Fielding, *David Simple*, 115.

26. Kristina Straub, "Frances Burney and the Rise of the Woman Novelist," in *The Columbia History of the British Novel*, ed. John Richetti (New York: Columbia University Press, 1994), 203.

27. *The Vicar of Wakefield* has traditionally been read in terms of its use of eighteenth-century religious discourse or its mixing of satire and sentiment. See Thomas R.

Preston, "Moral Spin Doctoring, Delusion, and Chance: Wakefield's Vicar Writes An Enlightenment Parable," *Age of Johnson* 11 (2000): 237–81. Christopher Flint likewise considers domesticity in *The Vicar of Wakefield* in *Family Fictions*, 1–2, 32–33. In a discussion of the novel's generic classification, George H. Haggerty argues that "if *The Vicar of Wakefield* is ironic, it is ironic in such a way that real pathos is evoked and sustained throughout the narration." "Satire and Sentiment in *The Vicar of Wakefield*," *The Eighteenth Century: Theory and Interpretation* 32, 1 (Spring 1991): 28. See also Barbara M. Benedict, *Framing Feeling: Sentiment and Style in English Prose Fiction, 1745–1800* (New York: AMS Press, 1994), 49; and Liz Bellamy, *Commerce, Morality and the Eighteenth-Century Novel* (Cambridge: Cambridge University Press, 1998), 138–44.

28. Peter M. Briggs develops this idea through a reading of the family's portrait. Peter M. Briggs, "Oliver Goldsmith and the Muse of Disjunction," *Age of Johnson* 9 (1998): 238–42.

29. Doody, *A True Story of the Novel*, 304.

30. Oliver Goldsmith, *The Vicar of Wakefield*, vol. 4 of *Collected Works of Oliver Goldsmith*, ed. Arthur Freeman (Oxford: Clarendon Press, 1966), 34. Subsequent references are cited parenthetically within the text.

31. As David Aaron Murray notes, Primrose's attempts to exercise fatherly authority generally fail, thus exposing a marked "disparity" "between his own image of himself and his actual authority." David Aaron Murray, "From Patrimony to Paternity in *The Vicar of Wakefield*," *Eighteenth-Century Fiction* 9, 3 (April 1997): 327.

32. Moretti, *The Way of the World*, 7.

33. Frances Burney, *Evelina; or, The History of a Young Lady's Entrance Into the World*, ed. Edward A. Bloom (Oxford: Oxford University Press, 1982), 25. Subsequent references are cited parenthetically within the text.

34. Timothy Dykstal, "*Evelina* and the Culture Industry," *Criticism* 37, 4 (Fall 1995): 561. As Elizabeth Kowaleski-Wallace reminds us, the timing of Burney's writings correspond "to the full implementation of retail practice," and the *OED* identifies the gerund "shopping" with Burney's early diaries. Kowaleski-Wallace, *Consuming Subjects*, 91–92.

35. *The Diary of Sophie von La Roche* (1786); quoted in Neil McKendrick, "Commercialization and the Economy," 79.

36. Ibid., 64.

37. Catherine Gallagher, *Nobody's Story: The Vanishing Acts of Women Writers in the Marketplace, 1670–1820* (Berkeley and Los Angeles: University of California Press, 1994), 214. See also Joanne Cutting-Gray, *Woman as 'Nobody' and the Novels of Fanny Burney* (Gainesville: University of Florida Press, 1992). Martha Koehler takes up the subject of paragon construction in *Evelina*, particularly in the character of Orville. See Martha Koehler, "'Faultless Monsters' and Monstrous Egos: The Disruption of Model Selves in Frances Burney's *Evelina*," *The Eighteenth Century: Theory and Interpretation* 43, 1 (Spring 2002): 22–28.

38. McKendrick, "Commercialization and the Economy," 63.

39. Alexander Stewart, *The Art of Hair Dressing; or The Ladies Director* (London, 1788), 6–18.

40. David Oakleaf, "The Name of the Father: Social Identity and the Ambition of Evelina," *Eighteenth-Century Fiction* 3, 4 (July 1991): 343; and Julia Epstein, *The Iron Pen: Frances Burney and the Politics of Women's Writing* (Madison: University of Wisconsin Press, 1989), 43.

41. This is contrasted with Deidre Shauna Lynch's argument that the patterns of consumerism that shape Evelina's appearance "invariably render the woman conspicuous only to make the 'real' woman disappear" (Lynch, *The Economy of Character*, 166).

42. Audrey Bilger, *Laughing Feminism: Subversive Comedy in Frances Burney, Maria Edgeworth, and Jane Austen* (Detroit: Wayne State University Press, 1998), 95.

43. Julia Epstein, "Marginality in Frances Burney's Novels," in *The Cambridge Companion to the Eighteenth-Century Novel*, ed. John Richetti (Cambridge: Cambridge University Press, 1996), 199; and Epstein, *The Iron Pen*, 97.

44. Gonda, *Reading Daughters' Fictions*, 117.

45. Steven J. Gores, *Psychosocial Spaces: Verbal and Visual Readings of British Culture, 1750–1820* (Detroit: Wayne State University Press, 2000), 49–64.

46. Young Branghton expresses his preference for the final night of the London season when hooligans clamor about: "Why, Lord, it's the best night of any; there's always a riot,—and there the folks run about,—and then there's such squealing and squalling!—and there all the lamps are broke,—and the women run skimper scamper" (195). Susan Staves has demonstrated the violence of Evelina's experiences of London's public spaces. Susan Staves, "*Evelina*; or, Female Difficulties," *Modern Philology* 73 (1976): 368–81.

47. Carol Houlihan Flynn, "Where the Wild Things Are: Guides to London's Transgressive Spaces," in *Orthodoxy and Heresy in Eighteenth-Century Society: Essays from the DeBartolo Conference*, ed. Regina Hewitt and Pat Rogers (Lewisburg, Pa.: Bucknell University Press, 2002), 45; and Yeazell, *Fictions of Modesty*, 123.

48. Charlotte Lennox, *The Female Quixote*, ed. Margaret Dalziel (Oxford: Oxford University Press, 1989), 281. Subsequent references are cited parenthetically within the text.

49. Spacks, *Desire and Truth*, 13.

50. The narrator explains that "Her Ideas, from the Manner of her Life, and the Objects around her, had taken a romantic Turn; and, supposing Romances were real Pictures of Life, from them she drew all her Notions and Expectations" (7).

51. Jane Spencer, "Not Being An Historian: Women Telling Tales in Restoration and Eighteenth-Century England," in *Contexts of Pre-Novel Narrative*, ed. Roy Eriksen (Berlin and New York: Mouton de Gruyter, 1994), 334; and Wendy Motooka, *The Age of Reasons: Quixotism, Sentimentalism and Political Economy in Eighteenth-Century Britain* (London and New York: Routledge, 1998), 131, 126. For a discussion of Lennox's appropriations of Cervantes, see Eric Rothstein, "Woman, Women, and *The Female Quixote*," in *Augustan Subjects: Essays in Honor of Martin C. Battestin*, ed. Albert J. Rivero (Newark: University of Delaware Press; London: Associated University Presses, 1997), 249–75.

52. Mary Molesworth Monck, "On a Romantic Lady," in *Poems and Translations upon Several Occasions* (London, 1716), 10–12.

53. Janet Todd, *The Sign of Angellica: Women, Writing and Fiction, 1660–1800* (London: Virago, 1989), 155.

54. Moretti, *The Way of the World*, 16.

55. Motooka, *The Age of Reasons*, 138.

56. Ibid. Scott Paul Gordon argues that Arabella's madness allows Lennox to preserve the category of romance. See Scott Paul Gordon, "The Space of Romance in Lennox's *Female Quixote*," *SEL* 38, 3 (Summer 1998): 499–516.

57. See Lennox, *The Female Quixote*, 414–15, 419–28. For a detailed account of Johnson's contributions, see Spacks, *Desire and Truth*, 14–24. Kate Levin, for example, contends that Lennox designed Arabella's cure in response to her own fear of the literary marketplace (Kate Levin, "'The Cure of Arabella's Mind': Charlotte Lennox and the Disciplining of the Female Reader," *Women's Writing* 2, 3 [1995]: 271–90). In contrast, Anne Hall Bailey argues that Arabella herself is Lennox's model of reason, not the clergyman who converts her (Anne Hall Bailey, "Charlotte Lennox's *The Female*

Quixote: The Reconciliation of Enlightenment Philosophies," *Tennessee Philological Bulletin* 38 [2001]: 9–18).

58. Spacks, *Desire and Truth*, 32.
59. Gallagher, *Nobody's Story*, 178.
60. Shaffer, "Not Subordinate," 54.
61. Timothy Dykstal, "The Story of O: Politics and Pleasure in *The Vicar of Wakefield*," *ELH* 62, 2 (Summer 1995): 343.
62. Samuel Richardson, *Pamela: Or, Virtue Rewarded*, vol. 3 (London, 1801), 2–3.
63. Toni Bowers, *The Politics of Motherhood: British Writing and Culture, 1680–1760* (Cambridge: Cambridge University Press, 1996), 155.
64. Susan C. Greenfield, introduction, in *Inventing Maternity: Politics, Science, and Literature, 1650–1865*, ed. Susan C. Greenfield and Carol Barash (Lexington: University Press of Kentucky, 1999), 1.
65. Bowers, *The Politics of Motherhood*, 156–67.
66. Dever, *Death and the Mother from Dickens to Freud*, 19.
67. *The Covent-Garden Repository* "contained sexually provocative stories, and advertisements for prostitutes and brothels, with the prices (five shillings 'for a temporary favour', and half a guinea 'for a night's lodging')" (Stone, *The Family, Sex, and Marriage In England, 1500–1800*, 336). *The Covent-Garden Repository* was also contemporaneous with *Harris' List of Covent Garden Ladies*, an annual directory of prostitutes that described each woman's particular skill, experience, and prices.
68. *The Covent-Garden Repository: Or, Ranger's Packet of Whim, Frolick, And Amusement. Number III* (London, n.d. [1788?]), 110.
69. Ibid., 111.
70. Ibid.
71. Ibid., 110.
72. Kristina Straub, *Divided Fictions: Fanny Burney and Feminine Strategy* (Lexington: University Press of Kentucky, 1987), 28.
73. Jill Campbell, "Lady Mary Wortley Montagu and the 'Glass Revers'd' of Female Old Age," in *"Defects": Engendering the Modern Body*, ed. Helen Deutsch and Felicity Nussbaum (Ann Arbor: University of Michigan Press, 2000), 229.
74. *The Letters of Horace Walpole*, ed. Paget Tynbee (Oxford: Oxford University Press, 1903), 1:84–85.
75. John Zomchick, "Satire and the Bourgeois Subject in France Burney's *Evelina*," in *Cutting Edges: Postmodern Critical Essays on Eighteenth-Century Satire*, ed. James E. Gill (Knoxville: University of Tennessee Press, 1995), 358.
76. Bilger, *Laughing Feminism*, 163.
77. Jane Austen, *Pride and Prejudice*. vol. 2 of *The Novels of Jane Austen*, ed. R. W. Chapman, 3rd ed. (Oxford: Oxford University Press, 1982), 71.
78. Ibid., 378.
79. Claudia L. Johnson, *Jane Austen: Women, Politics, and the Novel* (Chicago and London: University of Chicago Press, 1988), 73.
80. Austen, *Pride and Prejudice*, 378.
81. Ibid. William Deresiewicz reads *Pride and Prejudice* as fundamentally about how "community" produces Elizabeth (William Deresiewicz, "Community and Cognition in *Pride and Prejudice*," *ELH* 64.2 [1997]: 504); if so, then the novel's conclusion foregrounds how she, in turn, produces the community that will subsequently define her after marrying Darcy. The novel's conclusion subtly displaces the Bennets with the more genteel and more admirable Gardiners, Elizabeth's aunt and uncle: "With the Gardiners, they were always on the most intimate terms. Darcy, as well as Elizabeth, really loved them," we learn in the novel's final paragraph (388). Austen's novel devotes

hundreds of pages to the machinations of Mrs. Bennet and the impediments she raises, only to erase her presence from the plot after the marriage.

82. See Bilger, *Laughing Feminism*, 161, 185–87, and 189–219; and Claude Rawson, *Satire and Sentiment, 1660–1830* (Cambridge: Cambridge University Press, 1994), 267–98. Of course, *Evelina's* infamous footrace between two old women is another dramatic example of Burney's vicious satire.

83. Anne K. Mellor, "A Novel of Their Own: Romantic Women's Fiction, 1790–1830," in *The Columbia History of the British Novel*, ed. John Richetti (New York: Columbia University Press, 1994), 333.

84. Smith, *Eighteenth-Century Decoration*, 254.

85. Ibid., 254, 222.

86. Burney, *Journals and Letters*, 240–43. Burney's most recent biographer notes that "some posts at court allowed the holders to come and go almost at will, but Burney's required her constant presence." Janice Farrar Thaddeus, *Frances Burney: A Literary Life* (London: Macmillan; New York: St. Martin's Press, 2000), 100.

87. Lady Morgan explains: "I was just setting off for Ireland, the horses literally putting to—. . . Mr. C[olburn], taking up a scrubby MS. volume, which the servant was about to thrust into the pocket of the carriage, asked 'What was that?' I said it was 'one of the many volumes of odds and ends, *de omnibus rebus*;' and I read him the last entry I had made the night before, on my return from the opera. 'This is the very thing,' said the European publisher." Lady Morgan, Sydney Owenson, *The Book of the Boudoir* (1829), v–vi. Subsequent references are cited parenthetically within the text. However, the reviewer writing for *Blackwood's Magazine* snidely observes that "the world will never know to what particular accident or circumstance it is indebted for the Iliad of Homer, or the Agamemnon of Æschylus, or the dramas of Shakespeare; but our more fortunate posterity, to the end of time, will recall with fond veneration the decision and sagacity of the 'European publisher' at the critical moment when Lady Morgan was 'just setting off for Ireland.'" (Review of *The Book of the Boudoir* in *Blackwood's Magazine* 26 [July–December 1829]: 632).

88. Francesca Lacaita argues that Edgeworth and Lady Morgan share a common novelistic legacy insofar as they are "the initiators in Ireland of that genre in fiction called 'national tale'" (Francesca Lacaita, "The Journey of the Encounter: The Politics of the National Tale in Sydney Owenson's *Wild Irish Girl* and Maria Edgeworth's *Ennui*," in *Critical Ireland: New Essays in Literature and Culture*, ed. Alan A. Gillis and Aaron Kelly [Dublin: Four Courts, 2001], 148–54). For another feature of their literary relationship, see Robert Tracy, "Maria Edgeworth and Lady Morgan: Legality versus Legitimacy," *Nineteenth-Century Literature* 40, 1 (June 1985): 1–22.

89. Maria Edgeworth, *Belinda*, ed. Kathryn Kirkpatrick (Oxford: Oxford University Press, 1994), 10. Subsequent references are cited parenthetically within the text.

90. John Brewer, *Pleasures of the Imagination: English Culture in the Eighteenth Century* (New York: Farrar, Straus and Giroux, 1997), plate 2.

91. Edgeworth, *Letters from England, 1813–1844*, 25.

92. Elizabeth Kowaleski-Wallace, *Their Fathers' Daughters: Hannah More, Maria Edgeworth, and Patriarchal Complicity* (New York and Oxford: Oxford University Press, 1991), 110.

93. Ibid.

94. Colin B. Atkinson and Jo Atkinson, "Maria Edgeworth, *Belinda*, and Women's Rights," *Eire-Ireland* 19, 4 (Winter 1984): 94–118. Kowaleski-Wallace interprets Freke's name as a personification of "aberrant *female agency*" (Kowaleski-Wallace, *Their Fathers' Daughters*, 224n18).

95. Donoghue, *Passions Between Women*, 100; and Moore, *Dangerous Intimacies*, 77.

96. Kathryn Schwarz, *Tough Love: Amazon Encounters in the English Renaissance* (Durham and London: Duke University Press, 2000), 3.

97. See Susan C. Greenfield, *Mothering Daughters: Novels and the Politics of Family Romance, Frances Burney to Jane Austen* (Detroit: Wayne State University Press, 2002), 114.

98. Ibid., 112.

99. Heather Macfadyen, "Lady Delacour's Library: Maria Edgeworth's *Belinda* and Fashionable Reading," *Nineteenth-Century Literature* 48, 4 (March 1994): 423–24. Nicholas Mason reminds us that Lady Delacour's reformation depends upon her assuming the proper domestic role for an *aristocratic* woman. Nicholas Mason, "Class, Gender, and Domesticity in Maria Edgeworth's *Belinda*," *Eighteenth-Century Novel* 1 (2001): 271–85.

100. Armstrong, *Desire and Domestic Fiction*, 76.

101. Edgeworth's original sketch called for a Doctor Sane, perhaps modeled on Dr. John Moore or Dr. Erasmus Darwin (Butler, *Maria Edgeworth*, 31–34, 248).

102. Robert Whytt, *Observations on the Nature, Causes, and Cure of those Disorders which are commonly called Nervous, Hypochondriac, or Hysteric, To which are prefixed some Remarks on the Sympathy of the Nerves*, in *The Works of Robert Whytt* (London, 1768), 502.

103. See Greenfield, *Mothering Daughters*, 116–23; Moore, *Dangerous Intimacies*, 98–101; and Andrew McCann, *Cultural Politics in the 1790s: Literature, Radicalism and the Public Sphere* (London: Macmillan Press; New York: St. Martin's Press, 1999), 181–206.

104. Felicity A. Nussbaum, *Torrid Zones: Maternity, Sexuality, and Empire in Eighteenth-Century English Narratives* (Baltimore and London: Johns Hopkins University Press, 1995), 73.

105. Marjorie Lightfoot, "'Morals for Those That Like Them': The Satire of Edgeworth's *Belinda*, 1801," *Eire-Ireland* 29, 4 (Winter 1994): 118–19.

106. Doody, *True Story*, 15–16; and Hunter, *Before Novels*, 25–26. For additional discussion on this topic, see McKeon, *The Origins of the English Novel, 1600–1740*, 273–314 and Christine Roulston, "Histories of Nothing: Romance and Femininity in Charlotte Lennox's *The Female Quixote*," *Women's Writing* 2, 1 (1995): 25–42.

107. Sir Walter Scott, review of *"Emma*: A Novel," *Quarterly Review* 14 (1815–16): 188–201.

108. Marilyn Butler, *Jane Austen and the War of Ideas* (Oxford: Oxford University Press, 1975), 131.

109. Jane Spencer, "Women Writers and the Eighteenth-Century Novel," in *The Cambridge Companion to the Eighteenth-Century Novel*, ed. John Richetti (Cambridge: Cambridge University Press, 1996), 213–14. Ros Ballaster notes that the term "romance" was regularly used, though inaccurately, to describe what she calls the "amatory fiction" of Behn, Manley, and Haywood. Ros Ballaster, *Seductive Forms: Women's Amatory Fiction from 1684 to 1740* (Oxford: Oxford University Press, 1992), 42–49.

110. McKeon, *The Origins of the English Novel*, 145, 148. See also 39–64.

111. For an important discussion that resists interpreting Edgeworth's fictions as realist, instead calling them "romances of real life," see Michael Gamer, "Maria Edgeworth and the Romance of Real Life," *Novel* 34, 2 (Spring 2001): 232–66.

112. Mitzi Myers, "My Art Belongs to Daddy? Thomas Day, Maria Edgeworth, and the Pre-Texts of *Belinda*: Women Writers and Patriarchal Authority," in *Revising Women: Eighteenth-Century "Women's Fiction" and Social Engagement*, ed. Paula R. Backscheider (Baltimore and London: Johns Hopkins University Press, 2000), 130.

113. Greenfield, *Mothering Daughters*, 119–20.

CODA

"Duelling Designers: All Dolled Up," *House Beautiful* (March 2002): 50.

1. Third Earl of Shaftesbury [Anthony Ashley Cooper], *Second Characters, or The Language of Forms*, ed. Benjamin Rand (Bristol: Thoemmes Press, 1995), 61.

2. "Duelling Designers," 50.

3. Hilary Robertson, *Boudoir: Creating the Bedroom of Your Dreams* (London: Carlton Books, 2000), 5.

4. Nancy V. Workman, "From Victorian to Victoria's Secret: The Foundations of Modern Erotic Wear," *Journal of Popular Culture* 30 (Fall 1996): 61–73.

5. www.victoriassecret.com. Accessed 29 February 2004.

Bibliography

PRIMARY SOURCES

Addison, Joseph, and Richard Steele. *The Spectator*. Edited by Donald F. Bond. 3 vols. Oxford: Oxford University Press, 1965.

Adultery. The Trial of Mr. William Atkinson, Linen-Draper of Cheapside, For Criminal Conversation with Mrs. Conner, Wife of Mr. Conner, late of the Mitre, at Barney. London, 1789.

Alberti, Leon Battista. *The Family in Renaissance Florence*. Translated by Renée New Watkins. Prospect Heights, Ill.: Waveland Press, 1994.

———. *On the Art of Building in Ten Books*. Translated by Joseph Rykwert, Neil Leach, and Robert Tavernor. Cambridge and London: MIT Press, 1994.

Allestree, Richard. *The Ladies Calling*. 4th ed. London, 1676.

Ames, Richard. *The Folly of Love; or, An Essay Upon Satyr Against Woman*. London, 1691.

[Amhurst, Nicholas, and James Welton]. *The Art of Beauty: A Poem. Humbly address'd to the Oxford Toasts*. London, 1719.

The Art of Beauty, or, A Companion for the Toilet. London, 1760.

Astell, Mary. *The First English Feminist: Reflections Upon Marriage and Other Writings by Mary Astell*. Edited by Bridget Hill. New York: St. Martin's Press, 1986.

Austen, Jane. *The Novels of Jane Austen*. Edited by R. W. Chapman. 5 vols. 3rd ed. Oxford: Oxford University Press, 1982.

Barbauld, Anna Laetita. *The British Novelists; with an Essay; and Prefaces, Biographical and Critical*. 50 vols. London, 1810.

Beauties Treasury: or, the Ladies 'Vade Mecum.' London, 1705.

Behn, Aphra. *The Works of Aphra Behn*. Edited by Janet Todd. 7 vols. London: William Pickering, 1996.

Blackwood's Magazine, 26 (July–December 1829).

Boswell, James. *The Life of Johnson*. Edited by R. W. Chapman. Oxford: Oxford University Press, 1980.

[Breval, John]. *The Art of Dress: An Heroi-Comical Poem*. 2nd ed. London, 1717.

Browne, Thomas. *A Legacy for the Ladies, or, Characters of Women of the Age*. London, 1705.

Bruys, François. *The Art of Knowing Women; Or, The Female Sex Dissected*. London, 1730.

Burgh, James. *Thoughts on Education*. London, 1747.

Burke, Edmund. *A Philosophical Enquiry into the Origin of our Ideas of the Sublime and Beautiful*. Edited by James T. Boulton. Notre Dame: University of Notre Dame Press, 1986.

Burney, Frances. *Evelina; or, The History of a Young Lady's Entrance Into the World*. Edited by Edward A. Bloom. Oxford: Oxford University Press, 1982.

————. *Journals and Letters*. Edited by Peter Sabor and Lars E. Troide. London: Penguin Books, 2001.

Campbell, Colin. *Vitruvius Britannicus; or, The British Architect.* 1715–25. 3 vols. Facsimile reprint, New York: Benjamin Blom, 1967.

Care, Henry. *The Female Secretary: or, Choice New Letters.* London, 1671.

A Catalogue of all the Entire Live and Dead Stock. Implements in husbandry, Dairy and Brewing Utensils, and Household Furniture, of Mr. Tho'. Laugher, the Younger, at Aldington, in the Parish of Badsey, and County of Worcester. 1782.

A Catalogue of All the Genuine Household Furniture of John Trevor, Esq.; At his House, in Castle-Street, Canterbury. Canterbury, 1766.

A Catalogue of All the Household Goods, &c. &c. of Miss Lampreys In St. Alphage, Canterbury. 1764.

Catalogue of all the Houshold Furniture And Other valuable Effects of Edgeley Hewer, Esq.; (Deceas'd) Brought from his Seat at Clapham, to his House in Buckingham-street, York-Buildings. 1729.

A Catalogue of the Genuine Houshold Goods, Pictures, fine old China, Fire-Arms, &c. of his Excellency Don Thomas Geraldino. 1740.

A Catalogue of the Household Furniture, And Effects of the Hon. Col. John Mercer, Late of Demark-Street, Soho; And Nicholas Hawskmoor, Esq; Both Deceased. 1740.

A Catalogue of the Household Furniture Of Mrs. Masters, Deceas'd. 1760.

A Catalogue of the Rich Household Furniture, &c. of Edward Lisle, Esq. 1739.

A Catalogue of the Rich Household Furniture and valuable Cabinet of Curiosities of the Right Honourable the Countess Dowager of Gainsborough, Deceased. 1739–40.

A Catalogue of the Superb and Elegant Household Furniture . . . Late Property of Monsieur de Calonne. 1793.

Chloe Surprized; Or, The Second Part of the Lady's Dressing-Room. London, 1732.

Cibber, Colley. *An Apology for the Life of Colley Cibber.* London: Dent, 1976.

————. *A Letter From Mr. Cibber to Mr. Pope, Inquiring into the Motives that might induce him in his Satyrical Works, to be so frequently fond of Mr. Cibber's name.* 1742. Facsimile reprint, Los Angeles: William Andrews Clark Memorial Library, University of California, 1978.

Clarissa: Preface, Hints of Prefaces, and Postscript. Introduction by R. F. Brissenden. Augustan Reprint Society, Los Angeles: University of California Press, William Andrews Clark Memorial Library, 1964.

Clarissa Harlow; or the History of a Young Lady, consisting of Four Ballads in different periods of her Life, namely Her Morn of Happiness, Her Noon of Uneasiness, Her Eve of Brighter Prospects, Her Night of Death. London, n.d.

Collier, Jeremy. *A Short View of the Immorality, and Profaneness of the English Stage.* 1698. Edited by Arthur Freeman. Reprint, New York and London: Garland Publishing, 1972.

Congreve, William. *The Complete Works of William Congreve.* Edited by Montague Summers. 3 vols. New York: Russell & Russell, 1964.

[Cooper, Anthony Ashley.] Third Earl of Shaftesbury. *Second Characters, or The Language of True Forms.* Edited by Benjamin Rand. Bristol: Thoemmes Press, 1995.

Corbyn, Morris. *An Essay Towards Fixing the True Standards of Wit, Humour, Raillery, Satire, and Ridicule.* London, 1744.

A Court Lady's Curiosity; or, the Virgin Undress'd. Curiously surveying herself in her Glass, with one Leg upon her Toilet. London, 1741.

The Covent-Garden Repository: Or, Ranger's Packet of Whim, Frolick, And Amusement. Number III. London, n.d.

Dallaway, James. *Observations on English Architecture.* London, 1806.

Defoe, Daniel. *The London Ladies Dressing-Room: Or, the Shop-keepers Wives Inventory.* London, 1705.

Delany, Patrick. *Observations Upon Lord Orrery's Remarks On The Life And Writings of Dr. Jonathan Swift.* Dublin, 1754.

Dennis, John. *A True Character of Mr. Pope and His Writings.* 1716. Facsimile reprint, New York: Garland Publishing, 1975.

Dryden, John. *The Works of John Dryden.* Edited by Edward Niles Hootker, H. T. Swedenberg et al. 20 vols. Berkeley and Los Angeles: University of California Press, 1955–.

"Duelling Designers: All Dolled Up." *House Beautiful* (March 2002): 50.

D'Urfey, Thomas. *New Poems, Consisting of Satyrs, Elegies, and Odes.* London, 1690.

Edgeworth, Maria. *The Absentee.* Edited by W. J. McCormack and Kim Walker. Oxford: Oxford University Press, 1988.

———. *Belinda.* Edited by Kathryn Kirkpatrick. Oxford: Oxford University Press, 1994.

———. *Letters from England, 1813–1844.* Edited by Christina Colvin. Oxford: Clarendon Press, 1971.

Elmes, James. *Memoirs of the Life and Works of Sir Christopher Wren.* London: Priestly and Weale, 1823.

Evelyn, John. *The Diary of John Evelyn.* Edited by Guy de la Bédoyère. Dorchester, England: Dorchester Press, 1994.

Evelyn, Mary. *Mundus Muliebris; or, The Ladies Dressing-Room Unlock'd And her Toilette Spread.* London, 1690.

The Female Ægis; or, The Duties of Women from Childhood to Old Age, and in most Situations of Life Exemplified. London, 1798.

Female Taste: A Satire. London, 1745.

Ferguson, James, F.R.S. *Lectures on Select Subjects in Mechanics, Pneumatics, Hydrostatics, and Optics.* London, 1764.

Fielding, Henry. *Shamela.* Edited by Martin C. Battestin. Boston: Houghton Mifflin, 1961.

Fielding, Sarah. *The Adventures of David Simple.* Edited by Malcolm Kelsall. Oxford: Oxford University Press, 1987.

Fiennes, Celia. *Through England on a Side Saddle In the Time of William and Mary.* London: Field & Tuer, Leadenhall Press, 1888.

Filmer, Robert. *Patriarcha; or, The Natural Power of Kings.* London, 1680.

[Gauden, John]. *A Discourse of Artificial Beauty, In Point of Conscience Between Two Ladies.* London, 1692.

Gay, John. *The Poetical, Dramatic, and Miscellaneous Works of John Gay.* 1795. 6 vols. Facsimile reprint, New York: AMS Press, 1970.

The Gentleman's Study in Answer to the Lady's Dressing-Room. London and Dublin, 1732.

[Gildon, Charles]. *A Comparison between the Two Stages.* 1702. Facsimile reprint, New York: Garland Press, 1973.

Gillow Furniture Designs, 1760–1800. Edited by Lindsay Boynton. United Kingdom: Bloomfield Press, 1995.

Goldsmith, Oliver. *Collected Works of Oliver Goldsmith*. Edited by Arthur Freeman. 5 vols. Oxford: Clarendon Press, 1966.

Gould, Robert. *Love given o're; or, a Satyr against the Pride, Lust, and Inconstancy, &c. of Woman*. London, 1682.

Guerinot, J. V., ed. *Pamphlet Attacks on Alexander Pope, 1711–1744: A Descriptive Bibliography*. London: Methuen, 1969.

Hogarth, William. *Engravings by Hogarth*. Edited by Sean Shesgreen. New York: Dover Publications, 1973.

Hoole, Charles. *Joh. Amos Commenii Orbis Sensualium Pictus*. London, 1672.

Ince, William, and John Mayhew. *The Universal System of Household Furniture*. London, 1762.

The Inventory and Particular of All and Singular the Lands, Tenements, and Hereditaments, Goods, Chattels, Debts, and Personal Estate whatsoever of Stephen Child, Esq. 1721.

An Inventory of the Household Goods and other Effects of Edward Dennis, lately seiz'd by Virtue of a Warrant under the Hands and Seals of the Commissions of the Land-Tax, for the Year 1726.

Jeffrey, Francis. *Contributions to the Edinburgh Review*. New York: Appleton, 1879.

The Ladies Cabinet, or a Companion for the Toilet. London, 1743.

Lennox, Charlotte. *The Female Quixote*. Edited by Margaret Dalziel. Oxford: Oxford University Press, 1989.

Mabbe, James. "To the Memory of Master William Shakespeare." In *The Complete Works of William Shakespeare*, ed. Stanley Wells and Gary Taylor. Oxford: Clarendon Press, 1989.

Marlborough, Sarah, Duchess of. *Memoirs of Sarah, Duchess of Marlborough*. Edited by William King. London: George Routledge & Sons, 1930.

Marvell, Andrew. *The Complete Poems*. Edited by George deF. Lord. New York: Knopf, 1993.

Memoirs Of the Extraordinary Life, Works, and Discoveries of Martinus Scriblerus. Edited by Charles Kerby-Miller. Oxford: Oxford University Press, 1988.

Monck, Mary Molesworth. *Poems and Translations upon Several Occasions*. London, 1716.

Morgan, Lady, Sydney Owenson. *The Book of the Boudoir*. 1829.

North, Roger. *Of Building: Roger North's Writings on Architecture*. Edited by Howard Colvin and John Newman. Oxford: Clarendon Press, 1981.

Oldham, John. *The Poems of John Oldham*. Edited by Harold F. Brooks and Raman Selden. Oxford: Clarendon Press, 1987.

On the author of a dialogue concerning women, pretended to be writ in Defence of the Sex (ca. 1690). Manuscript X.d. 194. Folger Shakespeare Library.

The Original of Apparel: Or, the Ornaments of Dress. London, 1732.

Orrery, John, Earl of. *Remarks on the Life and Writings of Dr. Jonathan Swift, Dean of St. Patrick's, Dublin*. 1752. Facsimile reprint, New York and London: Garland Publishing, 1974.

Pamela Censured. London, 1741.

The Particular and Inventory of Richard Houlditch, Esq. 1721.

The Particular and Inventory of Sir Harcourt Master, Knt. 1721.

The Particular and Inventory of Sir John Blunt, Bart. 1721.

The Particular and Inventory of the Estate of Sir John Lambert, Bart. 1721.

The Particular Inventory of Richard Wooley. 1732.

Pepys, Samuel. *The Diary of Samuel Pepys: A New and Complete Transcription.* Edited by Robert Latham and William Matthews. 11 vols. Berkeley: University of California Press, 1970–83.

Pilkington, Laetitia. *Memoirs of Mrs. Laetitia Pilkington, Written by Herself.* 1754. In *Memoirs With Anecdotes of Dean Swift, 1748–1754.* Vol. 19. Facsimile reprint, New York and London: Garland Publishing, Inc., 1975.

A Pleasant Battle Between Two Lap Dogs of the Utopian Court. London, 1681.

Polygraphice; or, The Arts of Drawing, Engraving, Etching, Limning, Painting, Washing, Varnishing, Gilding, Colouring, Dying, Beautifying and Perfuming. London, 1673.

Pope, Alexander. *The Correspondence of Alexander Pope.* Edited by George Sherburn. 5 vols. Oxford: Oxford University Press, 1956.

————. *Poetical Works.* 1776.

————. *Selected Prose of Alexander Pope.* Edited by Paul Hammond. Cambridge: Cambridge University Press, 1987.

————. *The Twickenham Edition of the Poems of Alexander Pope.* General Editor John Butt. 11 vols. New Haven: Yale University Press, 1938–68.

————. *The Works of Alexander Pope Esq.* Edited by William Warburton. 9 vols. London, 1751.

Ramsay, Allan. *The Poems of Allan Ramsay.* 2 vols. London, 1800.

Richardson, Samuel. *Clarissa; or, the History of a Young Lady.* London, 1748.

————. *Clarissa, or the History of a Young Lady.* 3rd ed. 8 vols. London, 1751.

————. *Clarissa; or, the History of a Young Lady.* Edited by Angus Ross. New York: Penguin, 1985.

————. *The Correspondence of Samuel Richardson.* Edited by Anna Laetitia Barbauld. 6 vols. London, 1804.

————. *The History of Sir Charles Grandison.* 3 vols. Oxford: Oxford University Press, 1972.

————. *Pamela: Or, Virtue Rewarded.* 4 vols. London, 1801.

————. *Pamela; or, Virtue Rewarded.* Edited by T. C. Duncan Eaves and Ben D. Kimpel. Boston: Houghton Mifflin, 1971.

————. *Selected Letters of Samuel Richardson.* Edited by John Carroll. Oxford: Oxford University Press, 1964.

Robertson, Hilary. *Boudoir: Creating the Bedroom of Your Dreams.* London: Carlton Books, 2000.

Rousseau, Jean-Jacques. *La Nouvelle Héloïse (Julie, or the New Eloise).* Translated by Judith H. McDowell. University Park: Pennsylvania State University Press, 1968.

The St. James's Beauties: or, the Real Toast. London, 1744.

Sawney and Colley (1742). Edited by W. Powell Jones. Facsimile reprint, Los Angeles: William Andrews Clark Memorial Library, University of California, 1960.

Scott, Sir Walter. Review of *"Emma: A Novel." Quarterly Review* 14 (1815–16): 188–201.

Shakespeare, William. *The Riverside Shakespeare.* Edited by G. Blakemore Evans et al. Boston: Houghton Mifflin, 1974.

Sheraton, Thomas. *The Cabinet-Maker and Upholsterer's Drawing-Book*. 1802. Edited by Charles F. Montgomery and Wilfred P. Cole. New York: Praeger Publishers, 1970.

Soane, John. *Sketches in Architecture. Containing Plans and Elevations of Cottages, Villages, and Other Useful Buildings*. London, 1793.

Sprat, Thomas. *The History of the Royal Society of London, For the Improving of Natural Knowledge*. 3rd ed. London, 1722.

Stapylton, Sir Robert, trans. *Juvenal's Sixteen Satyrs, or, a Survey of the Manners and Actions of Mankind*. London, 1673.

Stewart, Alexander. *The Art of Hair Dressing; or The Ladies Director*. London, 1788.

Swift, Jonathan. *An Apology For the, etc*. London, 1704.

———. *Journal to Stella*. Edited by Harold Williams. 2 vols. Oxford: Oxford University Press, 1948.

———. *The Poems of Jonathan Swift*. Edited by Harold Williams. 3 vols. 2nd ed. Oxford: Oxford University Press, 1958.

———. *The Prose Works of Jonathan Swift*. Edited by Herbert Davis et al. 14 vols. Oxford: Oxford University Press, 1939–68.

———. *The Works of Jonathan Swift, D. D., Dean of St. Patrick's Dublin*. Edited by Sir Walter Scott. 12 vols. London, 1814.

Thomas, Elizabeth. *The Metamorphoses of the Town: or, A View of the Present Fashions*. 4th ed. London, 1738.

Thurston, Joseph. *The Toilette; In Three Books*. London, 1730.

Trial for adultery, in Westminster Hall, on Wednesday, December 9, 1789, before Lord Kenyon, John Parslow, Esq. plaintiff, and Francis William Sykes, Esq. defendant, for Criminal Conversation with the Plaintiff's Wife. Dublin, 1790.

The Trial of His R. H. the D. of C. July 5th, 1770 for Criminal conversation with Lady Harriet G———r. London, 1770.

The Trial, with the whole of the evidence, between the Right Hon. Sir Richard Worsley and George Maurice Bissett, Esq. defendant, for Criminal Conversation with the Plaintiff's Wife. London, 1782.

Vanbrugh, Sir John. *The Complete Works of Sir John Vanbrugh*. Edited by Geoffrey Webb. 4 vols. Bloomsbury, England: Nonesuch Press, 1927.

Waller, Edmund. *Poems, &c. Written by Mr. Edited by Waller*. London, 1645.

Walpole, Horace. *The Letters of Horace Walpole*. Edited by Paget Toynbee. 16 vols. Oxford: Oxford University Press, 1903–5.

Ward, Ned. *Apollo's Maggots in his Cups, or the Whimsical Creation of a Little Satyrical Poet*. 1729. In *Pamphlet Attacks on Alexander Pope, 1711–1744: A Descriptive Bibliography*, ed. J. V. Guerinot. London: Methuen, 1969.

———. *The London Terræfilius; Or, The Satyrical Reformer*. Nos. 1–6. London, 1707–8.

Wecker, Johann Jacob. *Cosmeticks; or, The Beautifying Part of Physick*. London, 1660.

Whytt, Robert. *Observations on the Nature, Causes, and Cure of those Disorders which are commonly called Nervous, Hypochondriac, or Hysteric, To which are prefixed some Remarks on the Sympathy of the Nerves*. In *The Works of Robert Whytt*. London, 1768.

Wilmot, John, Earl of Rochester. *The Complete Poems of John Wilmot, Earl of Rochester*. Edited by David M. Vieth. New Haven and London: Yale University Press, 1968.

[Wilmot, John, Earl of Rochester or Robert Gould?]. "A General Satyr on Woman." In *Female Excellence; or, Woman Displayed, In Several Satyrick Poems*. London, 1679.

Woman in Miniature: A Satire. London, 1742.

A Wonder of Wonders; or, A Metamorphosis of Fair Faces voluntarily transformed into foul Visages. London, 1662.

Wortley Montagu, Lady Mary. *The Complete Letters of Lady Mary Wortley Montagu*. Edited by Robert Halsband. 3 vols. Oxford: Oxford University Press, 1960.

———. *Essays and Poems and* Simplicity. A Comedy. Edited by Robert Halsband and Isobel Grundy. Oxford: Oxford University Press, 1977.

Wotton, Sir Henry. *The Elements of Architecture*. London, 1624.

Wren, Christopher. *Life and Works of Sir Christopher Wren, From the* Parentalia *or Memoirs by His Son Christopher*. Edited by Ernest J. Enthoven. London: Arnold, 1903.

Wren Society. 20 vols. Oxford: Oxford University Press, 1924–43.

[Wright, James]. *Historia Histrionica: An Historical Account of the English-Stage*. 1699. Facsimile reprint, New York and London: Garland Publishing, 1974.

Wycherley, William. *The Complete Works of William Wycherley*. Edited by Montague Summers. 4 vols. New York: Russell & Russell, 1964.

Young, Edward. *The Complete Works*. Edited by James Nichols. 2 vols. London, 1854.

The Young Ladies Companion, or, Beauty's Looking-Glass. London, 1740.

SECONDARY SOURCES

Aden, John M. "Those Gaudy Tulips: Swift's 'Unprintables.'" In *Quick Springs of Sense: Studies in the Eighteenth Century*, ed. Larry S. Champion, 15–32. Athens: University of Georgia Press, 1974.

Altman, Janet Gurkin. *Epistolarity: Approaches to a Form*. Columbus: Ohio State University Press, 1982.

Armstrong, Nancy. *Desire and Domestic Fiction: A Political History of the Novel*. New York and Oxford: Oxford University Press, 1987.

Atkinson, Colin B., and Jo Atkinson. "Maria Edgeworth, *Belinda*, and Women's Rights." *Eire-Ireland* 19, 4 (Winter 1984): 94–118.

Ayers, James. *Domestic Interiors: The British Tradition, 1500–1850*. New Haven and London: Yale University Press, 2003.

Bailey, Anne Hall. "Charlotte Lennox's *The Female Quixote*: The Reconciliation of Enlightenment Philosophies." *Tennessee Philological Bulletin* 38 (2001): 9–18.

Bakhtin, Mikhail. *Problems of Dostoevsky's Poetics*. Edited and translated by Caryl Emerson. Minneapolis and London: University of Minnesota Press, 1984.

Ballaster, Ros. *Seductive Forms: Women's Amatory Fiction from 1684 to 1740*. Oxford: Oxford University Press, 1992.

Bannet, Eve Tavor. *The Domestic Revolution: Enlightenment Feminisms and the Novel*. Baltimore and London: Johns Hopkins University Press, 2000.

———. "Rewriting the Social Text: The Female Bildungsroman in Eighteenth-Century England." In *Reflection and Action: Essays on the Bildungsroman*, ed. James Hardin, 195–227. Columbia: University of South Carolina Press, 1991.

Barker, Francis. *The Tremulous Private Body: Essays on Subjection*. 2nd ed. Ann Arbor: University of Michigan Press, 1998.

Barker-Benfield, G. J. *The Culture of Sensibility: Sex and Society in Eighteenth-Century Britain*. Chicago: University of Chicago Press, 1992.

Barney, Richard A. *Plots of Enlightenment: Education and the Novel in Eighteenth-Century England.* Stanford, Calif.: Stanford University Press, 1999.

Bean, Brenda. "Sight and Self-Disclosure: Richardson's Revision of Swift's 'The Lady's Dressing Room.'" *Eighteenth-Century Life* 14, 1 (February 1990): 1–23.

Beasley, Jerry C. "Richardson's Girls: The Daughters of Patriarchy in *Pamela, Clarissa,* and *Sir Charles Grandison.*" In *New Essays on Samuel Richardson,* ed. Albert J. Rivero, 35–52. New York: St. Martin's Press, 1996.

Bellamy, Liz. *Commerce, Morality and the Eighteenth-Century Novel.* Cambridge: Cambridge University Press, 1998.

Benedict, Barbara M. *Framing Feeling: Sentiment and Style in English Prose Fiction, 1745–1800.* New York: AMS Press, 1994.

Berg, Maxine. "New commodities, luxuries and their consumers in eighteenth-century England." In *Consumers and Luxury: Consumer Culture in Europe, 1650–1850,* ed. Maxine Berg and Helen Clifford, 63–85. Manchester and New York: Manchester University Press, 1999.

Berg, Maxine, and Helen Clifford. *Consumers and Luxury: Consumer Culture in Europe, 1650–1850.* Manchester and New York: Manchester University Press, 1999.

Bevis, Richard W. *English Drama: Restoration and Eighteenth Century, 1660–1789.* London and New York: Longman, 1988.

Bilger, Audrey. *Laughing Feminism: Subversive Comedy in Frances Burney, Maria Edgeworth, and Jane Austen.* Detroit: Wayne State University Press, 1998.

Bogel, Fredric V. *The Difference Satire Makes: Rhetoric and Reading from Jonson to Byron.* Ithaca: Cornell University Press, 2001.

Borch-Jacobsen, Mikkel. *The Freudian Subject.* Translated by Catherine Porter. Stanford, Calif.: Stanford University Press, 1988.

Bowers, Toni. *The Politics of Motherhood: British Writing and Culture, 1680–1760.* Cambridge: Cambridge University Press, 1996.

Boyle, Frank. *Swift as Nemesis: Modernity and Its Satirist.* Stanford, Calif.: Stanford University Press, 2000.

Braund, Susanna Morton. "Safe Sex? Dryden's Translation of Juvenal's Sixth Satire." In *John Dryden (1631–1700): His Politics, His Plays, and His Poets,* ed. Claude Rawson and Aaron Santesso, 139–57. Newark: University of Delaware Press, 2004.

Brewer, John. *Pleasures of the Imagination: English Culture in the Eighteenth Century.* New York: Farrar, Straus and Giroux, 1997.

Brewer, John, and Roy Porter, ed. *Consumption and the World of Goods.* London and New York: Routledge, 1993.

Briggs, Peter M. "Oliver Goldsmith and the Muse of Disjunction." *Age of Johnson* 9 (1998): 237–56.

Brooks, Cleanth. *The Well-Wrought Urn: Studies in the Structure of Poetry.* New York: Harcourt, Brace & World, 1947.

Brooks, Peter. *Body Work: Objects of Desire in Modern Narrative.* Cambridge and London: Harvard University Press, 1993.

Brophy, Elizabeth Bergen. *Women's Lives and the 18th-Century English Novel.* Tampa: University of South Florida Press, 1991.

Brown, Homer Obed. *Institutions of the English Novel: From Defoe to Scott.* Philadelphia: University of Pennsylvania Press, 1997.

Brown, Laura. *Ends of Empire: Women and Ideology in Early Eighteenth-Century English Literature.* Ithaca: Cornell University Press, 1993.

Bryant, Julius. *Marble Hill House, Twickenham.* London: English Heritage, 1988.

Burlingame, Anne Elizabeth. The Battle of the Books *in its Historical Setting.* New York: Biblo and Tannen, 1969.

Burroughs, Catherine B. *Closet Stages: Joanna Baillie and the Theater Theory of British Romantic Women Writers.* Philadelphia: University of Pennsylvania Press, 1997.

Butler, Judith. *Excitable Speech: A Politics of the Performative.* New York and London: Routledge, 1997.

———. "Imitation and Gender Insubordination." In *The Lesbian and Gay Studies Reader,* ed. Henry Abelove, Michèle Aina Barale, David M. Halperin, 307–20. New York: Routledge, 1993.

Butler, Marilyn. *Jane Austen and the War of Ideas.* Oxford: Oxford University Press, 1975.

———. *Maria Edgeworth: A Literary Biography.* Oxford: Oxford University Press, 1972.

Campbell, Colin. *The Romantic Ethic and the Spirit of Modern Consumerism.* Oxford: Basil Blackwell, 1987.

Campbell, Jill. "Lady Mary Wortley Montagu and the 'Glass Revers'd' of Female Old Age." In *"Defects": Engendering the Modern Body,* ed. Helen Deutsch and Felicity Nussbaum, 213–51. Ann Arbor: University of Michigan Press, 2000.

Carroll, John. "Richardson on Pope and Swift." *University of Toronto Quarterly* 33, 1 (October 1963): 19–29.

Castan, Yves. "Politics and Private Life." In *Passions of the Renaissance,* ed. Roger Chartier. Vol. 3 of *A History of Private Life,* ed. Philippe Ariès and Georges Duby, 21–67. Cambridge: Harvard University Press, 1989.

Castle, Terry. *Clarissa's Ciphers: Meaning and Disruption in Richardson's* Clarissa. Ithaca and London: Cornell University Press, 1982.

Chambers, E. K. *The Elizabethan Stage.* 3 vols. Oxford: Clarendon Press, 1923.

Chartier, Roger, ed. *Passions of the Renaissance.* Vol. 3 of *A History of Private Life,* gen. ed. Philippe Ariès and Georges Duby. Cambridge: Harvard University Press, 1989.

Christie, William. "'To Advantage Drest': Poetics and Cosmetics in *The Rape of the Lock.*" In *Imperfect Apprehensions: Essays in English Literature in Honour of G. A. Wilkes,* ed. Geoffrey Little, 133–47. Sydney: Challis, 1996.

Claridge, Laura. "Pope's Rape of Excess." In *Perspectives on Pornography: Sexuality in Film and Literature,* ed. Gary Day and Clive Bloom, 129–43. New York: St. Martin's Press, 1988.

Clark, Steve. "'Let Blood and Body bear the fault': Pope and misogyny." In *Pope: New Contexts,* ed. David Fairer, 81–101. London: Harvester Wheatsheaf, 1990.

Conway, Alison. *Private Interests: Women, Portraiture, and the Visual Culture of the English Novel, 1709–1791.* Toronto, Buffalo, and London: University of Toronto Press, 2001.

Copeland, Edward. "Remapping London: *Clarissa* and the Woman in the Window." In *Samuel Richardson: Tercentenary Essays,* ed. Margaret Anne Doody and Peter Sabor, 51–69. Cambridge: Cambridge University Press, 1989.

Coulton, Barbara. *A Shropshire Squire: Noel Hill, first Lord Berwick, 1745–1789.* Shrewsbury, England: Swan Hill Press, 1989.

Crary, Jonathan. *Techniques of the Observer: On Vision and Modernity in the Nineteenth Century.* Cambridge and London: MIT Press, 1996.

Cruise, James. *Governing Consumption: Needs and Wants, Suspended Characters, and the "Origins" of Eighteenth-Century English Novels.* Lewisburg, Pa.: Bucknell University Press, 1999.

Cryle, Peter. *Geometry in the Boudoir: Configurations of French Erotic Narrative.* Ithaca and London: Cornell University Press, 1994.

Cutting-Gray, Joanne. *Woman as 'Nobody' and the Novels of Fanny Burney.* Gainesville: University of Florida Press, 1992.

D'Agostino, Mary Ellin. "Privy Business: Chamber Pots and Sexpots in Colonial Life." *Archaeology* 53, 4 (July/August 2000): 32–37.

Daston, Lorraine. "Baconian Facts, Academic Civility, and the Prehistory of Objectivity." *Annals of Scholarship* 8, 3/4 (1991): 337–63.

———. "Objectivity and the Escape from Perspective." *Social Studies of Science* 22 (1992): 597–618.

Davis, Lennard J. *Factual Fictions: The Origins of the English Novel.* New York: Columbia University Press, 1983.

Dear, Peter. "From Truth to Disinterestedness in the Seventeenth Century." *Social Studies of Science* 22 (1992): 619–31.

Delon, Michel. *L'invention du boudoir.* Paris: Zulma, 1999.

Deresiewicz, William. "Community and Cognition in *Pride and Prejudice.*" *ELH* 64.2 (1997): 503–35.

DeRitter, Jones. *The Embodiment of Characters: The Representation of Physical Experience on Stage and in Print, 1728–1749.* Philadelphia: University of Pennsylvania Press, 1994.

Derrida, Jacques. *Of Grammatology.* Translated by Gayatri Chakravorty Spivak. Baltimore and London: Johns Hopkins University Press, 1976.

Deutsch, Helen. *Resemblance and Disgrace: Alexander Pope and the Deformation of Culture.* Cambridge and London: Harvard University Press, 1996.

Dever, Carolyn. *Death and the Mother from Dickens to Freud: Victorian Fiction and the Anxiety of Origins.* Cambridge: Cambridge University Press, 1998.

———. *Skeptical Feminism: Activist Theory, Activist Practice.* Minneapolis: University of Minnesota Press, 2004.

Dickson, P. G. M. *The Financial Revolution in England: A Study in the Development of Public Credit, 1688–1756.* London: Macmillan; New York: St. Martin's Press, 1967.

Dolan, Frances E. "Taking the Pencil out of God's Hand: Art, Nature, and the Face-Painting Debate in Early Modern England." *PMLA* 108, 2 (March 1993): 224–39.

Donoghue, Denis. *Jonathan Swift: A Critical Introduction.* Cambridge: Cambridge University Press, 1971.

Donoghue, Emma. *Passions Between Women: British Lesbian Culture, 1668–1801.* New York: HarperCollins, 1993.

Doody, Margaret Anne. *Frances Burney: The Life in the Works.* New Brunswick: Rutgers University Press, 1988.

———. *A Natural Passion: A Study of the Novels of Samuel Richardson.* Oxford: Oxford University Press, 1974.

———. "Swift among the Women." In *Critical Essays on Jonathan Swift,* ed. Frank Palmeri, 13–27. New York: G. K. Hall, 1993.

———. *The True Story of the Novel.* New Brunswick: Rutgers University Press, 1997.

DuPlessis, Rachel Blau. *Writing Beyond the Ending.* Bloomington: Indiana University Press, 1984.

Dutton, Ralph. *The English Interior*. London: B. T. Batsford Limited, 1949.

Dykstal, Timothy. *"Evelina* and the Culture Industry." *Criticism* 37, 4 (Fall 1995): 559–81.

———. "The Story of O: Politics and Pleasure in *The Vicar of Wakefield*." *ELH* 62, 2 (Summer 1995): 329–46.

Eagleton, Terry. *The Function of Criticism from* The Spectator *to Post-Structuralism*. London: Verso, 1987.

Ehrenpreis, Irvin. *The Personality of Jonathan Swift*. Cambridge: Harvard University Press, 1958.

Elias, Norbert. *The Court Society*. Translated by Edmund Jephcott. New York: Pantheon Books, 1983.

Epstein, Julia. *The Iron Pen: Frances Burney and the Politics of Women's Writing*. Madison: University of Wisconsin Press, 1989.

———. "Marginality in Frances Burney's Novels." In *The Cambridge Companion to the Eighteenth-Century Novel*, ed. John Richetti, 198–211. Cambridge: Cambridge University Press, 1996.

Ezell, Margaret. *Writing Women's Literary History*. Baltimore and London: Johns Hopkins University Press, 1993.

Fabricant, Carole. *Swift's Landscape*. Baltimore and London: Johns Hopkins University Press, 1982.

Ferguson, Rebecca. "'Quick as her Eyes, and as unfix'd as those': Objectification and Seeing in Pope's *Rape of the Lock*." *Critical Survey* 4, 2 (1992): 140–46.

Flint, Christopher. *Family Fictions: Narrative and Domestic Relations in Britain, 1688–1798*. Stanford, Calif.: Stanford University Press, 1998.

Flynn, Carol Houlihan. *The Body in Swift and Defoe*. Cambridge: Cambridge University Press, 1990.

———. *Samuel Richardson: A Man of Letters*. Princeton: Princeton University Press, 1982.

———. "Where the Wild Things Are: Guides to London's Transgressive Spaces." In *Orthodoxy and Heresy in Eighteenth-Century Society: Essays from the DeBartolo Conference*, ed. Regina Hewitt and Pat Rogers, 27–50. Lewisburg, Pa.: Bucknell University Press, 2002.

Fowler, John, and John Cornforth. *English Decoration in the 18th Century*. London: Barrie & Jenkins, 1974.

Foxon, D. F. *English Verse, 1701–1750: A Catalogue of Separately Printed Poems*. 2 vols. Cambridge: Cambridge University Press, 1975.

Fraiman, Susan. *Unbecoming Women: British Women Writers and the Novel of Development*. New York: Columbia University Press, 1993.

Freeman, Barbara. *Staging the Gaze: Postmodernism, Psychoanalysis, and Shakespearean Comedy*. Ithaca and London: Cornell University Press, 1991.

Freeman, Lisa A. *Character's Theater: Genre and Identity on the Eighteenth-Century Stage*. Philadelphia: University of Pennsylvania Press, 2002.

Gallagher, Catherine. *Nobody's Story: The Vanishing Acts of Women Writers in the Marketplace, 1670–1820*. Berkeley and Los Angeles: University of California Press, 1994.

Gamer, Michael. "Maria Edgeworth and the Romance of Real Life." *Novel* 34, 2 (Spring 2001): 232–66.

Garber, Marjorie. *Vested Interests: Cross-Dressing and Cultural Anxiety*. New York: HarperCollins, 1993.

Genster, Julia. "Belforded Over: The Reader in *Clarissa*." In *Clarissa and Her Readers: New Essay for The* Clarissa *Project*, ed. Carol Houlihan Flynn and Edward Copeland, 143–62. New York: AMS Press, 1999.

Gillis, Christina Marsden. *The Paradox of Privacy: Epistolary Form in* Clarissa. Gainesville: University Presses of Florida, 1984.

Gilmore, Thomas B., Jr. "The Comedy of Swift's Scatological Poems." *PMLA* 91, 1 (January 1976): 33–43.

Girouard, Mark. *Life in the English Country House: A Social and Architectural History*. New Haven and London: Yale University Press, 1978.

Goldberg, Rita. *Sex and Enlightenment: Women in Richardson and Diderot*. Cambridge: Cambridge University Press, 1984.

Gonda, Caroline. *Reading Daughters' Fictions, 1709–1834: Novels and Society from Manley to Edgeworth*. Cambridge: Cambridge University Press, 1996.

Gordon, Scott Paul. *The Power of the Passive Self in English Literature, 1640–1770*. Cambridge: Cambridge University Press, 2002.

———. "The Space of Romance in Lennox's *Female Quixote*." *SEL* 38, 3 (Summer 1998): 499–516.

Gores, Steven J. *Psychosocial Spaces: Verbal and Visual Readings of British Culture, 1750–1820*. Detroit: Wayne State University Press, 2000.

Goulemot, Jean Marie. "Literary Practices: Publicizing the Private." In *Passions of the Renaissance*, ed. Roger Chartier. Vol. 3 of *A History of Private Life*, ed. Philippe Ariès and Georges Duby, 363–95. Cambridge: Harvard University Press, 1989.

Greene, Donald. "On Swift's 'Scatological' Poems." *The Sewanee Review* 75, 4 (Autumn 1967): 672–89.

Greenfield, Susan C. *Mothering Daughters: Novels and the Politics of Family Romance, Frances Burney to Jane Austen*. Detroit: Wayne State University Press, 2002.

Greenfield, Susan C., and Carol Barash, ed. *Inventing Maternity: Politics, Science, and Literature, 1650–1865*. Lexington: University Press of Kentucky, 1999.

Griffin, Dustin. *Satire: A Critical Reintroduction*. Lexington: University Press of Kentucky, 1995.

———. *Satires Against Man: The Poems of Rochester*. Berkeley, Los Angeles, and London: University of California Press, 1973.

Gubar, Susan. "The Female Monster in Augustan Satire." *Signs* 3 (1977): 380–94.

———. "Reply to Pollak." *Signs* 3 (1978).

Guest, Harriet. *Small Change: Women, Learning, Patriotism, 1750–1810*. Chicago and London: University of Chicago Press, 2000.

Gurr, Andrew. *Playgoing in Shakespeare's London*. Cambridge: Cambridge University Press, 1994.

Guthkelch, A. *The Battle of the Books*. London: Chatto and Windus, 1908.

Gwilliam, Tassie. "Cosmetic Poetics: Coloring Faces in the Eighteenth Century." In *Body and Text in the Eighteenth Century*, ed. Veronica Kelly and Dorothea von Mücke, 144–59. Stanford, Calif.: Stanford University Press, 1994.

———. *Samuel Richardson's Fictions of Gender*. Stanford, Calif.: Stanford University Press, 1993.

Habermas, Jürgen. *The Structural Transformation of the Public Sphere: An Inquiry into a*

Category of Bourgeois Society. Translated by Thomas Burger. Cambridge: MIT Press, 1989.

Haggerty, George H. "Satire and Sentiment in *The Vicar of Wakefield.*" *The Eighteenth Century: Theory and Interpretation* 32, 1 (Spring 1991): 25–38.

Hagstrum, Jean. *The Sister Arts: The Tradition of Literary Pictorialism and English Poetry from Dryden to Gray.* Chicago and London: University of Chicago Press, 1958.

Halsband, Robert. *The Life of Lady Mary Wortley Montagu.* Oxford: Clarendon Press, 1956.

———. *The Rape of the Lock and its Illustrations, 1714–1890.* Oxford: Clarendon Press, 1980.

Harris, Jocelyn. "Grotesque, Classical and Pornographic Bodies in *Clarissa.*" In *New Essays on Samuel Richardson,* ed. Albert J. Rivero, 101–16. New York: St. Martin's Press, 1996.

———. "Protean Lovelace." *Eighteenth-Century Fiction* 2, 4 (July 1990): 327–46.

———. *Samuel Richardson.* Cambridge: Cambridge University Press, 1987.

Heffernan, James A. W. *Museum of Words: The Poetics of Ekphrasis from Homer to Ashbery.* Chicago and London: University of Chicago Press, 1993.

Hollingworth, Brian. *Maria Edgeworth's Irish Writing: Language, History, Politics.* London: Macmillan Press; New York: St. Martin's Press, 1997.

Howard, Jean E. *The Stage and Social Struggle in Early Modern England.* London and New York: Routledge, 1994.

Howe, Elizabeth. *The First English Actresses: Women and Drama, 1660–1700.* Cambridge: Cambridge University Press, 1992.

Hunter, J. Paul. *Before Novels: The Cultural Contexts of Eighteenth-Century English Fiction.* New York and London: W. W. Norton, 1990.

Hussey, Christopher. *English Country Houses: Early Georgian, 1715–1760.* London: Country Life Limited, 1965.

Ingrassia, Catherine. *Authorship, Commerce, and Gender in Early Eighteenth-Century England: A Culture of Paper Credit.* Cambridge: Cambridge University Press, 1998.

Jackson-Stops, Gervase, and James Pipkin. *The English Country House: A Grand Tour.* Boston: Little, Brown and Company, 1985.

Jaffe, Nora Crow. *The Poet Swift.* Hanover, N.H.: University Press of New England, 1977.

Jardine, Lisa. *Still Harping on Daughters: Women and Drama in the Age of Shakespeare.* Sussex: Harvester Press; Totowa, N.J.: Barnes and Noble Books, 1983.

Jed, Stephanie H. *Chaste Thinking: The Rape of Lucretia and the Birth of Humanism.* Bloomington and Indianapolis: Indiana University Press, 1989.

Johnson, Claudia L. *Jane Austen: Women, Politics, and the Novel.* Chicago and London: University of Chicago Press, 1988.

Jones, Richard Foster. *Ancients and Moderns: A Study of the Background of the* Battle of the Books. St. Louis: Washington University Studies, 1936.

Jones, Robert W. *Gender and the Formation of Taste in Eighteenth-Century Britain: The Analysis of Beauty.* Cambridge: Cambridge University Press, 1998.

Jones, Vivien. "Luxury, Satire and Prostitute Narratives." In *Luxury in the Eighteenth Century: Debates, Desires and Delectable Goods,* ed. Maxine Berg and Elizabeth Eger, 178–89. New York: Palgrave Macmillan, 2003.

Kahn, Madeleine. *Narrative Transvestism: Rhetoric and Gender in the Eighteenth-Century English Novel*. Ithaca and London: Cornell University Press, 1991.

Kaplan, E. Ann. "Is the Gaze Male?" In *Powers of Desire*, ed. Ann Snitow, 309–27. New York: Monthly Review Press, 1983.

Keymer, Tom. *Richardson's 'Clarissa' and the Eighteenth-Century Reader*. Cambridge: Cambridge University Press, 1992.

King, Thomas A. "'As if (she) were made on purpose to put the whole world into good Humour': Reconstructing the First English Actresses." *The Drama Review* 36 (Fall 1992): 78–102.

Klein, Lawrence E. "Gender and the Public/Private Distinction in the Eighteenth Century." *Eighteenth-Century Studies* 29, 1 (1995): 97–109.

Knellwolf, Christa. *A Contradiction Still: Representations of Women in the Poetry of Alexander Pope*. Manchester and New York: Manchester University Press, 1998.

Koehler, Martha. "'Faultless Monsters' and Monstrous Egos: The Disruption of Model Selves in Frances Burney's *Evelina*." *The Eighteenth Century: Theory and Interpretation* 43, 1 (Spring 2002): 19–41.

Kowaleski-Wallace, Elizabeth. *Consuming Subjects: Women, Shopping, and Business in the Eighteenth Century*. New York: Columbia University Press, 1997.

———. *Their Fathers' Daughters: Hannah Moore, Maria Edgeworth, and Patriarchal Complicity*. New York: Oxford University Press, 1991.

Kreissman, Bernard. "Pamela-Shamela: A Study of the Criticism, Burlesques, Parodies, and Adaptations of Richardson's 'Pamela.'" *University of Nebraska Studies*, 22 (May 1960).

Krieger, Murray. *Ekphrasis: The Illusion of the Natural Sign*. Baltimore and London: Johns Hopkins University Press, 1992.

Kupersmith, William. *Roman Satirists in Seventeenth-Century England*. Lincoln and London: University of Nebraska Press, 1985.

Lacaita, Francesca. "The Journey of the Encounter: The Politics of the National Tale in Sydney Owenson's *Wild Irish Girl* and Maria Edgeworth's *Ennui*." In *Critical Ireland: New Essays in Literature and Culture*, ed. Alan A. Gillis and Aaron Kelly, 148–54. Dublin: Four Courts, 2001.

Landa, Louis A. *Essays in Eighteenth-Century English Literature*. Princeton: Princeton University Press, 1980.

Laqueur, Thomas. *Making Sex: Body and Gender from the Greeks to Freud*. Cambridge and London: Harvard University Press, 1994.

Leacroft, Richard. *The Development of the English Playhouse*. Ithaca: Cornell University Press, 1973.

Leavis, F. R. *Determinations: Critical Essays*. London: Chatto and Windus, 1934.

Lee, Jae Num. *Swift and Scatological Satire*. Albuquerque: University of New Mexico Press, 1974.

Lenygon, Francis. *The Decoration and Furniture of English Mansions During the Seventeenth and Eighteenth Centuries*. London: T. Werner Laurie, 1949.

Levin, Kate. "'The Cure of Arabella's Mind': Charlotte Lennox and the Disciplining of the Female Reader." *Women's Writing* 2, 3 (1995): 271–90.

Levine, Joseph M. *The Battle of the Books: History and Literature in the Augustan Age*. Ithaca and London: Cornell University Press, 1991.

Levine, Laura. *Men in Women's Clothing: Anti-Theatricality and Effeminization, 1579–1642.* Cambridge: Cambridge University Press, 1994.

Lightfoot, Marjorie. "'Morals for Those That Like Them': The Satire of Edgeworth's *Belinda,* 1801." *Eire-Ireland* 29, 4 (Winter 1994): 117–31.

Lynch, Deidre Shauna. *The Economy of Character: Novels, Market Culture, and the Business of Inner Meaning.* Chicago: University of Chicago Press, 1998.

Macfadyen, Heather. "Lady Delacour's Library: Maria Edgeworth's *Belinda* and Fashionable Reading." *Nineteenth-Century Literature* 48, 4 (March 1994): 423–39.

Mack, Maynard. *Alexander Pope: A Life.* New York: W. W. Norton, 1988.

McCann, Andrew. *Cultural Politics in the 1790s: Literature, Radicalism and the Public Sphere.* London: Macmillan Press; New York: St. Martin's Press, 1999.

McKendrick, Neil, John Brewer, and J. H. Plumb. *The Birth of a Consumer Society: The Commercialization of Eighteenth-Century England.* Bloomington: Indiana University Press, 1982.

McKeon, Michael. *The Origins of the English Novel, 1600–1740.* Baltimore and London: Johns Hopkins University Press, 1987.

Mandell, Laura. *Misogynous Economies: The Business of Literature in Eighteenth-Century Britain.* Lexington: University Press of Kentucky, 1999.

Markley, Robert. *Fallen Languages: Crises of Representation in Newtonian England, 1660–1740.* Ithaca and London: Cornell University Press, 1993.

Mason, Nicholas. "Class, Gender, and Domesticity in Maria Edgeworth's *Belinda.*" *Eighteenth-Century Novel* 1 (2001): 271–85.

Maus, Katharine Eisaman. "'Playhouse Flesh and Blood': Sexual Ideology and the Restoration Actress." *English Literary History* 46 (1979): 595–617.

Mellor, Anne K. "A Novel of Their Own: Romantic Women's Fiction, 1790–1830." In *The Columbia History of the British Novel,* ed. John Richetti, 327–51. New York: Columbia University Press, 1994.

Michie, Allen. *Richardson and Fielding: The Dynamics of a Critical Rivalry.* Lewisburg, Pa.: Bucknell University Press, 1999.

Miller, Julia Anne. "Acts of Union: Family Violence and National Courtship in Maria Edgeworth's *The Absentee* and Sydney Owenson's *The Wild Irish Girl.*" In *Border Crossings: Irish Women Writers and National Identities,* ed. Kathryn Kirkpatrick, 13–37. Tuscaloosa and London: University of Alabama Press, 2000.

Miller, Nancy K. "Gender and Narrative Possibilities." In *Sade and the Narrative of Transgression,* ed. David B. Allison, Mark S. Roberts, and Allen S. Weiss, 213–27. Cambridge: Cambridge University Press, 1995.

Moglen, Helene. *The Trauma of Gender: A Feminist Theory of the English Novel.* Berkeley and Los Angeles: University of California Press, 2001.

Moore, Lisa L. *Dangerous Intimacies: Toward a Sapphic History of the British Novel.* Durham and London: Duke University Press, 1997.

Moretti, Franco. *The Way of the World: The Bildungsroman in European Culture.* London: Verso, 1987.

Morrissey, Lee. *From the Temple to the Castle: An Architectural History of British Literature, 1660–1760.* Charlottesville and London: University Press of Virginia, 1999.

Motooka, Wendy. *The Age of Reasons: Quixotism, Sentimentalism and Political Economy in Eighteenth-Century Britain.* London and New York: Routledge, 1998.

Mui, Hoh-Cheung, and Lorna H. Mui. *Shops and Shopkeeping in Eighteenth-Century En-*

gland. Kingston, Montreal, London: McGill Queen's University Press; London: Routledge, 1989.

Mulvey, Laura. "Visual Pleasure and Narrative Cinema." In *Feminisms*, ed. Robyn Warhol and Diane Price Herndl, 438–48. New Brunswick: Rutgers University Press, 1997.

Murray, David Aaron. "From Patrimony to Paternity in *The Vicar of Wakefield*." *Eighteenth-Century Fiction* 9, 3 (April 1997): 327–36.

Myers, Mitzi. "My Art Belongs to Daddy? Thomas Day, Maria Edgeworth, and the Pre-Texts of *Belinda*: Women Writers and Patriarchal Authority." In *Revising Women: Eighteenth-Century "Women's Fiction" and Social Engagement*, ed. Paula R. Backscheider, 104–46. Baltimore and London: Johns Hopkins University Press, 2000.

The National Trust. *Ham House*. London: Balding + Mansell for National Trust Enterprises, 1995.

Neal, Larry. "The Finance of Business during the Industrial Revolution." In *The Economic History of Britain Since 1700*. Vol. 1, *1700–1860*, ed. Roderick Floud and Donald McCloskey, 2nd ed., 151–81. Cambridge: Cambridge University Press, 1994.

Nicoll, John Allardyce. *A History of English Drama, 1660–1900*. 6 vols. Cambridge: Cambridge University Press, 1952.

Norris, Christopher. "Pope among the Formalists: Textual Politics and 'The Rape of the Lock.'" In *Post-Structuralist Readings of English Poetry*, ed. Richard Machin and Christopher Norris, 134–61. Cambridge: Cambridge University Press, 1987.

Nussbaum, Felicity. *The Brink of All We Hate: English Satires on Women, 1660–1750*. Lexington: University Press of Kentucky, 1984.

———. *Torrid Zones: Maternity, Sexuality, and Empire in Eighteenth-Century English Narratives*. Baltimore and London: Johns Hopkins University Press, 1995.

Oakleaf, David. "The Name of the Father: Social Identity and the Ambition of Evelina." *Eighteenth-Century Fiction* 3, 4 (July 1991): 341–58.

Ordish, T. Fairman. *Early London Theatres*. London: Elliot Stock, 1894.

Orlin, Lena Cowen. *Private Matters and Public Culture in Post-Reformation England*. Ithaca and London: Cornell University Press, 1994.

Pateman, Carole. *The Sexual Contract*. Stanford, Calif.: Stanford University Press, 1988.

Paulson, Ronald. *The Fictions of Satire*. Baltimore: Johns Hopkins University Press, 1967.

———. *Satire and the Novel in Eighteenth-Century England*. New Haven and London: Yale University Press, 1967.

Payne, Deborah C. "Pope and the War Against Coquettes; Or, Feminism and *The Rape of the Lock* Reconsidered—Yet Again." *The Eighteenth Century: Theory and Interpretation*, 32, 1 (1991): 3–24.

———. "Reified Object or Emergent Professional? Retheorizing the Restoration Actress." In *Cultural Readings of Restoration and Eighteenth-Century Theater*, ed. J. Douglas Canfield and Deborah C. Payne, 13–38. Athens and London: University of Georgia Press, 1995.

Phillimore, Lucy. *Sir Christopher Wren: His Family and His Times*. London: Kegan Paul, Trench, & Co., 1883.

Pollak, Ellen. *The Poetics of Sexual Myth: Gender Ideology in the Verse of Swift and Pope*. Chicago: University of Chicago Press, 1985.

Poovey, Mary. *A History of the Modern Fact: Problems of Knowledge in the Sciences of Wealth and Society*. Chicago and London: University of Chicago Press, 1998.

————. *The Proper Lady and the Woman Writer: Ideology as Style in the Works of Mary Woll-stonecraft, Mary Shelley, and Jane Austen.* Chicago and London: University of Chicago Press, 1984.

Posner, Donald. *Watteau: A Lady at her Toilet.* London: Allen Lane of Penguin Books, 1973.

Preston, Thomas R. "Moral Spin Doctoring, Delusion, and Chance: Wakefield's Vicar Writes An Enlightenment Parable." *Age of Johnson* 11 (2000): 237–81.

Pritchard, Will. "Masks and Faces: Female Legibility in the Restoration Era." *Eighteenth-Century Life* 24, 3 (2000): 31–52.

Rackin, Phyllis. "Androgyny, Mimesis, and the Marriage of the Boy Heroine on the English Renaissance Stage." *PMLA* 102 (1987): 29–41.

Rambuss, Richard. *Closet Devotions.* Durham and London: Duke University Press, 1998.

————. *Spenser's Secret Career.* Cambridge: Cambridge University Press, 1993.

Ranum, Orest. "The Refuges of Intimacy." In *Passions of the Renaissance,* ed. Roger Chartier. Vol. 3 of *A History of Private Life,* ed. Philippe Ariès and Georges Duby, 210–29. Cambridge: Harvard University Press, 1989.

Rawson, Claude. *Gulliver and the Gentle Reader: Studies in Swift and Our Time.* London: Routledge & Kegan Paul, 1973.

————. *Order from Confusion Sprung: Studies in Eighteenth-Century Literature from Swift to Cowper.* London: George Allen & Unwin, 1985.

————. *Satire and Sentiment, 1660–1830.* Cambridge: Cambridge University Press, 1994.

Redford, Bruce. *The Converse of the Pen: Acts of Intimacy in the Eighteenth-Century Familiar Letter.* Chicago and London: University of Chicago Press, 1986.

Rees, Christine. "Gay, Swift, and the Nymphs of Drury-Lane." *Essays in Criticism* 23, 1 (January 1973): 1–21.

Romm, Sharon. *The Changing Face of Beauty.* St. Louis, Mo.: Mosby Year Book, 1992.

Rosenthal, Laura J. "'Counterfeit Scrubbado': Women Actors in the Restoration." *The Eighteenth Century: Theory and Interpretation* 34, 1 (1993): 3–22.

————. *Playwrights and Plagiarists in Early Modern England: Gender, Authorship, Literary Property.* Ithaca and London: Cornell University Press, 1996.

Rosslyn, Felicity. "'Dipt in the rainbow': Pope on Women." In *The Enduring Legacy: Alexander Pope Tercentenary Essays,* ed. G. S. Rousseau and Pat Rogers, 51–62. Cambridge: Cambridge University Press, 1988.

Rothstein, Eric. "Woman, Women, and *The Female Quixote.*" In *Augustan Subjects: Essays in Honor of Martin C. Battestin,* ed. Albert J. Rivero, 249–75. Newark: University of Delaware Press; London: Associated University Presses, 1997.

Roulston, Christine. "Histories of Nothing: Romance and Femininity in Charlotte Lennox's *The Female Quixote.*" *Women's Writing* 2, 1 (1995): 25–42.

Rousseau, G. S. "From Swift to Smollet: The Satirical Tradition in Prose Narrative." In *The Columbia History of the British Novel,* ed. John Richetti, 127–53. New York: Columbia University Press, 1994.

Rubin, Gayle S. "The Traffic in Women: Notes on the Political Economy of Sex." In *Toward an Anthropology of Women,* ed. Rayna P. Reiter, 157–77. New York: Monthly Review Press, 1975.

Rumbold, Valerie. *Women's Place in Pope's World.* Cambridge: Cambridge University Press, 1989.

Salvaggio, Ruth. *Enlightened Absence: Neoclassical Configurations of the Feminine*. Urbana and Chicago: University of Illinois Press, 1988.

Sarti, Raffaella. *Europe at Home: Family and Material Culture, 1500–1800*. Translated by Allan Cameron. New Haven and London: Yale University Press, 2002.

Schwarz, Kathryn. *Tough Love: Amazon Encounters in the English Renaissance*. Durham and London: Duke University Press, 2000.

Sedgwick, Eve Kosofsky. *Between Men: English Literature and Male Homosocial Desire*. New York: Columbia University Press, 1985.

———. *Epistemology of the Closet*. Berkeley and Los Angeles: University of California Press, 1990.

Seidel, Michael. *Satiric Inheritance: Rabelais to Sterne*. Princeton: Princeton University Press, 1979.

Shaffer, Julie. "Not Subordinate: Empowering Women in the Marriage Plot — The Novels of Frances Burney, Maria Edgeworth, and Jane Austen." *Criticism* 34, 1 (1992): 51–73.

———. "Romance, Finance, and the Marketable Woman: The Economics of Femininity in Late Eighteenth- and Early Nineteenth-Century English Novels." In *Bodily Discursions: Genders, Representations, Technologies*, ed. Deborah S. Wilson and Christine Moneera Laennec, 39–56. Albany: State University of New York Press, 1997.

Shapin, Steven, and Simon Schaffer. *Leviathan and the Air-Pump: Hobbes, Boyle, and the Experimental Life*. Princeton: Princeton University Press, 1985.

Shapiro, Barbara J. *A Culture of Fact: England, 1550–1720*. Ithaca and London: Cornell University Press, 2000.

Siebert, Donald T. "Swift's *Fiat Odor*: The Excremental Re-Vision." *Eighteenth-Century Studies* 19, 1 (Fall 1985): 21–38.

Sitwell, Sacheverell. *British Architects and Craftsmen: A Survey of Taste, Design, and Style during Three Centuries, 1600–1830*. New York: Charles Scribner's Sons, 1946.

Smith, Charles Saumarez. *Eighteenth-Century Decoration: Design and the Domestic Interior in England*. New York: Harry N. Abrams, 1993.

Solomon, Harry M. "'Difficult Beauty': Tom D'Urfey and the Context of Swift's 'The Lady's Dressing Room.'" *SEL* 19 (1979): 531–44.

Spacks, Patricia Meyer. *Desire and Truth: Functions of Plot in Eighteenth-Century English Novels*. Chicago and London: University of Chicago Press, 1990.

———. *Privacy: Concealing the Eighteenth-Century Self*. Chicago and London: University of Chicago Press, 2003.

———. "Some Reflections on Satire." *Genre* 1 (1968): 13–20.

Spencer, Jane. "Not Being An Historian: Women Telling Tales in Restoration and Eighteenth-Century England." In *Contexts of Pre-Novel Narrative*, ed. Roy Eriksen, 319–40. Berlin and New York: Mouton de Gruyter, 1994.

———. "Women Writers and the Eighteenth-Century Novel." In *The Cambridge Companion to the Eighteenth-Century Novel*, ed. John Richetti, 212–35. Cambridge: Cambridge University Press, 1996.

Stadler, Eva Maria. "Defining the Female Body within Social Space: The Function of Clothes in Some Early Eighteenth-Century Novels." In *Proceedings of the XIIth Congress of the International Comparative Literature Association*, ed. Roger Bauer and Douwe Fokkem, III, 468–73. München: Iudicium Verlag, 1990.

Stafford, Barbara Maria. *Body Criticism: Imaging the Unseen in Enlightenment Art and Medicine*. Cambridge: MIT Press, 1991.

Starkman, Miriam Kosh. *Swift's Satire on Learning in* A Tale of a Tub. Princeton: Princeton University Press, 1950.

Staves, Susan. "*Evelina*; or, Female Difficulties." *Modern Philology* 73 (1976): 368–81.

———. *Married Women's Separate Property in England, 1660–1833*. Cambridge and London: Harvard University Press, 1990.

Stewart, Alan. "The Early Modern Closet Discovered." *Representations* 50 (Spring 1995): 76–100.

Stone, Lawrence. *The Family, Sex, and Marriage in England, 1500–1800*. New York: Harper & Row, 1979.

Straub, Kristina. *Divided Fictions: Fanny Burney and Feminine Strategy*. Lexington: University Press of Kentucky, 1987.

———. "Frances Burney and the Rise of the Woman Novelist." In *The Columbia History of the British Novel*, ed. John Richetti, 199–219. New York: Columbia University Press, 1994.

———. "Reconstructing the Gaze: Voyeurism in Richardson's *Pamela*." *Studies in Eighteenth-Century Culture* 18 (1988): 419–31.

———. *Sexual Suspects: Eighteenth-Century Players and Sexual Ideology*. Princeton: Princeton University Press, 1992.

Styles, John. "Custom or Consumption? Plebeian Fashion in Eighteenth-Century England." In *Luxury in the Eighteenth Century: Debates, Desires and Delectable Goods*, ed. Maxine Berg and Elizabeth Eger, 103–15. New York: Palgrave Macmillan, 2003.

Summers, Montague. *The Restoration Theatre*. New York: Macmillan, 1934.

Sykes, Christopher Simon. *Country House Album*. Boston: Bulfinch Press, 1989.

Thaddeus, Janice Farrar. *Frances Burney: A Literary Life*. London: Macmillan; New York: St. Martin's Press, 2000.

Thornton, Dora. *The Scholar in His Study: Ownership and Experience in Renaissance Italy*. New Haven: Yale University Press, 1997.

Thurley, Simon. *Hampton Court Palace*. Great Britain: Historic Royal Palaces 2000, 1996.

Thurley, Simon, and Anna Keay. "Charles II, Louis XIV, and the English Royal Bedchamber." Lecture at the Newberry Library, 12 March 2002.

Todd, Janet. *The Sign of Angellica: Women, Writing and Fiction, 1660–1800*. London: Virago, 1989.

Tracy, Robert. "Maria Edgeworth and Lady Morgan: Legality versus Legitimacy." *Nineteenth-Century Literature* 40, 1 (June 1985): 1–22.

Traugott, John. "*Clarissa's* Richardson: An Essay to Find the Reader." In *English Literature in the Age of Disguise*, ed. Maximillian E. Novak, 157–208. Berkeley: University of California Press, 1987.

Tristram, Philippa. *Living Space in Fact and Fiction*. London and New York: Routledge, 1989.

Trumbach, Randolph. *Sex and the Gender Revolution: Heterosexuality and the Third Gender in Enlightenment London*. Chicago and London: University of Chicago Press, 1998.

Turner, Edward Raymond, and Gaudens Megaro. "The King's Closet in the Eighteenth Century." *The American Historical Review* 45, 4 (July 1940): 761–76.

Turner, James Grantham. "Lovelace and the Paradoxes of Libertinism." In *Samuel Richardson: Tercentenary Essays*, ed. Margaret Anne Doody and Peter Sabor, 70–88. Cambridge: Cambridge University Press, 1989.

Van Sant, Ann Jessie. *Eighteenth-Century Sensibility and the Novel: The Senses in Social Context*. Cambridge: Cambridge University Press, 1993.

———. "Satire and Law: The 'Case' against Women." *REAL: The Yearbook of Research in English and American Literature* 18 (2002): 39–64.

Varey, Simon. *Space and the Eighteenth-Century English Novel*. Cambridge: Cambridge University Press, 1990.

Vickers, Nancy J. "Diana Described: Scattered Woman and Scattered Rhyme." In *Writing and Sexual Difference*, ed. Elizabeth Abel, 95–109. Chicago: University of Chicago Press, 1982.

Vickery, Amanda. *The Gentleman's Daughter: Women's Lives in Georgian England*. New Haven and London: Yale University Press, 1998.

Victoria's Secret. www.victoriassecret.com

Vries, Jan de. "Between Purchasing Power and the World of Goods: Understanding the Household Economy in Early Modern Europe." In *Consumption and the World of Goods*, ed. John Brewer and Roy Porter, 85–132. London and New York: Routledge, 1993.

Wall, Cynthia. "Gendering Rooms: Domestic Architecture and Literary Acts." *Eighteenth-Century Fiction* 5, 4 (July 1993): 349–72.

Warner, William B. *Licensing Entertainment: The Elevation of Novel Reading in Britain, 1684–1750*. Berkeley and Los Angeles: University of California Press, 1998.

———. *Reading Clarissa: The Struggles of Interpretation*. New Haven and London: Yale University Press, 1979.

Watt, Ian. *The Rise of the Novel: Studies in Defoe, Richardson, and Fielding*. Berkeley and Los Angeles: University of California Press, 1957.

Weatherhill, Lorna. *Consumer Behavior and Material Culture, 1660–1760*. London: Routledge, 1988.

———. "The meaning of consumer behaviour in late seventeenth- and early eighteenth-century England." In *Consumption and the World of Goods*, ed. John Brewer and Roy Porter, 206–27. London and New York: Routledge, 1993.

Weinbrot, Howard. *Alexander Pope and the Traditions of Formal Verse Satire*. Princeton: Princeton University Press, 1982.

Wheeler, Angela J. *English Verse Satire from Donne to Dryden: Imitation of Classical Models*. Heidelberg: Carl Winter Universitätsverlag, 1992.

Wigley, Mark. "Untitled: The Housing of Gender." In *Sexuality & Space*, ed. Beatriz Colomina, 327–89. New York: Princeton Architectural Press, 1992.

Williams, Carolyn D. *Pope, Homer, and Manliness: Some Aspects of Eighteenth-Century Classical Learning*. London and New York: Routledge, 1993.

Williams, Neville. *Powder and Paint: A History of the Englishwoman's Toilet, Elizabeth I–Elizabeth II*. London: Longmans, Green, 1957.

Wilson, John Harold. *All the King's Ladies: Actresses of the Restoration*. Chicago: University of Chicago Press, 1958.

Wilson, Penelope. "Feminism and the Augustans: Some Readings and Problems." *Critical Quarterly* 28, 1, 2 (Spring, Summer 1986): 80–92.

Wohlgemut, Esther. "Maria Edgeworth and the Question of National Identity." *SEL* 39, 4 (Autumn 1999): 645–58.

Workman, Nancy V. "From Victorian to Victoria's Secret: The Foundations of Modern Erotic Wear." *Journal of Popular Culture* 30 (Fall 1996): 61–73.

Wykes-Joyce, Max. *Cosmetics and Adornment: Ancient and Contemporary Usage*. New York: Philosophical Library, 1961.

Wyrick, Deborah Baker. *Jonathan Swift and the Vested Word*. Chapel Hill and London: University of North Carolina Press, 1988.

Yeazell, Ruth Bernard. *Fictions of Modesty: Women and Courtship in the English Novel*. Chicago: University of Chicago Press, 1991.

Ytzhak, Lydia Ben. *Petite Histoire du Maquillage*. Paris: Éditions Stock, 2000.

Zimbardo, Rose. "The Semiotics of Restoration Satire." In *Cutting Edges: Postmodern Critical Essays on Eighteenth-Century Satire*, ed. James E. Gill, 23–42. Knoxville: University of Tennessee Press, 1995.

Zomchick, John P. *Family and the Law in Eighteenth-Century Fiction: The Public Conscience in the Private Sphere*. Cambridge: Cambridge University Press, 1993.

———. "Satire and the Bourgeois Subject in France Burney's *Evelina*." In *Cutting Edges: Postmodern Critical Essays on Eighteenth-Century Satire*, ed. James E. Gill, 347–66. Knoxville: University of Tennessee Press, 1995.

Index